Structural Injustice

Structural Injustice

Structural Injustice

Power, Advantage, and Human Rights

MADISON POWERS AND RUTH FADEN

Oxford University Press is a department of the University of Oxford. It furthers
the University's objective of excellence in research, scholarship, and education
by publishing worldwide. Oxford is a registered trade mark of Oxford University
Press in the UK and certain other countries.

Published in the United States of America by Oxford University Press
198 Madison Avenue, New York, NY 10016, United States of America.

Library of Congress Cataloging-in-Publication Data
Names: Powers, Madison, author. | Faden, Ruth, author.
Title: Structural injustice : power, advantage, and human rights / Madison Powers.
Description: New York : Oxford University Press, 2019. |
Includes bibliographical references and index.
Identifiers: LCCN 2018057225 (print) | LCCN 2019980504 (ebook) |
ISBN 9780190053987 (cloth : alk. paper) | ISBN 9780190054014 (ebook)
Subjects: LCSH: Social justice. | Power (Social sciences) | Human rights.
Classification: LCC HM671 .P684 2019 (print) | LCC HM671 (ebook) |
DDC 303.3/72—dc23
LC record available at https://lccn.loc.gov/2018057225
LC ebook record available at https://lccn.loc.gov/2019980504

9 8 7 6 5 4 3 2

Printed by Integrated Books International, United States of America

For Penn and Tom

CONTENTS

PREFACE AND READERS' GUIDE

This book has its roots in an invitation from the University of Zurich to participate in a two-day conference on our book *Social Justice: The Moral Foundations of Public Health and Health Policy*. It was held in 2012 and hosted by the Institute of Biomedical Ethics and the University Research Priority Program for Ethics. The conference featured two dozen speakers and commentators, representing a mix of academics and activists from eleven countries. This volume is the result of our expansion and refinement of the ideas in *Social Justice* that so excited this group, and in turn excited us.

For readers familiar with *Social Justice*, we note several ways in which our thinking has evolved. In order to ward off a variety of potential misinterpretations, where we once spoke of "essential dimensions" of well-being we now use the less problematic phrase "core elements." The earlier book was structured around the positive and negative aims of justice, where the positive aim is to secure a basic level of well-being and the negative aim is to prevent or combat densely woven, unfair patterns of disadvantage. In a series of exploratory papers in the intervening years, we referred to the theory's twin aims. Ultimately, in *Structural Injustice*, we opted for a twin focus on human rights and fairness norms.

We devoted a very brief section of *Social Justice* to how our conception of well-being might be used to ground an interest theory of human rights. This book picks up on that suggestion and uses our conception of well-being to defend such a theory. We also establish extensive links between human rights norms and structural fairness norms.

Our thinking about fairness norms has evolved considerably since *Social Justice*. In that book, we used the phrase "systematic disadvantage" to encompass a plurality of ways in which unfair patterns of advantage become cemented into place. We left open the possibility that unfair patterns of advantage emerge from the unintended, largely benign, uncoordinated actions of individuals and institutions, while also devoting attention to morally more complex patterns of interaction involving unfairness in relations of power. In this book, we focus on the latter trajectory. We now place greater emphasis on the inherent unfairness of certain power relations, and we highlight the instrumental role asymmetric power routinely plays in creating and sustaining deep disadvantage.

In *Social Justice*, we claimed applicability of our theory to both domestic and global contexts. Since that book went to press in 2005, much has been written on this topic. It has required us to address powerful arguments against the global extension of the fairness norms we propose. In *Structural Injustice* we draw a careful distinction between the norms we defend and the kinds of norms of justice that critics and some proponents have in mind when they argue for or against global application of norms of justice.

Finally, although we developed our theory in *Social Justice* in conversation with specific issues in public health and health policy, we indicated that we believed our theory was not limited to health. In fact, we rejected the general thesis that social justice fundamentally differs in its requirements in "separate spheres," along with the assumption that matters of structural justice could be addressed adequately in one sphere in isolation from injustices in other sectors of social life. In this book, we make good on these claims by putting forward a theory of structural injustice that is intentionally freed from a special focus on health and that continues to emphasize the interconnected and interdependent relations between different core elements of well-being and different kinds of structural unfairness.

There are also two features of *Structural Injustice* that were not present in our earlier volume and that we want to note for all readers. First, many of the chapters are accessible as stand-alone discussions of interest to audiences with various levels of prior exposure to the justice literature. Although the book is designed as a sequence of chapters through which we develop our overall theory of structural injustice, distinguish it from existing alternatives, demonstrate its relevance within different nation-states and across national boundaries, and defend the justifiability of forms of resistance, many chapters are also written so that they can be read on their own. For example, a reader interested in what makes norms of justice different from other moral norms can read chapter 3, or a reader interested in debates about the foundations of human rights can read chapter 5. Both provide surveys of the central issues in key debates, even though the ultimate purpose of each chapter is to take sides on some hotly contested points that are central to our theory. Chapter 4 offers a useful place for diving into contemporary debates about structural injustice, including controversies pertaining to the moral significance of membership in social groups such as those defined by race, gender, or economic class. Chapter 6 provides a self-contained discussion of the nature, rationale, and limits of nation-state responsibility for addressing human rights claims in tandem with the underlying structural conditions that make their violation more likely.

Second, certain parts of the book are intended to be particularly relevant and accessible to readers who do not have a background in philosophy but who have expertise in mitigating and preventing structural injustices on the ground, including participants in social movements, investigative journalists, and staff at non-governmental organizations (NGOs), philanthropic institutions, government agencies, and international organizations. Our selection of focal readings recommended for these readers is more complicated, given the range of backgrounds and interests of the intended audience. For example, some readers might come to the book with a practical understanding of human rights and the role they play in global discourse, but they may have a less firm grasp of what is distinctive about fairness norms, or they may have given less thought to how fairness norms and human rights are intertwined in real-world scenarios. Other readers may have questions about how to frame the moral issues arising in situations in which human rights, on their own, seem inadequate or fail to capture some aspects of what is morally problematic. For all of these readers, we suggest starting with section 2.1 for an explanation of how fairness norms and human rights interact, followed by 3.4, which provides a broadly accessible, but more detailed introduction to notions of unfairness.

Section 1.1, together with chapter 2, provides a basic understanding of our overall theory and how it differs from other structural theories of justice that may be familiar already, at least in broad outlines, to a diverse array of journalists, activists, NGO staff members, philanthropies, government agencies, and international organizations. Chapter 4 discusses the question of what makes a theory of justice a structural theory. Even though we intend the chapter to engage specialist audiences on highly contested issues of contemporary importance in the philosophical literature, we think that the general idea of structural injustice is so much a part of political conversations today that many readers will find rewarding the extra effort required to work through the main lines of argument. For example, issues of how race, gender, and economic class intersect, and how the relative social position of members of each social group shapes their daily experience and life prospects, are central concerns in popular feminist literature, labor activist circles, and social movements such as Black Lives Matter.

Readers working on issues of global economic justice are likely to find relevant the discussion in chapter 6.5, where we provide a moral framework for engaging in debates about state sovereignty, the global power of multinational corporations, and the role of supranational institutions such as the World Bank, International Monetary Fund, and World Trade Organization. Readers with an interest in environmental justice may want to read sections 7.1 and 7.2 for their discussions of the commonalities of sacrifice zones from Appalachia to Zambia. Readers with a focal interest in many of the issues posed by the Black Lives Matter movement should find much of interest in 7.3, and global slum activists and students of global development should find 7.4 of special interest.

A range of readers may find the general discussion of the ethics of resistance in chapter 8 of particular value. Since "resistance" is so much a part of the vernacular of contemporary social movements, we hope that this discussion offers a framework useful for generating more extensive conversations about its ethical dimensions. As it turns out, the philosophical literature is quite sparse, while the public discussion of efficacious strategy and tactics is saturated with moral concerns about what actions are appropriate when ordinary channels of reform appear blocked by those at the center of concentrations of power and advantage.

We close these brief remarks by expressing our indebtedness to the many colleagues, students, and postdoctoral fellows who read successive iterations of chapter drafts or who participated in seminars in which we presented our evolving thinking over the years. Thank you for helping us mature our theory. Without your input, *Structural Injustice* would not be the book it is.

CHAPTER 1 | Introduction

1.1. Structural Injustice

Structural injustice is an increasingly popular topic in the philosophical literature and a tragic state of affairs for millions of people. For these people and for social activists, investigative journalists, and non-governmental organizations (NGOs) that advocate for them, structural injustice is much more than an abstract concept. It is a defining feature of the institutional arrangements and web of social norms in which they live. Desperate poverty, human trafficking, police misconduct, institutional racism, exclusionary gender norms, environmental sacrifice zones, international trade rules, voter suppression tactics, sweatshop labor, and global land grabs are all too familiar examples.

Our book is fundamentally philosophical, but it is also responsive to and inspired by structural injustices in the here and now. We put forward a theory that captures the central injustices of large-scale forms of social organization, both within and across national boundaries. These injustices take the form of unfair patterns of advantage and unfair relations of power, including subordination, exploitation, and social exclusion, as well as human rights violations and deprivations in well-being that contribute to and grow out of unjust social structural conditions. In our theory, human rights violations, disadvantage, and unfair power relations interact and are mutually reinforcing. They are both cause and effect of each other. Together, they are the hallmark of serious structural injustices that typically implicate multiple institutions and agents having differing degrees of culpability for the wrong that results. In many cases, these are the kinds of injustices that motivate, and also justify, social movements of resistance.

Five features of this book distinguish our approach from many other accounts of structural injustice. First, our account is designed for the world as we find it. It is built to fit a real-world characterization of deprivation, human rights violations, disadvantage, and unfair power relations. Second, we defend an integrated theory of structural injustice in which human rights violations and structural unfairness are routinely intertwined in both their origin and their solution. Third, our theory addresses what we view as basic or fundamental injustices that arise both within and across national boundaries. Fourth, we provide a novel response to criticisms about the universal applicability of theories like ours that rely on an account of human well-being. Like so much of our thinking, our response is informed by and responsive to critical perspectives found in social justice movements. To that end, we devote substantial space to four extended examples that illustrate our theory. Fifth, the primary practical aims of the theory are different from those of other accounts. We offer guidance for conditions that are all too commonplace where states (and other institutional agents) cannot or will not protect basic well-being interests or create fair patterns of advantage and fair relations of power.

1.1.1. The World as We Find It

We differ from John Rawls, Iris Young, and other prominent theorists in the way we characterize the social structural phenomena of central interest. Rawls's distributive principles are designed for a "nearly just" society. His focus is on the threats that deep social class differences pose to an ideal of socioeconomic fairness in circumstances of moderate scarcity, where basic needs and basic liberties are already secured. The social structural phenomena of interest to us, however, are quite different. Our theory is concerned with structural injustices that take a more complex and malignant form but that are routine in the world as we know it. These injustices are characterized by deep pockets of multidimensional deprivation and entrenched disadvantage, born of power differentials across social groups. They are injustices in which millions have unmet basic needs and no secure liberties, and human rights violations, including violations of equal standing based on characteristics like race and gender, are commonplace. As a consequence, relationships grounded in exploitation or social exclusion are easily created and sustained.

Like us, Young rejects the idealizing assumptions in Rawls's theory, and so our work shares much more common territory with her than with Rawls. However, in her later work Young distinguishes sharply between classic instances of intentional oppression and structural injustices that are the cumulative effect of multiple, uncoordinated, morally benign decisions of diverse agents. While we do not claim that structural injustices can never emerge in this way, we think they seldom do. Instead, we focus on patterns of structural injustice that are fundamentally different in origin and in the underlying social processes in which these injustices are produced and sustained. In circumstances ranging from institutional racism to the global dumping of hazardous waste, our diagnosis of the structural origins and systematic consequences of unfair structural conditions and human rights violations reveals a mix of agents and motivations that is very different from Young's perspective.

1.1.2. Theoretical Integration of Human Rights Violations and Structural Injustice

Unlike most theorists who have written about structural injustice, we make a theoretical case that human rights violations and unfair social arrangements should be analyzed as intertwined in one theory of structural injustice.

Some, like Rawls, presuppose the satisfaction of human rights as lexically prior to his principles of fairness, whereas others often describe structural injustices as constituting human rights violations. Some theorists argue that various issues that are typically understood as human rights violations should instead be analyzed primarily as systematic injustices, while others highlight reasons for drawing a sharp distinction between the kinds of problems that should be addressed by human rights norms and those that should be addressed by norms regulating structural unfairness. By contrast, we argue that human rights violations and structural unfairness are inseparably connected in ordinary contexts and belong in one theory of structural injustice. We use our integrated theory to defend the novel view that states' fulfillment of human rights responsibilities—not only their duties to citizens, but also in some cases to non-nationals—requires simultaneous attention to combating and preventing the onset of conditions of serious structural unfairness.

1.1.3. Structural Injustice within and across States

We also argue that considerations of structural justice constrain nations from taking actions that create and sustain conditions that erode the ability of other states to fulfill their duties to uphold the human rights of those within their territorial jurisdictions. The practical standpoint from which our theory proceeds thus differs from that of many other approaches because of the kinds of questions we pursue. For example, unlike John Rawls, we do not propose a set of principles that are meant to be jointly sufficient for the regulation of social relations in a single, self-contained, politically unified society. Nor do we propose a separate set of principles that would characterize a "reasonably just" global order. Instead, our theory is meant to apply to domestic *and* global contexts. Our theory, therefore, is neither a theory of domestic justice, or one meant solely for application in a particular political context, such as liberal democratic societies, nor a theory intended exclusively for the regulation of some aspect of global affairs, such as the relations between sovereign states. To put matters slightly differently, our theory focuses on the most basic, fundamental matters implicating the core elements of well-being characteristic of a decent human life. It does not attempt to specify further, potentially more demanding requirements of a fully just, liberal democratic society or a reasonably just global order.

Beyond the fact that the core well-being interests at stake are of universal moral importance, our theory is meant to apply both within and beyond national boundaries and to a diversity of national contexts, for three additional reasons. First, there are many parallels across state contexts in the way social relations, well-being outcomes, and overall life prospects are structured. Many of the relevant incentive structures, social dynamics, political preconditions, and interdependencies that characterize the most pernicious forms of structural injustice routinely exist in a variety of national contexts. In a nutshell, our structural theory emphasizes that what happens here, wherever here is, often happens elsewhere.

Second, although social structural factors that are closest to home are still the most relevant to the formation of structural injustices, globalization adds a new layer of structural influence. The reality of the current phase of globalization is that increasingly what happens here affects what happens elsewhere, and what happens elsewhere affects what happens here.

Third, in the new global order, state sovereignty, once both a threat to and a guarantor of human rights and fairness, has been eroded. A combination of politically unaccountable supranational institutions and increasingly powerful multinational corporations exacerbates the loss of ability of sovereign political institutions to chart their own course in economic development and social policy and secure human rights within their borders.

1.1.4. Insights from Social Movements

Our theory is built around an account of well-being that is applicable to a diverse array of nations and to interactions that stretch across national boundaries. However, unlike some theorists, we do not believe that the justification of our conception depends on its prospects for universal endorsement from within every existing ethical framework. We take persistent disagreement about well-being and norms of justice to be a given, but we believe that the most important disagreements are not between the West and the rest. Rather, the cleavages that are most fundamental are those rooted in deep differences in perspectives between activists in social movements and other advocates for change, on the one hand, and defenders of existing relations of power and dominant social policies, on the other.

We take seriously the perspectives of participants in social movements around the world, and we attempt to provide a rigorous theoretical framework that integrates lessons gleaned from the experiences of persons who are engaged in everyday struggles for justice. In this way, we supply a model of how practical ethics can reposition itself as an academic enterprise and a form of public intellectual engagement.

Nearly one-third of the book is devoted to the exposition of conditions of structural injustice around the world, bringing into conversation the points of view commonly expressed within social movements. We discuss a number of transnational injustices in chapter 6, and in chapter 8 we address issues of daily importance to activists concerned about strategies of resistance to injustice. Our most extensive engagement appears in chapter 7, where we present four extended examples of our theory's application to a range of settings and its resonance with the perspectives of activists.

Two of our broad examples are drawn from deep pockets of deprivation, disadvantage, and power differentials found in sites of intensive resource extraction, as they arise in the United States and lower- and middle-income countries alike. The second pair of examples portray socially marginalized and predominantly poor communities in urban settings, one in the United States and the other in several lower- and middle-income countries. All of these communities are themselves diverse and have singular histories and cultures, but there are several important respects in which they are more alike than different.

All of these communities are burdened by a legacy of external control. All are structured by coercive institutional rules and a web of informal, but highly consequential social practices, market realities, and dynamics of entrenched social stratification. All are subject to the predatory behaviors of more powerful social groups who have both the capacity and the incentive to exploit the vulnerable and the desperate. Differences in relative social position and socially created patterns of advantage and disadvantage ensure that current options for members of the community are few and overall life prospects for residents are poor or in decline. All are effectively excluded from or, at best, exist on the margins of the mainstream institutions and social processes through which a decent life for others around them is made possible. The result is that many of their residents live in the shadows, falling between the cracks of frayed or non-existent social safety nets, often struggling to secure necessities such as food, shelter, and health care for themselves and their children.

Another common denominator is the extent to which structural injustice all too often arises out of and persists because of an explicit or implicit judgment that some lives matter less than others. This is a central message of the Black Lives Matter movement. Its critique of the condition of Black America begins with, but goes far beyond, the disproportionate number of black lives lost to police-involved shootings or the urban and suburban concentration of poverty.

Although the racial backdrop of structural injustice in the US is to some extent distinctive, urban counterparts are found across the globe. Slum activists routinely complain that they are viewed as disposable, especially women who endure not only the health risks from unsafe and impermanent housing, but also constant threats of private and state violence and a level of durable economic dislocation and disadvantage beyond what men typically experience.

Rural communities caught in the grip of control by extractive industries from the outside, and often subject to unresponsive or even brutal governments from within, have come to be known around the world as "sacrifice zones." The name signals the same underlying complaint made by activists in the Black Lives Matter movement and the slums of the global South.

1.1.5. When States Cannot or Will Not Respond to Structural Injustice

The upshot of the conditions highlighted in these four examples, together with the ways in which external global influences increasingly shape the domestic context, is that states all too often do not deliver on their responsibilities. Unlike most theories of structural injustice, our account offers practical guidance for the times when states and other institutional agents cannot or will not protect basic well-being interests that ground human rights or create fair patterns of advantage and fair relations of power. The guidance we offer is markedly different from that of theorists who share many of our assumptions about unjust power relations and real-world structural injustices but who emphasize proposals for creating or improving the functioning of democratic institutions as a response.

By contrast, our focus is on what activists are justified in doing in direct defense of their interests. In the last chapter, we propose a moral framework for analyzing the justifications of and limits on different targets and modes of resistance. These modes of resistance include "name and shame" strategies and boycott and divestment campaigns, as well as organized activities intended for self-defense and the defense of others when states either fail to protect their citizens or themselves become perpetrators. We hope that our analysis will be helpful to activists and advocates who take seriously the task of defining and defending their strategies of resistance on moral grounds.

1.2. Plan of the Chapters

In what follows we offer a brief summary of the chapters. In addition, readers may wish to consult our preface, which offers a guide to the book tailored to both philosophically oriented readers and readers who work to address structural injustices in the here and now, including socially engaged activists and advocates, investigative journalists, and staff members of NGOs, governmental and international organizations, and philanthropies.

In chapter 2, we present and defend the conception of human well-being on which our theory of structural injustice rests. The core elements are health; knowledge and understanding; personal security from physical and psychological harm, as well as the threat of such harm; personal attachments constitutive of valuable forms of human relationship; equal respect manifested in equal social and political standing in which individuals and groups experience treatment as moral equals; and a self-determining life, in which individuals shape its broad contours and have some significant say over its general course.

We begin the chapter by explaining three ways that our conception of human well-being undergirds the human rights and structural unfairness components of our theory. First, our conception identifies unjust deprivations in the core elements of well-being, in particular deprivations that constitute violations of human rights. Second, our conception pinpoints the patterns of structural disadvantage that are deeply unfair because of their longer-term, systematic impact on the core well-being prospects, or chances for a decent life, of members of socially situated groups. Third, our conception highlights power relations that are fundamentally unfair because of the unjustified forms of control some groups have over the most vital well-being interests of other groups.

We devote the bulk of the chapter to a series of arguments that support our selection of the core elements. We explain why our list is not meant as a general conception of well-being but as a conception tailored to the assessment of social structural arrangements. We take up a series of objections that arise from persistent disagreement over some of the elements included on our list, and we distinguish our theory from some other moral norms that rely on a conception of well-being. We end the chapter by highlighting some key differences between the foundational role of well-being within our theory of justice and some other theories of justice.

In chapter 3, we explain why our theory is a theory of justice. Specifically, we explain how we understand both human rights claims and fairness claims to be matters of justice, and not matters that fall under other categories of moral norms. Although there is no consensus on the features of moral norms that explain why they should be classified as norms of justice, we consider five that command enough attention to be useful: importance, stringency, claimability, specificity, and rightful enforceability. Using these five features of norms allows us to make clear what we think is at stake in describing as matters of justice the social phenomena we assess in our theory.

We end the chapter by elaborating upon unfairness as a distinctive normative phenomenon. We begin by way of examples of how we use ordinary language to describe moral complaints in everyday life. From this foundation, we construct the more complex notion of structural variants of unfairness, focusing in particular on three forms that figure prominently in our theory. In the case of subordination, some persons are subjected to control by members of another social group in ways that are unfair because of the nature, extent, or means of the power exercised over them. In the case of exploitation, some are unfairly taken advantage of for the benefit of another, more powerful person or social group. And in the case of social exclusion, some are unfairly excluded from, or permitted only marginal participation in, some valuable activity or social interaction.

In chapter 4, we explain what makes our theory of injustice a structural theory. We survey four key features of structural theories of justice that vary from one theory to another, and we explain and defend what is distinctive about our own. First, theories differ in their inventory of the morally significant impacts traceable to social structural influences. For example, our theory differs from others that focus on the structural impact on economic distribution or the impact on individual choice and available options. By contrast, we focus on the impact of structural influences on the core elements of well-being.

Second, theories vary in their understanding of the primary structural components that have the relevant kind and degree of impact. The structural components of interest to us are characterized by impact that is profound, pervasive, asymmetric, and near-inescapable, and we elaborate on these characteristics through illustrative examples.

Third, theories diverge in the differentially positioned, differentially affected social groups selected for heightened moral scrutiny. We explain how differences in power and advantage are crucially important markers of the relevant social groups under our theory, including groups defined by race, gender, and social class.

Fourth, theories differ in their background assumptions regarding the circumstances constitutive of the social structural phenomena to which they apply. As we have already noted, we part company with both Rawls and Young, who tailor their theories to circumstances in which injustices largely emerge from morally benign social processes. Our theory addresses what we see as the more typical pattern, where there are individually identifiable agents of injustice whose wrongful conduct is manifested in unfair power relations and in their roles in creating or sustaining structural injustices.

In chapter 5, we present and defend an account of human rights that relies on our conception of human well-being as a crucial part of the rationale or justification for rights. We defend a variant of interest-based conceptions of human rights against a number of objections. These objections include criticisms raised by proponents of both control theories and dignity-based theories. We also address objections from critics who maintain that the function of human rights is not limited to considerations of how human rights matter to right-holders whether rights are understood as protecting their well-being interests or securing their control over certain matters.

We end the chapter by reflecting on the way we understand the interactive nature of how well-being interests are advanced or compromised in ordinary social contexts, where rights violations are often rooted in interlocking patterns of structural unfairness. In the worst instances of concern under our theory, deprivations arise from human rights violations that are neither random nor isolated events. These violations are rooted in a web of social norms, mutual expectations, public rituals, and behavioral regularities that are embedded not only in political and other rule-governed institutions but also in market mechanisms and informal social practices.

We defend a pragmatic approach to the problem of specification of duties that builds on the contingent but widespread empirical linkage between structural unfairness and human rights. We discuss both the specification of counterpart duties that correlate with particular human rights claims and more general responsibilities of institutional agents, paradigmatically nation-states, for maintaining background conditions of structural fairness.

In chapter 6, we examine the nature and limitations of the moral responsibility of nation-states for both human rights and structural justice. We begin with a discussion of what makes states unique moral agents and explore the implications for the assignment of responsibility for human rights and the structurally unjust conditions that give rise to many human rights violations. We conclude that there are responsibilities that only states, within the current global order, have the politically legitimate authority and institutional capacity to discharge.

However, we reject the position that nation-states have a near-exclusive role in preventing and remedying structural unfairness and human rights violations and, even then, only for the sake of their own citizens and residents. We examine several lines of argument, including the claim that there is no positive rationale for states to concern themselves with inequalities in power or advantage beyond their borders, along with arguments that defend the stronger thesis that it would be unjust to do so. Instead, we argue for a particular way of expanding state responsibilities for structural injustice and the human rights violations it facilitates beyond its borders. Specifically, we defend a Principle of Interstate Reciprocity that establishes conditions under which the pursuit of national benefit, global advantage, and the exercise of power over others is morally constrained.

We conclude the chapter by examining the global overlay of non-state concentrations of advantage and power that does much to determine the fates of nations and limits the ability of states to pursue domestic justice, especially within low- and middle-income countries (LMICs). We utilize examples drawn from social activist critiques of the existing global order as a vehicle for distinguishing and highlighting the moral significance of four unfair forms of control exercised by various supranational institutions, often in combination with powerful states and other non-state institutional agents.

In chapter 7, we illustrate and explicate our theory by way of our four extended examples. We explain why it is important to highlight both the kinds of structural injustices characteristic of urban settings and the kinds that are concentrated in rural sites of resource extraction and the processing and disposal of the hazardous byproducts of modern industrial life. There are many structural interconnections in national policy, local and global market dynamics, and the concentration of national and geopolitical power that explain some important similarities of structural injustices across different national settings and that also explain links between the fates of rural and urban dwellers.

In the first two sections, we examine how structural injustice operates in "sacrifice zones" both in the US and in LMICs. We explore the commonalities in market dynamics and the use of national and international political power in communities across the globe that are ongoing or historical sites of resource extraction and other activities involving an extensive concentration of environmental hazards. Our focus is the impact on children and future generations.

In the next two sections, we provide a portrait of the overlapping, mutually reinforcing mechanisms of structural injustice that, despite important contextual differences, operate both in US cities and in the rapidly growing urban centers of LMICs. We look at the US urban context primarily through the lens of the experiences of communities of color, especially in areas of concentrated poverty, with an emphasis on the dynamics of direct and egregious misuse of state power and state-facilitated economic exploitation by private entities. We then explore how both of these dynamics operate in the slums of rapidly growing urban areas within LMICs, but here the primary focus is the experience of women.

Finally, in chapter 8 we examine remedies for or justified responses to structural injustice other than the comprehensive approach to structural injustice available only to nation-states. Absent a global state with the features that make states normatively unique, and without some supranational entity for the enforcement of the principle of interstate reciprocity, there remain large gaps in the remedies available to many vulnerable, powerless people. These are people who live in politically unresponsive states or people who are subject to transnational injustices that transcend the capacities of politically legitimate authority to address, or both.

What, then, do we do in the face of these domestic and global gaps? This question arises as an important part of the overall assignment of responsibility for addressing structural injustice when states do not protect the human rights of their own citizens or violate the human rights of non-nationals. This can occur under conditions involving failed or failing states, corruption of democratic processes, extensive de-democratization, violations of the strictures established by the Principle of Interstate Reciprocity, or other compromises of state legitimacy.

We examine remedial strategies directly available to the aggrieved in these unfavorable circumstances. In particular, we consider the conditions under which forms of resistance that involve direct action designed to halt unjust activities or force the divestment of undeserved benefits are justified. We examine some counterarguments, including the contention that widely recommended forms of direct action constitute morally impermissible vigilantism or indiscriminately affect innocent beneficiaries.

We end the chapter and the book with some thoughts about how direct action, while far from the comprehensive forms of prevention and remedial action that structural injustice demands, is nevertheless of value. Direct action offers an avenue not only for social change otherwise structurally blocked but also for enhanced realization of the core elements of well-being for those who are deeply disadvantaged and relatively powerless.

CHAPTER 2 | Well-Being

OUR THEORY OF STRUCTURAL injustice is built upon an overarching conception of human well-being. In this chapter, we defend and explicate the six core elements of well-being that are at the center of this concept. The core elements are health; knowledge and understanding; personal security from physical and psychological harm, as well as the threat of such harm; personal attachments constitutive of valuable forms of human relationship; equal respect manifested in social and political standing in which individuals and groups experience treatment as moral equals; and a self-determining life, in which an individual shapes its broad contours and has some significant say over its general course.

In section 2.1, we begin by outlining how our conception of human well-being underpins our theory of structural injustice. We distinguish three respects in which the well-being of socially situated groups is unjustly subject to the differential influence of social structural arrangements. First, our conception identifies unjust deprivations in the core elements of well-being, in particular deprivations that constitute violations of human rights by those under duties to protect and promote them. Second, our conception pinpoints patterns of structural disadvantage that are deeply and fundamentally unfair because they have longer-term, systematic impact on the core well-being prospects, or chances for a decent life, of some socially situated groups. Third, our conception highlights unfair power relations that are particularly urgent to address because they permit some social groups to have unjustified forms of control over the most vital well-being interests of other groups.

In section 2.2, we develop the first two of four lines of argument to defend the selection of our six core elements of well-being. In the Socratic Argument, we rely on a variant of the method of Socratic reflection to make the initial, intuitive case that each of these elements belongs in an account of well-being intended to underpin a theory of what makes social arrangements structurally unjust. In order to make vivid the vital interest everyone has in protecting and promoting each element, our Socratic Argument proceeds by asking what all persons would want for themselves, whatever else they might want. The Structural Dependence Argument piggybacks on the main lines of the Socratic Argument as a way of tailoring the list so that it includes only those elements that most people cannot securely realize for themselves by individual choice and action alone. Our assumption is that a theory of structural justice should be concerned with elements of well-being that generally require institutionalized formal protections, assistance from political and legal institutions, and supportive social arrangements and practices to be securely realized.

In section 2.3, we present the six core elements of well-being in more detail. We elaborate the key points of our understanding of each element and discuss how they meet the tests set out by the Socratic and the Structural Dependence Arguments.

In section 2.4, we add a third layer of argument, primarily directed against conceptions of well-being whose lists of core elements are far less inclusive and, as a consequence, considerably less demanding in their implications than ours. Such lists hew closely to what is necessary for biological survival. Our main objective in this section is to argue directly against these under-inclusive conceptions of well-being—frequently touted as the most that can be claimed to be of universal value—by showing how a life lacking in some dimensions on our list is contrary to a highly plausible conception of a decent human life.

In section 2.5, we press a fourth line of argument. We argue against the view that only quite modest conceptions of well-being can be justified because only they will meet with universal endorsement. We also argue against the opposing view that more comprehensive conceptions of well-being can be defended as justifiable to a wide, if not universal audience from within the perspectives of diverse ethical outlooks. We turn the tables on both views. We raise doubts about the shared assumption that an adequate conception of well-being should be expected to put an end to persistent disagreement in the ways theorists in both camps think necessary for its justification. Instead, we put forward a different line of defense for our account of well-being that embraces disagreement as a necessary feature of the core complaints found within a range of social justice movements across diverse cultural and institutional settings.

In section 2.6, we conclude by highlighting three implications of our understanding of the roles that our conception of well-being plays in our theory of justice. We first distinguish the function that well-being plays in a theory of justice from its role in theories of beneficence or humanitarian assistance. Second, we explain why our theory's concern about well-being is not exclusively backward-looking, attending only to deprivations or diminished life prospects that the social structure has already caused. Third, we build upon these two points to elaborate on a theme introduced in section 2.1 about how the conception of well-being figures differently in the foundations of human rights than it does in our account of the unfairness of differential patterns of advantage and asymmetric power relations.

2.1. The Place of Well-Being in Our Theory

Our first task is to show how our conception of well-being underpins our theory of structural injustice. Our theory's focus on well-being is developed in two distinct ways. The most straightforward way is through a direct moral concern for actual deprivation of well-being of the sort that constitutes a human rights violation. Our conception of well-being identifies deprivations that are particularly unjust, either by direct harm to the well-being interests protected by human rights or by a violation of a duty by agents obligated to protect or promote those interests. Thus, in our account, well-being plays a central role in the justification for human rights, and with some important qualifications, it has much in common with interest-based theories of human rights. The hallmark of such theories is the claim that well-being interests occupy a central place among the primary justificatory grounds or rationale for human rights.[1] These well-being interests are said to be of such weighty and universal importance that the creation of effective institutional protections against deprivation is among the highest priorities of justice.[2]

The second distinct way in which our theory builds on and develops its focus on well-being is through the instrumental role of deprivation as a contributor to unfair patterns of advantage and unfair power relations, and the role of these two forms of structural injustice as risk factors for deprivation.

---

[1] John Tasioulas, "On the Foundations of Human Rights," in *Philosophical Foundations of Human Rights*, ed. Rowen Cruft, Matthew Liao, and Massimo Renzo (Oxford: Oxford University Press, 2015), 45–70.

[2] Henry Shue, for example, describes the aim of protections against human rights violations as a matter of ensuring a floor below which no one is allowed to fall. Henry Shue, *Basic Rights: Subsistence, Affluence, and U.S. Foreign Policy*, 2nd ed. (Princeton, NJ: Princeton University Press, 1996), 18–19.

Our theory is concerned not only with actual deprivation, but with the elevated risk of deprivation experienced by some social groups. More precisely, it is concerned with differential prospects for a decent life for members of social groups who are differentially affected by the arrangement of the social structure. Differential life prospects are structurally unfair when they involve forms of disadvantage that systematically impede the realization of something of value to all who are affected by them. However, not all objects of value are on a moral par, and consequently not all patterns of systematic disadvantage jeopardize objects of comparable moral significance. Our theory focuses on the patterns of unfair advantage that are present in the most fundamental or most basic forms of structural unfairness. Differential life prospects for members of social groups are fundamentally structurally unfair, on our theory, when they involve forms of disadvantage that systematically impede the realization of the core elements of well-being, which our theory describes as characteristic of a decent life. In other words, our conception of well-being is used to explain *why* some unfair patterns of (dis)advantage are structurally unfair in the morally most urgent, most basic sense.

Systematic disadvantage, in the relevant sense used within our theory, occurs whenever any social structural impediment profoundly, pervasively, asymmetrically, and near-inescapably diminishes an individual's most important well-being prospects, or in other words her prospects for a decent human life. Such impediments are often multiple and mutually reinforcing, and they systematically favor some often at the very great expense of others. Moreover, these disadvantaging effects are often compounded, perpetuated, and sustained over the course of a lifetime and, frequently, over the course of generations.

Unlike the concept of deprivation, which tracks well-being outcomes, the notion of an individual's life prospects is a probabilistic one. Having an advantage involves being in a condition that confers a superior position, relative to others, in the pursuit of various goods or valued ends (including, paradigmatically for us, the core elements).

Disadvantage, unlike deprivation, is a concern that arises when some have the benefit of a significant, social "leg up" in their chances for a decent life that those who are systematically disadvantaged do not.[3] Our

---

[3] To be advantaged is to have the benefit of a competitive edge, a leg up, to be in a position to gain the upper hand, to get the drop on the competition, or to occupy the higher ground (so as to go forward with the benefit of a superior line of sight against the enemy in battle, as the Middle English word *avantage* connoted).

interest is not simply disadvantage in any of its imaginable guises, where social conditions impede the realization of something of value, but only disadvantage in the prospects for realizing the core elements of well-being characteristic of a decent life. To put matters more crisply, if the social arrangements within which you lead your life disadvantage you in one or more core respects, those arrangements change your life prospects. You may beat the odds, as it were, but your chances for well-being have been altered for the worse. And odds are, your being disadvantaged will end up depriving you of well-being in one way or another.

There are, of course, important connections between well-being and advantage, and between deprivation and disadvantage, but the connections are purely contingent, not conceptual. Advantage can fail to produce well-being, well-being can fail to translate into advantage, and so on. Some people fail to make the most of their advantages, just as some people manage to rise above disadvantages. Disadvantage therefore may or may not translate into actual deprivation for each member of a disadvantaged social group, and deprivation does not guarantee disadvantage.

However, this is the point at which our instrumental concern with deprivation arises and the link to human rights begins to come into focus. Under reasonable empirical assumptions, deprivation shades into disadvantage, and disadvantage, in turn, begets further deprivation. For those who are deprived of one or more core elements of well-being—paradigmatically, through human rights violations—the stage is set for new and more deeply entrenched forms of disadvantage. Deprivation then matters on our theory, first, insofar as it produces outcomes of the sort that constitute violations of human rights, and deprivation matters also insofar as it is instrumental in producing unfair patterns of advantage, unjust on our account, even though some affected individuals slip through the net and manage to avoid further, consequential deprivations.[4]

Unfair patterns of advantage and disadvantage do not exhaust the categories of structural unfairness under our theory. Disadvantage does not magically materialize out of thin air. Nor does it arise entirely in some organic way, say, as the cumulative but unintended outcome of numerous, morally benign decisions and actions. Somewhere in the origin story of

---

[4] Our theory treats deprivation and disadvantage as distinct, in contrast to accounts of disadvantage that focus primarily on capabilities and only secondarily on well-being outcomes, or actual functioning. See Jonathan Wolff and Avner De-Shalit, *Disadvantage* (New York: Oxford University Press, 2007). For our discussion of key differences, see Madison Powers and Ruth Faden, "Health Capabilities, Outcomes, and the Political Ends of Justice," *Journal of Human Development and Capabilities* 12, no. 4 (2011): 565–670.

systematic disadvantage we routinely find evidence of differential power relations that are unjust in themselves and out of which patterns of disadvantage and, ultimately, concentrated pockets of deprivation are created and sustained.

Much more will be said in subsequent chapters about our position on three unfair forms of power, but a few preliminary points are useful to fix ideas of what lies ahead. Subordination or domination involves being subjected to control by members of another social group in ways that are unfair because the nature, extent, or means of power exercised is without sufficient moral justification. Exploitation involves being unfairly taken advantage of for the benefit of another, more powerful person or social group.[5] And social exclusion involves being unfairly excluded from, or permitted only marginal participation in, some valuable activity or social interaction.

Our conception of well-being is not meant to explain the basic wrongness of these unfair power relations. Being in someone's grip, as a mere instrument of another's will, or being treated as an object of exploitation, or being made the subject of social exclusion: all these are, in themselves, morally objectionable. However, the seriousness or gravity of the injustice rises as the moral significance of the well-being interests at stake increases. In other words, what gives each form of structurally unfair power relationship its particular added moral punch within our theory is the fact that the core elements of well-being are at stake.

In assessing both unfair power relations and unfair patterns of disadvantage, our theory thus takes its cue from the influence each has on the core elements of well-being. The reason is simply that we are interested in the most basic, most fundamental forms of egregious patterns of structural injustice rather than the full range of circumstances in which moral complaints about unfairness and the exercise of power in social relations arise.

Our theory's reliance on the conception of well-being as a rationale for human rights and as the basis for identifying the most fundamental forms

---

[5] Positions on the issue of what makes exploitation wrong, given that the transactions are presumed to be both voluntary and mutually beneficial, tend to divide between theories that identify some aspect of human dignity that is implicated and ones that emphasize the unfairness of the differential benefits extracted by the party having greater bargaining power. For excellent treatments of the dignity view, see Ruth Sample, *Exploitation: What It Is and Why It Is Wrong* (Lanham, MD: Rowman & Littlefield, 2003). For a powerful case for the unfairness view, see Alan Wertheimer, *Exploitation* (Princeton, NJ: Princeton University Press, 1996). We follow what is by now a fairly common view that no single conception of what makes exploitation wrong explains all instances of exploitation and in fact, in many instances, both wrong-making features are present.

of structural unfairness in patterns of advantage and relations of power points to some stark differences between our theory and some prominent alternatives.

Compare Rawls, for example. His theory is concerned focally with differential life prospects, specifically the socioeconomic opportunities available to the least advantaged economic classes. By contrast, our concern regarding disadvantage pertains to structural impediments to the successful realization of a decent life for members of diverse social groups. The notion of life prospects, on our theory, is both more granular and more encompassing than what is captured in differentials of income and wealth. Rawls's theory assumes background conditions in which basic human rights, including subsistence rights, have been realized, and concerns for fairness in life arise only on this foundation of rights fulfillment. We make no such idealizing assumption with regard to background conditions. Instead, the central concern of our theory is structural injustice in the world as we know it, in which deprivation and human rights violations are widely present.

Rawls also assumes that concerns about disadvantage arise under conditions in which morally problematic power relations are absent. Moreover, disadvantages that arise out of normal market and political processes, and potentially translate into unjust power differentials, are both transient and politically manageable in what he calls a nearly just society. In this society, the central concerns about injustices merely emerge from the cumulative, but unintended effects of multiple personal decisions and public policies that are presumed to be morally benign or even salutary.

For us, the morally most significant and empirically most typical form of structural injustice is far more complex than this emergent conception reveals.[6] It is rooted in a particular kind of normative phenomenon that is very present in the world as we know it and very different from a nearly just society. The patterns of structural injustice examined under our theory are characterized by diverse motivations and variations in degree of moral culpability among a variety of agents. We acknowledge here and elsewhere the in-principle possibility that structural injustice, characterized by densely woven patterns of systematic disadvantage, might simply emerge out of a largely morally untainted causal trajectory.[7] However, that is not

---

[6] For a discussion of the general notion of structural injustice as an emergent phenomenon, see Kevin Vallier, "Social Injustice as Emergent Property," *Bleeding Heart Libertarians* (blog), May 22, 2013, http://bleedingheartlibertarians.com/2013/05/social-injustice-as-emergent-property/.

[7] Madison Powers and Ruth Faden, *Social Justice: The Moral Foundations of Public Health and Health Policy* (New York: Oxford University Press, 2006), 16, 29–30, 64–79 (hereafter, Powers and Faden, *Social Justice*).

an accurate description of the phenomena we take as our focus. We claim that most reasonably plausible empirical scenarios, and certainly the normatively most important kind to examine, have far from benign origins.

The background assumption of our theory is that deprivations in the core elements of well-being, including ones associated with human rights violations, are often best explained by reference to their deep causal roots in unfair social structures. These deprivations in turn translate into new sources of disadvantage and set the stage for new or more consequential unfair power relations to take hold. Unfair social structures are unjust, in part, when their disadvantaging mechanisms undermine prospects for a decent life. They are also unfair when these mechanisms are under the control of social groups that can use their power to set the terms of social interaction in ways that permit them to dominate, exploit, and exclude other social groups from the very activities that make possible a decent life. Deprivation, unfair disadvantage, and unfair power dynamics are thus best understood as both inputs and outputs of the normative phenomena of interest under our theory. Not only does each one matter for its own sake, but each one matters additionally because of its instrumental role in creating and sustaining social conditions that foster and reproduce each of the other forms of injustice.

2.2. The Socratic and Structural Dependence Arguments

Our theory begins with an ancient and enduring idea about the primacy of a pluralist conception of human well-being within normative theories. The idea is widely associated with the moral and political philosophy of Aristotle, but it is shared by philosophical approaches as diverse as natural law theory,[8] objective list and similar variants of utilitarianism,[9] the

---

[8] John Finnis, a prominent contemporary natural law theorist, describes his own list of natural rights as ones resting on seven "basic values of human existence," which provide the "evaluative substratum of all moral judgments." John Finnis, *Natural Law and Natural Rights* (Oxford: Oxford University Press, 1980), 59. His list includes knowledge, life, play, aesthetic experience, sociability (friendship), practical reasonableness, and religion (59–95).

[9] James Griffin, for example, develops what he calls an "objective list of prudential values," which include various components of existence, such as the presence of the senses, integrity of limbs and bodily functioning, and freedom from pain and great anxiety, as well as understanding and knowledge of oneself and the world, enjoyments, having deep personal relations, and the various material goods and liberties that keep body and soul together and allow one to act on a conception of a worthwhile life and "choose one's own course through life." James Griffin, *Well-Being: Its Meaning, Measurement, and Moral Importance* (Oxford: Oxford University Press, 1986), 64–68. Even J. S. Mill, now widely regarded as endorsing a pluralist conception of the human good, famously says in chapter IV of *Utilitarianism* that "[t]he ingredients of happiness are very various, and each of them is desirable in itself, and not merely when considered as swelling an

capabilities approach,[10] basic needs theories,[11] and interest-based theories of the grounding or foundation of human rights.[12] They are, broadly speaking, *teleological* theories. The common denominator is that each approach defends a conception of the diverse elements of the human good that have a kind of primacy over other normative concepts.

Any claim of theoretical primacy within philosophy is, however, certain to mislead unless spelled out with some care. The philosophical literature contains divergent definitions of teleology, some of which rest on deeply controversial or discredited metaphysical doctrines that play no part in our conception.[13] The heart of the kind of primacy claim that we

---

aggregate. . . . They are desired and desirable and for themselves; besides being a means, they are a part of the end." John Stuart Mill, *The Collected Works of John Stuart Mill, Volume X: Essays on Ethics, Religion, and Society*, ed. John M. Robson, intro. F. E. L. Priestley (Toronto: University of Toronto Press; London: Routledge & Kegan Paul, 1985), 235. For prominent examples of pluralist interpretations of Mill, see Elizabeth Anderson, "John Stuart Mill and Experiments in Living," *Ethics* 102, no. 1 (1991): 4–26; and Fred Berger, *Happiness, Justice and Freedom: The Moral and Political Philosophy of John Stuart Mill* (Berkeley: University of California Press, 1984).

[10] The capabilities approach, as elaborated by Martha Nussbaum, begins with a list of functional capabilities, or valuable things that a person "can do or be." Her list includes life, bodily health, bodily integrity, senses, imagination and thought, emotions, affiliation, practical reason, living with other species, play, and control over one's environment. Martha Nussbaum, *Women and Human Development: The Capabilities Approach* (Cambridge: Cambridge University Press, 2000), 78–80; Martha Nussbaum, *Creating Capabilities* (Cambridge, MA: Belknap Press, 2001), 33–34.

[11] Gillian Brock argues for five basic needs that have universal moral importance and enjoy widespread support. Gillian Brock, "Needs and Global Justice," *Royal Institute of Philosophy Supplement* 57 (2005): 51–72. She argues as follows: "In order to deliberate and choose one will need at least a certain amount of (1) physical and mental health, (2) sufficient security to be able to act, (3) a sufficient level of understanding of what one is choosing between, and (4) a certain amount of autonomy. Because of its important role in developing (and maintaining) (1)–(4), I also add a fifth basic need which underlines the importance of our social needs, namely, (5) decent social relations with at least some others" (63).

[12] John Tasioulas's is an example of an interest theory that assumes the relevant interests grounding human rights are aspects of a person's well-being. His list is open-ended, but it is not restricted to a notion of well-being that encompasses only basic needs. Tasioulas, "On the Foundations of Human Rights."

[13] Aristotle's theory is generally seen as the paradigmatic example of a teleological principle, though it is saddled with a variety of complications that contemporary teleological theories hope to avoid. Problems arise from a pair of metaphysical claims. For Aristotle, all living things (and perhaps all things) are members of a "natural kind," each of which has its own distinctive final end, or *telos*. For each natural kind, including human beings, there are essential defining attributes or capacities, which if fully developed, constitute a person's perfection, or state of optimal flourishing. The essential properties of a flourishing human being in Aristotle's theory are its virtues or excellences, both moral and intellectual. Many contemporary teleologists working in the broadly Aristotelian tradition, by contrast, focus on human traits and capacities, which when sufficiently developed are thought valuable simply because experience shows that they tend to make life go well. They do not endorse the essentialist claim about which of these attributes make us distinctively human or argue that what is good for us is a matter of perfecting our essential nature. Contemporary teleological theories, including our theory, thus identify ways of living that our nature makes possible and which reflective persons value, not forms of living that are valuable because they represent the perfection of our essential nature. For a discussion of these and

make is encapsulated in Richard Kraut's summary of the teleological approach: "According to this way of thinking, the *point* of social institutions, social interactions, and individual projects should be to enhance someone's well-being or to eliminate impediments to well-being."[14]

Well-being—"eudaimonia" in Aristotle's language—refers not only to what is good for a person but also, more precisely for Aristotle, what makes for the best life.[15] In contemporary parlance, however, the core elements of what is often described as a good or decent or dignified life are generally referred to as elements of the prudential good rather than the more ambitious notion of eudaimonia. We employ the modern notion of prudential good in order to express the central idea that well-being is a matter of what is *good for* a person, what tends to make a person's life go well. Our concern is for core elements that contribute to a characteristically decent life, not the best life possible.[16]

2.2.1. Socratic Reflection

We begin the defense of our conception of human well-being by relying on an argumentative strategy that resembles a method widely understood

---

other controversies surrounding the teleological aspects of Aristotle's theory, see Jonathan Lear, *Aristotle: The Desire to Understand* (Cambridge: Cambridge University Press, 1988).

[14] Richard Kraut, *What Is Good and Why: The Ethics of Well-being* (Cambridge, MA: Harvard University Press, 2007), 15 (emphasis in the original).

[15] Some critics of teleology have a particular target in mind. They tend to equate teleological theories with Aristotle's or other perfectionist doctrines, which assume there is one kind of human excellence, for which it is the aim of ethical or political theory to maximize. See John Rawls, *A Theory of Justice* (1971), rev. ed. (Cambridge, MA: Harvard University Press, 1999), 285–286 (hereafter, Rawls, *TOJ*); Thomas Hurka, *Perfectionism* (Oxford: Oxford University Press, 1993), 55–68. Current teleological theories, including ours, however, tend to be more concerned with the distinctive elements of a good life that should matter for anyone, not comprehensive questions, such as whether the best life is the contemplative life or the life of the statesman, or whether we should prefer the life of the aesthete or the ascetic.

[16] A prudential conception of the good—a conception of what is good for an individual because it makes her life go well—contrasts with two other familiar philosophical conceptions of the good. One contrast is with moral goodness. For example, it may be prudentially good for someone to be healthy, but not necessarily something that makes a person morally good. Aristotle famously thought the prudential good of certain virtues or excellences and the moral goodness of individuals converged. Not everyone then or now shares Aristotle's optimism. A second contrast is with a conception of the impersonal goodness of certain states of affairs. G. E. Moore and some contemporary philosophers such as Derek Parfit make use of arguments of this kind. For example, Moore's "method of isolation," which Parfit often relies upon, asks us to consider a thought experiment in which World A contains more species, more beauty, less inequality, and so on, than World B. Is World A better than World B? This is a different question than one that asks what makes an individual better off. G. E. Moore, *Principia Ethica*, rev. ed., ed. T. Baldwin (Cambridge: Cambridge University Press, 1993), 142, 145–147, 236, 256; Derek Parfit, *Reasons and Persons* (Oxford: Oxford University Press, 1986).

as the centerpiece of Aristotle's own approach to questions of what makes a life go well. Aristotle begins his philosophical reflection on the constituents of a good life by examining the opinions of the wise and the many.[17] He employs this method of Socratic reflection, as it is known, not because he assumes that the judgments it renders are decisive, but simply because there is no place to begin other than the available stock of carefully considered judgments rooted in human experience. Indeed, Aristotle assumes that most opinions are in significant part wrong, but nonetheless widely held or favored by the practically wise because they reveal a kernel of truth that further, more refined reflection can make clearer and less prone to error.[18]

A prominent interpretation of Aristotle's theory supposes that he endorses a pluralist account of the elements of well-being and that, upon reflection, certain elements would be ones that human beings would want, whatever else they would want for themselves.[19] Whether or not this position is the best overall interpretation of Aristotle is a matter of some dispute.[20] We need not take sides on which reading of the historical Aristotle is textually superior. The important point is that the method of Socratic reflection often attributed to Aristotle remains central to debates among philosophers who attempt to understand the nature of human well-being and utilize that understanding as a basis for assessing how well social arrangements serve the most vital interests of everyone materially affected by them.

2.2.2. Caveats and Clarifications to Our Method of Socratic Reflection

Our contemporary version of this reflective method is a plausible first step, within an extended justificatory chain of arguments, in defending our list, subject to three important caveats or clarifications. First, it is crucially important to emphasize the reason we are interested only in what anyone would want, whatever else it might be reasonable for particular persons to

---

[17] G. E. L. Owen, *"Tithenai ta phainomena,"* in *Logic, Science and Dialectic* (1961) (London: Duckworth, 1986), 239–251.

[18] Ibid.

[19] Prominent articulations and defenses of the "inclusivist" interpretation include J. L. Ackrill, "Aristotle on Eudaimonia," in *Essays on Aristotle's Ethics*, ed. A. O. Rorty (Berkeley: University of California Press, 1980); and Roger Crisp, "Aristotle's Inclusivism," *Oxford Studies in Ancient Philosophy* 12 (1994): 111–136. The inclusivist interpretation rests, in part, on Aristotle's explication of eudaimonia as a self-sufficient or complete life, or one "lacking in nothing."

[20] For a carefully argued contrarian view, see Robert Heinaman, "The Improvability of Eudaimonia in the *Nicomachean Ethics*," *Oxford Studies in Ancient Philosophy* 23 (2002): 99–145.

want. The point of this restriction is to exclude various things that particular individuals might count as centrally important to their own conception of a worthwhile or personally fulfilling life but, nonetheless, are not
assumed by them to be among the things that anyone necessarily thinks
of as having comparable value for everyone else. Climbing the world's
tallest mountain peaks, mastering classical Greek, and becoming an expert
wood carver are examples of potentially worthwhile personal conceptions,
but even avid climbers, classicists, and carvers would agree that there are
no good reasons to think that these goals are or should be valuable to
everyone or that society has strong reasons to see to it that its members
can realize these values in their own lives. Moreover, judgments about
what constitutes the best life for an individual are left to the individual
to determine. This commitment follows directly from our inclusion of
self-determination as a core element in our conception. This and the other
elements of our account, such as being healthy and secure from personal
violence, are tailored to the task of identifying aspects of well-being that
are universally valuable.

Second, it is equally important to understand the limited implications
of our conception of well-being for questions about the worthwhileness
or value of particular persons' lives. At times, some of Aristotle's remarks
suggest that the conception of well-being suitable for the assessment of
political and social arrangements can serve as a basis for deciding whether
life is worth living. For example, when some elements, such as friendship
(broadly construed as involving many valuable forms of human attachment), are lacking, Aristotle makes the strong claim that such a life cannot
be a worthwhile life.[21] However, the conception that we need for a theory
of structural injustice makes no such claims, and as a result, we avoid two
deeply unpalatable implications.

We do not claim that anyone who is lacking in one or more of these
core elements cannot have a decent life. Quite the contrary; a life marked
by pain, illness, and physical infirmity is a familiar enough example of a
life that, when viewed by the person who experiences these conditions as
well as by others, is often judged a worthwhile or decent life, or even an
extraordinary life. Also on our view, it is even reasonable for particular
individuals to value specific personal projects and commitments so highly

---

[21] For the suggestion that friendship is a good without which life itself would not be worth living,
see *NE* I.7.1097b11; *NE* IX.9.1169b16–20; *Rhet.* I.5.1360b14–23. All references to Aristotle are
found in Aristotle and Jonathan Barnes, *The Complete Works of Aristotle: The Revised Oxford
Translation* (Princeton, NJ: Princeton University Press, 1984).

that, for example, they would accept a substantial risk to a core dimension like personal security or health in order to pursue them. In short, our theory is not prescriptive with regard to how individuals should assess the quality of their own lives.

Moreover, a life greatly lacking in the realization of one or more core elements does not warrant a social judgment that this life is less important or not entitled to the same moral concern as others. Again, quite the contrary; our theory's commitment to equal respect rules out of consideration treating persons who live lives of severe deprivation in any of the core elements of well-being as less worthy of societal concern.[22]

Third, we do not claim that the core elements on our list are always beneficial in all circumstances for all people. This point of clarification is aimed at a potential misunderstanding that Aristotle warned against in his era. For example, he noted that being courageous—one of his enumerated constitutive excellences that are good for persons to have—can lead to arrogance, excessive risk-taking, or diminished empathy for others, or impede friendship. On our list, health is valuable, whatever else one wants, but good health can also lead some people to excessive risk-taking or diminished empathy for those with disabilities. The list of core elements of well-being appropriate for political and institutional purposes only reflects what is generally *good for* everyone, and thus the list is relevant to judgments of how we should fashion institutional and social arrangements that affect their realization.[23]

A conception of well-being that is appropriate for use in the arena of political and social institutions should take notice only of general facts

---

[22] In previous work, we described the core dimensions as essential dimensions. We tried to preempt various points of confusion by use of the phrase "moderate essentialism." Powers and Faden, *Social Justice*, 16, 29–30. Since then, we have abandoned any reference to what is essential because of the misunderstanding or confusion that this way of putting matters invites. See Madison Powers and Ruth Faden, "Social Practices, Public Health, and the Twin Aims of Justice: Responses to Comments," in "Symposium on *Social Justice: The Moral Foundations of Public Health and Health Policy*," *Public Health Ethics* 6, no. 1 (2013): 45–49.

[23] John Tasioulas makes this same kind of Aristotelian point by noting that the source of confusion results from "conflating what *generally* serves our well-being in *some* respect with that which will best serve our *overall* well-being in any *particular case*." Tasioulas, "On the Foundations of Human Rights," 49 (emphasis in the original). He is arguing in defense of his interest-based theory of human rights by responding to an objection by Amartya Sen. Sen argues that many of the freedoms that protect our human rights do not serve our interests. This is an example of the same sort of confusion that Aristotle noted when elucidating what it means to say that something is in our interest or contributes to our well-being. Understood in the context in which our concern is for the way that social arrangements should be configured, what we want to know are the kinds of interests that generally matter to all, quite independently of how much they matter to particular persons in particular cases.

about what makes life go well, and these facts should inform judgments about what policies, practices, and norms tend to contribute to the well-being of all of those who are materially affected. In the political arena, for example, the objective cannot be to tailor policies to fit the specific needs of each person on a case-by-case basis. The lawmaker's task is thus different from, say, that of a parent or teacher who is in a position to recognize that a particular child might not benefit from what children in general need to thrive. Our theory is not meant to provide guidance in such cases. It is thus no objection to our conception of well-being that the elements on our list do not always make a net positive contribution to the overall well-being of particular persons in specific circumstances.

These three caveats or clarifications inform the way we see the point of Socratic reflection in the current context of thinking about structural injustice. The purpose of reflection is not to generate a ranked list of what is subjectively most valuable within the life of any particular individual or to help individuals decide what the best or most worthwhile life is. It is not meant to help individuals or society decide if a particular life is worth living or its quality unacceptably low. It is not constructed in order to provide practical guidance in all sorts of arenas of personal decision where knowledge of concrete specifics is essential to wise choice. Rather, the point is to generate a list that can and should inform the configuration of political institutions and social arrangements and guide collective decision-making in ways that are just and also leave room for the individual pursuit of a personal ideal of a worthwhile life.

2.2.3. The Structural Dependence Argument

The Structural Dependence Argument claims that each element matters greatly to structural justice, not only because it is intrinsically important to individuals, but also because the successful realization of the element is virtually impossible within most contemporary forms of organized social life without the appropriate structure and configuration of background social arrangements and institutions. That is, each dimension is so highly influenced by the structure of institutions and social practices that it is difficult to imagine how these elements of well-being could be sufficiently realized under deeply antagonistic social structures.

The Structural Dependence Argument is crucial at the ground level in order to understand one of the key purposes behind our conception of well-being and how deprivation figures in our structural theory. We do not focus on deprivations or the prospect of deprivation in the core well-being interests simply because they are particularly bad for those affected. We focus on deprivations that, when viewed from the perspective of those subject to the highly consequential influence of social structures, generate claims against institutional or other agents who play central roles in their creation and maintenance. That structural arrangements matter in this normatively specific way arises from the fact that certain core well-being interests are not realizable without social contribution to what individuals cannot feasibly and securely achieve for themselves. The relevant social contribution can take a variety of forms, including the provision of public goods, the establishment of social safety nets, a functioning criminal justice system, and the public regulation of economic transactions and other private activities that have significant spillover effects on the core elements.

We will have more to say about social contribution in section 5.4, where we discuss responsibility for human rights fulfillment. Here we want to emphasize how the central insights of the Structural Dependence Argument rely on the premise that deprivation in any of the core elements often has two kinds of cascading effects that can be addressed only by action taken at the level at which social arrangements are structured.

First, deprivations in each core element of well-being tend to cascade into deprivations in the other core elements unless institutions and social processes are configured in ways that stop the slide through which deprivations beget other deprivations. Second, not only do deprivations worsen through cascading causal processes, but deprivations in the core elements of well-being are important sources of disadvantage, implicating a person's longer-term chances for a decent life, and they are a source of increased vulnerability to unfair forms of power, including subordination, exploitation, and social inclusion.

2.3. The Core Elements

In this section, we provide a fuller elaboration of the six core elements, relying in part on the first two lines of argument we employ in their defense. The intuitive case we press thus depends upon showing, for each element, both its intrinsic value for human beings generally and the social contribution that is generally necessary for its realization. Along the way we also take up some potential objections to the elements that make up our list.

2.3.1. Health

There are many accounts of the concept of health, some embedded in particular cultural traditions and healing professions and others constructed for specific theoretical purposes. We work with what is essentially an ordinary language understanding of physical and mental health. While health is a state or condition that in many respects can be described in organic or functional terms, we reject an understanding of health deprivation that is restricted to biological malfunctioning or impairments of some functional ability such as mobility, sight, or hearing. Instead, we have chosen a conception that is broad enough to avoid the arbitrary exclusion of some deficits from what counts as a concern of justice, on the grounds that those deficits are not produced through the vectors of illness or injury or because they cannot or should not be classified as diseases.

At the same time, our conception is not so broad as to encompass every other element of well-being. In this, we reject the oft-cited World Health Organization (WHO) definition, which views health as a state of emotional, physical, and economic well-being.[24] The problem with the WHO account is that it conflates virtually all elements of human development under a single rubric and thereby converts almost any deficit of well-being into a health deficit.

Health is for us a distinctive moral concern. It reflects the rich and diverse set of considerations of focal concern to both public health and clinical health services, including premature mortality and preventable morbidity, malnutrition, pain, loss of mobility, mental health, the biological basis of behavior, reproduction (and its control), and sexual functioning. Being in pain, even if that pain does not impede proper biological functioning, is also incompatible with health. So, too, are sexual dysfunction and infertility.

There is probably no more paradigmatic example of an aspect of well-being that is intrinsically valuable to all persons, whatever else they might want for themselves, than health. Health is also a paradigmatic example of an aspect of well-being that individuals cannot generally secure for themselves without significant institutional support of states and civil society more generally. Good health is possible only under complex social arrangements that allow for research, education, and training of professionals who are necessary for the development and delivery of

---

[24] World Health Organization, Preamble to the Constitution of the World Health Organization as adopted by the International Health Conference, New York, June 19–22, 1946.

health care and public health services. More important perhaps, among the major determinants of health are factors beyond the capacity of individuals to secure for themselves or to acquire solely through bilateral market exchanges. Poor health in early childhood puts health across the life span at risk. For both adults and children, sanitation facilities and clean water, population-wide vaccinations, environmental quality, food availability and safety, and much more all require substantial social coordination within any reasonably complex society. The nexus of necessary social contributions and its intrinsic value make health an obvious element of well-being relevant to what structural justice demands.

2.3.2. Knowledge and Understanding

"Knowledge and understanding" is our umbrella term for discussing the moral importance of possessing a broad set of diverse skills and abilities commonly classified in philosophical discussions under the headings of "theoretical reason" and "practical reason." As the Aristotelian point is sometimes put, theoretical reasoning skills aid us in answering empirical questions and forming our understanding of what there *is*, while the skills of practical deliberation aid us in deciding what we *ought* to do or how we *ought* to live and the kinds of choices we should make.

Within the psychology literature both practical and theoretical reasoning are essential to the acquisition, development, and successful use of knowledge and understanding. The broad account of such reasoning abilities includes a "combination of skills, including attention, learning, memory, praxis (skilled motor behaviors), and the so-called executive functions, such as decision making, goal setting, and judgment."[25]

The successful exercise of theoretical reasoning involves the use of basic intellectual skills and habits of mind necessary for persons to understand the world. Such skills include sensory perception, analytical ability, imagination, logical inference, the ability to form beliefs based on evidence, the ability to reflect on what counts as relevant evidence for those beliefs, and the ability to weigh the probative value of each, and in modern societies, numeracy and literacy. Successful use of these skills results in understanding, knowing, and good judgment.

The abilities we associate with practical reason include those needed to form and revise a conception of how we each wish to live, to conform

---

[25] Peter Whitehouse, Eric Juengst, Maxwell Mehlman, and Thomas Murray, "Enhancing Cognition in the Intellectually Intact," *Hastings Center Report* 27 (1997): 14–22.

behavior to ideals and ends that are a part of that conception, and to deliberate among alternative means to the achievement of those ends. Practical reason is valuable for more than just the development of individual life plans or the setting of one's personal goals and ends, however. It is necessary for the very possibility of other-regarding morality. In order to function as a member of a moral community, we need to be able to deliberate with others about the reasonableness of our actions and choices and to reflect on those actions and choices from the perspectives of others affected by them. In addition, we need to coordinate our actions, engage in reciprocal transactions, and make strategic evaluations of options and emotionally astute assessments of the motives and intentions of those with whom we interact.[26]

Although theoretical reasoning is distinguishable from practical reasoning, judgments of what to do necessarily piggyback on basic theoretical abilities. The abilities that allow us to form beliefs about the natural and social world provide us with a reliable factual basis for forming practical conclusions. Theoretical reason and practical reason thus work together, allowing us to navigate both the natural and social worlds. As with the other categories of well-being on our list, without both forms of cognitive success we lack something of huge and distinctive significance to a decent human life, no matter what other dimensions of well-being we may experience. Knowledge and understanding, then, is something that everyone has reason to want, no matter what else they would want.

Knowledge and understanding, like health, is critically dependent on instructional structures within which the transmission of human knowledge is facilitated. In the modern world, securing the knowledge and understanding characteristic of a decent life generally requires a process of

---

[26] Practical reasoning also involves taking up a critical, self-reflective stance toward our own desires, preferences, values, and ideals so that we are able to revise them if they are found wanting. Harry Frankfurt, "Freedom of the Will and the Concept of a Person," in *The Importance of What We Care About* (Cambridge: Cambridge University Press, 1998). We need the ability to subject our current or immediate desires and preferences to scrutiny so that we may better harmonize them with our longer-term goals and aspirations. See also Griffin, *Well-Being*. In addition, the skills of practical reasoning allow our judgments of value to be examined in light of how well they cohere with our more global personal ideals for our own character. Practical reasoning abilities also include some capacity to examine the origins of our moral beliefs, value judgments, and personal ideals and to reflect upon the process by which those commitments were acquired. John Christman, "Autonomy and Personal History," *Canadian Journal of Philosophy* 21, no. 1 (1991): 1–24. As Mill frequently observes in *On Liberty*, the skills of reflective persons include the ability to step back from one's beliefs and opinions about how one should live and to "adopt" them as one's own rather than simply "inherit" them. John Stuart Mill, *The Collected Works of John Stuart Mill, Volume XVIII: Essays on Politics and Society, Part I*, ed. John M. Robson, intro. Alexander Brady (Toronto: University of Toronto Press; London: Routledge & Kegan Paul, 1977).

formal education that is not possible without the institutional arrangements that provide schools and produce teachers, and the resources necessary to support them, including research and government oversight. Even when education is privatized at the consumer level, private schools and home instruction are directly dependent on these institutional structures. Moreover, the need for access to information about the world does not end in adulthood or with formal schooling. Information necessary for the competent exercise of theoretical and practical reasoning is constantly in flux. Individuals cannot secure access to this information on their own. They are dependent on state policies to protect freedom of speech and prohibit censorship or the control of information by the privileged and powerful. Increasingly, they are dependent as well on the infrastructure and resources needed for access to information sources such as the internet.

More foundationally, possession of knowledge and understanding depends critically on what happens in early childhood and even prior to birth. Environmental and disease exposures, malnutrition, inadequate social interaction and affection, and insufficient stimulation can have profound negative effects on cognitive development, effects that in some cases are lifelong.[27] Each of these potential assaults on cognitive capacity has a supporting social structural nexus, whether it be providing social supports for parents and families or otherwise ensuring that all children are properly cared for and protected from environmental and other threats to their development of knowledge and understanding.[28]

2.3.3. Personal Security

Virtually all conceptions of well-being, and in particular those that serve as a basis for human rights theories, recognize the importance of personal security as a vital human interest.[29] It is extremely difficult if not impossible to live a decent life if one is in constant fear of physical or psychological abuse. Experiencing the fear or threat of such abuse is surely a

---

[27] Y. Ben-Shlomo and D. A. Kuth, "A Life Course Approach to Chronic Disease Epidemiology: Conceptual Models, Empirical Challenges, and Interdisciplinary Perspectives," *International Journal of Epidemiology* 31 (2002): 285–293.

[28] There are overlaps between health and knowledge and understanding, for example, insofar as healthy brain development is necessary for the realization of knowledge and understanding that has its special moral salience in the prudential value that it adds to human life and it is a value that is not reducible to a notion of biological functioning. Powers and Faden, *Social Justice*, 19–22.

[29] William Blackstone, for example, argued that the right to personal security is one of the three "absolute natural rights of man." William Blackstone, *Commentaries on the Laws of England*, 1753.

setback to well-being, regardless of who we are or what values we might otherwise have. Injustices involving assault, enslavement, degradation, and rape, for example, typically violate multiple interests simultaneously, including the interest we have in our health and other elements of well-being, such as leading a self-determining life. But the focus on personal security highlights the distinct interest everyone has in safekeeping against violation or threats of violation of bodily integrity. Independently of whether bodily harm or other adverse consequences accompany threats to this interest, a life of perpetual insecurity, marked by the experience of extreme vulnerability and awareness of the risk of arbitrary physical and psychological mistreatment at the hands of another, is a life of greatly reduced quality, and its adverse effects pervade and color all other aspects of one's well-being. The systematic use of terror and intimidation is among the chief weapons of social control employed by totalitarian regimes, colonial powers, foreign occupiers, and the leaders of violent racist social movements, as well as by abusive family members, particularly in male-dominated communities.

Our account of personal security contrasts sharply with the umbrella concept found in the 2005 report of the United Nations World Summit. The notion of security and the human right to security endorsed there, and subsequently reaffirmed by the United Nations General Assembly, encompasses an expansive range of human rights, including the right to subsistence and the freedom from fear, as well as quite a few specific rights contained in the Universal Declaration of Human Rights.[30] For some observers, this trend has much to be said for it. Rhonda Powell, for example, argues that "security is nothing more than a referent to goods, attributes, and things we want to secure" and "thus, [it] represents the endurance of certain valuable interests without threat."[31]

On our view, the UN definition is overbroad in the same way we think the WHO definition of health is too broad to be useful. Our general point is that a conception of well-being loses its capacity for reasonably determinate practical guidance when matters of distinct moral

---

[30] World Summit Outcome Document, Article 143, 2005; United Nations General Assembly Resolution 66/290. For the text of the Declaration, see United Nations General Assembly, "Universal Declaration of Human Rights," 1948, http://www.un.org/en/universal-declaration-human-rights/index.html.

[31] Rhonda Powell, "The Relational Concept of Security" (DPhil diss., University of Oxford, 2006), quoted by Liora Lazarus, "The Right to Security," in *Philosophical Foundations of Human Rights*, ed. Rowen Cruft, S. Matthew Liao, and Massimo Renzo (Oxford: Oxford University Press, 2015), 432.

salience are blurred. Instead, it is more useful to recognize, as we do, that in so many instances in which there is a deprivation in one element of well-being or where it is put at grave risk, other elements of well-being suffer a similar fate. An overarching concern for each of the elements on our list is the importance of its secure realization. However, the moral importance of secure realization should not lead us to conflate the various threats to distinct elements of well-being by adopting a definition of personal security that drags in every other moral concern under one conceptual umbrella.

Another key point regarding our account of personal security is that it is something that an individual on her own cannot securely realize for herself and those who depend upon her. For this we need institutions for the maintenance of public order, the enforcement of criminal law, and the protection of equal status under the law, as well as personal liberties. Personal security is not possible without laws that treat violence and threats of violence against all persons with equal concern and with functioning law enforcement that properly upholds those laws, as well as fire departments and other institutions of public safety, courts, and the military. Although the very wealthy can protect themselves with armed guards and gated communities, even they require social institutions to protect them from external threats to their security. Diplomacy and international relations also matter. They can mitigate threats from war and armed conflict, and social policies of all sorts can reduce violence and group animus and promote solidarity among peoples.

2.3.4. Equal Respect

At minimum, having the respect of others involves being recognized and treated as a moral being deserving of equal moral standing. Concretely, that means that whatever consideration is due to the most urgent moral interests of some must be given to everyone, lest those denied equal standing suffer a host of indignities and personal affronts. These include social and economic marginalization, cultural stigmatization that marks some persons as naturally inferior and not worthy of the treatment due to others, and public shame and humiliation of the sort that the US Supreme Court in its celebrated school desegregation case labeled as a badge of inferiority. On our view, it is enough that a person can suffer gravely from the humiliating experience of being disrespected even if she is perfectly aware that she does not merit the insult or remains confident that she is not less worthy of respect.

This is true in the typical case of disrespect as a function of group membership. Equal respect is characteristically under assault when an individual is the object of discrimination based on judgments of intrinsic inferior social status, often linked to properties of group membership, such as ethnicity, gender, sexual orientation, religion, and social class, or characteristics like cognitive or physical disabilities. Respect in the sense we intend is part of what all persons would want for themselves and yet it is what is lacking in invidious judgments of persons on the basis of their group membership, as in the phenomenon of racism or sexism.

Although it is possible for individual members of a socially disfavored group to retain their self-respect under discriminatory and oppressive social conditions, escaping without diminished self-respect is extremely difficult, especially when the disrespect is systemic and long-standing. However, that some members of oppressed groups maintain their self-respect does nothing to vitiate the injustice and the reduced quality of life that derive from being disrespected by others. Being regularly subjected to small and large humiliations, denied courtesies accorded others, dismissed as unworthy of attention, addressed as inferiors, or simply not being seen or heard are all failures of equal respect and are ways of living that are incompatible with anything like a decent human life.

Social institutions are among the primary mechanisms that determine whether an individual or social group is publicly recognized as worthy of equal respect, for whom morally comparable interests are given comparable weight. Many social institutions, formal and informal, adjudicate and validate public perceptions of individual worth by determining, for example, who is eligible to live, play, or work where, and who is deserving of what forms of address, and by controlling the primary determinants of social distinction.

The nexus of social contribution is vitally important here, as it is for other elements of well-being on our list. Equal respect cannot be experienced by groups who are treated unequally under the law, nor can it be experienced by groups who are subject to entrenched social practices and norms of inferiority, whether sanctioned by the law or not. Moreover, the prospect that individuals and groups will experience the equal respect of others is nearly impossible, absent the recognition of equal political standing.[32] In concrete terms, full recognition of equal moral standing will require equal rights of political

---

[32] For children, the relevant consideration is that they will be accorded equal political standing upon maturity.

participation.[33] Second-class political status is emblematic of social judgments of second-class standing as a moral being. While morally acceptable modes of political participation might vary across societies, the non-negotiable requirement for any form of political organization is that none is treated as less deserving or less eligible to play a role in shaping public life.

Moreover, equal moral and political standing is incompatible with the view that a person's interests are well-enough accounted for and represented by the voices of others who are presumed to speak on her behalf, say, as her guardian, protector, or superior. Perhaps even more than the role that institutions play in economic distribution, their contributions to socially shared judgments of worth do so much to profoundly shape and pervasively color a person's entire life experience.

For reasons of the intrinsic value to the individual, and because of the heavy influence of institutional arrangements on the very possibility of its realization, the respect of others as equals is an important good on our list of core elements of well-being that are of central concern to structural justice.

A critic might object that conceptualizing the value of equal respect in prudential terms fails to locate properly the fundamental moral objection to social phenomena such as marginalization and stigmatization. Tim Scanlon characterizes stigmatization as an evil of a special sort. For example, what is wrong with marking members of some groups as inferior to other human beings is that it offends a deep egalitarian value. What is wrong is the inequality itself, not, for example, the diminishment of well-being that it occasions. What is wrong is that failures of respect violate a deontological constraint, a kind of moral category that marks absolute demands of morality, independent of whether some form of treatment reduces or adds to human well-being.[34] The charge is that we have made a simple category mistake within moral theory.

Let us suppose that Scanlon is right to claim that what is most directly wrong with stigmatized status is the simple wrongness of the kinds of

---

[33] We can think of several concrete cases for further exploration. For convicted felons, it could be claimed that political participation should be returned to them after time served. For non-nationals, we might consider whether not having equal political standing means that it is nearly impossible for them to experience equal moral standing. By contrast, there may be exceptions. Those with profound and permanent cognitive disabilities may be denied equal rights of political participation, but this then poses important questions about what further steps are required to ensure that equal respect is accorded to them and that their interests are adequately represented.

[34] T. M. Scanlon, *Why Does Inequality Matter?* (Oxford: Oxford University Press, 2018), 19, 26–29.

inequality it embodies. It is unjust even if no one is aware of the disrespect, and it is unjust even if no one experiences any deprivation of well-being as a consequence. That is a very plausible claim, but even if we accept it, as we do, it does not follow that there is one and only one way in which someone is wronged by failures of equal respect. We are not claiming that our theory's concern with deprivation of equal respect has gotten to the bottom of all that matters morally, especially with regard to the assessment of the bigot's conduct and character.

Indeed, in subsequent discussions of human rights and structural fairness we argue for a different, though complimentary way in which a commitment to moral equality enters into our theory at a foundational level. We thus recognize that much more is at stake. Here, we merely claim that it is important for the way we arrange political institutions and social practices to understand that this kind of disrespect is also deeply unjust for a particular kind of reason. It is unjust because it is *bad for* persons who are members of disrespected groups. Whatever animus the bigot harbors within such arrangements should not be allowed to spill over in ways that result in serious deprivation for others.

We also claim that forms of disrespect built into forms of domination, social exclusion, and exploitation are unjust because they are seriously and unfairly disadvantaging, even if some members of an affected group avoid the worst outcomes. When this kind of disrespect plays a motivating role in creating and maintaining unjust forms of social relations, as is often the case, the stigmatization and marginalization of persons based on group membership unfairly disadvantage them and in turn, become part and parcel of the mechanisms through which all too familiar forms of subordination, social exclusion, and exploitation are created and sustained.

To reiterate, although our account rests on the prudential value of respect, it does not reject the Kantian or other deontological claims that failures of respect can be morally wrong even if no aspect of human well-being is harmed and the predictable disadvantaging and disempowering consequences fail to materialize. As a matter of general morality, the demands of respect very likely go well beyond the prudential importance of avoiding serious deprivation in well-being and its instrumental role in establishing and sustaining unfair patterns of disadvantage and positions of powerlessness.

Indeed, we do not presuppose a general theory of morality that assumes that the moral salience of our conception of the core elements of well-being within our theory of structural justice exhausts the moral significance of respect. Hence, the deontological account is not incompatible with our claim that an important part of what makes social structural arrangements unjust is when the bigot's worldview is instantiated in those arrangements. Individuals and groups who are not accorded equal respect suffer in terms of experienced deprivations in well-being. And as we argue in more detail in subsequent chapters, it is also unjust when failures of equal respect eventuate in unfair disadvantage and durable patterns of unfair control.

2.3.5. Personal Attachments

Having deep bonds of personal attachment is one of the most central dimensions of human well-being. Such bonds are found in friendships, in romantic relationships and life partnerships, within families and between parents and children, as well as in a sense of solidarity or fellow feeling with others within one's community or among those with similar life experiences. Personal attachments involve experiencing love, friendship, emotional engagement, and sympathetic identification with others. Few people would choose a life without these experiences. Such a life would seem empty, emotionally arid, and devoid of a special kind of purposefulness that commitment to mere projects, professional ambitions, and causes lack, however meaningful these may be within a personal conception of a worthwhile life.

The value of personal attachments is distinct from all other elements of well-being. For example, although having the respect of others is an element of human well-being that emerges in social relations, it is not the same as being loved by or loving others. Respect is impersonal. It is a posture appropriate to all persons with whom one is connected in some manner. However, it lacks the emotional depth that comes with a more robust attunement to the deepest needs and longings of another. As important as being respected is, if all one's relationships were characterized only by respect, without the added aspect of reciprocal emotional involvement, something of great intrinsic value to a decent life would be absent. Consider Bernard Williams's well-known example of a man who must decide which of two drowning persons he should save. One is his beloved wife and the other is a world-renowned surgeon who would go on to save many more lives. If the man pauses to deliberate, he simply fails to recognize what makes relationships of deep personal attachment valuable. He has, in Williams's words, "one thought too many."

It might seem that, however plausible the claim that personal attachment is a core element characteristic of a decent human life, its successful realization is largely independent of the way that social arrangements and institutions are structured. However, that would be a mistake. It is no doubt true that society and its political institutions cannot simply provide its members with friends and loved ones. Nonetheless, when institutional arrangements and social values are antagonistic to these valuable forms of personal attachment, their realization is extremely difficult. For example, institutions like schools and workplaces can undermine prospects for friendship if their configuration reinforces norms of human interaction in which others are viewed primarily as mere rivals or opportunistic vehicles for self-aggrandizement or economic acquisition. Laws and social practices that prohibit or make illicit loving relationships between people of the same gender or of different ethnicities or classes or castes similarly deprive some individuals of important forms of personal attachment.

More foundationally, social institutions and practices that support young parents and that work to ensure that all children are properly cared for, whether they have parents or not, can profoundly affect whether young children will experience close, stable bonds of attachment with caring adults. Absent such attachments early in life, a person's prospects for forming meaningful emotional relationships with others as an adult are severely compromised. Thus, in childhood as well as later in life, institutional structures and social practices have the capacity to undermine the realization of one of the most important sources of human satisfaction, and in so doing can lead to human deprivation that is deeply unjust.

2.3.6. Self-Determination

The value of self-determination, the lynchpin of liberal political theory, is a broad and encompassing category of human good. It is widely endorsed in many moral and political systems, even among those who complain that in specific cultures or concrete cases too much concern is placed on individual choice. The value of self-determination underlies many accounts of the importance of political liberty. Mill, for example, offers a plethora of arguments in defense of its importance for well-being, some of which famously concentrate on the good consequences of leading a self-directed life—or a life that is guided and shaped by one's own choices and values. Mill's ultimate concern, and ours, however, is not simply for the cultivation of the capacity for self-direction but for the successful living of a self-directed life.[35] Moreover, it is for the intrinsic value of living such a life.

---

[35] Mill's most eloquent discussions of these background factors appear throughout *The Subjection of Women*. John Stuart Mill, *The Collected Works of John Stuart Mill, Volume XXI: Essays on*

Commentators often note the high instrumental importance that Mill attaches to successful self-direction. For example, Mill argues that living a substantially self-determining life facilitates the advancement of knowledge, understanding, and self-discovery, and even the perfection of all of the rest of an individual's faculties. However, one of Mill's most significant justifications is the most straightforward and points to its intrinsic value. It is his contention that being self-directed, or living one's life from the inside according to one's own inclinations and values, under suitably favorable social conditions, is itself an important constituent of human well-being: "there is a greater fullness of life" and, beyond that, a life lacking in an irreplaceable constituent of a decent life, for which no amount of other ingredients of happiness can compensate for its absence.[36]

The force of Mill's insight regarding the direct value of leading a self-determining life, a life not substantially controlled by others or encumbered by significant social impediments, can be explicated by a simple thought experiment. Imagine a life in which the other core dimensions of well-being are present. A person is healthy, has strong bonds of attachment, enjoys the respect of others as a moral equal, is secure in his person, and has knowledge and understanding that allows him to participate in the social and political environments in which he lives. However, from his earliest years onward, he has been told what his path in life will be. All aspects of his life have been determined for him, including how much and what kind of schooling he will have, how he will make a living, with whom he will be friends, where he will live, whether he will have children and with whom, and so on. Although his life in many ways goes well, he has been denied any opportunity to shape its contours through his own choices, and thus has been denied the chance to make something of his life through his own efforts. Such a life would be rich in all other respects but seriously lacking in what is required for a decent life.

A number of other philosophers have made the case for values of the general sort we have in mind under the label of "self-determination," using slightly different terminology. For example, Isaiah Berlin sums matters up this way: "I wish to determine myself, and not be directed by others, no matter how wise or benevolent; my conduct derives an irreplaceable value

---

Equality, Law, and Education, ed. John M. Robson, intro. Stefan Collini (Toronto: University of Toronto Press; London: Routledge & Kegan Paul, 1984).

[36] Mill, *The Subjection of Women*, especially 290, 336–340. For a discussion of how we interpret Mill on these key points, see Madison Powers, Ruth Faden, and Yashar Saghai, "Liberty, Mill, and the Framework of Public Health Ethics," *Public Health Ethics* 5, no. 1 (2012): 6–15.

from the sole fact that it is my own, and not imposed on me."[37] Joseph Raz puts matters in similar fashion, claiming that an important, irreducible dimension of well-being consists in "people controlling, in some degree, their own destiny, fashioning it through successive decisions throughout their lives."[38] James Griffin offers a comparable description of what he takes to be among the most important elements of well-being: "Choosing one's own course through life, making something out of it according to one's own lights, is at the heart of what it is to lead a human existence."[39]

Central to the arguments of Berlin, Raz, and Griffin is the assumption that, in addition to the knowledge and understanding that are necessary to set and revise our own ends, our well-being consists in being in a condition in which our ends contribute effectively to the shaping of the course of our lives. It is "controlling [our] own destinies," or "the making of something out of" our lives, that is the irreplaceable value that these accounts and our own take as the ultimate aim.

The social structural nexus of support required for self-determination is straightforward. Self-determination is not possible in the presence of coercive interferences by the state or others that make it impossible for individuals to control even the basic contours of their lives. We should be clear, however, that self-determination, for us and for those whose views we see as similar in their implications, requires social institutions and conditions to go beyond what they do to ensure the absence of coercive or manipulative constraints on choices or envisioned futures. Without the proper economic, legal, and social structures, one's chances of being self-determining are thwarted.[40] For example, certain material conditions are indispensable to our being self-determining. People who live from meal to meal, who do not know if tomorrow there will be food for themselves or their children, who regularly experience exposure, starvation, or exhaustion are not positioned to be self-determining in any meaningful respect. As Rousseau noted, "[N]ecessitous men are not free men." People who are

---

[37] Isaiah Berlin, *Four Essays on Liberty* (Oxford: Oxford University Press, 1969), xliii.

[38] Joseph Raz, *The Morality of Freedom* (Oxford: Clarendon Press, 1986), 369.

[39] Griffin, *Well-Being*, 67.

[40] Griffin's more recent contribution to the human rights debate makes clear how much his understanding of what he now calls "normative agency" resembles the way we have developed the notion of self-determination, here and in our previous work. Normative agency, which is the foundation of his theory of human rights, is understood as composed of three elements: *autonomy*, or the capacity to choose a conception of a worthwhile life; a political guarantee of *liberty* to pursue that conception; and *material provision*, generally and with respect to education in particular, for the successful pursuit of that conception. James Griffin, *On Human Rights* (Oxford: Oxford University Press, 2008).

entirely beholden to others for their very survival cannot be said to play any substantial part in directing their own lives.

Our defense of self-determination as a core dimension of well-being thus rests on a simple and, we believe, widely shared view about the importance of having some control over who we are and who we will become, and on the fact that even a modest level of self-direction is not possible without appropriate economic, legal, and social structures.

There are, of course, critics who argue that the value of self-determination is not widely shared, that it is a distinctively Western liberal value, or that it should not inform an account of just social structural relationships within a global context. We return to these issues later in this chapter. Another more immediate criticism is that our conception may demand too much in terms of how much in control the individual needs to be. Indeed, there are limits on what is reasonable to demand, and Aristotle's account of a mariner helps illuminate our view that self-determination has plausible boundaries.[41]

The mariner sets a course on an open ocean, but does not command the winds or determine the distances between land and sea. Her choices are therefore bounded. She cannot decide to sail upon the land, and she cannot will the wind to blow in the desired direction or at the desired velocity. She does not choose her course wholly without regard to necessity or need, and she does not proceed on any course without the help or hindrance of luck. And yet the mariner charts her own course within the parameters of these external influences. At the same time, however, it is impossible for her to chart a course when the seas are so rough and her vessel so damaged that she must work feverishly just to keep from drowning. Self-determination requires some material and political basis for its exercise—a sturdy enough boat, so to speak.

For joint enterprises, involving a common objective with others, the cooperation of other crew members is required. Many journeys are not conceivable on one's own. Like the image of the mariner, our notion of self-determination is not some fixed state that can be asymptotically approached or a quantity that can be maximized. It is not something that depends on individual talent and skill alone, or that can be achieved outside a web of interdependencies, or that needs only an absence of human interference. Rather, self-determination is a valuable state or condition that is central to our well-being, without which the prospects for a decent

---

[41] Aristotle, *Politics* 1279a1–5, cited in Thomas May, "The Concept of Autonomy," *American Philosophical Quarterly* 3, no. 2 (1994): 139.

life are undermined in ways not reducible to deficits in the other valuable dimensions of well-being. Moreover, whether individuals can experience the self-determination needed for a decent human life is importantly dependent on how much control others exercise over their shared environment. It is not possible for all persons to have enough control over the contours of their own lives as long as some maintain far greater control over vast bits of the social machinery that exert a profound, pervasive, asymmetric, and near-inescapable impact on the core elements of well-being.

The successful exercise of self-determination, like the successful navigation by the mariner, depends crucially on the presence of laws and policies that protect a range of interests critical to self-determination. Laws and policies as well as social practices are also critical to ensuring that people are not so necessitous that charting any aspect of their life course is completely out of reach. Like all of the elements on our list, self-determination is virtually impossible to achieve when social arrangements and the structure of institutions are inimical to it. Also, the securing of self-determination, like all the elements on our list, depends on favorable circumstances in which other dimensions of well-being, health, personal security, attachment, equal respect, and knowledge and understanding are present.

2.4. A Decent Human Life

We have thus far relied upon the Socratic and Structural Dependence Arguments to make the intuitive case for the core elements that make up our account of human well-being. We now turn to a third line of argument that relies upon an overarching ideal to provide additional justificatory support for each constituent of well-being. In searching for this overarching ideal, we could cast the net narrowly, for example, adopting the position that we need an account of well-being suitable for the ideal of life as a citizen in a liberal democratic society. Instead, however, we cast the net more widely. The point of our inquiry is to establish a well-being conception that is applicable to all persons *qua* human beings, and not one that is specific to a person's fulfilling her role as a citizen in a particular kind of society.[42] To that end, we conceive of the overarching ideal to be a decent human life, which we take to be an appropriate and meaningful

---

[42] Elizabeth Anderson provides an example of the democratic citizenship approach. Elizabeth Anderson, "What Is the Point of Equality?" *Ethics* 109, no. 2 (1999): 287–337; Elizabeth

ideal for social organization for all persons, regardless of who they are or where they live.

It is possible to interpret an overarching ideal of a decent human life quite restrictively as including only elements that track the most basic of human biological needs.[43] The presumptive advantage of such an interpretation is that it is arguably less controversial than some more inclusive alternatives. John Rawls, for example, is well known for citing Henry Shue's account of the basic human right to subsistence, which is but one component of Shue's larger portfolio of human rights.[44] Rawls rejects Shue's larger portfolio of rights but commends the right to subsistence because it tracks the very basic human needs presumed to be universal moral prerequisites for the application of his own principles of distributive justice.[45]

In our view, a decent life requires more than mere subsistence or biological preservation, but less than a maximally flourishing life for all. Our conception of well-being assumes that what it means to live a decent life must reflect *relational* as well as biological considerations. By that we mean aspects of a person's quality of life that go well beyond the satisfaction of basic biological needs to encompass the quality of a person's social relations with others. This is one reason that our core list of elements of well-being includes equal respect and personal attachments. And it is one

---

Anderson, "Justifying the Capabilities Approach to Justice," in *Measuring Justice*, ed. Harry Brighouse and Ingrid Robeyns (Cambridge: Cambridge University Press, 2010).

[43] Sometimes the relevant point is put in terms of a minimally decent life. How minimal the various writers intend the overarching standard to be, or whether the account of everyone who employs the label necessarily differs from our own account of a decent life, is not always clear. Gillian Brock, for example, speaks of the basic ingredients of a decent life, or basic needs as a shorthand, but her notion of needs is quite similar to our richer list of core elements. Gillian Brock, *Global Justice: A Cosmopolitan Account* (Oxford: Oxford University Press, 2009), 63, 69. For references to a "minimally decent life" see David Miller, *National Responsibility and Global Justice* (Oxford: Oxford University Press, 2007); Massimo Renzo, "Human Rights, Human Needs," in *Philosophical Foundations of Human Rights*, ed. Rowen Cruft, Matthew Liao, and Massimo Renzo (Oxford: Oxford University Press, 2015).

[44] John Rawls, *The Law of Peoples* (Cambridge, MA: Harvard University Press, 1999), 65 n. 1 (hereafter, Rawls, *LOP*). Shue's theory involves a portfolio of human rights that go well beyond what Rawls recognizes. It also includes liberty rights, which he interprets expansively to include some rights of political participation. Shue, *Basic Rights*, 153–180. Moreover, it is not clear how modest the subsistence requirement in Shue's theory really is, given the kinds of social guarantees he thinks necessary for the enjoyment of this right, together with occasional remarks suggesting that the purpose of human rights generally is to prevent the vulnerable from being at the utter mercy of the powerful. For some of Rawls's other remarks on human rights to subsistence, see John Rawls, *Political Liberalism* (New York: Columbia University Press, 1995), 7 (hereafter, Rawls, *PL*); and John Rawls, *Justice as Fairness: A Restatement* (Cambridge, MA: Harvard University Press, 2001), §17.1 (hereafter, Rawls, *JAF*).

[45] Shue, *Basic Rights*, 18.

reason that our list includes the universal value of self-determination. Our argument here—one of several stages of argument, we should emphasize—is that the absence of these elements in a conception of well-being and their omission from the scope of universal human rights would be *contrary* to a decent life. So, too, would a failure to see the profound unfairness of social structures that stack the deck against the prospects of some groups being able to realize these elements.

A decent life is not one that is marked by servility, slavishness, the necessity to grovel, or deep dependence on the goodwill or whim of others for the most basic requirements of life. A decent life is not one marred by the most degrading aspects of poverty, including squalor, helplessness, extreme vulnerability, and the inability to provide for one's own children and family.[46]

A decent life is not one in which someone is treated as less than a full member of the human community or as someone whose most vital concerns are accorded no weight or less weight than is accorded to the same concerns of others. Indeed, to be treated as a second-class citizen within one's own society is to be treated as a second-class human being, as someone who is not due the full measure of respect and concern accorded to other members of a single political community.[47]

A decent human life is one in which someone is not subjugated, marginalized, stigmatized, infantilized, or deprived of the full use of her mature faculties.[48] Much more might be said along these lines, but the essential point we make here is that these relational aspects of well-being earn a place on the list of constituents of a decent human life as securely as the concerns about health, knowledge and understanding, and physical security that are typically included in bare-bones conceptions of well-being and typically endorsed by human rights minimalists.

2.5. An Alternative to Universal Endorsement Approaches to Justification

All theories of justice that are grounded in a conception of the core elements of human well-being are open to the same, familiar reproach. No matter how the core elements are cast or defended, some critics contend that

---

[46] Powers and Faden, *Social Justice*, 138–141; Avishai Margalit, *The Decent Society* (Cambridge, MA: Harvard University Press, 1996), 229.

[47] Margalit, *The Decent Society*, 155.

[48] Many of these points are developed in Mill's *The Subjection of Women*.

theories relying upon such conceptions cannot be properly justified unless they meet with universal endorsement. They assume that in order for such a theory of justice to be justifiable, it must be capable of being justified *to* all persons from within their existing ethical outlooks.[49] The explanation of how we know whether a conception of justice can be justified to all persons from within their diverse existing outlooks is developed in two distinct ways in the literature. Either it can be empirically demonstrated that the commitments of a particular theory of justice are actually endorsed by all of these ethical outlooks or it can be argued that there are interpretative resources available within these outlooks that participants themselves would have reason to recognize as supporting the theory's commitments.

The empirical approach often relies on evidence from cross-cultural data, typically generated using social science methods, about the values people hold and the normative implications they attach to them. By contrast, the interpretative approach often adapts Rawls's idea of an overlapping consensus to the global context. It maintains that even if people adhering to specific ethical outlooks do not explicitly endorse a particular normative principle or value, it may be possible to find a rationale that would support its endorsement within their ethical outlooks.

The inference that some draw from the challenging demand for universal endorsement is that only the most minimal conception of human interests is likely to pass this test, empirically or as a matter of interpretation.[50] Others are more hopeful about finding a robust overlapping evaluative consensus on a global scale, relying largely on an interpretative strategy.[51] Both approaches share the assumption that demonstrating the existence of or potential for achieving universal endorsement is a necessary condition for justifying any theory of justice that relies on a conception of universal interests.

We take a different position. We do not look for an airtight argument for universal endorsement, based either on empirical evidence or on

---

[49] Tasioulas, "On the Foundations of Human Rights," 70. We borrow the phrase "ethical outlook" from Joshua Cohen, "Minimalism About Human Rights: The Most We Can Hope For?," *Journal of Political Philosophy* 12, no. 2 (2004): 190–213. An ethical outlook is a generic notion capacious enough to include cultural or religious traditions or any tradition or perspective that involves a cluster of norms and values.

[50] Michael Ignatieff, *Human Rights as Politics and Idolatry* (Princeton, NJ: Princeton University Press, 2001). The universal norms of justice discussed by Ignatieff are human rights, and his minimalist position holds that the only human rights are negative rights that protect against harms to universally agreed upon aspects of well-being such as life and bodily integrity. These are interests Ignatieff describes as "for any kind of life at all." Cohen, "Minimalism About Human Rights," 210.

[51] Nussbaum, *Creating Capabilities*, 169.

interpretative processes. Because both approaches have been the object of considerable scrutiny we will be brief in our comments, focusing only on the criticisms that set the stage for our alternative.

2.5.1. Empirical Approaches and Minimalist Conclusions

A familiar argument for a minimalist approach is motivated by anxieties about reliance on parochial Western values that could not be accepted outside of the context of liberal democratic cultures. For example, in the context of debates about universal human rights—for many, the only part of justice that is universal in scope—the claim is that these rights must be narrowly tailored to include only ones that protect an individual's interests in what is needed for biological survival, preservation of life, and physical security. Rawls, for example, holds that universal human rights include only ones that protect life and bodily integrity, ensure the fulfillment of subsistence needs, and guarantee a very basic set of civil and political liberties, without which the interests undergirding the other rights on the list are too much at risk.[52] Rawls assumes that the prospect for agreement on a richer menu of rights and well-being interests is foreclosed by the existence of deep, persistent, but reasonable disagreement about the nature of human good. For Rawls, the implication is clear. The value of national self-determination takes on considerable moral weight, warranting a large measure of deference to the judgments of different peoples or nation-states.

Rawls's theory is widely criticized, and in our view, rightly so, for failing to appreciate how these collective entities ("peoples" in Rawls's terminology) often fail to speak for their most disadvantaged, subordinated members.[53] Rawls is not engaged in a justificatory exercise that requires universal endorsement from within each individual's ethical outlook. Instead, justification is directed to a collective entity presumed to be an authoritative expositor of a local tradition of a homogeneous people.

A more circumspect version of the human rights minimalist position responds to critics who doubt that socially dominant and politically empowered groups speak authentically for their most disadvantaged, subordinated members. They add a caveat that preserves the underlying

---

[52] Rawls, *LOP*, 78–81. James Nickel construes the rationale behind Rawls's truncated list in this way, and that seems to us a plausible hypothesis. James Nickel, *Making Sense of Human Rights*, 2nd ed. (Malden, MA: Blackwell, 2007), 98–103.

[53] Seyla Benhabib, *The Rights of Others: Aliens, Residents and Citizens* (Cambridge: Cambridge University Press, 2004); Martha Nussbaum, "Women and the *Law of Peoples*," *Politics, Philosophy & Economics* 1, no. 3 (2002): 283–306.

commitment to justifying a theory of justice to individuals from within each individual's ethical outlook. Deference to collective judgments is justified only as long as those judgments are not simply the expression of group domination and the imposition of value preferences of the powerful on the powerless.[54]

With this caveat in place, the core of the objection to a more fulsome account of well-being and human rights shifts to concerns of the sort that motivated Rawls in the first place. Rawls's worry is that if the world community adopted universal standards of critical appraisal, departures from the standards would trigger presumptive reasons for coercive, external intervention in the affairs of independent states and peoples. This worry has been met in the literature by numerous arguments for delinking standards of critical appraisal from intervention triggers. We will not rehearse them here, except to signal our broad concurrence.[55] We can envision numerous ways in which universal agreement on human rights can be decoupled from criteria for justified intervention in the affairs of an internationally recognized nation-state.

Even if delinking successfully responds to worries about triggering intervention, empirical worries about universal endorsement remain. Empirical evidence confirming universal endorsement is hard to come by, beyond some very modest minimum list of elements of well-being and the abbreviated schedule of rights they are thought to generate. However, placing great weight on such worries comes at a high cost. As long as the commitment to requiring empirical evidence for universal justification remains in place, social movements that aim to mitigate structural injustices are likely to find themselves limited in the kinds of critical judgments and rights claims they can make. The commitment to universal endorsement

---

[54] Joshua Cohen adds this proviso, limiting deference to national self-determination to states or societies for which the overall ethical outlook is not a product of group domination. Cohen, "Minimalism About Human Rights," 211. The absence of such a proviso is the basis of trenchant criticism of a similar ideal in Rawls's *Law of Peoples*.

[55] Jean Cohen provides one example of this argument. She proposes the division of human rights into two separate categories, each with differentiated functions. On the one hand, there are human security rights, the violation of which potentially warrants international action. On the other hand, there is the catalog of rights that function as internal standards by which citizens, activists, and social movements hold their own government accountable. Jean Cohen, *Globalization and Sovereignty* (Cambridge: Cambridge University Press, 2012), 216; Ranier Forst, "A Critical Theory of Human Rights: Some Groundwork," in *Critical Theory in Critical Times*, ed. Penelope Deutscher and Christina Lafont (New York: Columbia University Press, 2017), 80. For a collection of recent essays on the debate, see Adam Etinson, *Human Rights: Moral or Political?* (Oxford: Oxford University Press, 2018).

puts a thumb on the scales in favor of the ethical outlooks that hew closely to dominant cultural views.[56]

2.5.2. Interpretative Approaches

Reservations about the prospects for the empirical approach may incline proponents of universal endorsement to explore the interpretative approach. As we noted already, the aim of the interpretative approach is to find an overlapping consensus on relevant values by showing that a great deal of ethical overlap can be generated from within the internal interpretative resources of many ethical outlooks.[57] If the aim is to find genuinely universal overlap through the interpretative resources available across all ethical outlooks, we think that this is a tall order, for two reasons.[58]

First, to the extent that we seek agreement on the requirements of justice, we need more than overlapping endorsement of the various elements on our list or any other conception of well-being. For example, it is not enough for diverse ethical outlooks to agree that some deprivation in well-being—deprivation of health or knowledge and understanding, for example—matters morally. It must be shown that it matters in a comparable way. As Charles Beitz puts it, at minimum, in order to mirror the full normative implications of an ideal of justice, and human rights in particular, we have to understand the further normative and institutional implications of the values identified.[59] For example, for an ethical outlook to value an element of well-being in a way that tracks its value within a theory of justice, that element would have to be understood as having significant presumptive weight against trade-offs when it comes into

---

[56] Of course, there are more optimistic proponents of an empirical approach. Jack Donnelly might be read as endorsing such an empirical approach insofar as his argument at crucial places seems to turn on instances of actual cross-cultural agreement about the substance of human rights. Jack Donnelley, *Universal Human Rights in Theory and Practice*, 3rd ed. (Ithaca, NY: Cornell University Press, 2013), chap. 5. We simply record here our own reservations.

[57] Cohen, "Minimalism About Human Rights," 192, 203; Miller, *National Responsibility and Global Justice*, 172–175.

[58] There are reasons to doubt just how seriously we should take the proponents' aspirations for genuine universal endorsement. One question is whether the appropriate method is one that seeks an interpretative overlap across all societies and traditions or one that exists only among societies that already adopt what Rawls, in the domestic context, describes as a reasonable conception of the good. Charles Beitz argues that the latter method is the one most faithful to Rawls's original understanding. The consensus that can be generated is by definition one that holds only among societies and traditions that already have ethical outlooks with quite a bit in common such that the range of disagreement is narrowed at the outset. Charles Beitz, *The Idea of Human Rights* (Oxford: Oxford University Press, 2009), 76.

[59] Ibid., 281.

competition with other collective aims. Valuing something highly and valuing something in the distinctive way that justice generally and human rights in particular presuppose are thus importantly different in their practical significance. Moreover, as Thomas Nagel puts it, behind the idea of justice lies the notion of individual inviolability, which he says is not simply the value of not suffering some harm but the value of each person being protected against harm to some vitally important interest and of each knowing that she or he is protected.[60] In our view, it is highly problematic to suppose that a robust overlapping consensus can be generated through the internal resources available in many of the world's ethical outlooks, beyond a shallow agreement that this or that element of well-being matters morally. And if we are correct in this, then insistence on universal endorsement through an interpretative approach is likely to freeze out dissident and reformist perspectives.

Second, and relatedly, central to the concerns of many social movements is the demand for what amounts to recognition as a moral equal, with corresponding claims to political equality and harm protections that others routinely receive but that are not extended to marginalized or subordinated social groups. There are powerful reasons to doubt whether many ethical outlooks embraced by dominant social groups have the kind of internal resources available to address this demand. David Miller argues that such commitments are not always easy to extract, even with the most creative interpretation, for example, from the textual materials of some religious traditions, particularly those that prop up patriarchal political and social ideologies. Of course, the proponent of an overlapping consensus justification is not bound by any particular interpretation of a theological or cultural tradition. Neither must we take the dominant interpretations defended within religious hierarchies or supported by members of politically powerful ethnic majorities as authoritative. But as Miller rightly observes, we have ample evidence of the ways in which the facial commitment to equality of moral status turns out to be not that robust and is routinely "overshadowed" or effaced in many of the most widely observed

---

[60] Thomas Nagel, "Personal Rights and Public Space," *Philosophy and Public Affairs* 24 (1995): 83–107. Joseph Raz also speaks of a distinctive feature of rights as pointing to the value of having rights as different from the value of the underlying interest. The added value comes from the security of being able to exercise control over what affects one's interest or being secure in the knowledge that the interest is protected by institutional mechanisms that articulate a system of rights and duties and enable their reliable enforcement. Joseph Raz, "Human Rights in the Emerging World Order," in *Philosophical Foundations of Human Rights*, ed. Rowen Cruft, S. Matthew Liao, and Massimo Renzo (Oxford: Oxford University Press, 2015), 220–221.

interpretations of some religious and cultural traditions. A familiar fact is the widespread existence of hierarchical judgments of moral worth within societies. These judgments typically reflect gender or ethnic norms that in effect differentiate between those whose intrinsic qualities are presumed to merit not only different treatment but, more fundamentally, differences in moral standing as makers of legitimate claims on others.

The point is not that the failure of overlapping consensus strategies is guaranteed. However, it is instructive to observe just how much interpretive agility is required in order to make good on the prospect for an overlapping consensus on a conception of well-being that can serve as a foundation for agreement on norms of justice.[61]

2.5.3. What a Justification for a Theory of Structural Justice Should Seek to Achieve

The plausibility of a theory of the minimum requirements of structural justice—including human rights and fairness norms—and the conception of well-being which supplies its principal rationale, depends upon the purposes that the theory is intended to serve. We do not defend a theory that is meant to garner universal allegiance within the current global order. We do not seek an in-principle global consensus that might result from a careful examination of the interpretative resources within otherwise divergent ethical outlooks. Nor do we seek a conception of well-being suitable for the construction of a theory that can serve as a practical guide for establishing the legitimate scope of state sovereignty or identifying the moral triggers that might justify external intervention, economic sanction, or diplomatic censure.

Instead, we seek a theory, and an underlying conception of well-being, that track and provide theoretical defense for the *core evaluative concerns, diagnostic complaints, and normative aspirations exhibited in a variety of social justice movements worldwide.* Of course, we cannot claim that our theory or the conception of well-being it rests upon is a precise match in every detail endorsed by every participant within every movement. However, we do believe that our view, including the six elements that comprise our account of well-being, encapsulates and gives expression to what is centrally important to an array of social justice movements. These

---

[61] It is worth remembering that critics from the outset raised doubts about the likely breadth and depth of any overlapping consensus, even within the deliberative context of liberal democracies, much less globally. See Kurt Baier, "Justice and the Aims of Political Philosophy," *Ethics* 99, no. 4 (1989): 771–790.

movements are far-ranging and diverse but illustrative of many of the key claims we argue for in this book.

Social justice movements share a diagnosis of the structural injustices that are often at the root of human rights violations. They also share a conception of the most important elements of well-being that are harmed by human rights violations and the structural context within which they routinely occur in their most pernicious forms. Central to such contexts are grossly unfair norms that govern the institutions, social practices, and religious and cultural hierarchies that structure the overlay of local and global entanglements within which the world's poorest, least powerful, and most vulnerable individuals, groups, and countries interact with the affluent, the powerful, and the resilient.

We therefore offer a theory of justice that resembles the tradition of critical theory. The specific purpose of our theory is to provide a systematic grounding and diagnosis of some of the gravest human rights abuses and the primary sources of structural unfairness that facilitate and perpetuate their occurrence. A critical theory, as we understand it, is similar in ambition. It also begins with an empirical understanding of complex social relations and the overarching institutions and social practices that structure those relations. From that vantage point, it takes seriously and articulates the concerns and complaints of various social justice movements, often unnoticed or dismissed by the perpetrators and beneficiaries of injustice.[62] Our assumption is that there are deep divisions in ethical outlook

---

[62] Ranier Forst elaborates on what makes his approach to human rights "one of *critical theory*," namely that it starts from the participant's perspective in social struggles and reconstructs the basic emancipatory claim of human rights." Forst, "A Critical Theory of Human Rights," 75. Terry Pinkard observes that "[t]he defining aim of Frankfurt critical theory since its founding has been to mesh philosophy and empirical theory with the goal of producing a kind of thinking that would itself contribute to human emancipation." Terry Pinkard, "Review of *Kritik von Lebensformen* by Rahel Jaeggi," *European Journal of Philosophy* 25, no. 2 (2017): 540. The founders of the Frankfurt school of critical theory describe their task as scrutinizing inherited social practices and normative frameworks, particularly practices and norms that many of its participants, adherents, and especially its beneficiaries have come to see as natural, inevitable, or unchangeable. As Adorno memorably put it, the task is to examine all aspects of a normative order that has come to be experienced as a kind of "second nature." Theodor Adorno, *History and Freedom: Lectures, 1964–1965*, ed. Rolf Tiedemann (Cambridge: Polity, 2006), 135. In the same era, R. H. Tawney in the UK developed a similar approach to the mix of empirical and philosophical argument, with an emphasis on the way in which the injustices identified by leaders of social movements often go unnoticed generally. "Institutions which have died as creeds sometimes live on, nevertheless, to survive as habits . . . Just as "[m]en are rarely conscious of the quality of the air they breathe" . . . the gradations of the social hierarchy are preserved and emphasized . . . What requires our attention, if social divisions are to be eliminated, is the habit of mind that regards them as natural and inevitable." R. H. Tawney, *Equality* (1929), 4th ed., into. Richard Titmuss (London: Unwin Books, 1964), 34–37.

separating the affluent, the powerful, and the resilient from the poor, the powerless, and the vulnerable. Indeed, such claims are integral to the critiques of the status quo.

We take seriously the likely differences in perspectives between representatives of social movements and the points of view of those more comfortable with the status quo. We see these differences in perspectives as signaling the depth and breadth of the divide in ethical outlooks, which better track cleavages of power and privilege than liberal versus non-liberal cultures or supposed differences between the West and the rest. Moreover, the likelihood of such divergence should come as no surprise to anyone familiar with the relevant social science literature or the statements of social movement activists, NGOs, and investigative journalists.

The reality of social distance between dominant and subordinate social groups under the same set of social conditions is as much a fact of great moral significance as the existence of disagreement rooted in evaluative pluralism across cultural and religious traditions.[63] This is a point emphasized by Aristotle in his *Politics*. Vast differences in power, wealth, and life experiences often mean that the powerless poor and the powerful rich do not "walk the same path." The metaphor points to the ways in which social cleavages are both rooted in and result in vastly different life experiences and vastly different judgments about unfairness and well-being. The privileged often have limited insight into the lives of the disadvantaged; they know little of the magnitude and pervasiveness of the threats they face, the obstacles they endure, or the nature of the frustrations, resentments, fears, or insecurities that they sometimes feel. Vast disparities in advantages often render unintelligible to the better-off the daily threats to the core interests of the worse-off and obscure their understanding of how much they differ in judgments of what counts as reasonable responses to their circumstances. Quite often, differentially situated social groups simply do not share a widely overlapping understanding of the social world. Social distance readily exacerbates the differences in understanding, even in instances of close geographic proximity. Consider, for example, how many traditions refuse to extend rights of self-determination or recognize equality of moral status to women or members of marginalized ethnic groups within their own communities.

As we indicated in chapter 1, where we outlined some of the basic features of the domestic and transnational examples we have chosen to

---

[63] Daniel Putnam, "Equality of Intelligibility," in *The Equal Society: Essays on Equality in Theory and Practice*, ed. George Hull (Lanham, MD: Lexington, 2015).

highlight in this book, we do not claim to speak authoritatively about how the participants in social movements understand the central evaluative and normative commitments at issue. Nor we do claim to speak for them.[64] Our intention is to supplement traditional philosophical arguments throughout the book by taking seriously their voices and perspectives as the touchstone of empirically informed, critically oriented theorizing. Our aim is to incorporate into our theory some key insights gleaned from the voluminous literature surrounding these examples and explore ways in which our theory might in turn contribute to the public debates. Our extended examples are found in chapter 7, after the main lines of argument of the book are completed, and before the final chapter, where we examine the permissible responses of affected individuals and groups in resisting injustice or seeking remedies where institutional agents fail in their duties.

2.6. Three Implications of the Roles of Our Conception of Well-Being

We conclude this chapter by highlighting three implications of the roles that our conception of well-being plays within our theory of justice. We first distinguish the role that well-being plays in a theory of justice from its role in theories of beneficence or humanitarian assistance. Second, we explain why our theory's concern about well-being is not exclusively backward-looking, attending only to deprivations or diminished life prospects that have already been caused by the social structure. Third, we build upon these two points to elaborate on our earlier claim about how the conception of well-being figures differently in the foundations of human rights than it does in our account of the unfairness of differential patterns of advantage and asymmetric power relations.

2.6.1. Deprivation in Well-Being Is Not the Unique Concern of Justice: What Is Distinctive About Our Theory?

Because well-being and its deprivation are not uniquely concerns of justice, we need to explain how the role that well-being plays in our theory

---

[64] Linda Alcoff, "The Problem of Speaking for Others," *Cultural Critique*, no. 20 (Winter 1991–1992): 5–32.

differs from the role it plays in other moral norms. Although we address in greater detail in chapter 3 what makes norms of justice different from other moral norms, we offer two points here about how concerns about well-being matter within our theory of justice.

First, although individuals have general duties of beneficence and other presumptive moral reasons to alleviate remediable deprivation experienced by others, these are general duties that are independent of any social structural nexus. They are not specific duties owed to particular individuals who have justice-based claims against specific persons or institutions who are under a duty to those claimants. Duties of beneficence, for example, are quite general in their beneficiaries. They are not grounded in any shared history of how deprivations arose, nor are they grounded in concerns about establishing fair terms of interaction for the future. Duties of beneficence are responsive to suffering, while our duties of structural justice are responsive to the requirements of shared living.

Second, the conception of well-being that underlies many other moral norms tends to be more comprehensive than our deliberately pruned list of core elements. We focus on a much narrower slice of the constituents of human well-being. That too makes our theory very different from principles of general beneficence, where the nature of well-being that should be promoted tends to be open-ended.

However, because our conception identifies some especially salient dimensions of well-being, the application of our conception could be extended beyond its intended purposes within our theory. For example, it could serve as a kind of blueprint or checklist for individuals or institutions thinking about how to prioritize the fulfillment of their duties of beneficence. A philanthropic strategy, for example, might focus on the core dimensions of well-being that are most centrally relevant to securing conditions of structural justice. Though the aim of beneficence, unlike the aims of our theory of structural justice, is the general improvement of well-being or the alleviation of suffering in any of its forms, there are reasons to consider targeted beneficence. Targeted beneficence, based on our core conception of well-being, can serve additional moral ends by securing conditions of structural justice, even if, for the sake of argument, there are no justice-based claims by specific individuals or groups directed against a particular donor. Deprivation might be relieved, as is often the goal of philanthropic strategies, and life prospects also might be improved through changes in patterns of advantage and power relations, strategically reconfigured by deliberately targeted policies.

2.6.2. How Does Our Structural Justice Theory Deal with Deprivation Not Caused by the Social Structure?

We also need to be clear about our understanding of the social structural nexus linking deprivation to specific duties owed to particular individuals. Social structural theories of justice, including our own theory, attach great moral significance to the existence of densely woven webs of social interaction that are highly determinative of the well-being and overall life prospects of those who are subject to its influence. However, the question arises about how our theory deals with risks to, or deprivations in, the core elements that are not caused by social structural factors or where the complex causal pathways are poorly understood. For example, some deprivations and diminished life prospects are due to the voluntary personal choices of individuals, presumed differences in natural endowment, or natural disasters. It is possible that some such cases might arise in circumstances in which there are no prior human rights violations and no unfair power relations or unfair patterns of disadvantage.

Some discussions of social justice suggest that these deprivations fall outside the purview of a theory of structural justice, or that the proper concern is not the remedy of "cosmic inequalities" due to natural forces or natural factors or the inequalities attributable to the improvident choices of individuals, where clear social structural causes are absent.[65]

However, we disagree with purely backward-looking accounts that tether responsibility for preventing or mitigating deprivation only to those deprivations that are clearly traceable to structural causes. Under our theory, deprivations in the core elements, however they are caused, also matter instrumentally and prospectively. When left unaddressed at the level of social organization, deprivation in core elements of well-being have reverberating effects that alter and reconstitute the social structure. Deprivation, whether or not it arises from a human rights violation or existing structural unfairness, is always a crucial instrumental concern of structural justice for a quite straightforward reason. Deprivation, however caused, exposes people to the threat of greater, entrenched disadvantage, deeper entanglement in unfair power relations, and the increased likelihood of human rights violations.[66] In our view, an important part of what

---

[65] Allen Buchanan, Dan W. Brock, and Norman Daniels, "Genes, Justice, and Human Nature," in *From Chance to Choice: Genetics and Justice*, ed. Allen Buchanan, Dan W. Brock, Norman Daniels, and Dan Wikler (Cambridge: Cambridge University Press), 61–103.

[66] For the application of this general approach to questions about responsibilities for addressing racial disparities in health and health care access, where causal trajectories are complex and uncertain, see Madison Powers and Ruth Faden, "Racial and Ethnic Disparities in Health Care: An

a social structural theory is intended to illuminate is missed if these pro-spective, or forward-looking, concerns are not given prominent billing.[67]

2.6.3. How Does the Connection Between Our Conception of Well-Being and Human Rights Differ from Its Connection to Unfairness Norms?

We said at the outset of this chapter that our conception of well-being figures differently in the foundations of human rights than it does in our account of unfairness in patterns of advantage and power relations. Our conception of well-being plays a central role in the rationale for human rights, explaining the kinds of interests which ground a variety of duties aimed at protection against serious forms of deprivation. Violation of those duties constitutes a distinct injustice. By contrast, we utilize the core elements of our conception of well-being to answer a very different question about structural unfairness. The conception of core elements of well-being allows us to identify which instances of structural unfairness are most egregious, simply because the moral stakes are highest.

Structural unfairness and human rights violations are thus different normative concerns under our theory. Each is rooted in our conception of the core elements of well-being but in functionally distinct ways, and both are best understood as both cause and consequence of an interactive process. Human rights violations and serious deprivations of well-being generally usher in structural unfairness in patterns of advantage and relations of power, and both sorts of structural unfairness jointly incubate human rights violations and, more generally, serious deprivations in the core elements of well-being. This interactive process is the central message of our theory of structural injustice. It demonstrates the rationale for an integrated account of social conditions characterized by two forms of structural unfairness and the kinds of human rights violations typically embedded in, and instrumental in producing and reproducing, those conditions.

Ethical Analysis of When and How They Matter," in *Unequal Treatment: Confronting Racial and Ethnic Disparities in Health Care*, ed. Brian D. Smedley, Adrienne Y. Stith, and Alan R. Nelson, Committee on Understanding and Eliminating Racial and Ethnic Disparities in Health Care, Board on Health Sciences Policy (Washington, DC: National Academy of Sciences, Institute of Medicine, 2002), 463–475.

[67] For more discussion of alternative accounts of retrospective and prospective approaches in theories of structural justice, see Madison Powers, "Social Justice," in *Encyclopedia of Bioethics*, 4th ed., ed. Bruce Jennings (Farmington Hills, MI: Macmillan, 2014), 2966–2973.

CHAPTER 3 | What Justice Is

OUR THEORY IS A theory of structural injustice. In chapter 4, we elaborate on what makes our theory a structural theory. The overarching question posed in this chapter is, what makes our theory—indeed, any normative theory—a theory of justice? Insofar as justice is appropriately a distinct category within morality, this is a question of great significance. It is more difficult to answer than might be thought, and it matters for reasons that go well beyond the aim of achieving greater conceptual clarity. The answer holds the key not only to an explication of the types of moral norms that qualify as norms of justice, but to central issues regarding the nature and assignment of associated duties, the permissible enforcement remedies for duties that are breached, and the rationale for distinguishing types of justice norms.

The philosophical literature contains many references to justice understood as more or less coextensive with all questions of right and wrong action.[1] However, as John Passmore observed, "The question of whether it is wrong to act in certain ways is not the same as whether it is unjust to do so."[2] We and many others concur. The view that justice is

---

[1] Aristotle noted that sometimes the term "justice" is used in a comprehensive way rather than as a label that marks any distinctive category of morality. He noted that in classical Greek society "justice" was used to refer to complete virtue, or the sum of all moral virtues, and at other times, used to designate a specific set of virtues. These are best thought of as homonyms, each designating a different subject matter.

[2] John Passmore, "Civic Justice and Its Rivals," in *Justice*, ed. Eugene Kamenka and Alice Erh-Soon Tay (London: Edward Arnold, 1979), 47. Examples of the comprehensive usage today include Michael Sandel's seeming equivalence between justice and the notion of the right thing to do. Michael Sandel, *Justice: What's the Right Thing to Do?* (New York: Farrar, Straus& Giroux, 2010).

not coterminous with all of ethics, but is rather its own distinctive domain, is today the dominant view in moral and political thought. That said, there is less consensus on the features of moral norms that explain why they should be classified as norms of justice. There are several widely discussed criteria, however, that command enough attention that it is useful to consider their relevance and significance for our theory. The main criteria fit under five headings: special importance, stringency, claimability, specificity, and rightful enforceability. We develop our position with respect to each one, and we conclude with a discussion of what further distinguishes the fairness norms that are central to our theory.

In section 3.1, we explain special importance and stringency and spell out the implications of each. In section 3.2 we examine claimability and specificity. We respond to critics who object that many of the rights defended by human rights theories and advocates are not genuine rights, but moral standards of some other sort because they lack both pre-institutionally identifiable duty-bearers, against whom claims of justice can be made, and sufficiently specific duties.

In section 3.3, we address the problem of rightful enforceability. At issue is whether norms of justice presuppose an identifiable moral agent who has both moral standing and effective capacity to enforce justice claims, and the identity of such agents. We argue against the view that the only category of moral agent positioned to fill that role is the state. On our view, rightful enforceability should be conceived less restrictively, given the existence of circumstances in which states and other entities are unwilling or unable to fulfill their duties to protect. A consequence of our view is that justified enforcement remedies available to the aggrieved move to the forefront.

In section 3.4, we segue from these general criteria for norms of justice to an elaboration of the specific norms of unfairness that are centrally important under our theory. We begin with an explanation of what we see as intuitively distinctive about claims of unfairness in each of their specific forms. We look first at the ordinary language used to articulate these claims in less weighty, less complex situations of everyday experience. We then extrapolate from our most basic intuitions about relatively simple patterns of unfairness in interpersonal relationships to gain a better understanding of our theory's fairness norms, applicable in more complex contexts where an array of institutions and social practices structure relationships between social groups.

3.1. Moral Importance and Stringency

Perhaps the least controversial of the proposed distinguishing features of theories of justice are the notions that whatever human interests ground justice norms they must be matters of special moral importance and that the norms that secure these important interests are particularly stringent. Special moral importance reflects reasons to think that some things of value are too important to be left to the uncertainty of open-ended balancing against other things of value. Stringency is the notion that norms of justice have a certain peremptory force when placed in competition with other social goals or moral norms. Stringency does not entail absolute priority over other moral norms or social goals, but at minimum it must be understood as strongly resistant to being overridden by competing considerations.

Theories as different as those developed by J. S. Mill and John Rawls converge on these two criteria and, arguably, for much the same reasons. Mill describes justice as "the chief part, and incomparably the most sacred and binding part, of all morality."[3] On his view, rights are the centerpiece of the domain of justice, and he explicates their grounding and their stringency in a number of often-quoted statements. For example, the rights that are central to justice track "the most vital of all interests."[4] Rights not only track important interests, judged from the perspective of an individual reflecting on what life would be like without them; rights provide "a security that no human being can possibly do without."[5] These interest-protecting norms are variously described as the "very groundwork of our existence" or "the most indispensable of all necessities."[6]

Mill's references to "the most indispensable of all necessities" and "a security that no human being can possibly do without" are revealing. They suggest that some interests are picked out as normatively special, not simply because they are elements of a life most highly prized by individuals. These interests are designated as special because they serve as a kind of bulwark against the worst consequences that might affect what we most care about as human beings. As a consequence, Mill thinks that norms of justice owe their stringency in part to the added importance of

---

[3] J. S. Mill, *Utilitarianism*, in *The Collected Works, Volume X*, 255.
[4] Ibid., 251.
[5] Ibid.
[6] Ibid.

deeply embedding mechanisms for their protection within the normative architecture of social organization.

We think Mill's two crucial points explaining the architectural role of norms of justice are captured in the Socratic Argument and the Structural Dependence Argument discussed in chapter 2. First, our Socratic Argument emphasizes how an element of well-being is a core concern on our theory, not because it is essential for a fully flourishing life, but because (in part) its absence signifies an especially grave loss of what all individuals have sufficient reason to want for themselves. Moreover, concerns about deprivation take on such fundamental moral importance not because the core elements of well-being are needed for successful participation in a particular form of social organization, such as a democracy or a hypercompetitive economy. The interests that ground justice norms are especially important for a more basic reason. Deprivation of these interests detracts from what is characteristically important for the sake of a decent life, wherever that life may be.

Second, norms of justice matter in a morally unique way, not only because of the weighty interests that they protect, but because the interests at stake are also subject to grave threats that, absent appropriate social mechanisms, leave them in constant, morally intolerable jeopardy. Put another way, the vital interests that are the concern of justice require consistent, unwavering protection by society for their secure realization. This point is reflected in our Structural Dependence Argument, which restricts what we count as core elements of well-being to those that human beings generally cannot secure for themselves, on their own, but that require societal assurance or assistance.

While Mill's own account of the special moral importance of certain interests, and the stringency of justice norms upon which they are grounded, is confined to rights—arguably, negative rights only—other theories of justice assign the same sort of priority to fairness norms, for the same sorts of reasons.

Rawls, for example, argues for the lexical priority of his fairness norms of justice, giving special protection to both the opportunity for, and the distribution of, certain all-purpose goods that are presumed to have special value for anyone, whatever their overall life plan.

Although Rawls and Mill differ in the particular set of norms of justice recognized within their theories, both treat justice norms as stringent because of the architectonic role they play in the way social life is organized. In language similar to Mill's description of rights as securing the very groundwork of our existence, Rawls describes his own norms of fairness as securing background justice,[7] essential to establishing what he calls fair terms of social cooperation within which individuals can pursue their own life plans. Just as the architecture of a building provides the foundation, scaffolding, and design that determine its very shape, the norms of justice set the contours of the shape, the supporting moral structure, in which social interactions of all types take place.

Perhaps the architectonic, special normative organizing role of justice norms is part of what Brian Barry had in mind in his well-known attempt to mark a distinction between duties of justice and duties of humanity (or duties clustered under similar headings, such as humanitarian assistance, beneficence, and charity). Barry's example involved issues of resource distribution. Duties of humanity instruct us to use our resources to assist those in need, while principles of justice, among other things, establish the legitimacy of resource holdings in the first place.[8] So understood, justice norms play an architectonic role within the overall normatively governed social framework that is analogous to the role they play in theories proposed by Mill and Rawls.

The larger point we can extract from Mill, Rawls, and Barry is this. Considerations of justice—both the fulfillment of individual rights and the satisfaction of norms of fairness—take precedence over other moral principles, social goals, and discretionary judgments of individuals. The reason is that norms of justice establish the moral architectural framework within which both the public pursuit of social goals and the private use of resources and discretionary power are constrained.

It is important to be clear, however, about what is not entailed by the normative priority, as we construe it. The normative priority we assign to justice should not be conflated with the view that justice entails a fixed hierarchy of duties applicable in all situations.

Suppose, for example, that a massive famine is under way. Suppose also that a large part of the cause of the famine is some clear injustice on the part of identifiable human rights violators or an injustice attributable to those who have established and continue to benefit from deeply unfair, disadvantaging schemes of global market organization. These facts tell

---

[7] Rawls, *PL*, 267–268; Rawls, *JAF*, §§ 13.2 and 15.

[8] Brian Barry, "Humanity and Justice in Global Perspective," in *NOMOS XXIV, Ethics, Economics and the Law*, ed. J. Roland Pennock and John W. Chapman (New York: Harvester Wheatsheaf, 1982), 244–250. A source of Barry's concern about the need to draw such a distinction was the influence of Peter Singer's discussion of global duties to aid those who suffer deprivation, however it was caused. See Peter Singer, "Famine, Affluence, and Morality," *Philosophy and Public Affairs* 1, no. 3 (1975): 229–243.

us nothing about the morally most urgent duties at the moment of crisis. What may be morally most urgent in the moment is likely to be humanitarian assistance from whatever source, independent of any causal roles in bringing about the crisis. The failures of some identifiable agents to acquit their duties of justice do not get everyone else off the moral hook for immediate humanitarian assistance. Still, we might reserve an especially harsh judgment for the perpetrators of injustice, and we might justifiably look to them first for compensation or mitigation of harm. Put another way, the peremptory force of justice norms over charity norms should not be construed as a context-free priority rule for ranking one category of moral norms over other normative categories.

Suppose further that the humanitarian duties of famine relief in this example can be fulfilled only by temporarily imposing curfews and other restrictions on nearby populations engaged in local hostilities in order to secure safe passage for famine relief workers. Whether the urgency of the humanitarian crisis outweighs the violation of the human right to freedom of movement depends upon a number of factors, including, for example, whether there is no less restrictive way to effect famine relief. In such cases, duties of justice as a type, including in this instance to respect a human right, do not necessarily trump all instances in which competing duties of assistance are in play. Duties of justice, in roughly the way Barry sets up the classificatory schema, establish background norms of the sort that we see as matters of structural justice. These norms are stringent because, in the ordinary course of things, they are the kinds of norms that make possible forms of social life that Mill and Rawls both imagined as taking priority within a normatively configured framework of social organization.

The justice norms in our theory play a similarly architectural role in establishing the normative framework for social organization. Human rights norms involve entitlement claims made by individuals for forbearance, protection of an individual's core well-being interests, or provision or guarantee of the availability of some good or service that secures these interests. By contrast, the claims of fairness highlighted by our theory reflect a group relational orientation. They are based primarily in concerns of individuals as members of one or more socially situated groups and how the patterns of ongoing relations between social groups are structured with regard to advantages and power. These norms protect the core well-being interests in a different way than human rights entitlements that secure a welfare floor. They rule out as unfair social arrangements that result in or perpetuate corrosive forms of differential advantage, involve exploitation, or result in social exclusion of some groups from valuable forms of ongoing social interaction that is the context within which a decent life is possible.

3.2. Claimability and Specificity

Claimability and specificity are features of norms of justice often explicated by the distinction between perfect and imperfect duties. While there are some disagreements regarding the best understanding of this distinction, a familiar account consists of two key parts. Duties of justice are said to be perfect duties. They are perfect in the sense that the duty-bearer who is responsible for fulfilling justice claims is fixed. They are perfect also in the sense that the deontic content of the duties is fixed; that is to say, the actions or forbearance required of the duty-bearer for the fulfillment of justice claims is fully and determinately specified. Duties of justice then are claimable against identified addressees, namely duty-bearers who owe the claimant specific duties.

Duties of beneficence or charity, by contrast, are imperfect in both senses. They neither involve a particular duty-bearer to whom a particular claim is addressed, nor require a specific, determinate action. Duty-bearers have a wide range of discretion or latitude in the choice of beneficiaries and actions. Because it is within the discretion of the benefactor to determine who the beneficiary is, as well as the kind and level of benefit that are bestowed, there are no potential beneficiaries who are in the position to claim that the benefit was owed to them, much less claim that they are entitled to a particular kind or level of benefit.

Claimability and specificity, understood as hallmarks of justice, apply to all justice norms, though some of the most detailed arguments have been worked out in the context of debates over human rights. Onora O'Neill, for example, argues that justice-based claims to a benefit, such as human rights claims to health care, education, subsistence, or a minimum economic standard of living, run into a conceptual problem that justice-based claims to forbearance avoid. There is no definitive way to assign counterpart duties to the former category of rights without knowing facts about institutional arrangements. According to O'Neill, genuine rights, in particular human rights claimable by everyone, must have pre-institutionally fixed duty-bearers and fixed duties that are not dependent on empirical contingencies for their specification.[9] By contrast, negative duties such as

---

[9] Onora O'Neill, *Towards Justice and Virtue* (Cambridge: Cambridge University Press, 1996), 128–136.

the right against torture, are paradigmatic examples of pre-institutionally fixed duties. They are fully assignable and determinate in what is required in the absence of any facts about institutional arrangements. They would exist in the proverbial state of nature, and they would have their normative force even for stateless persons.

Negative rights on O'Neill's view are thus different from positive rights. They pass the pre-institutional test because we know who has what duties to whom and, in fact, such rights are generally described as doubly universal. For example, everyone has a right against everyone else not to be tortured, and everyone is assigned the duty not to torture anyone. The existence of the duty not to torture does not depend on the presence of nation-states or other institutional structures. We know the identities of claimants and of duty-bearers, and we know the actions that constitute violations of the right, prior to the establishment of any such institutional arrangements.

O'Neill frames the challenge faced by proponents of positive human rights as a dilemma:

> Only if we jettison the entire normative understanding of rights in favour of a merely aspirational view, can we break the normative link between rights and their counterpart obligations. If we take rights seriously and see them as normative, . . . we must take obligations seriously. If . . . we opt for a merely aspirational view . . . then we would also have to accept that where human rights are unmet there is no breach of obligation, nobody at fault, nobody who can be held to account, nobody to blame and nobody who owes redress. We would in effect have to accept that human rights claims are not real claims.[10]

The underlying notion of human rights that O'Neill defends reflects its origins in a juridical approach, where justice norms are modeled on an analogy to legal norms.[11] One strategy for responding to O'Neill's challenge is to reject the juridical model outright. The argument is that we do not need to know to whom a duty is directed or the identity of claimants

---

[10] Onora O'Neill, "The Dark Side of Human Rights," *International Affairs* 81, no. 2 (2005): 430. Note that O'Neill's definition of counterpart duties is more restrictive than ours. She uses the phrase to refer to what she calls primary duties of individuals, in contrast to institutional duties which she calls secondary duties. We refer to all duties that correlate with and satisfy rights claims as counterpart duties.

[11] H. L. A. Hart, "Are There Any Natural Rights?" *Philosophical Review* 64, no. 2 (1955): 175–191.

in order to know the substance of a duty. Knowing that the duty is to a particular person does not explain what makes it a duty corresponding to a human right or something that everyone is entitled to on the basis of their humanity. We look for our answers in the importance of the underlying interests that universally deserve to be protected.[12]

The difficulty with this strategy is that it removes a crucial piece of information that explains why this or that agent should do something or other with respect to another's well-being interest. For example, it is uncontroversial that a scheme of social cooperation that fails to secure the most vital interests of its participants is a bad state of affairs. But knowing that it is a bad state of affairs does not entail an identifiable agent of injustice, or an identifiable action, or an omission that constitutes a breach of duty, whether that breach of duty involves some sort of unfairness in the way relations are structured or a human rights violation. Without some account of claims of specific agents against specific addressees who are under a reasonably determinate duty to those agents, we are left with little basis for discriminating between duties of justice and duties of beneficence, charity, and so on. Without the linkage between claimants and addressees, we have, as O'Neill argues, no one specifically to blame, no one to hold accountable, and no one to whom to address our complaints whenever the state of the world is unsatisfactory.[13]

Absent something normatively unique about claims of justice, we are left with a world in which every regrettable state of affairs is either everyone's moral responsibility or a mere tragedy for which literally no one is morally responsible. We need some distinctive notion of justice in order to grasp the full moral significance of states of affairs in which there

---

[12] Tim Hayward, "On Prepositional Duties," *Ethics* 123, no. 2 (2013): 264–291.

[13] Of course, some accounts of justice are untroubled by this implication. Consider Larry Temkin's characterization of a luck egalitarian view of justice. "I believe egalitarians have the deep and (for them) compelling view that it is a bad thing—unjust and unfair—for some to be worse off than others through no fault of their own." Larry S. Temkin, "Inequality," *Philosophy and Public Affairs* 15, no. 2 (1986): 101. For a discussion of disagreements between egalitarian theories on this point, see Martin O'Neill, "What Should Egalitarians Believe?," *Philosophy & Public Affairs* 36, no. 2 (2008): 119–156. Moreover, non-relational theories hold that inequalities between two wholly unrelated states of affairs can be instances of injustice, independent of the existence of any socially structured relationships. Their conclusion does not rest on any empirical facts about the ways the lives of the participants in social practices have been or might become intertwined, and so by definition, they do not require the existence of an identifiable agent of injustice who has wronged an identifiable victim. For discussions of non-relational theories, see Simon Caney, *Justice beyond Border* (Oxford: Oxford University Press, 2005), 111; and Chris Armstrong, *Global Distributive Justice: An Introduction* (Cambridge: Cambridge: University Press, 2012), 30–32.

is some sort of wronging of someone by agents who should be held accountable for their part in the way things are.

3.2.1. Pre-Institutional Benchmark of Existence or Pragmatic Normative Innovation?

While we agree with O'Neill that the cost of abandoning the normative link between claimants and addressees is too high, we can still ask why we should endorse her conclusion that the only—or best—way to hold onto the link is by retaining the pre-institutional benchmark. In one sense, the answer might seem obvious. Human rights seem like an extension of natural rights theories of the early modern era, when the rhetorical emphasis was on an ideal of justice that transcends mere convention and has binding force before and after the creation of sovereign states. Moreover, the general idea behind the natural law conception of timeless moral norms, "out there" awaiting discovery, remains congenial to many ordinary ethical outlooks, especially ones that are secular descendants of religious traditions.[14]

Consider, however, the merits of a more pragmatic approach to matters of structural justice and human rights. Our suggestion is that these norms are best understood as components of morality that necessarily involve a considerable degree of normative innovation. Norms that constitute what we call the architecture of a social order need revision as circumstances change. As contingent threats to human well-being shift, and new constellations of hierarchical power and clusters of advantage replace or layer upon existing ones, norms of justice need to adapt to them.

The thought behind the idea of a legitimate sphere of normative innovation is that norms that structure our most consequential social arrangements become unmoored from the basis for their justification unless they are understood as open to adaptation and change in response to contingent problems that our existing moral repertoire seems inadequate to address. The norms morph, even as our core human interests remain unaltered by contingent circumstances.[15] In other words, core interests remain the same

---

[14] For suggestions about the relation between theological assumptions that are difficult to extricate from interpretations of modern moral theorizing, see Jeremy Waldron, *God, Locke, and Equality* (Cambridge: Cambridge University Press, 2002).

[15] John Tasioulas, for example, makes a similar point. He cites the dynamic character of human rights, with their deontic content not fixed "once and for all" as a theoretical virtue. John Tasioulas, "The Moral Reality of Rights," in *Freedom from Poverty as a Human Right*, ed. Thomas Pogge (Oxford: Oxford University Press, 2007), 94.

over variations in time and place, but because the conditions that put them at risk change and the justifiable and feasible options for their protection and promotion evolve, normative innovation is not only permissible, but sometimes required.[16]

Consider the circumstances facing Locke and others pondering the threats posed by the emergence of powerful states. The concentrated power in the hands of hereditary absolute monarchs (who viewed their authority as both absolute in its scope and beyond the need for justification to those affected) put core human interests at risk in arguably historically unprecedented ways. However, the prevailing norms of justice offered no remedy for the aggrieved. Until late in the sixteenth century, political authority throughout European Christendom reflected the consensus view that the authority of the king derives from an irrevocable grant from the people, or from divine authority, or some combination, and that resistance to constituted authority undermines the very interests that the divine institution of political authority was designed to secure (and God's will, of course).[17]

Anti-absolutists began to put forward a radically revisionist view. They argued that such a grant (assuming there was one) was both conditional at the outset and revocable whenever the exercise of authority was contrary to the rights and interests of individuals. This was normative innovation in pure form. Moreover, in Locke's theory, even the mix of rights and duties that are properly assigned to individuals in the state of nature is altered with the change of institutional conditions, even as the underlying interests remain unaltered. Under the Lockean bargain for entry into political association, individuals surrender their personal power (rights) possessed in the state of nature to interpret and execute what Locke calls the "Fundamental Law of Nature." They do so in return for the security and order provided by the state when it assumes those functions.[18] This, too,

---

[16] Our position resembles one of the arguments by Elizabeth Ashford. She argues that duties of justice include some unspecific duties to protect. Such duties are imperfect, in the sense that they are inherently open-ended, shared by everyone prior to institutional assignment, and require individuals to create institutions that can address large-scale injustices. Elizabeth Ashford, "Duties Imposed by the Right to Basic Necessities," in *Freedom from Poverty as a Human Right*, ed. Thomas Pogge (Oxford: Oxford University Press, 2007), 194–201.

[17] The Augustinian Doctrine gave theological support for the political absolutism that was universal throughout Europe up through most of the seventeenth century. It was based on an interpretation of Romans 13: "Let everyone be subject to the governing authorities, for there is no authority except that which God has established. The authorities that exist have been established by God." Accordingly, resistance against earthly princes, no matter how odious, is a sin and the authority of the prince is absolute and irrevocable.

[18] The Fundamental Law of Nature in the pre-political context is set forth in the *Second Treatise*, § 6: "Everyone is obliged to preserve himself and not opt out of life willfully, so for the same

represents a profound normative transformation, revising norms and the way duties are delineated and assigned for the sake of securing the underlying interests that informed the older norms.

Although the kinds of problems that motivated Locke and the kinds of solutions he proposed were most likely unique to his era, what remains true today are the reasons for thinking that significant institutional transformation justifies significant transformation in our normative outlook. Part and parcel of such a normative transformation is a rethinking of the content and assignment of duties with regard to both human rights and fairness norms within an altered context of power, advantage, and interdependency.

We think that Locke's theory—while greatly different from our own—reveals the reasons that we need to abandon the pre-institutional benchmark. But what then? We believe that there is no alternative to reliance upon the resources of practical reasoning, starting from a conception of human well-being, as the basis for both the assignment and specification of duties. This involves working from empirical premises regarding the kinds of institutions and social practices that are in place, the contingent threats they pose to enduring, core human interests, and an appraisal of the capacities and deficiencies of existing institutional arrangements to respond to structural realities.

The upshot of our pragmatic approach is that there is no permanent list of addressees of a portfolio of claims that arrives on the scene, ready-made, straight out of the mythical state of nature, never to be altered, and normatively bound by a conceptual straitjacket. This way of thinking about the unalterable content and addressees of justice norms makes sense, if at all, only within a context that neither Locke nor we inhabit.[19] In chapter 6, we utilize a more flexible, pragmatic approach to develop an account of

---

reason everyone ought, when his own survival isn't at stake, to do as much as he can to preserve the rest of mankind." The fundamental law that the sovereign is charged with interpreting and executing is very different in the *Second Treatise*, § 134: "[T]he first and fundamental natural law—which should govern even the legislature itself—is the preservation of the society and (as far as the public good allows it) the preservation of every person in it." John Locke, *Two Treatises of Government*, ed. Peter Laslett (Cambridge: Cambridge University Press, 1988). The priority that the individual is permitted (and required) to give to his own life is not mirrored in the responsibility of the legislature, where the well-being of the society as a whole takes precedence over that of each individual. The transformation of norms from pre-political to political society is quite profound, more so than many expositions of Locke often highlight. Ruth Grant is a notable exception. Ruth W. Grant, *John Locke's Liberalism* (Chicago: University of Chicago Press, 1991).

[19] Shue's arguments for the normative superiority of what he describes as a model of "institutionally-mediated duties" over the pre-institutional model fit well with this view. Henry Shue, "Mediating Duties," *Ethics* 98, no. 4 (1988): 687–704. In *Basic Rights*, he argues that his approach involving a plurality of duties assigned to multiple addressees allows for a moral division of labor that distributes the complex burdens of fulfillment. Shue, *Basic Rights*, 59–60. It ensures

the claims of justice applicable to the current global institutional context. We examine the rationale for claims of individuals and socially situated groups addressed to their own nation-state, other nation-states, powerful non-state entities, and transnational institutions, as well as claims properly addressed by nation-states to other nation-states and to supranational institutions.

3.2.2. Specificity and the Problem of Multiple Realizability

An implication of endorsing claimability as a criterion of justice norms is that it highlights the importance of a high degree of specificity in the deontic content of the duties of fulfillment and the challenges posed by proposals to relax requirements of determinacy of duty. Kant, for example, offers one of the most familiar and powerful arguments for specificity, at least in the context where coercive state enforcement of claims is at issue. He suggests that coercive state enforcement would be unfair unless the deontic content of the duty were sufficiently determinate or specific in the requirements imposed on an addressee. To enforce a duty that is neither specific in what it requires nor grounded in the claims of identifiable others aggrieved by a breach of duty owed to them seems at least unreasonable, and generally unfair. The necessity of an antecedently known addressee of a duty, as well as a determinate and publicly known (or knowable) content of that duty, has become the sin qua non of contemporary notions of the rule of law. No one should be held to legal account, especially when loss of liberty is at stake, without clear, antecedently delineated and institutionally assigned duties.

It thus seems indisputable that justice-based claims should not be so elastic that addressees cannot know and act upon the requirements imposed upon them. Elasticity is therefore a worry that is magnified somewhat by our pragmatic approach. On our view, however, there are countervailing reasons in favor of less determinate standards of duty. In many instances, it is implausible to suppose that there is one and only one way to address emergent threats to human interests. If there is a human right to health care, for example, it is not obvious that there is only one way of organizing health care delivery to fulfill it. Employer-based, market-oriented health funds of the sort found in Germany, Canadian-style single-payer systems involving state funding and private care providers, or national health

---

fairness by avoiding unreasonably burdensome demands on individuals (161–166); and it enables a more efficient matching of duty with capacity (165–166). Cf. Shue, "Mediating Duties," 703.

services might do equally well in terms of meeting the demands of this human right. By contrast, a health care delivery system that excludes some individuals or groups or fails to ensure access to important, basic services would not satisfy requirements of justice.

A similar point applies to norms of fairness. Deeply embedded forms of labor exploitation might be combated, for example, by elimination of the background economic conditions in which some people are so desperate. The existence of such conditions motivates workers to accept harsh workplace environments and motivates manufacturers to search the world over for labor obtainable at the lowest cost. Or alternatively, tighter regulation of labor conditions and wages, perhaps through internationally enforceable treaties or trade agreements, might serve the purpose of combating exploitation. What is clear, however, is that a combination of extreme inequality of wealth, concentration of market power, and the limited options of labor is likely to result in one of the kinds of social relationship that our theory counts as deeply unfair, and thus a significant form of structural injustice. Equally clear is that the multiplicity of ways to mitigate unfairness of this sort provides reasons to challenge the rigid requirement of specificity embedded in the idea of a perfect duty. In a complex and dynamic social structure, the view that a claimant's demand is a demand of justice only if it can be satisfied in one and only one way, by one and only one set of pre-institutionally designated agents is both naive and archaic.

How much, then, should Kant's initial worries about the undesirable consequences of lack of specificity concern us when confronted with the fact of multiple realizability of justice norms? In our view, not much at all. The reason is that Kant's objections applied to state enforcement of interpersonal norms of justice. In that context, heightened demands for specificity of justice norms seems warranted as a core feature of the rule of law. However, from the perspective of structural justice, it is far more plausible to contemplate relaxation of specificity requirements as our examples above suggest. In the structural context, the norms of justice are used for the evaluation of forms of social arrangement, for example, of the sort that we find within nation-states. Latitude in the manner of fulfillment of justice norms that are applicable to states or other social orders is not problematic in the way that latitude is generally problematic in the norms of justice that govern interpersonal relations of the sort that Kant had in mind. In chapter 5, we consider some further issues regarding indeterminacy of human rights norms, along with suggestions about how our theory can offer guidance for reducing indeterminacy in those instances in which indeterminacy takes on greater moral significance.

3.3. Rightful Enforceability

To say that norms of justice are rightfully enforceable is merely to assert that these are norms for which some enforcement effort is always presumptively justified.[20] Enforcement efforts can include steps to compel fulfillment, forms of resistance, self-protective action against the activities of those who fail to do their duties, or demands against agents who are under a duty to protect against injustices toward others. There may be instances in which competing reasons counsel against enforcement or in favor of some mechanisms of enforcement over others, but a defining feature of injustice is that it *always* presumptively warrants a response aimed at enforcement of a norm.[21]

Rightful enforceability seems to follow quite naturally from the four features of justice norms already surveyed: they are grounded in especially important human interests, the threats to those interests justify especially stringent moral requirements, and the proper understanding of these norms resides in claims or demands for reasonably determinate kinds of performance against identifiable addressees. Given these features of justice norms, it would seem odd to deny the general appropriateness of some robust response aimed at a norm's enforcement and of vindication of grievances where the norm is violated.

---

[20] The link between justice and the rightful enforceability of claims has a long and distinguished pedigree, with numerous contemporary expositors. See, e.g., Immanuel Kant, *Metaphysical Elements of Justice* (1797), trans. John Ladd (Indianapolis: Hackett [1997] 1999); Mill, *Utilitarianism,* chap. 5; Joel Feinberg, "The Nature and Value of Rights," *Journal of Value Inquiry* 4 (1970): 243–257; Robert Nozick, *Anarchy, State and Utopia* (New York: Basic Books, 1974); Miller, *National Responsibility and Global Justice,* 261; and Laura Valentini, "Cosmopolitan Justice and Rightful Enforceability," in *Cosmopolitanism versus Non-Cosmopolitanism,* ed. Gillian Brock (Oxford: Oxford University Press, 2013), 9–11.

[21] It may be true, as sometimes is argued, that the breach of other, non-justice moral norms also should be enforced or met with resistance. For example, it has been argued that it is permissible to coercively enforce some scheme by which individual duties of beneficence are fulfilled. A coercively enforced scheme might be necessary to solve coordination problems arising among potential voluntary contributors responding to some morally weighty concern such as a humanitarian crisis or to ensure effective governmental policies pertaining to population health, even if no rights claims are at stake. The crucial difference, however, is that norms of justice are always presumptively rightfully enforceable, unlike other norms which carry no such presumption but which may warrant enforcement in specific cases. See Allen Buchanan, "Justice and Charity," *Ethics* 97, no. 3 (1987): 558–575; Pablo Gilabert, *From Global Poverty to Global Equality* (Oxford: Oxford University Press, 2012), 18; Laura Valentini, *Justice in a Globalized World* (Oxford: Oxford University Press, 2012), 184; David Miller, *Principles of Social Justice* (Cambridge, MA: Harvard University Press, 1999), 76; and Miller, *National Responsibility and Global Justice,* 248–249.

3.3.1. The Legacies of Mill and Locke

One prominent way in which rightful enforceability is often understood equates justice norms with ones that warrant coercive state enforcement. Mill famously equates rights with justice and then says that to have a "right . . . is . . . to have something which society ought to defend me in possession of."[22] Kant, as noted in the preceding section, rests much of his case for limiting the inventory of norms of justice to ones that are highly specific in their duty requirements, in large part, on the supposition that such claims generate secondary claims against the state for enforcement. This "juridical model" of rightful enforceability, as it is sometimes called, has earned a prominent place in contemporary philosophical literature.[23]

Many who follow Kant and Mill seem to suppose that the understanding of the idea of rightful enforcement is centrally located in an aggrieved party's claim to protection through coercive interventions by the state.[24] In addition, some political theorists construe the conceptual link between rightful enforceability and state enforcement in an even stronger way. They take the existence of a state mechanism for enforcement to be a prerequisite for the existence of a right.[25] The argument is that unless actual state mechanisms of enforcement are in place, the talk of human rights and their violation is obscure and often a source of false hopes among those who suffer grave hardships. This argument for the existence of effective enforcement mechanisms as a precondition for the existence of human rights—not just institutionally recognized legal rights—represents a further expansion of the influence of the legal or juridical model.[26]

The problem with the juridical model is that it is by no means obvious why it should exert such wholesale influence over our understanding of human rights (or any justice norms) and our perspective on what makes them rightfully enforceable. It makes rather obvious sense in the legal context to restrict permissible state enforcement to legal rights antecedently

---

[22] Mill, *Utilitarianism*, 250.

[23] John Tasioulas and Loren Lomasky both adopt this terminology, only to raise doubts about it, though not the doubts we raise. Tasioulas, "The Moral Reality of Rights," 85–86; Loren E. Lomasky, *Persons, Rights, and the Moral Community* (New York: Oxford University Press, 1987), 105–110.

[24] Buchanan, "Justice and Charity," 564.

[25] Raymond Geuss, *History and Illusion in Politics* (Cambridge: Cambridge University Press, 2001), 146; Susan James, "Realizing Rights as Enforceable Claims," in *Global Responsibilities: Who Must Deliver on Human Rights?* ed. Andrew Kuper (New York: Routledge, Taylor & Francis, 2005).

[26] E.g., Tasioulas, "The Moral Reality of Rights," 85–86; Lomasky, *Persons, Rights, and the Moral Community*, 105–110.

recognized within a scheme of promulgation and enforcement, if for no other reasons than Kant's points about the rule of law and its requirements of procedural fairness and due process.

However, in the realm of human rights it would be perverse to say that the only bearers of human rights are those who are fortunate to live under conditions in which their rights are effectively enforceable. By conceptual fiat, stateless people and residents of failed, failing, ineffective, corrupt, or complicit states would be excluded from the class of human rights–bearers, as would people who are members of groups in states where they are not recognized as legitimate claimants to some or all human rights. Often, these are the very persons who are least likely to have their morally most important interests protected and who are most vulnerable to rights violation.[27]

More generally, the idea that rightful enforceability is reducible to what states can or will deliver is odd. Not only does the strictly juridical model leave out people who live in dysfunctional states or in states that refuse to recognize their status as bearers of human rights, it is also an anomaly even within the history of rights theory.

In our view, the historically entrenched and philosophically most plausible understanding of rightful enforceability is not limited to what states or any other juridical body (e.g., international courts) are permitted or required to do in order to vindicate claims of justice. The idea of rightful enforceability also should encompass what aggrieved parties, and others presumptively on their behalf, are entitled to do in response to injustice or the threat of injustice. Indeed, the notion of what individuals may do in the absence of reliable mechanisms for state enforcement has a long history and a direct connection to individual claims of justice.

Consider the Lockean tradition as a case in point. Locke maintained that some injustices provide presumptive grounds for direct resistance by the victim of injustice. Built into this account is the recognition that there will not always be an available agent of organized society who can be counted on to vindicate a person's rights. His point is not at odds with the Millian thesis that aggrieved parties have secondary enforcement claims against society; rather, it supplements it.

Norms of justice, on this more encompassing view, may be rightfully enforced by society, and aggrieved individuals have claims against society to do so. However, sometimes they are rightfully enforceable directly by

---

[27] Susan James acknowledges these implications and yet holds firm to her position. James, "Realizing Rights as Enforceable Claims," 91.

the aggrieved party or by non-state agents acting on behalf of the victims of injustice. Rightful enforceability, on this more capacious reading, simply means that there are a number of potentially justified ways to prevent or respond to injustice, all of which aim at the enforcement or vindication of claims of justice. Where coercive state mechanisms of enforcement are absent or ineffective, and the injustice is palpable, focusing on what we are entitled to demand of states or other coercive institutions to do on our behalf deflects attention from other rightful ways of enforcing claims of justice.

In chapter 8, we take up the questions of when and under what conditions responses to injustice by victims or their non-state advocates are justified. These are difficult and insufficiently explored matters beyond the extreme cases of state oppression that Locke addressed in his arguments for rebellion against existing state authorities. Our central point for now is that the most plausible interpretation of rightful enforceability does not confuse one contingently available enforcement mechanism (e.g., Mill's or Locke's) with an exclusive way of understanding enforceability of claims of justice. Nor is it plausible to suppose that there is no injustice when there is no coercive state agent in place who will enforce our claims on our behalf. The whole point about claimability is that claims are personal to the claimants, and so too are the justified demands for their enforcement.

3.3.2. Taking Stock

Thus far in this chapter we have presented our construal of five criteria for norms of justice. The interests at stake are morally important. They are the core elements of human well-being. The norms for their protection are stringent. They justify both institutional schemes of human rights protection and institutional mechanisms for the continuous adjustment of structural arrangements in order to prevent or undo unfair concentrations of power and clusters of differential advantage.

Injustices of all kinds under our theory are normatively distinctive also insofar as they give rise to claims of identifiable parties against identifiable agents of injustice who have breached a duty or failed to discharge their responsibilities. Injustice is therefore normatively different from a bad state of the world. However, neither the content of such duties nor the assignment of responsibilities comes ready-made, straight out of the mythical state of nature. We inevitably look to the resources of practical reason to make a pragmatic case for their more specific content and proper assignment. This case must be made as part of a division of moral labor within a portfolio of duties in light of the host of institutional factors and contingent threats to the underlying interests at stake. Accordingly, the centrally important duties of justice are not necessarily as specific as the juridical model supposes and they are contingently assignable in light of multiple factors.

Finally, rightful enforceability is not merely a matter of the actions that individuals or groups may demand from states or other institutional entities charged with some duties to protect. Rightful enforceability sometimes is a matter of what affected individuals and groups or participants in social movements may pursue on their own. Sometimes it is only aggrieved individuals and social groups, and the social movements they galvanize, that can bring about social change blocked by institutional barriers, secure a degree of self-protection that institutions fail to provide, and work toward remedies that are largely out of reach within the established social order.

3.4. Unfairness Norms

We close the chapter with some general remarks about fairness as a distinct kind of norm of justice and some specific features of our account of structural unfairness. First, we offer some observations about the relation between fairness norms and human rights norms. There is widespread agreement that human rights are not the whole of justice, and perhaps not even the whole of what justice minimally demands.[28] Ranier Forst summarizes the prevailing view, noting that human rights "are a central part of the full picture of social justice, but they're only a part."[29]

There are, of course, widespread disagreements about where to draw the line between human rights norms and other justice norms. The sharpest demarcation assumes that the domain of universal human rights is limited to a bundle of negative rights that protect basic political and civil liberties.[30] More commonly perhaps, human rights are thought of as including some guarantees of minimum material entitlements, for example, rights to basic necessities, the provision of goods and services sufficient to secure a minimum standard of living or what is understood to be a

---

[28] Samuel Moyn, *Not Enough: Human Rights in an Unequal World* (Cambridge, MA: Belknap Press, 2018).

[29] Forst, "A Critical Theory of Human Rights," 85.

[30] E.g., O'Neill, "The Dark Side of Human Rights"; Geuss, *History and Illusion in Politics*; and Lomasky, *Persons, Rights, and the Moral Community*.

decent life.[31] Typically, such entitlements are part of what is often called non-comparative justice. They are norms guaranteeing a minimum welfare floor, not comparative norms setting limits on socioeconomic inequalities, such as economic opportunity or distribution of wealth and income. Some theories of human rights also incorporate certain fairness standards, such as the right to a fair trial or rights against exclusion from political participation.

No matter how the lines are drawn, there is broad agreement that various other fairness norms fall outside the domain of human rights. James Griffin, for example, rejects the "wholesale inclusion" of a range of requirements of justice as human rights, including matters best characterized under distinct headings of "distributive justice and fairness."[32]

Our structural theory therefore is not unique in assuming that justice norms include both human rights and norms of fairness that fall outside the domain of human rights. However, unlike other theories that identify norms of fairness that are purely domestic in application, for example, Rawls's Principle of Fair Equality of Opportunity and the Difference Principle, our fairness norms are more basic and universal in the same way that human rights norms are. They are norms that are rooted in universal ideals of moral equality, also foundational for human rights. Moreover, our fairness norms do not focus on socioeconomic inequalities that are thought unjust because of politically localized concerns, such as the way they undermine democratic institutions. Rather, our fairness norms go beyond the

---

[31] These more expansive accounts differ among themselves. Shue famously argues for rights to subsistence, which he describes as a "morality of the depths" specifying the "line beneath which no one is to be allowed to sink." Shue, *Basic Rights*, 18. Griffin includes what he calls rights of minimum provision of resources and capabilities sufficient to be able to act in pursuit of an individual's view of a worthwhile life. Griffin, *On Human Rights*, 33. Rawls's theory construes a right to life as including the means to security and subsistence. Rawls, *LOP*, 65 n. 1. Miller includes a range of "social needs" that go beyond mere biological or physical needs because they matter centrally to a distinctively good life for humans. Miller, *National Responsibility and Global Justice*, 181–182 n. 27. Miller also describes the function of rights as securing the minimum conditions for "a decent life" (184). The minimum of human rights guarantees is often glossed as the requirements for a "decent or minimally good life" or "a dignified or minimally good life." Nickel, *Making Sense of Human Rights*, 14, 62, 65, 138. For Nussbaum, the minimum is a bundle of capabilities that overlap with human rights, which constitute "a life worthy of human dignity"; Nussbaum, *Creating Capabilities*, 33–34. Others refer to the guarantees that secure "a minimally decent life." Matthew Liao, "Human Rights as Fundamental Conditions for a Good life," in *Philosophical Foundations of Human Rights*, ed. Rowan Cruft. S. Matthew Liao and Massimo Renzo (Oxford: Oxford University Press, 2015), 81. Renzo also uses the language of "a minimally decent life," but he takes that to include a number of social needs, including a minimum level of social recognition and degree of social interaction. Renzo, "Human Needs, Human Rights," 577–583.

[32] Griffin, *On Human Rights*, 186.

local and the socioeconomic, and set limits on structural inequalities of power or advantage in relations between moral equals that are broadly and globally applicable.

3.4.1. Intuitive Cases

This last section of the chapter is meant to build up the case for the moral distinctiveness and universal relevance of our fairness norms, beginning with simple intuitive cases and eventually illuminating forms of unfairness in more complex structural phenomena. In chapter 4 we describe in detail how the forms of unfairness that are the focus of our theory are inherent in social relationships that are structured by both formal institutional rules and informal but regularized social practices. Here, we provide an intuitive case for our fairness norms by looking first at the ordinary language used to articulate different claims of unfairness in less weighty, less complex situations of everyday experience.

Complaints of unfairness are pretty easy to spot in daily conversation. For example, we object to the person who jumps the queue at a bus stop, even if we do not get bumped as a consequence. People are supposed to wait their turn.

We protest when the referee calls a foul only on our team when it was actually members of both teams who broke the rules. Even if we go on to win the game, and even if we admit that our side also committed a foul, we continue to harbor the complaint. In sports competitions, everyone similarly situated expects to be treated in a similar fashion, with no special advantages conferred on either team.

We object to the conduct of the teacher who, without any apparent good reason, lets one student have an extra week to complete an assignment. The objection holds even if we end up with a better grade. Students, like athletes, expect to be treated similarly when it comes to the rules that govern competitive activities, including assignments and grades; teachers are not supposed to have favorites or at least not dispense favors to those who are.

We recognize all of these scenarios as instances of unfair disadvantage, and we think of our complaints as justified even if what is at stake is relatively trivial, even if any setback we might experience is not that significant to us. It's not the certainty of harm to our interests that explains why something is unjust. It is the differential effect on our prospects for realizing something we value, whether it's a bus ride, winning a game, or a receiving good grade, in circumstances in which we expect institutional rules and informal norms to treat comparable interests in comparable ways.

We object not only to the fact of disadvantage, or to failures of institutions or persons to guard against unfair disadvantage. We also object when we think that others are taking advantage of us. We object to "being used," as the saying goes. Imagine that your roommate eats all of the leftover lasagna (which you made) and leaves the dirty dishes in the sink for you to clean up. Not a lot hangs on what your roommate did; it was fairly ordinary, relatively inconsequential behavior. But if your moral sensibilities are in good working order, the conduct is readily recognizable as part and parcel of a relationship that is tainted by a specific kind of unfairness, especially if your roommate behaves this way repeatedly. The nub of the complaint is against being exploited. One roommate gains the unearned benefits of another roommate's labor, and in the process also imposes additional burdens on her.

We lodge a quite different kind of complaint of unfairness when we are excluded from participation in some aspect of the common social life within which we find ourselves. Think of the child who sits alone at lunch and is the only one in her sixth grade class not invited to a birthday party, or the office worker who notices that conversation stops whenever he approaches the water cooler and is never asked to join his colleagues for drinks on Friday nights. Although there maybe defensible reasons why the child and the office worker are excluded from the common social life of their classmates and co-workers, what is happening to them certainly seems and feels unfair, and it would certainly seem reasonable for them to complain that they are being treated unfairly.

There is yet another context in which we complain of unfairness. Imagine a marriage in which one spouse makes all the decisions, controls all the finances, and routinely tells the other spouse what to do. Or think of an extended family in which one member exerts so much control over everyone else that all that is left for the others is to effectively follow orders. We would be quick to conclude that the degree and pervasiveness of the power that the one person has is wrong and that the others are being treated unfairly. Or consider a somewhat more complicated case in which a company establishes policies that constrain the conduct of its employees in their non-working lives, claiming that employee decorum even outside the workplace is necessary to protect the corporation's brand and public image. Many might protest that it is unfair for an employer to have this degree of intrusive control over how its employees lead their lives.

3.4.2. From Subterranean Layers to Wider Social Contexts

Now consider variants of these cases in which the moral gravity is ratcheted up a considerable notch. Some of the scenarios described above are relatively mundane in their circumstantial details, but they can be altered slightly in order to reveal subterranean layers of graver injustice. We can imagine situations in which it is not just one referee favoring one team that is objectionable but rather the rules of a youth league that, by requiring expensive uniforms or charging exorbitant entry fees, differentially favor teams from affluent communities. Instead of examining the unfairness of one spouse controlling another, we can change the scenario by identifying the domineering spouse as the husband, where gendered patterns of relationships are likely to be at issue. Instead of the objection to co-workers excluding a colleague, we can see what else is at stake if the excluded colleague is the member of an ethnic minority or if we extend the example to race-based exclusion from some workplace settings. Instead of thinking about managerial overreach by individual employers, we can reflect on the range of decisions affecting our collective well-being that have been privatized or removed from the purview of democratic accountability.

We know that broad social consequences accompany the private club that has different signs above two separate entrances, a main door marked "members" and a side door marked "ladies' entrance." We know what is at stake when the sign over the courthouse water fountain reads "whites only." Typically, these practices are emblematic of a much larger pattern of social exclusion in which individuals are effectively excluded, on the basis of group membership, from full participation in the social and economic life of the wider community. The systematic disadvantage that is produced and reproduced by outright social exclusion, in its most egregious forms, is in some respects more extreme than the unfairness of exploitation. Systems of racial and gender discrimination simply push some to the margins of society where much of what makes valuable life prospects possible is out of reach. The available options, likely outcomes, and rewarding relationships available to others are foreclosed simply on the basis of membership in a social group that is not accorded the same standing as other social groups.

Or take the classroom scenario. With the modification of a few details, multiple vectors of disadvantage come into view, each in itself a form of unfairness but, taken as a whole, of greater, longer-lasting consequence than the immediate impact. Instead of the favoritism shown toward a particular student we can reframe the description of the scenario to take account of the variety of ways that favoritism toward "golden boys" is manifested in the high school classroom. The boys interrupt the girls, re-state what the girls say, and at the end of each class session the teacher glosses over or ignores the girls' contributions or, worse yet, predictably and incorrectly attributes the good ideas to the boys. As a consequence, some girls get lower grades, experience a loss of self-confidence and a di-minished sense of agency, and get letters of reference that do not reflect the quality of their academic performance. Along the way, the teacher and the boys contribute to the creation of conditions in which much more insid-ious, durable, and pervasively impactful forms of injustice occur. The boys grow into men who are able to subordinate women, render them powerless and ineffectual, exploit their subordinate status in order to extract benefit for themselves, and marginalize or effectively exclude women from full participation as equals in valuable forms of social interaction.

The force of these examples is that they show that we are able to start from our most basic intuitions about patterns of unfairness in our interper-sonal relationships and uncover further subterranean veins of other mor-ally salient factors. As our modifications of the examples illustrate, we can also extrapolate from complaints arising within interpersonal contexts to the larger societal contexts within which relationships between social groups are structured in more fundamental ways.

Our ordinary language is therefore well equipped to make the leap to an assessment of larger-scale, institutionally dense, causally more com-plex structural injustices. We all know what is being said when we hear someone say in reference to society or the economy that the game has been fixed or that the rules are rigged. We object when we see ourselves as weighed down with more burdens than others who are not like us, or when expectations that our interactions will take place on a level playing field are not met. We complain when members of some groups have to overcome hurdles or break through barriers that the occupants of other, more privileged or circumstantially favored social positions do not have to navigate. We protest when someone with advantages open only to the affluent gets the better of us in ways that run counter to our expectations as participants in some social process or shared social practice. We ob-ject to being sidelined. We object in particular to circumstances that let a privileged few determine the rules about who gets to play and under what terms.

We object most strenuously to all of these forms of unfairness when they constitute serious, high-stakes forms of structural disadvantage that undermine the secure realization of core elements of well-being. These more complex, higher-stakes complaints are thus not only about the way our relations to other social groups are structured by institutionalized rules and procedures, but also about how these institutional vectors combine with webs of expectations and behavioral patterns that define our social position within less formal social settings and practices.

3.4.3. The Place of Unfair Power Relations within Our Theory

In both our mundane and socially complex scenarios, we have taken pains to illustrate the intuitive differences, first, between unfair advantage and unfair exercises of power and, second, between distinct forms of unfair power that we categorize under the headings of exclusion, exploitation, and subordination. In our analysis of complex patterns of structural injustice, where densely woven patterns of systematic disadvantage and power differentials occur, it is crucially important to identify each constituent feature of unfair exercises of power for what it is. Exploitation, exclusion, and subordination must be understood as morally distinct complaints, each captured by various metaphors deeply rooted in our ordinary discourse and often beginning in and ending with systematic disadvantage. Each one marks the presence of an inherently objectionable constitutive feature of the way in which the relationship between the wrongdoers and those treated unfairly is structured, and each one functions as a vector resulting in compounded patterns of structural injustice.

One form of unfair power is the subordination of an individual or group to the will of others whose authority over us is not justified. Typically, in the most egregious instances, that authority is exercised across a wide range of matters. We take special exception to being under the thumb of another, having little or no say in what happens to us, especially when control is exercised over matters that we think are both weighty and largely our own concern. We also object to being asymmetrically dependent upon their good graces, often subject to monitoring and surveillance aimed at enforcing compliance and locked into a position of relative powerlessness. We recoil at being beholden to or at the mercy of others, especially those who are contemptuous or suspicious of our capacities to make personal choices or who are indifferent to our preferences. We remonstrate against those who counsel us to know our place, accept our assigned lot in life, and get along by doing as we are told or as "society" expects. We bristle at being silenced, rendered invisible, or infantilized by those who assert their prerogative to decide how things go, with no questions asked. We know full well the nature of the judgment we reach about those who claim the prerogative to "name the tune to which others must dance." We resent being treated as subordinates by those who act as if they were our superiors when they are really no more than our equals, as if we were by nature fit only to follow the instruction of our betters. The heart of the objection, then, is to the exercise of control by persons or institutions that do not rightly possess authority over us.[33]

While we object to the exercise of authority by those who are not entitled to exercise power over us, such power typically involves the further injustices of exploitation and social exclusion. Differential power typically results in differential advantages and, ultimately, in better outcomes for the powerful and worse outcomes for those who are not. Power is routinely used to extract an unearned benefit, to arbitrarily marginalize or exclude the less powerful from beneficial forms of interaction, or simply to fix the rules of interaction in ways that distribute advantages and disadvantages in self-serving, self-perpetuating ways.

Racial and gender injustices are obvious examples, but so too are the injustices in the organization of the domestic and transnational economic order. Multiple and mutually reinforcing structural injustices often gain a foothold because of the prior exercise of unjust forms of social control. Economic and political domination, as well as cultural patterns of subordination such as patriarchy readily permit dominant social groups to fix the terms of the economy for their own advantage, impose exploitative terms of participation on those groups who are vulnerable and dependent on their goodwill, skim the benefits and offload the risks, and marginalize or exclude subordinated groups altogether from participation in the mainstream of social and economic life.

Structural injustice, as we view it in its most ordinary context, does not simply emerge as an unintended consequence of morally innocuous actions and policies. Matters are far more complex than the portrayal of emergent injustice in its pure form suggests. Patterns of systematic disadvantage of interest under our theory also typically involve discrete forms of unfairness in power relations, including exploitation, exclusion, and subordination. The upshot is that our theory is concerned focally with the advantages that accrue to some groups by virtue of the disadvantages

---

[33] We employ the term "subordination" to give expression to the general objection to being subject to unjustified control. Both "domination" and "subordination" are used more or less interchangeably in the literature, but the precise understanding of the kinds of control that fit under either of these labels varies. In the last section of chapter 6, we rely upon a series of examples of unjust power over others in the international arena, pointing to a family of ways in which the exercise of authority over others is unjustified. See, e.g., Frank Lovett, *A General Theory of Domination and Justice* (Oxford: Oxford University Press, 2010).

faced by others under conditions that are morally unjustifiable ways of structuring or organizing social relations.

The objection is not simply to the way things are, but to the way things have been brought about. The benefits extracted or the risks imposed by the exploiting party are not up to the perpetrators to determine unilaterally. The exclusion of some from entering public places, engaging in shared social practices, or expressing themselves within discursive spaces should not be left to the prerogative of powerful groups, under social arrangements that enable them to use their power to isolate members of some groups and make them feel unimportant or unworthy of participation on a par with others. The least powerful segments of society often find themselves having to choose between effective exclusion from the economy and other aspects of social life or participation on the basis of asymmetrically imposed exploitative terms. Quite often it is not mere circumstance that generates vulnerability to multiple forms of unfairness but the cumulative concentration of power in the hands of members of dominant groups. The colloquial expression "my way or the highway" captures the nature of the difficult choice that members of vulnerable, dependent groups routinely face.

3.4.4. Common Assumptions in Fairness and Human Rights Claims

Embedded in each of these morally distinct complaints of unfairness is an explicit or implicit judgment that our lives and our interests do not matter in the same way that the lives and interests of others matter. We are wrongly viewed as legitimate candidates for subordination to the will of others, suitable targets for exploitation and the one-sided extraction of benefits, and appropriate subjects for social exclusion. Subordination, exploitation, and exclusion are thus hallmarks of relationships rooted in especially deep inegalitarian assumptions about who really matters, and hence the kinds of patterns of disadvantage and external control that are morally tolerable. It is on the basis of what moral equality minimally demands that we assert that there are limits to patterns of disadvantage appropriate to relationships among moral equals, that we are not mere instruments of the will of others, that we are not resources to be exploited, and that we are not social inferiors to be shut out of social life on the say of others.

The underlying assumption of equality is also at work when we assert our status as bearers of human rights. We are presupposing that our most basic well-being interests are on a moral par with others and that forms of structural unfairness that involve differential threats to those interests join human rights claims as among the most fundamental moral demands of human beings. Our normative approach therefore rests on a bedrock ideal that rejects the existence of a natural hierarchy among humans. The world as we know it of course contains many individuals and expositors of cultural traditions who appear to think otherwise.

We conclude this chapter by restating an important point about unfairness and human rights and the different ways they are connected to our conception of well-being. Human rights violations directly affect the elements of well-being that ground our rights. Structural unfairness in both relations of power and patterns of advantage are wrong in themselves, but the egregiousness of such wrongs and the special moral urgency of addressing them are a function of the moral weightiness of the interests implicated by the way social structures are arranged. We turn next in chapter 4 to our understanding of the characteristic features of complex social structural phenomena and thus why our theory is a theory of structural justice.

CHAPTER 4 | What Structural Injustice Is

WHAT MAKES STRUCTURAL INJUSTICE "structural"? Structural theories of justice share one overarching assumption. It is the assumption that social arrangements, including certain institutions and social practices, have highly consequential, differential, and sometimes unjust effects on individuals because they are members of identifiable social groups. The primary task of a structural theory of justice is to explain what makes some social structural impacts unjust, and on this task theories differ.

However, most contemporary theories of structural justice share the basic idea of differential or relative social position. For example, the distributive problem in Rawls's theory begins with a recognition that "people are born into different social positions with different and unequal life prospects."[1] Iris Marion Young also constructs her theory of structural injustice from the observation that societies are composed of "group[s] of persons who are similarly positioned in interactive and institutional relations that condition their opportunities and life prospects."[2]

The concept of relative social position has a long history in the social sciences. In the late 1920s, for example, R. H. Tawney observed that to a significant extent "the destiny of the individual is decided . . . by his place in the social system, by his position as a member of this stratum or of that."[3] This way of thinking allowed Tawney and subsequent generations of social scientists to retain Marx's understanding of a social order as composed of social groups differentially affected by political, economic, and social arrangements, without endorsing his views about economic class. These social scientists rejected the idea that economic

---

[1] Rawls, *TOJ*, 7.

[2] Iris Marion Young, *Inclusion and Democracy* (Oxford: Oxford University Press, 2000), 97.

[3] Tawney, *Equality*, 73.

class, defined by position within the system of production, is the only socially positioned group appropriate for empirical study or significant from the perspective of justice. As Tawney put it, "[T]he sections of a community" that might be subject to sharp differences stemming from institutions and policies are "infinite in number," including not only socioeconomic classes, but also sharp divisions that have "coloured the relations between the sexes . . . religions, and members of different races."[4]

Tawney's analysis rests on assumptions that are central to our own theory. He observes that the "systematic differences in the manner of life" found in hierarchical social orders are based in the "powers and advantages which different classes in practice enjoy."[5]

An important implication of Tawney's analysis is that patterns of unjust social stratification are matters of social contingency.[6] Relative social positions, based on differentials of power and advantage, are not fixed. They come into existence or fade from prominence as patterns of human interaction evolve and shift over time. Political unification and subdivision, colonialism and de-colonization, warfare, migration, religious animosities, gender relations, changes in industrial organization and economic concentration, the rise and fall of the economic importance of regionally located natural resources, and global market integration are examples. We should not assume the permanence of any existing patterns of interaction, but we should assume that the normative significance of certain kinds of fact patterns, characterized by self-perpetuating, group-based differentials in power and advantage, does endure. The best we can hope for in a theory of structural injustice is that it will have something to say about the world as it is, but still remain applicable to the world as it might become.

Political philosophers must lean heavily on the empirical foundations supplied by the social sciences, at least in broad strokes, in order to construct theories of structural justice. Political theorizing depends on empirically based assumptions about the key components of social structures that create and sustain differences in power and advantage among differentially positioned social groups.

In this chapter, we survey four key features of structural theories of justice that vary from one theory to another, and we explain and defend

---

[4] Ibid., 57.

[5] Ibid., 113, 111; cf. 158–159.

[6] This contingency, as Young's remark reveals, is due to the fact that "[s]tructural social groups are relationally constituted in the sense that one position does not exist apart from the differentiated relation to other positions." Iris Marion Young, "Equality of Whom? Social Groups and Judgments of Justice," *Journal of Political Philosophy* 9, no. 1 (2001): 12.

what is distinctive about our own. First, theories differ in their inventory of the morally significant impacts traceable to social structural influences. Second, they vary in their understanding of the primary structural components that have the relevant kind and degree of impact, based on membership in one or more socially positioned groups. Third, theories diverge in the differentially positioned, differentially affected social groups they select for special scrutiny. Fourth, they differ in their background assumptions regarding the circumstances constitutive of the social structural phenomena to which they apply.

In section 4.1, we provide an overview of some contemporary approaches, examining the first three features together. The emphasis is on differences in the kinds of impact that theories highlight as morally significant. In section 4.2, we discuss in more detail the characteristics of the structural components central to our theory, along with examples illustrating those characteristics. In section 4.3, we dive deeper into some current issues pertaining to the selection of relevant social groups, and in section 4.4, we examine assumptions about background circumstances.

4.1. Significant Impacts, Structural Components, and Social Groups

A theory's selection of the impacts of a social structure that are worthy of moral examination are closely linked to what it counts as the relevant components of the social structure and the social groups that constitute its normative focus.

The impacts of particular concern in Rawls's theory, for example, pertain to the fair distribution of a society's joint economic product. These impacts extend both to the actual distribution of income and wealth and to differential economic life prospects, by which Rawls means what individuals can expect as a consequence of their membership in a social group. More specifically, his concern is for the least advantaged group in relation to other, more advantaged socioeconomic groups that receive a greater share of income and enjoy better lifetime economic prospects because of their superior advantages. The least advantaged class here is the class of unskilled workers.[7] The Fair Equality of Opportunity Principle

---

[7] For Rawls, the income shares of unskilled workers are the lowest. He concedes that the idea of the least advantaged to whom priority is due might be spelled out in a variety of ways, but within his theory, "the representative man who is worse off, in this case [is] the representative unskilled worker." Rawls, *TOJ*, 67–68, 83.

corrects for differential economic advantages, especially those present from early childhood among socioeconomic classes that can provide education and other resources that enlarge their children's economic opportunities. The Difference Principle, by contrast, guarantees an economic floor to the least advantaged, in the sense that it requires that the "basic structure" be arranged in a way that maximizes their distributive share of income and wealth.

While the basic structure is not precisely defined, its components include such things as laws, the market, and the social organization of the family.[8] Given that the focal concern is economic distribution across socioeconomic classes, it makes sense that his examples of the relevant structures are ones that have highly consequential effects on distributive outcomes (e.g., wealth and income) and socioeconomic opportunities or prospects (e.g., access to jobs). Formal legal rules, forms of market organization, the social position of the family within which one is born and raised, along with systems of education and training are thus central components of the social structure in Rawls's theory because of their highly consequential impact on economic outcomes and economic life prospects.

As critics have long contended, there are numerous other approaches to the way social structural impact might be understood. Concentrating on multiple forms of deprivation that can be alleviated through the enhancement of basic human capabilities is one familiar alternative that, at least indirectly, places its focus on well-being more broadly.[9] Another alternative involves rejecting the "distributive paradigm," at least in part, by not only attending to the structural impediments to well-being, but also examining the structural factors that contribute to domination, subordination, and other unjust exercises of power. Iris Young, for example, sometimes speaks of the dual aims of relieving structurally mediated deprivation and eliminating domination.[10]

Both shifts—away from economic shares to matters of well-being and toward the inclusion of concerns about power relations—open the door to rethinking the relevant social groups that are affected in multiple ways.

---

[8] Rawls's notion of a social structure, which he refers to as the "basic structure" is "the way in which the major social institutions distribute fundamental rights and duties and determine the division of advantages from social cooperation." Rawls, *TOJ*, 7. This description highlights three things: (1) the centrality of institutions rather than informal social norms; (2) institutions as important under his theory insofar as they function as instruments of economic distribution; and (3) a special role for the kinds of institutions that distribute fundamental rights and duties, a task that only states can perform through the exercise of rules backed by coercive power.

[9] E.g., Nussbaum, *Creating Capabilities*.

[10] Iris Marion Young, *Responsibility for Justice* (Oxford: Oxford University Press, 2011), 52.

Once the inventory of morally significant impacts expands, along with the list of implicated social groups, a broader array of components of the social structure becomes relevant. Our theory follows this trajectory. It is concerned with the effects on six core elements of well-being of members of social groups marked by differentials of power and advantage. These effects are produced through multiple components of the social structure, including but going well beyond those institutions and practices primarily affecting economic distribution.

Some theories of structural justice tend to place an overarching emphasis on the unjust influence that structural arrangements have on individual choices and available options, an emphasis that we think requires modification. For example, when Rawls explains what is at stake when differential advantages among socioeconomic groups affect their access to economic goods, the diagnosis of what is unjust turns on how lack of access undermines the ability of individuals to form and execute their life plans. At times, Iris Young emphasizes how the dynamic between social groups differentially affected by structural arrangements serves to "constrain the options of some at the same time as they expand the options of others."[11] The emphasis on the moral significance of individual choice and the availability of choiceworthy options is a dominant feature in much of the capabilities literature as well. For example, Martha Nussbaum identifies the political goal of justice as "the capability to function well if one so chooses," noting that this formulation distinguishes between achievement and the freedom to achieve.[12]

Our theory concurs with judgments regarding the importance of such concerns, first by including a reasonable measure of self-determination on our list of core elements of well-being, and second by treating certain kinds of power relations as fundamentally unfair. However, as important as choice and the availability of meaningful options are, the moral significance of structural influence on members of differentially situated social groups is far from exhausted by the constraints on individual choice.[13]

---

[11] Young, "Equality of Whom?," 11. In a similar vein, she speaks of "the socially collective or institutional conditions . . . which limit options and actions" (10).

[12] Nussbaum, *Creating Capabilities*, 45, 51. We offer more extensive critiques of the capabilities approach and defenses of our own position in *Social Justice*, 37–41, and Powers and Faden, "Health Capabilities, Outcomes."

[13] As noted earlier, Young sometimes gives equal billing to deprivation and domination as the kinds of impacts of unjust structures. Nonetheless, many of her sympathetic critics interpret the focus of her work narrowly. Serena Parekh, for example, notes that "[s]tructural injustice refers to

There are many structural constraints on the likely outcomes that members of a social group can expect, regardless of the options available to them or the choices they can make.[14] Two types of cases reveal what is at stake.

First, the disadvantages experienced in childhood, in particular, illustrate how the lifetime prospects of members of any social group are structured by numerous social determinants that are independent of how individual choice is affected, often from the earliest stages of life. For example, impoverished children, in both extremely poor countries and highly economically stratified affluent countries, face structural barriers that limit the range of individual choices they will have, but they also face much more. They start life with a low ceiling on what is probable for them, a ceiling that is extremely difficult to crack no matter what personal efforts or choices they might make as adults. Growing up in severe poverty is likely to involve a compromised developmental trajectory, diminished by a heavily polluted and unhealthful physical environment and a social community that fails to provide adequate educational, health care, police, and other social services. The children of the very poor are much more likely than other children to be unhealthy and to experience nutritional deficiencies, developmental delays, and cognitive impairments. Depending on the circumstances, they also can be physically insecure, under constant stress, and emotionally traumatized.

The deprivations and disadvantages that come in their wake are set in place well before issues regarding the quality of their options or the range of choices they can make even arise. When levels of well-being compatible with a decent life are not secured in childhood, as is frequently the case with extreme poverty, deprivation at this critical stage in human development can be so profoundly destructive of well-being and so profoundly disadvantaging across a lifetime as to make later gains virtually

---

structural limitations that unfairly constrain the opportunities of some while granting privileges to others." Serena Parekh, "Getting to the Root of Gender Inequality: Structural Injustice and Political Responsibility," *Hypatia* 26, no. 4 (2011): 676. Christian Barry and Laura Ferraciola similarly take note of the way Young frames her account of structural injustice in opposition to both libertarian and luck egalitarian conceptions of the moral significance of individual choice. Christian Barry and Laura Ferraciolia, "Young on Responsibility and Structural Injustice," *Criminal Justice Ethics* 32, no. 3 (2013): 248–249. Jeffrey Reiman also views the effects on individual possibilities for action and choice as central to Young's account of structural injustice. Jeffrey Reiman, "The Structure of Structural Injustice: Thoughts on Iris Marion Young's *Responsibility for Justice*," *Social Theory and Practice* 38, no. 4 (2012): 748–749.

[14] Sally Haslanger, "What Is a (Social) Structural Explanation?," *Philosophical Studies* 173, no. 1 (2016): 113–130. Haslanger speaks of possibility sets composed of options and end states. We mark what we take to be the same distinction by substituting "outcome" for "end state."

impossible. What a focus on children reveals is that prospects for a decent life often are truncated by social forces that are well beyond what individuals can adequately address through the exercise of individual choice or otherwise mitigate through efforts on their own behalf.[15]

Second, for adults as well as children, the expansion of choiceworthy options is a normatively incomplete public policy response to some kinds of structural impediments to a decent life. Adults on their own cannot protect themselves from the risks of some of the most severe, most disadvantaging deprivations that social arrangements often engender or free them from the grips of control by others. Many forms of protection of core elements of well-being lie beyond the capacity of most individuals to address. Health deprivations, for example, when caused by our environment, our food, our water supply, or pharmaceuticals or by aspects of the health care system, the workplace, or dangers on the road and in the skies, are not always amenable to a model of justice that places central emphasis upon increasing the range of choiceworthy options. These are threats to well-being that require management through collective action. They can be mitigated only minimally by education, consumer information, or expansion of the range of individual choices that help individuals to avoid these threats through their own efforts. Moreover, a failure to address these threats through collective action leaves individuals subject to the unilateral, unchecked decisions of powerful private actors.

While giving people choiceworthy options is an important moral concern, too much emphasis on the structural impediments to personal choice masks the kinds of remedies needed in order to address many of the deeper sources of deprivation in dimensions such as health and personal security. Examples of structural impacts on both children and adults reveal why we ought not endorse a social structural theory that misleadingly suggests that freeing up structural constraints in order to allow individuals to make more and better choices will be sufficient for what structural justice requires.

---

[15] Martha Nussbaum argues that the case of children provides an exception to the general view that justice is centrally about capabilities and the availability of choiceworthy options. Nussbaum, *Creating Capabilities*, 26; Nussbaum, *Women and Human Development*, 76; Martha Nussbaum, *Frontiers of Justice: Disability, Nationality, Species Membership* (Cambridge, MA: Harvard University Press, 2006), 172. However, that move strikes us as especially odd, given that social justice is commonly understood as concerned with the arrangement of social structures that have their impact on a person's long-term prospects for well-being across a full life span and across generations.

4.2. Social Structural Components and Their Systematic Influence

4.2.1. Defining Characteristics of Unjust Structural Influences

In our theory, we understand the relevant social structural arrangements to include both domestic and international institutions and social practices that are, in their totality, a *systematic social framework within which regular, ongoing, highly consequential interactions among individuals, social groups, and various institutional (governmental and non-governmental) agents take place.*[16] Not all influences that institutions and social practices have are sufficiently weighty or systematic, however, to count on our theory. Those that do share four centrally defining characteristics. They are asymmetric, near-inescapable, profound, and pervasive.

Asymmetric impact: The impact of unjust structural arrangements on socially situated groups is at its core fundamentally asymmetric. The very structures that advantage some groups, open up options, confer benefits and social standing and power, protect them from deprivation and abuse, and render them relatively impervious to natural and social risks and the predatory behavior of others have precisely the opposite effect on other social groups. For adversely affected social groups, these asymmetric impacts further entrench patterns of severe disadvantage. They foreclose options and make them less choiceworthy, impose burdens, reduce the control these groups have over their own lives, diminish their social standing, expose them to greater vulnerability to deprivation and abuse, and make them more susceptible to various natural and social hazards and predation by others, including human rights violations.

Near-inescapable impact: The near-inescapable (or largely unavoidable) nature of the impact of unjust social structural arrangements is crucially important. It renders individuals and groups captive to social forces that overwhelm their capacity to enter into alternative arrangements. The predictable effects of such arrangements are more or less hardwired into the very fabric of social relations. And as a consequence, these effects are difficult if not impossible for most members of negatively positioned social groups to avoid or escape.[17]

---

[16] Our generic account is a variation of one that Rawls describes as "the background social framework within which the activities of associations and individuals take place." Rawls, *JAF*, 10.

[17] Both Young and Rawls seem to express this point somewhat differently. They focus on groups positioned by social structures that affect the life prospects of those similarly positioned in ways largely beyond their control, not as a matter of sheer luck, but because of the way humanly

To put matters slightly differently, systematic effects are not mere anomalies or clusters of unpredictable events that are more or less randomly distributed in the way that accidents or isolated bad financial decisions might be. Nor are they effects that are largely within the power of individuals to control or shape significantly on their own. They are the regular, predictable, routine consequences of the way that one or more causally important aspects of social institutions and practices are configured. The high probability of occurrence of adverse systematic effects on core elements of well-being, as well as the low probability of their avoidance or mitigation without fundamental structural change, is densely woven into the fabric of the social structure within which specific kinds of interactions routinely take place.

The near-inescapable influence of structural arrangements is evident in the influence they often have on social mobility. Social mobility refers to the movement of individuals, families, households, or other categories of people within or between social strata in a society. Social class immobility is one kind of socially mediated resistance to change in relative social position. Members of disadvantaged or disempowered social groups experience reduced ability to move from one social class to another. A different kind of socially structured resistance to change in relative position occurs when a social group, for example, one defined by race or gender, experiences reduced ability to alter its group's social position relative to other groups. Near inescapability of social position, then, can refer to two ways of being locked in: being locked into a social group that is difficult to move out of or being a member of a social group whose relative social position is resistant to change.

Systemic impact that is near-inescapable can emerge in some instances from the outsized effect of one catalytic socially mediated factor or characteristic. A gendered social and economic system, for example, can shape all the core elements of a decent life, across an entire life, and in deeply psychologically insidious ways.

In virtually all empirically plausible scenarios, however, near-inescapable impact emerges from multiple strands of the fabric of ongoing social interaction that work in concert.[18] Women disadvantaged by

---

alterable social arrangements differentially position some social groups. Young, "Equality of Whom?," 6–8, 16.

[18] In chapter 3 of *Social Justice*, we present a more formal analysis, with some examples of (i) single causal factor, singular effect on an element of well-being; (ii) multiple causal factors, singular effect; (iii) single causal factor, multiple effects; and (iv) multiple causal factors, multiple effects. Powers and Faden, *Social Justice*, 64–70.

gendered social and economic systems are usually affected by features of the social structure that negatively affect other social groups to which they also belong, such as racial minorities. That combination also accounts for the near inescapability of systematic injustice. Many additional factors combine to entrench serious deprivation, deep disadvantage, and multiple, overlapping forms of unfairness in power associated with social position. The relevant factors at work might include the hierarchical organization of family life, the lack of legal remedies or clearly defined and secure property rights within a nation, the dominance of a single, low-wage employer within a region, and cultural norms supporting the subordination of ethnic or religious groups. A regime of economic austerity imposed by global creditors and the International Monetary Fund on a debtor nation, imbalances in trade rules that limit entry into and competitive access to lucrative global markets, and unaffordable costs of water due to privatization and consequent loss of political accountability for the delivery of essential services can also be significant contributors.

The list of potentially causative and reinforcing mechanisms that affect quality of life, distribute advantages and disadvantages, and structure power relations among groups is both lengthy and familiar. The potential adverse effects are especially great within existing deep pockets of deprivation and disadvantage, where many of the world's poorest and most vulnerable people also live at the intersection of multiple forms of domination. These forms of domination include the control exerted by domestic autocrats, patriarchal families, multinational corporations, and foreign governments that exercise highly asymmetric power to advance their own parochial geopolitical interests.[19] The further effects of such power differentials and relative differences in social position include the magnification and entrenchment of the vulnerability of whole classes of persons, made subject to exploitative forms of interaction or outright social exclusion from participation in potentially rewarding forms of interaction. Because the power to subordinate often carries with it the power to exploit or exclude, those who are caught up in densely woven webs of disadvantage, often constructed by and for the powerful, frequently have few, if any, feasible avenues of escape.

---

[19] For similar remarks on multiple and overlapping forms of domination, see Cecile Laborde, "Republican Global Distributive Justice: A Sketch," *European Journal of Political Theory* 9, no. 1 (2010): 48–69; Ranier Forst, "Towards a Critical Theory of Transnational Justice," in *Global Justice*, ed. Thomas Pogge (Oxford: Blackwell, 2001), 169–187; and James Bohman, "Republican Cosmopolitanism," *Journal of Political Philosophy* 12, no. 3 (2004): 336–352.

Regardless of whether systematic impact in any given circumstance is a function of a single, predominant social structural factor or a constellation of factors, the morally significant results are the same. As a consequence of a densely woven causal web of influence affecting a substantial portion of a life, it is extremely difficult for individuals acting on their own, or frequently, even in concert with other members of an adversely situated social group, to fundamentally alter the terms of their interaction with others or to avoid its effects.

Profound impact: Not only are the structural effects of interest to our theory asymmetric and near-inescapable, they are also profound. These effects can permanently and significantly advance or set back the core elements of well-being characteristic of a decent life. The magnitude of their impact is substantial, not minor or incidental, and the elements of well-being affected are among the most fundamental of all human interests. These are the kinds of interests that matter deeply for anyone's experience of what makes a life go well, and they are the kinds of interests harmed in paradigmatic instances of human rights violations.

The adverse impacts on the actual well-being or overall life prospects for a decent life of differentially positioned social groups are profound in a dual sense. Their morally significant effect is reckoned in terms of both the degree of harm produced or put at risk by social arrangements and the moral significance of the affected interests. Moreover, these impacts are rarely limited to one element of well-being; deprivations in one element tend to cascade in their effects on other elements, exerting a negative influence on multiple aspects of well-being nearly simultaneously. Even when deprivation arising from social structural conditions does not result in a standard of living that is at or near the survival level, or is not brought about in a way that constitutes a clearly delineated human rights violation, the most pernicious social structural injustices involve an extraordinary degree of precariousness. The hallmark of such diminished life prospects is the constant threat of severe deprivation in one or more crucially important elements of well-being. This threat of severe deprivation is generally accompanied by increased vulnerability to both compounded and cascading patterns of deep disadvantage and wholesale subjection by those who have power over others.

Pervasive impact: The fourth characteristic of the influence of social structures subject to evaluation under our theory is the pervasiveness of their structural impact. The relevant set of institutions and practices exert pervasive effects on individuals, in two related ways. First, these effects generally last over a complete life or large parts of a life and, second, they tend to bleed into every aspect of a person's life experience. More specifically, we are concerned with social structures that have near-ubiquitous effects on overall well-being, prospects for a decent life, and the kinds of unfair relations that are unjust in themselves and unjust because they are among the worst incubators of human rights violations.[20]

By way of contrast, Rawls's focus on lifetime economic impact emphasizes the effects of the social class into which a person is born and raised, especially in light of his assumption that citizens can expect to spend their whole lives in the country of their birth. Our position is that social arrangements have a more pervasive influence on chances for a decent life than a focus on economic prospects alone captures. Moreover, pervasiveness of impact is not restricted to lifelong residency as a citizen of one country. Pervasive influence can also arise as a result of a person's status as an immigrant or a refugee under the rules that regulate the status of non-citizens both among nation-states and within countries.

Because we do not concentrate our focus on durable economic effects alone, the moral stakes are even higher. What matters fundamentally on our account are the pervasive effects on a decent life that result from aspects of the social structure that contribute significantly to serious deprivation in core elements of well-being, the creation of long-term disadvantage, or the establishment and perpetuation of structurally reinforcing patterns of domination, exploitation, and social exclusion.

The relevant effects of social arrangements of interest to us are thus pervasive in a dual sense. They are durable or highly influential on the morally most significant life prospects of persons for long periods of time, if not across the entire life span. These pervasive effects also tend to have a penetrative, formative effect on the consciousness of persons whose lives are affected and, as a consequence, they tend to color much of their subsequent life experiences.[21]

---

[20] Our understanding of the pervasiveness of impact differs from Rawls's in ways we have described throughout this chapter. His emphasis is on the economic life prospects of an individual, while our notion of life prospects is much broader and more fundamental to human well-being than protection of the narrowly economic prospects of the members of the least-advantaged socioeconomic groups.

[21] Rawls suggests something similar but with different purposes in view. He recognizes that the basic structure, as he understands it, does more than influence persons' economic life prospects. It "influences their life prospects, what they can expect to be and how well they can hope to do." Rawls, *TOJ*, 6–7. Even individual character is shaped by the basic structure. Rawls, *TOJ*, 89; *JAF*, 10. The "social system shapes wants and aspirations that its citizens come to have." Rawls, *TOJ*, 229; cf. Rawls, *JAF*, 10; *JAF*, §§ 4.2; 12.3. However, Rawls's point in making these observations is simply to highlight how socioeconomic prospects ultimately get shaped by these kinds of impacts. By contrast, our point is that we are focally and directly concerned with these effects, and why they

These four characteristics, in concert, are indicative of a specific kind of systematic, structural injustice that can be prevented or remedied in a comprehensive way only, or primarily, at the level of social and political organization.

Although we offer no comprehensive list of components of the social structures that have a highly consequential influence on the lives of those affected, in the next section we provide some examples of formal institutional arrangements and less formal norm-governed social practices, both of which are found in global and domestic contexts.

4.2.2. Institutional Structures

Legal systems are important for both economic and non-economic reasons. They provide many of the explicit, formal rules of social interaction. Constitutions, statutory laws, court decisions, and administrative regulations establish rules of property, contract, investment, inheritance, taxation, and criminal offenses. Laws—and equally significant, the absence of legal regulation—also determine the extent to which the actions of some individuals and groups that affect others are subject to social constraint. An important aspect of legal systems, for example, is whether they allow or restrain negative economic and environmental externalities that are imposed on others as a consequence of bilateral economic transactions. In this and other ways, laws raise or lower the social and interpersonal costs of courses of action, and create economic incentives and disincentives. They shape market outcomes, including the distribution of resources, opportunities, and risks through regulations that make some opportunities and options more or less costly or more or less prevalent. Laws also remove some ways of meeting human needs from competitive markets by, for example, providing for public goods and individualized social safety nets.

Legal regimes thus figure centrally in our account of the primary components of the social structure, but not only for reasons of economic distribution as they do in Rawls's theory. They matter for more basic reasons, affecting a broad array of well-being interests and overall life prospects. Laws establish conditions for entering into sustaining personal relationships and for participation in the life of the community. They affect whether people are given recognition as equals under the law and, more

---

matter in their own right, because of how they figure in a person's prospects for a decent life, not as instrumental concerns affecting economic life prospects.

generally, seen as moral equals. Laws have enormous impact on health and personal security, and they shape access to and standards for education that, on our view, matter for reasons other than the narrow instrumental value in securing employment and a fair share of economic rewards and access to economic opportunity.

Legal rules also affect power relations. These formal rules set the terms of interaction between employers and employees, between men and women, and between the state and the individual. They establish the degree of state deference to hierarchical organizations such as religious institutions and corporate entities, the degree of discretion given to agents charged with implementing the coercive power of the state, the degree of independence of states from the external influence of other states and powerful non-state actors, and so on.

It is no wonder, then, that social structural theories generally pay close attention to legal regimes. Formal rules, especially rules that are backed by state coercion and that authoritatively assign legally binding duties and responsibilities to everyone within the political jurisdiction of a nation-state, are a major way in which institutions systematically influence human well-being and prospects for a decent life.

However, there are also many global institutional factors at work. They often influence in rather dramatic ways the life prospects of residents of low- and middle-income countries or countries that are particularly subject to the political and economic influence of richer and more powerful nations. They can also have profound effects on the lives of less powerful people in high-income countries. Some effects are the direct product of institutional rules emanating from sources beyond the state, and even the regularities of markets depend on these background institutions. Consider, for example, the influence of international treaties, the World Trade Organization, the corporate organization of global supply chains, the policy prescriptions of the World Bank and International Monetary Fund, the investment decisions of multinational corporations, and global commodity and financial markets. Consider, also, transborder flows of migrants and refuges, scarcities of natural resources, shifts in global consumption patterns, and the spillover effects of armed conflicts and international competition for geopolitical power.

4.2.3. Informal Structural Influences

As important as national and global institutional influences are, we give equal weight to informal social practices and processes and the social norms they perpetuate. These social influences have effects that extend across all the core elements of well-being and infuse power relations at every level. They affect not only economic status and economic life prospects that are of central concern under Rawls's theory, but a whole array of further structural factors that in turn affect the core elements of well-being, shape overall prospects for a decent life, and lock into place positions of differential power within a host of personal, economic, cultural, and political relationships.

The grip of informal practices, even when they are not augmented by formal, institutionalized rules and coercive backing, should not be underestimated. When social practices are most influential, participants in the community in which they are operative also believe and act on the belief that the norms provide them with reasons for action, apart from the disvalue attached to any sanctions. For example, they may believe that acting in accordance with the norm contributes to the social good or to their own prudential well-being, that it is their right, obligation, or entitlement to do so, that it advances some morally worthwhile goal, or that it fulfills some moral or religious requirement. These beliefs might be well grounded, or alternatively they may be rooted in deep prejudices or be a product of false consciousness or adaptive preferences.[22]

If an individual considers defying a norm because she has private reservations about its justification, it is often enough to secure her conformity for her to believe that her defiance will result in some sanction that she disvalues, for example, public stigma, private shunning, or a loss of desirable associational opportunities. Doubts about the purpose or value of the norm, of course, can loosen its grip, and even more so when doubts arise about the probability that sanctions will be imposed. Also, a decrease in the perceived disvalue attached to the sanctions (who cares what they think) or an increase in perceived value to be gained from non-complying conduct can loosen the norm's grip and, ultimately, undermine its durability and structural influence. But for many people and for many social norms, the grip is tight. Compliance is unquestioned and in some cases near-automatic.

---

[22] See, e.g., Jon Elster, *Sour Grapes: Studies in the Subversion of Rationality* (New York: Cambridge University Press, 1983).

4.2.4. Institutional and Informal Influences Combined

As the examples of gendered norms show, informal social norms and institutional rules generally work in tandem. They continuously interact, each begetting, reshaping, sustaining, or undermining the other. Informal social norms are likely to parallel or prompt formal institutional rules, implemented and upheld by the beneficiaries of those rules and norms. Sometimes, however, the trajectories of formal rules and informal social norms diverge. Adherence to informal norms sometimes continues after formal rules governing the relevant conduct are abandoned, especially if the perceived disvalue of the social sanctions is great. Similarly, when the sanctions attached to non-compliance are great enough, informal norms can undermine compliance with conflicting formal institutional rules. Consider, for example, the perpetuation of de facto school segregation in the US or the perpetuation of female genital mutilation in Somalia even after both practices were declared formally illegal.

Informal and formal components of social structures in tandem determine access to resources and establish or sustain existing power relationships. They determine the conditions under which the production of the material basis of life occurs and the distribution of economic and personal opportunities, health and environmental risks, and various social burdens.

Formal rules and less formal norms governing group relations also work in tandem to produce and sustain various attitudes, beliefs, values, and preferences that penetrate deep into the psyche. They jointly define the parameters of the conceptions of a worthwhile life that members of all groups, advantaged and disadvantaged, powerful and powerless, are likely to form. They generate social expectations, penalize or reward personal decisions and policy alternatives, channel the way imagination and critical faculties are employed, confer or withhold intellectual and cultural authority, and in countless ways shape the architecture of choice and prospects for well-being of every person, social group, and institutional agent subject to their influence. Formal rules and social norms shape ideals of what we care about, objects of admiration and disapproval, ambitions and aspirations, attitudes of hopefulness and despair, and moral and intellectual horizons. They foster in others social attitudes of respect or contempt, glorification or stigmatization of behavior, and attributions of excellence or deficiency. They inform everyone's understanding of the kinds of things that are up to persons as individuals to decide, the things that should be kept private, and the proper boundaries of interaction and interpersonal influence. They determine the kinds of autobiographical narratives that can gain discursive traction in a culture, frame the judgments of taste and decorum, and structure the stance—whether it is acceptance, skepticism, resignation, or resistance—that is adopted by disadvantaged groups toward the rules and norms through which they find themselves forced to navigate.[23]

In these and many other ways, social structures constrain not only the options, but the outcomes and life prospects of all affected. And for occupants of disadvantaged and disempowered social positions, social structures often cement their subordinate place within a web of power relations.

4.3. Power, Advantage, and Social Position

At the beginning of the chapter we stated that differences in power and advantage provide crucially important markers of the social groups that merit both empirical examination and heightened scrutiny under a theory of structural injustice. We noted also that theories of social structural justice are most plausible and useful when they are open-ended and pluralistic. Here we elaborate on both points.

The social groups subject to structural injustice must be seen as open-ended because we cannot assume a priori that group-based injustices prevalent at one time will persist in a radically changed social context. Nor can we assume that no new cleavages of power and advantage will emerge in the future. Dynamism is an ever-present feature of human interaction, from the intimate to, increasingly, the global. How social groups are characterized and how they relate to one another does change over time. In some cases, relations between groups demarcated by ethnicity, religion, gender, or sexual orientation evolve positively and sometimes they deteriorate, as clusters of advantage and constellations of power shift around them. And groups that once had little contact enter into new and more durable forms of relationship.

In these and other ways, over time, more and different people are put into new and often more consequential situations of mutual impact. They have more influence on one another's life prospects, they establish or modify social hierarchies, and they substitute new forms of power for

---

[23] Cf. Miranda Fricker, *Epistemic Injustice: Power and the Ethics of Knowing* (Oxford: Oxford University Press, 2007).

old ones (e.g., global economic power for colonial rule). Shifts in relative bargaining power occur as geopolitical alliances unravel or consolidate. Patterns of power and influence morph as commodities and raw materials gain or lose their market importance or as new competitors displace established producers. Environmental changes redraw the map of human settlement, create new migration flows, and forge or unwind commercial ties, often redirecting and compounding existing struggles for control over land, labor, and the way of life of previously more insular communities.

Our theory is pluralist because we think that group-based differences in power and advantage can arise and manifest in different ways. Illustrative passages below reveal some important similarities and differences, depending on the choice of social position emphasized or included in a social structural theory. We look first at social position defined by role in the process of economic production and then at race, and we make some comparisons to related points made about gender in section 4.2.

4.3.1. Relative Position within Relations of Production

R. H. Tawney describes the differences in the experiences of individuals based on their positions in the process of economic production. Tawney rejects the orthodox Marxian prediction of a sharp binary divide between owners of property and those who survive only by wage labor. However, he makes the case that power and advantage lie in the control of economically concentrated enterprises.[24]

> For the characteristic of modern industry, and of the financial arrangements associated with it, is not only that it increases . . . man's power over nature, but . . . in the absence of deliberate restraints imposed by society, it heightens that of some men over others, by organizing and concentrating it . . . Its method is mass-production . . . makes all, nearly all, types of economic activity interdependent, so that those who control a key service can impose their terms on the remainder. It increases the scale of enterprise, and thus increases both the number and length for the threads which can be manipulated by the staff work of a single headquarters . . . The number of those who take the decisions upon which the conduct of economic affairs,

---

[24] Tawney argues that the standard Marxian notion of socioeconomic class focuses too narrowly on the division of labor and whether individuals receive their income from the ownership of capital or from wage labor. One reason is that the binary of capital-based income and wage-based income is no longer an accurate portrayal of the complexity of socioeconomic class stratification. High- and low-wage earners differ greatly in their access to capital. Tawney, *Equality*, 58, 67–72.

and therefore the lives of their fellow-men, depend is diminished; the number of those affected by each decision is increased.[25]

The differences in power and advantage, rooted in relative position in the productive system, "as employer, employee, capitalist, wage laborer, landlord, and so on"[26] are manifested not only in differential economic rewards but also in people's whole "manner of life."[27] Tawney's catalog of differences is extensive, but his description tracks all six core elements of our conception of well-being.

Those who hold positions of economic advantage benefit from differences in "the degree of security or insecurity of their economic position" and "the expression of varying degrees of authority and subordination" routinely experienced "in status, in influence, and sometimes in the consideration and respect they are shown."[28] While some become "accustomed . . . to exercise direction," for others "the normal lot is to be directed by others."[29] Such differences in position within relations of economic production also involve "sharp disparities . . . of environment, health and education,"[30] as well as of individuals' "family connections, their leisure and their amusements"[31] and the "degree of public influence" over their social and economic condition.[32]

Tawney's conception of the significance of socioeconomic class has implications that diverge from Rawls's theory. Rawls calls for the amelioration of disadvantaging social conditions built into the competitive structures of market economies by reducing inequalities in employment and educational opportunities, thereby facilitating greater social class mobility, along with policies that assign the working class a larger share of the economic rewards of joint production. By contrast, on our view and Tawney's, a comprehensive theory of structural injustice should recognize that control over the lives of others by powerful economic elites is an important moral concern that cannot be adequately addressed by merely altering patterns of resource distribution or changing the structure of

---

[25] Ibid., 16.
[26] Ibid., 60, 62, 73, 113.
[27] Ibid., 62.
[28] Ibid., 61.
[29] Ibid., 60.
[30] Ibid., 112.
[31] Ibid., 61.
[32] Ibid., 75.

market advantages. What also is required is a fundamental change in the relations of power.[33] It's not just about the money.

4.3.2. Race

Many critical race theorists point out that relative social position based on racial differences manifests in ways that overlap with relative social position based on socioeconomic group. However, relative social position also manifests in ways that are distinct and independent from membership in a socioeconomic group. Any reference to race as a social group, however, requires us to be clear about what such differences consist in and what is not being claimed. Paul Taylor, for example, rejects the idea that just because science discredits the idea of race as an essential biological category it no longer functions as an explanatory concept on which social criticism can be mounted.[34] "[R]ace-talk really is about the populations and phenomena that it seems to be about, and that most of us think it's about."[35] The critical perspective is not one that implies anything particular about self-identification or how persons should see themselves. It is a "matter of ascription, or how others categorize them and treat them differently as a consequence."[36] It follows that "[i]f you stop letting yourself notice, statistically, who's Asian or black or whatever, then you'll have a hard time noticing patterns that may point you to systemic problems."[37]

In a similar vein, Charles Mills notes the hazards of failing to treat race as "central to structuring the modern world, preferring some sort of 'class'

---

[33] Tawney is clear that the lack of attention to issues of power, together with insufficient attention to effects on well-being, provides grounds for rejecting an overreliance on socioeconomic class differences defined primarily as a function of standard of living and too much attention to their distributive economic share. Ibid., 63. The issue of power is a major theme in Elizabeth Anderson, *Private Government: How Employers Rule Our lives (and Why We Don't Talk About It)* (Princeton, NJ: Princeton University Press, 2017).

[34] Paul C. Taylor, *Race: A Philosophical Introduction*, 2nd ed. (Cambridge: Polity Press, 2013), 88–116.

[35] Ibid., 88.

[36] Ibid., 108. Compare Young, who discusses groups that are identifiable by reference to a special affinity members have with one another, rooted in their similar experiences and way of life, rather than a set of shared characteristics attributed to them or observable by third parties such as skin color. Sexual orientation is one of her examples. That said, she notes that such groups often share a certain social status and a common history that has been either forced upon them or forged by them in response to the ways others categorize them and treat them. Iris Marion Young, *Justice and the Politics of Difference* (Princeton, NJ: Princeton University Press, 1990), 44.

[37] Young, *Justice and the Politics of Difference*, 113.

reductionism (race is really class in disguise) or some other kind of racial eliminativism of a distinctively Marxist/critical theoretic variety."[38]

The relative social position rooted in ascribed racial differences involves differentials of power and advantage that manifest in ways to which a critical theorist should be alert. As Mills puts it, "If race and white racial privilege are not acknowledged to be among those key structures of the modern world . . . then there will be little sense of white domination as a social reality that molds us all, influencing recognized moral standings, civic statuses, doxastic tendencies, patterns of consciousness, opportunities and handicaps, wealth and poverty, for life chances in general."[39] For example, in the United States, long after the repeal of formal laws of the Jim Crow era that assigned second-class citizenship status to African Americans, there remains a de facto two-tier system of criminal justice. Black and brown people are stopped, frisked, questioned, and even beaten or killed by police at rates, relative to their share of the population, that vastly outstrip those at which white people experience similar patterns of engagement with law enforcement officers. Affluence, educational attainment, and formal laws against unequal treatment offer inadequate protection against the risk of suffering life-altering or life-ending setbacks on the basis of skin color.[40] Here again, it's not just about the money.

And so we agree with the view that race is indicative of a distinctive social position of independent significance. It should be recognized as a separate category of inquiry within any plausible theory of structural justice.

4.3.3. Gender

Gender, like race, is a distinctive social position of independent significance within any plausible theory of structural justice. The employment options available to women, and the terms and circumstances of daily life for women in jobs ranging across the occupational spectrum, are not the same as for men, even when, contrary to the usual case, pay differentials are not dramatic.[41] Gender norms operate behind the scenes, percolating

---

[38] Charles Mills, "Criticizing Critical Theory," in *Critical Theory in Critical Times*, ed. Penelope Deutscher and Christina Lafont (New York: Columbia University Press, 2017), 236.

[39] Ibid., 240.

[40] There are numerous references to and discussions of these issues in chapter 7, but a very powerful discussion of unjust aspects of the US criminal justice system that is both structural and difficult to explain without reference to the depth of anti-black animus of many of those who implement its policies, see Paul Butler, *Chokehold: Policing Black Men* (New York: New Press, 2017).

[41] For an insightful discussion of how gender norms fundamentally shape the nature of work reserved for women across very different societal and cultural contexts around the world, see

up into formal legal rules and market norms. They affect the kinds of employment available to women and men, their levels of compensation, the distribution of power at work and at home—where non-paid domestic and caretaking work becomes "women's work." Gender norms also affect the composition of political decision-making bodies that act—or fail to take action—in ways that both reflect and create gendered relations of power. Some government systems exclude women from the public sphere and political participation, restrict freedom of movement and association, and deny them not only the rights of property and employment but also education, personal security, bodily integrity, and independence from patriarchal control.

These gender-based differentials, like race-based differentials, are not reducible to economic differences, even though economic injustice can fuel and exacerbate gender or racial injustice.[42] From the moment of birth, children are subject to a vast array of expectations regarding gender roles, expressions of sexuality, intellectual and physical capacities, ideals of manliness and femininity, and the appropriate division of labor, power, and intellectual authority within households. These norms take root at an early age, and they shape other social arrangements, including the nature of the family, available reproductive options, and the extent to which violence against women and girls and sexual harassment and assault are tolerated. When it comes to differentials of power and advantage on the basis of gender, once again, it's not just about the money.

Alison Jagger, "Are My Hands Clean? Responsibility for Global Gender Disparities," in *Poverty, Agency, and Human Rights*, ed. Diana T. Meyers (Oxford: Oxford University Press, 2014). Discussions of the differences in daily experience between women and men in the workplace are found under the hashtag #MeToo. For a wide-ranging exploration of misogyny, with observations similar to ones in the literature of anti-black racism, and the motivational puzzles raised by seemingly deep psychological animus, see Kate Manne, *Down Girl: The Logic of Misogyny* (New York: Oxford University Press, 2018).

[42] In a recent series of papers, Nancy Fraser examines what a Marxian analysis can add to the understanding of gender injustice (and other issues), even when acknowledging the existence of multiple, irreducible sources of injustice. For example, she points to its ability to explain the distinctive shape of women's subordination under capitalism. Women's unpaid labor remains outside of regular labor markets and thereby contributes to the background conditions that make possible the kinds of wage labor exploitation central to orthodox Marxian theory. Nancy Fraser, "Behind Marx's Hidden Abode: For an Expanded Conception of Capitalism," in *Critical Theory in Critical Times*, ed. Penelope Deutscher and Christina Lafont (New York: Columbia University Press, 2017), 141–159.

4.3.4. The Importance of Groups and of Intersectional Group Memberships

This brings us to a final point on groups and structural injustice. The likelihood of adverse impact based on group membership is further complicated by the fact that individuals occupy multiple social positions, marked by differentials of power and advantage, and therefore are members of multiple social groups. The vulnerability of any individual is a function of how group memberships intersect, either to mitigate or to magnify their risk of injustice. This means that a social structural theory of justice benefits by being able to take into account the effects that result from the interplay of multiple group-level structural factors.

For Rawls, by contrast, there is no theoretical space within which to raise issues of unfairness that arise on the basis of gender, ethnicity, or other non-economic factors. Many of his most trenchant critics, as noted earlier, object because a consequence of this kind of theorizing is that other, sometimes more pressing sources of structural injustice fail to receive adequate philosophical airing, are given less attention, and are not treated as problems of comparable moral significance. We concur with the underlying point of this critique.[43]

The facts about the intersection of groups becomes critical to a granular understanding of the dynamics of power and advantage. Being a member of an affluent socioeconomic class can confer advantages and protections against domination, exploitation, and social exclusion that other members of racial minorities lack because of the immunity to certain hardships that money can buy. The converse is also true, and perhaps more likely. If a person is also a member of an ethnic minority especially vulnerable to overzealous, aggressive policing tactics, the protections of wealth are likely to be, at best, attenuated. Being a woman in a misogynistic culture and being poor almost anywhere confers greater disadvantage and adds to the risk of domination, exploitation, or exclusion, and greater susceptibility to a range of human rights violations, beyond what membership in either social group alone would involve.

In sum, we see powerful reasons to opt for a brand of theorizing that sheds light on a plurality of interacting and dynamic forms of group-level injustice. This approach puts theorizing on a different trajectory than the Rawlsian tradition. It expands the scope of inquiry to encompass a richer vein of empirical discussion of how group-level effects interact in

---

[43] Charles W. Mills, "'Ideal Theory' as Ideology," *Hypatia* 20, no. 3 (2005): 165–183.

morally problematic ways. For these reasons, we favor an approach that is pluralistic, intersectional, and open-ended, sensitive to the empirical circumstances and histories of different group experiences as they evolve.[44]

4.4. Background Assumptions

Every theory of structural justice relies on some background assumptions. There are very different kinds of background assumptions at work in different theories. Sometimes the distinction between ideal and non-ideal theory has been invoked to explain these differences in assumptions, but the differences often do not track the various ways in which the ideal/non-ideal distinction is drawn.

Some assumptions function as stipulations of the kinds of normative phenomena to which the theory is intended to apply. Other assumptions are straightforward counterfactuals with a very specific argumentative aim. They are not intended as accurate characterizations of existing social conditions or even forecasts of what is likely. Instead, these assumptions are designed to advance our understanding of a single moral problem and its solution by removing other, complicating moral problems from view. Also, every theory rests on some empirical assumptions about the way the world works, assumptions about human motivations, political processes, market dynamics, resource constraints, and so on. The purpose of this section is to set forth our various background assumptions, by way of contrast with Rawls and Young.

4.4.1. Moderate Scarcity and Human Rights Fulfillment

Rawls's theory is intended only for societies characterized by moderate scarcity, not for economies where scarcity is commonplace and deprivation is often severe, as in many low- and even some middle-income countries. Moreover, Rawls frames the problem of selecting principles of economic distribution as one that arises under favorable social conditions in which basic human rights are in place, including social guarantees for the satisfaction of basic human needs. The distributive problem, then, is restricted to contexts in which we need guidance for dividing the joint

---

[44] The claim that social groups subject to structural disadvantage and disempowerment can "vary dramatically across times and places" is commonplace among social scientists who study social stratification. Charles Tilly, "Inequality, Democratization, and De-democratization," *Sociological Theory* 21, no. 1 (2003): 37.

economic product of social cooperation where neither extreme scarcity nor deep pockets of deprivation exist. This is a reasonable stipulation, as long as we recognize that stipulation constrains the application of his theory to only infrequently observed social conditions.

Our theory's intended application, by contrast, is much broader. We intend for our theory to provide an account of the most basic, fundamental demands of justice that are applicable to prosperous countries with pockets of poverty amidst plenty and where human rights deficits coexist with democratic institutions, as well as to low- and middle-income countries, even those with significantly constrained resources. This is because our theory specifies what we construe as the moral minimum of structural justice—the most basic normative architecture of any just social order.

4.4.2. Closed Economic Systems

Rawls restricts the application of his distributive principles to a domestic political system, understood as a closed system, where neither external political entities nor exogenous economic forces are assumed to exert morally significant influence on the distributive shares or economic life prospects of its citizens. Such a society is described as "a more or less self-sufficient association of persons bound together by rules that specify a system of cooperation."[45] Exogenous factors such as global market prices for commodities, external interference by other nation-states, and economically disruptive geopolitical disturbances are not part of the primary explanatory structure of how the lives of its members are shaped.

This closed-system restriction strikes us as quite different from Rawls's deliberately idealized, counterfactual assumptions about moderate scarcity and human rights fulfillment. We think that even in the context of prosperous and geopolitically well-positioned countries of the sort to which Rawls's theory is meant to apply, it is a normatively distorting starting place. There are three points to consider.

First, consider the issue of empirical accuracy. An important implication of his closed-system assumption is that the pursuit of structural justice within a domestic context does not need to take account of the economic or geopolitical impact of how other societies pursue their internal distributive goals or foreign policy objectives. Nor must it consider the impact of multinational corporations or supranational institutions on the well-being, life prospects, and relative positions of power of its citizens. Rawls, of

---

[45] Rawls, *TOJ*, 4.

course, intended this as a simplifying assumption so that questions about fair distribution of a joint domestic economic product could be explored without the complications of cross-border economic impact. Our theory, by contrast, does not make this simplifying assumption because it excludes from examination much of what is most important about the realities of transnational interaction in an increasingly globalized world.

Second, many economists, from all parts of the ideological spectrum, would say that the notion of economic self-sufficiency is not an attractive normative ideal. The reason is the potential net benefits to human well-being derivable from global integration, as long as the right kinds of institutional constraints are in place.[46] The ideal of self-sufficiency thus strikes us as misguided, even if self-sufficiency in some respects (e.g., food security) is an important national goal or even if many existing patterns of cross-border economic interaction are destructive of local markets, damaging to democratic institutions, or have an adverse impact on the global poor.[47]

Rawls's assumption that the fates of citizens of each nation are largely shaped by endogenous policy choices and domestic market dynamics is problematic for yet a third reason. This assumption rules out the very idea of any transnational issues of structural justice, beyond the need for some modest norms of interstate bargaining, commitments to non-interference, or respect for the human rights of non-nationals. How much and what kinds of cross-border influences are consequential are empirical questions. If, however, the cross-border influence is as modest as Rawls assumes, nation-states have a wide berth in pursuing their geopolitical objectives, securing scarce resources from around the world for the benefit of their own citizens, gaining access to foreign markets on favorable terms, and locating facilities of production wherever labor costs are low and governmental regulations are minimal.

Embedded in Rawls's assumption is a further assumption that even the poorest and least powerful nations can take care of themselves, at least when this involves the core well-being interests of their own citizens. By

---

[46] Joseph Stiglitz, *Globalization and Its Discontents* (New York: W. W. Norton, 2003); Dani Rodrik, *The Globalization Paradox* (New York: W. W. Norton, 2010); William Easterly, *The Tyranny of Experts: Economists, Dictators, and the Forgotten Rights of the Poor* (New York: Basic Books, 2013); Jeffrey A. Frieden, *Global Capitalism: It's Fall and Rise in the Twentieth Century* (New York: W. W. Norton, 2006.

[47] Madison Powers, "Food, Fairness, and Global Markets," in *Oxford Handbook of Food Ethics*, ed. Anne Barnhill, Mark Budolfson, and Tyler Dogget (New York: Oxford University Press, 2018), 367–398.

contrast, we find this description of the world implausible and empirically inaccurate in a wide range of instances in the current context and foreseeable future.

4.4.3. Free and Equal Citizenship

For Rawls, many issues of structural injustice, for example, issues of gender and racial injustice, are set aside. These issues are bracketed in order to isolate a specific question: What principles of socioeconomic justice would be justified under conditions in which the focal source of structural disadvantage is tied to the socioeconomic class into which one is born and raised? The purely counterfactual assumption is employed in order to ask a deliberately narrow question of justice, as it would arise from a society that already embodies what Rawls calls ideals of free and equal citizenship. More generally, the free and equal citizenship assumption holds that the societies under evaluation are well-ordered communities. They are governed by democratic principles; they conform to the rule of law; they are organized in ways that support their commitments to liberal ideals of equality between citizens; and they effectively block impediments to economic opportunity and political participation on invidiously discriminatory grounds.[48]

Rawls is under no illusion about the ways in which current economic inequalities are rooted, for example, in a long and ongoing history of racial injustices, but these are described as matters of corrective justice. His theory is designed to specify ideal distributive principles, not to deal with matters of non-ideal theory, where practical guidance is needed to address the legacy of slavery, Jim Crow, and racial inequality more generally. However, critics mount two main objections. First, given the prominence of the civil rights movement at the time he was writing, they ask why it is that neither Rawls nor many prominent Rawlsians ever got around to what are among the more pressing issues of justice. Second, they worry about how practically useful such an idealized theory is when these complicating, intersecting factors are sidelined.[49] These are troubling questions, not just for Rawls, but for the way scholars engage with social issues more broadly.[50]

---

[48] Rawls, *JAF*, § 18.

[49] E.g., Mills, " 'Ideal Theory' as Ideology," and Mills, "Criticizing Critical Theory."

[50] Other critics of Rawlsian ideal theory make claims similar to that of Mills. David Schmidtz, for example, argues that reliance on certain types of idealization handicaps the capacity of normative

To sum up matters so far, Rawls focuses on the residual threats to an ideal of socioeconomic fairness posed by deep social class differences within a kind of society that he describes as a "nearly just" one.[51] Human rights are not ordinarily at stake; the problem of fairness is one that arises in circumstances of moderate scarcity, where basic needs are met and basic liberties are secured. Gross discriminatory violations of equal standing based on race or gender or other invidious group characteristics are not the normal state of affairs.[52] More generally, social conditions are not favorable for creating and sustaining unfair power relationships involving exploitation or social exclusion.

This profile of the social phenomena of focal interest to Rawls has several implications. The only significant threat of unfair power relations under these assumptions arises as an outcome of largely benign patterns of market transactions and morally permissible interpersonal interactions. He assumes that over time market processes tend to concentrate economic rewards in certain socioeconomic classes. Presumably, these rewards tend to become concentrated because of the differential benefits that predictably accrue to those who possess and develop certain marketable skills and specialized talents, aided by competitive advantages often present from birth. Moreover, he assumes that familial partiality, while a positive personal attribute, will contribute to the clustering of wealth and competitive advantages within families and their social network. As a side effect of economic concentration, political power within a society also tends toward consolidation, and the likely result is that the more advantaged are able to tailor the rules of economic cooperation and competition in ways that exacerbate and entrench socioeconomic inequalities.

Ultimately in Rawls's theory, the morally significant impacts are socioeconomic. Broader indicators of well-being, lifetime well-being prospects,

---

theory to guide action in the real world. David Schmidtz, "Nonideal Theory: What It Is and What It Needs to Be," *Ethics* 121, no. 4 (July 2011): 777. By contrast, John Simmons, citing Rawls, believes that once ideal theory is in place, "the remaining problems of justice will prove more tractable in the light of it." A. John Simmons, "Ideal and Nonideal Theory," *Philosophy & Public Affairs* 38, no. 1 (2010): 10. Not all distinctions between ideal and non-ideal theory track what Rawls had in mind. The current literature reveals a number of ways in which the distinction can be drawn and it raises questions about the sort of abstractions and idealized conditions we might wish to avoid in theorizing. For surveys and suggestions for navigating through the diverging ways the terminology has been deployed, see Laura Valentini, "Ideal vs. Non-Ideal Theory: A Conceptual Map," *Philosophy Compass* 7, no. 9 (2012): 654–664; and Alan Hamlin and Zofia Stemplowska, "Theory, Ideal Theory, and the Theory of Ideals," *Political Studies Review* 10, no. 1 (2012): 48–62.

[51] Rawls, *TOJ*, 319.

[52] Rawls, *JAF* § § 18.4–18.6, especially 64–66.

or concerns about unfair power and advantage are not of focal interest, except insofar as they implicate socioeconomic interests. The relevant groups of concern under the theory are defined by their position as members of a socioeconomic class, not their gender, race, or other markers of differential power and advantage. And to the extent that there remains a potential for structural injustice to gain traction in this nearly just society, it involves the impersonal processes of market forces and the largely morally benign choices of individuals. The jeopardy to justice comes only from a societal failure to keep concentrations of socioeconomic resources in check so that they do not undermine democratic processes that in turn maintain a nearly just social order.

4.4.4. The Emergence of Injustice

This brings us to our final point about background assumptions. As we have seen in section 4.1, Young disagrees with Rawls on which morally significant impacts to emphasize, the identification of social groups unjustly affected, and, accordingly, the multiple, added components of the social structure that matter.

However, there are some similarities to Rawls in the way Young sets up the problem of how structural injustice emerges and the best way to think about responsibility for change. In *Responsibility for Justice*, Young sets aside the kinds of structural injustices that involve deliberate patterns of oppression of social groups based, for example, on race, gender, or sexual orientation.[53] Specifically, Young's new focus is on a type of structural injustice that is the output of complex social processes in which many agents contribute by pursuing their own goals and interests through conduct that is generally recognized as morally acceptable.[54] Her assumption is that "[i]t is possible, and indeed even likely, that some people can rightly claim that their individual interactions with others are impeccable, and at the

---

[53] Young, *Responsibility for Justice*, 15, 69–70, 73–75.

[54] Ibid., 62–63: "Social structure, then refers to the accumulated outcomes of the actions of the masses of individuals enacting their own projects, often uncoordinated with many others. The combination of actions affects the conditions of the actions of others, often producing outcomes not intended by any of the participating agents." These structural injustices typically involve thousands or millions of individuals pursuing their own interests, "usually acting within institutional rules and according to practices that most people regard as morally acceptable. Ibid., 95. "Those who participate . . . are usually minding their own business and acting within accepted norms and rules." Ibid., 106. "Most of us contribute . . . because we follow the accepted rules and conventions of the communities and institutions in which we act." Ibid., 107.

same time they contribute a great deal to the production and reproduction of structural injustice."[55]

Young's way of framing this specific kind of problem of structural injustice thus assumes that individual decisions and transactions often involve no wrongdoing and that there is no particular unjust law or policy in place, but nonetheless the cumulative effect of such decisions and policies is deprivation, unfair disadvantage, domination, and exploitation.[56]

In such circumstances, blameworthy conduct is not a central feature of the causal trajectory by which structural injustice emerges.[57] In part, her exculpatory approach is based on what she sees as our "habitual" ways of acting, characterized by "lack of explicit reflection on the wider implications of what we are doing, having in the foreground of our consciousness and intention those immediate goals we want to achieve."[58] Moreover, she encourages an alternative to the "fault model" for assigning responsibility for remedying this kind of structural injustice and what she sees as the need to avoid the "blame game" and the risk of oversimplification by attributing power and wrongdoing to some agents while failing to appreciate the effects of actions undertaken by others who are comparatively without power and blameless.[59] Her earlier work also reflects an understanding of structural injustice as radically discontinuous with agent-centered injustices, that is to say, ones committed by identifiable, morally culpable agents. Her contention is that a focus on fault somehow "obscures the structural and institutional framework of oppression."[60]

Here, we part company with Young. We do not share her assumption that we can isolate those cases in which the origins of structural injustice are relatively benign from morally more tainted cases. As we have already noted, the kinds of structural injustice that we think most important to address do not come ready-made in neat analytic categories, with exploitation, subordination, and exclusion appearing in one scenario and largely benign causal origins of structural injustices in another. The more ordinary pattern involves a mix of agents, with differing degrees of culpability in their own interpersonal transactions and in their roles in creating or sustaining structural injustices.

---

[55] Ibid., 73.

[56] Ibid., 46–47.

[57] Ibid., 95: "[W]hen injustice is structural, there is no clear culprit, to blame and therefore no agent clearly liable for rectification."

[58] Young, *Responsibility for Justice*, 107.

[59] Ibid., 116–117.

[60] Young, *Justice and the Politics of Difference*, 196.

While there may be many relatively blameless agents, as Young supposes, that is not the whole story. There are individual and institutional agents that exercise unfair forms of power over others, knowingly. They avoidably benefit from and uphold unjust systems of advantage, and use their superior bargaining power to extract undeserved benefits that cause harm to or impose disadvantage upon others. And there are many institutional agents that fail to fulfill their duties to protect.

While Young worries about the risk of too much focus on issues of culpability, we worry about the risk of too little.[61] Isolating a category of structural injustices, assumed to be largely benign in origin, ignores some morally very important facts about any reasonably complex pattern of social structural injustice. In these more complex and, indeed, more typical cases, we should not tamp down efforts to try to identify and hold differentially responsible specific wrongdoers, as well as not-so-blameless beneficiaries of structural injustice.

Our examples in chapters 6 and 7 fit this more complex pattern. In chapter 8, our discussion of justified resistance to structural injustice builds upon these fact patterns and, in particular, insists on the importance of drawing distinctions among agents based on different kinds and degrees of culpability, in part in order to determine the appropriate targets and modes of resistance.

---

[61] Andrea Sangiovanni recently raised doubts about the extent to which Young's criticisms impugn his own "agent-oriented, fault-oriented" approach and concludes that "Young is too hasty in exculpating those who together sustain and reinforce structures of oppression." Andrea Sangiovanni, *Humanity Without Dignity: Moral Equality, Respect, and Human Rights* (Cambridge, MA: Harvard University Press, 2017), 167.

CHAPTER 5 | Well-Being and Human Rights

IN THIS CHAPTER, WE utilize arguments based on our conception of well-being to defend a variant of interest-based theories of human rights (hereafter, "interest theories"). Our approach differs from standard interest theories because it has resources that allow us to deflect some of the challenges typically lodged against them, as well as to accommodate some of their limitations. These resources are described in sections 5.1 through 5.3. The last and most substantial section of the chapter explains how our position on the grounding of human rights figures within our overall theory of structural justice. Here we describe how our fairness norms contribute to the resolution of problems of specification of the counterpart duties of human rights and, more generally, responsibility for addressing systematic patterns of injustice.

In section 5.1, we develop two responses to a challenge to the core thesis of interest theories. Critics claim that the best moral explanation of why rights matter to right-holders is the value of having control over some matter, not the personal well-being interests served by having a right. Our first response is that our conception of well-being accommodates concerns about the moral significance of a right-holder's control over certain matters. Our second response is that other examples of the moral significance of exercising control present problems for an interest theory that purports to ground all rights, but not for an interest account, like ours, that is restricted to human rights.

In section 5.2, we respond to a two-pronged challenge raised by proponents of dignity-based theories (hereafter, "dignity theories"). One criticism is that interest theories cannot explain who qualifies as a bearer of human rights. We respond by showing how our interest theory draws upon insights provided by dignity theories to supplement the grounding of human rights. The second objection claims that interest theories, unlike dignity theories, cannot provide grounds for rights commonly recognized as part of the egalitarian core of human rights, for example, rights protecting equality of social and political status. We show how our conception of well-being has the practical resources necessary to meet this challenge.

In section 5.3, we respond to an objection often made against both interest theories and control conceptions. This objection maintains that the function of human rights is not necessarily limited to considerations of how human rights matter to the right-holder, whether understood as providing protection of her well-being interests or securing her control over certain matters. Our response is that human rights are justified not only by their value to the right-holder but also by the broader societal function that such rights serve.

In section 5.4, we present two principles that flesh out what we described in chapter 3 as our pragmatic approach to the problem of specification and assignment of duties. Our approach is an alternative to the pre-institutional position defended by O'Neill. We discuss both the specification of institutional counterpart duties that correlate with particular human rights claims, as well as more general responsibilities of institutional agents, paradigmatically nation-states, for maintaining background conditions of structural fairness.

5.1. The Function of Rights

5.1.1. The Central Thesis of Interest Theories

Joseph Raz is perhaps the most prominent contemporary proponent of an interest theory of rights. His formulation is as follows:

> X has a right if X can have rights, and, other things being equal, an aspect of X's well-being (his interest) is a sufficient reason for holding some other person(s) to be under a duty.[1]

A more detailed formulation says that a right-holder's well-being interest is sufficient to ground a duty to protect or promote the right-holder's interest only when it makes a difference to the well-being of the right-holder in a significant way.[2] Excluded from the duties generated by rights are general obligations to do whatever might in some indirect, marginal, or

---

[1] Raz, *The Morality of Freedom*, 166.
[2] Ibid., 183.

diffuse way improve the right-holder's well-being. This is an important qualification. As Raz notes, rights generate duties that have a peremptory character. They constrain the realm of discretionary action of duty-bearers by limiting trade-offs for the sake of other social goals or personal objectives.[3]

John Tasioulas, unlike Raz, defends the interest theory approach for human rights only, not as a general theory of all rights, including legal and other kinds of moral rights.[4] He follows Raz's understanding of what qualifies as an interest. An illustrative statement of his interest theory of human rights is as follows:

> [A] [human] right exists if an individual's interest in the object of the putative right (for example, freedom from torture, access to healthcare, opportunities for political participation) has the requisite sort of importance to justify the imposition of duty on others variously to respect, protect or advance that interest by securing to that individual the object of his right.[5]

These clarifying remarks by Raz and Tasioulas mirror important points that we made in chapter 3. Any norms of justice, including human rights norms, must meet a high burden of justification because of their peremptory character. They are especially stringent moral requirements that are central to the moral architecture of any social order. Norms of justice structure both the public pursuit of social goals and the private use of resources and discretionary power. Their special stringency does not entail absolute priority over other moral norms or social goals, but at minimum, norms of justice are strongly resistant to being overridden by competing considerations.

We also argued in chapters 2 and 3 that the core elements of well-being that undergird human rights norms must satisfy the demands of what we called the Structural Dependence Argument. Core well-being elements are restricted to elements that human beings generally cannot secure for themselves, on their own, but instead require societal assurance or assistance. The interests that provide the foundation for human rights thus must be both of special moral importance and also dependent in critical ways on societal structures.

---

[3] Ibid.

[4] Tasioulas, "The Foundations of Human Rights," 45 n 2.

[5] Ibid., 50.

There is potential for misreading what it means for something to be in the right-holder's interest. Tasioulas points out that the relevant interest need not be one that necessarily contributes to any particular right-holder's overall well-being.[6] Instead, the kinds of interests that should be the grounds for human rights refer to categories of goods that generally and importantly contribute to the well-being of persons. Raz makes the same point. Rights are what Raz and others sometimes call "intermediate generalizations."[7] The assertion of a right begins from quite general premises about what in ordinary circumstances contributes to human well-being in significant measure. It is simply a mistake to suppose that human rights or norms of justice, more generally, proceed from anything but quite general premises about what in ordinary circumstances contributes to the realization of universally important facets of human well-being.

We took essentially the same position in chapter 2, where we presented the justification of our core elements of well-being and how they should figure in the arrangement of social institutions. Following Aristotle, we argued that the core elements of well-being are ones that all persons have reason to want for themselves, whatever else they want. To argue that a constituent of well-being is an appropriate object for promotion by political associations is simply to say that it is good for human beings generally, not that it makes life better for any particular human being in some specific set of circumstances.

5.1.2. The Challenge from Control Theories

A fundamental criticism of interest theories maintains that their emphasis on well-being interests entails a misunderstanding of the way rights function as the basis of the moral claim that right-holders make against duty-bearers. Specifically, this criticism argues that the primary normative function of any right is not the protection of the vital interests that a right-holder has in some aspect of her own well-being. Rather, the primary normative function is to assign to the right-holder a particular kind of power of control. Control theories focus on one or more aspects of a right-holder's power to exercise control over some matter, independently of whether the right-holder's own well-being interests are served by exercising that control.

---

[6] Ibid., 51.

[7] Raz, *The Morality of Freedom*, 183. For a similar view of rights as "intermediate generalizations" that begin from an account of what generally contributes to human well-being, see Finnis, *Natural Law and Natural Rights*.

H. L. A Hart argues for a control theory of rights as an alternative to interest theories. On this view, the distinctive normative function of a right is to give its holder control over another's performance of a duty. As Hart famously put it, "[T]he individual who has the right is a small-scale sovereign to whom the duty is owed."[8] The "will theory," as it is also called, takes its name from a passage in Kant. In the *Metaphysics of Morals*, he says that a duty-bearer is bound to another person in the sense that he is constrained to pursue the end of that other person's will.[9] The constraint, of course, is normative. The right-holder has the power to make various moral claims on the duty-bearer, for example, to demand performance of a duty, waive its performance, or insist upon the particular manner of its fulfillment. The holder of this sort of "claim-right" has the normative authority "to resist, complain, remonstrate, and perhaps use coercive measures of other kinds . . . , including, perhaps, to gain compensation if the right is violated."[10]

There are well-known objections to control theories, however. Chief among them is the concern that those who will never possess agential capacities are excluded from the status of bearers of rights. A right-holder can only be someone who has (or at some point will acquire or resume having) possession of sufficient agential capacities to make demands or claims upon a duty-bearer. Kant made clear that one implication of control theories is that a right-bearer *and* a duty-bearer can only be someone who has the capacities to undertake and discharge reciprocal moral obligations. To suppose otherwise involves a fallacy of "mistaking his duty with regard to other beings for a duty *to* those beings."[11] Although there may be duties to promote the welfare of those who lack the requisite capacities, such as non-human animals or humans permanently lacking agential capacity, the beneficiaries of such duties do not have the moral status of rights claimants, and the duty-bearer owes nothing *to them*.

Some control theorists acknowledge these and other counterintuitive implications, but they insist that they are a tolerable price to pay, given that

---

[8] H. L. A. Hart, *Essays on Bentham: Studies in Jurisprudence and Political Theory* (Oxford: Clarendon Press, 1982), 183.

[9] Immanuel Kant, *The Metaphysics of Morals* (1797), in *Practical Philosophy*, ed. and trans. M. J. Gregor, Cambridge Edition of the Works of Immanuel Kant (Cambridge: Cambridge University Press, 1999), 563.

[10] Stephen Darwall, *The Second-Person Standpoint: Morality, Respect, and Accountability* (Cambridge, MA: Harvard University Press, 2006), 18. Cf. John Skorupski, *The Domain of Reasons* (Oxford: Oxford University Press, 2010), XII.6, XIV.2–3.

[11] Kant, *The Metaphysics of Morals*, 563.

human rights do not exhaust our moral reasons for duties to care for and prevent harm to human beings.[12]

Interest theories and control theories thus have their own shortcomings, but both continue to attract adherents. Each approach captures important insights about the desirable functions of rights. Sometimes what matters most to the right-holder is the exercise of control; sometimes what matters most is the protection of important interests. It is tempting to combine the two in some fashion, and one hybrid option involves making room within an interest theory for the kinds of agency interests that control theorists identify. For example, some interest theories, including our own, argue for an expanded inventory of well-being interests that includes agency interests.[13] By that we mean the intrinsic value of exercising control over the contours of one's own life. Specifically, as we defended in chapter 2, our conception of well-being adds self-determination to the inventory of relevant interests. This self-determination interest provides the basis for grounding a host of rights and related duties that track much of what control theories emphasize as crucially important. These range from duties of non-interference with certain types of choices to protections of the conditions within which choice might be exercised.

We explored reasons for including self-determination among our core elements of well-being in chapter 2. We take our cue from Mill's position in *The Subjection of Women*. He argues there that being self-directed, or living one's life from the inside, according to one's own inclinations and values, under suitably favorable social conditions, is itself an important constituent of human well-being. Not only is there "a greater fullness of life" in doing so, but when self-determination is absent, the individual lacks an irreplaceable constituent of a decent life, for which no amount of other ingredients of happiness can compensate.[14]

Our more expansive account of the core elements of well-being allows interest theories to include agency interests and the importance of exercising a significant degree of control over matters of great consequence to a decent life. Our wider conception of well-being interests thus captures within an interest theory what control theories rightly identify as one—but only one—very important function of human rights.

The expansion of what an interest theory includes among the well-being interests that ground rights suggests another kind of hybrid approach

---

[12] Griffin, *On Human Rights*.
[13] E.g., Tasioulas, "The Foundations of Human Rights," 67.
[14] Mill, *The Collected Works: Volume XXI*, 290, 336–340.

that veers more in the direction of the control theory's central claim. On this account, rights also pertain to a right-holder's well-being, as interest theories assume, but the central function of rights remains the exercise of control by the right-holder. This hybrid model thus assigns control rights to Hart's "small scale sovereign," but those rights extend only to the exercise of control over matters that bear upon her own well-being.[15]

However, we still have not gotten to the heart of the disagreement, as control theorists see it. Their main point is that rights of control extend to matters other than ones pertaining to a right-holder's own well-being interests, however capaciously those interests are construed. A standard example illustrating this point is taken from legal theory. There are cases in which a person has both a right and a duty to act as a fiduciary or trustee for someone else. In these cases, the right-holder exercises control for the sake of the interests of another. Here, we seem to have an example of a genuine right: the fiduciary has the right to manage the funds as she sees fit. But contrary to the premise of interest theories and the hybrid theory just described, this is not a right grounded in the importance of the right-holder's own well-being interests. This objection tells against any version of interest theory that contends that the right-holder's well-being interest is a necessary condition of any right.[16] And equally, it undermines the hybrid account that focuses on control only over the right-holder's well-being interest. As a completely general account of rights, interest theories and this hybrid variant fail to capture many of the ways that rights function in our ordinary moral discourse.

The legal fiduciary example, then, suggests a reason to search for a different kind of hybrid. Lief Wenar proposes that we abandon both interest and control theories, each of which are single-function theories, as well as the hybrid that restricts the scope of agential control to the agent's own well-being interests. Instead, he argues that we should adopt a "several functions" approach. On this view, both the protection of a right-holder's well-being interests and control over matters—including but not limited to one's own well-being interests—are among the several distinct functions of diverse types of rights.[17] The several functions approach is motivated in

---

[15] Gopal Sreenivasan, "A Hybrid Theory of Claim-Rights," *Oxford Journal of Legal Studies* 25, no. 2 (2005): 257–274.

[16] For an example of this modest version of a right's grounding formulated in response to another objection we take up later, see Matthew Kramer, "Some Doubts About Alternatives to the Interest Theory," *Ethics* 123, no. 2 (2013): 245–263.

[17] Wenar's "several functions" theory also recognizes rights that neither give the right-holder discretionary power over the duty of another nor promote the well-being of the right-holder. Lief Wenar, "The Nature of Rights," *Philosophy and Public Affairs* 33, no. 3 (2005): 223–253.

part by the observation that this non-reductionist way of conceptualizing the grounds for rights better captures our ordinary understanding of the plurality of the kinds of rights there are and the diversity of functions they fulfill.[18]

We concede that Wenar's argument supplies powerful prima facie reasons for abandoning the position that a right-holder's interest is a necessary ground for *all* rights. However, we doubt the significance of this concession for an interest theory of *human rights*. The standard examples of rights grounded in something altogether unrelated to the well-being of the right-holder typically involve fiduciaries and trustees. These rights are artifacts of specific areas of law, and as we view them, they are far afield from what is central to human rights discourse. Where rights of control are central concerns of human rights, they are paradigmatically matters directly involving control over the well-being of right-holders themselves.[19]

Our claim in this section is that for any justified human right, there will be one or more important well-being interests that figure as an important part, if not the most fundamental part, of the rationale for that right. The right-holder's well-being interest, therefore, is a necessary condition for grounding all human rights, though neither necessary nor sufficient as part of the grounding of all rights. In many instances, the right-holder's well-being interest is best served by the assignment to the right-holder of a measure of control over her own well-being, but in some instances, individual well-being is best served by others who are under a duty to promote or protect that interest, for example, where individuals cannot feasibly do so on their own. The upshot is that an interest theory that subsumes the importance of retaining control under a more general umbrella of an interest theory is superior to the kind of hybrid that views the sole function of rights as securing control over the right-holder's well-being interests. In all cases, what matters is the right-holder's well-being; in some if not all cases, well-being matters in such a way that control is an ineliminable moral concern.

---

[18] Ibid., 238.

[19] A potential objection might be that parental rights are human rights, and these rights are grounded in the well-being interests of their children. We take no position on whether parental rights are human rights, as compared with some sort of moral right, but if they are human rights, one aspect of what grounds them is a core well-being interest they have in participation in the kinds of human relationships in which the value of personal attachment necessarily involves a standing commitment to act for the sake of the other. We make the case for such relationships as a core element of well-being in chapter 2.

5.2. Dignity and Well-Being Interests

In this section, we examine two additional objections to interest theories of human rights. Both are based in a conception of human dignity that is said to provide the foundation for human rights that interest theories cannot supply. The first objection is that interest theories are not sufficient to answer moral status questions regarding who should count as a bearer of rights and why. The second objection is that an interest theory cannot provide foundations for some specific kinds of rights generated from a conception of dignity and its deeply embedded ideals of moral equality.

5.2.1. The Moral Status Question

The first criticism of interest theories is that they do not provide the fundamental grounds for rights. According to this criticism, fundamental grounding rests on a conception of human dignity, understood as a marker for the inherent equal moral worth of each individual.

Frances Kamm, for example, argues that the notion of dignity is foundational to the justification of human rights because it can explain who is entitled to moral standing as a bearer of rights. Dignity thus offers a deeper foundation than well-being interests because it addresses what she and some other critics of interest theories view as the most basic question that a foundational account of rights must answer—who has rights and why. Questions about "what is good for the person, or what is in his interest" are said to be secondary in the sense that we first need to know what it is about the nature of a being whose interests are worth protecting.[20]

Competing conceptions of dignity differ in their attempts to answer what is seen as this most basic question. For example, some theories highlight the capacity for agency, self-direction, or choice, while other theories attribute human rights to individuals on the basis of properties that track species membership. These competing conceptions of dignity will answer moral status questions differently, but a comprehensive theory of human rights will need to articulate and defend its position on the moral status issue. Whatever the answer, the precise point of the criticism against interest theories is that, on their own, they cannot explain who is entitled to the special protection afforded by human rights.

---

[20] F. M. Kamm, *Intricate Ethics: Rights, Responsibilities, and Permissible Harm* (New York: Oxford University Press, 2007), 247.

We concede this point, but how should an interest theorist respond? We think that John Tasioulas has the right answer. Tasioulas also defends an interest theory of human rights, but he accepts a foundational role for some conception of human dignity as a way of answering moral status questions. However, he rejects dignity as playing a foundational role in generating the content of specific rights.

> The interests . . . are always the interests of individual human beings, and understanding their normative significance requires that we grasp the intrinsically valuable status equally possessed by all human beings, grounded in the fact that they are humans. What emerges is a form of the interest-based theory which regards the interests in question as generative of human rights in crucial part because they are the interests of human beings who possess equal moral status: human dignity and universal human interests are equally fundamental grounds of human rights, characteristically bound together in their operation.[21]

We agree with Tasioulas. A conception of dignity—or some theory of equal moral status, however it is denominated—can provide answers to questions about the properties of human beings that confer equal moral status as right-bearers that interest theories on their own cannot supply.[22] However, these questions are distinct from questions about what grounds the human rights of those who enjoy equal moral status, and it is to these questions that a conception of well-being provides the better answer.

5.2.2. What Rights We Have

Jeremy Waldron also argues that dignity plays an indispensable foundational role. However, he argues that it is important to distinguish two kinds of possible justificatory roles that dignity can play. He draws a distinction between dignity as a status or rank and dignity as a kind of well-being interest (a "value," in his terminology). Waldron's point is that dignity understood as rank is used to indicate the status of a right-holder, telling us who the bearers of rights are, while dignity as a kind of well-being interest provides the ground for specific rights. His point is that these distinct

---

[21] Tasioulas, "The Foundation of Human Rights," 53–54.

[22] We interject this caveat because the role that the concept of dignity plays in explicating equal moral status is contested. Thus, "dignity" simply serves as a placeholder for us. E.g., see Sangiovanni, *Humanity Without Dignity.*

usages should not be conflated.[23] "Dignity is what some of our rights are rights *to*; but dignity is also what grounds all of our rights."[24]

The idea "that dignity is what some of our rights are rights *to*" is precisely the claim that Tasioulas says we should reject. One commonly stated reason for such a judgment is the worry that dignity is much too abstract to generate any specific rights.[25] However, others argue that this conclusion is too hasty. The charge is that some plausible human rights now widely recognized can be generated only with the help of a conception of human dignity. As Jeremy Waldron observes, many human rights documents suggest this conclusion. He points to the preamble to the International Commission on Couple and Family Relations, which says that the rights contained in the covenant "derive from the inherent dignity of the human person."[26]

Examples include prohibitions in Common Article 3 of the Geneva Conventions against "outrages upon personal dignity, in particular humiliating and degrading treatment."[27] Article 5 of the Universal Declaration of Human Rights also protects people "against a very specific evil of gross humiliation, particularly in situations like detention, incarceration, hospitalization, and military captivity—situations of more or less comprehensive vulnerability with total control by others of a person's living situation."[28] These are examples of concerns pertaining to what rights attach to the equal moral status of human beings, and the answer is that we know them from the fact that their violation characteristically involves shame, humiliation, or degradation.

Other notions of dignity that figure prominently in human rights discussions are proposed as grounds for the generation of a very different bundle of human rights. For example, James Griffin uses the concept to refer to a bundle of agency interests that generate rights designed to protect and promote the development and successful exercise of the rightholder's capacities for human agency.[29]

---

[23] See Jeremy Waldron, *Dignity, Rank, and Rights* (Oxford: Oxford University Press, 2012), 14; and generally, Jeremy Waldron, "Is Dignity the Foundation of Human Rights?," in *Philosophical Foundations of Human Rights*, ed. Rowen Cruft, Matthew Liao, and Massimo Renzo (Oxford: Oxford University Press, 2015).

[24] Waldron, *Dignity, Rank, and Rights*, 19.

[25] It is the notion of dignity as marking a determinate set of interests perhaps that leads some to conclude that dignity, as a basis for the generation of specific human rights, is fatally vague. Ruth Macklin, "Dignity Is a Useless Concept," *British Medical Journal* 327 (2003): 1419.

[26] Waldron, *Dignity, Rank, and Rights*, 17.

[27] Ibid., 34–35.

[28] Ibid., 19.

[29] Griffin, *On Human Rights*.

At the very least, the difference between dignity as a marker for agency concerns and dignity as a stand-in for a bundle of concerns about equal moral status suggests that there is no univocal conception of dignity from which specific human rights are generated. However, this divergence simply doubles the challenge to the interest theory's capacity to generate specific rights of the sort that dignity theorists think only they can defend.

Waldron concedes that dignity is a vague notion, but he thinks that it nevertheless points to the existence of a single, coherent bundle of concerns that ground the various human rights that proponents of dignity theories see as a deficiency of interest theories. He speculates that "maybe we should say that there are all sorts of rights, with all sorts of foundations."[30] This way of thinking, which suggests that well-being is not essential to the foundation of all human rights, runs counter to our position that well-being interests play a necessary justificatory role in the generation of all human rights. In order to defend our alternative claim, we need to show that our conception of well-being is capacious enough to accommodate human rights that critics seem to think of as connected to conceptions of human dignity and equal moral status, such as those against humiliating and degrading treatment or those focused on agency. To do so, we have to respond to critics who object that the attempt to ground all human rights in a conception of well-being stretches the notion of well-being too far.

Allen Buchanan is one such critic.[31] He argues that non-discrimination and equal status provisions of contemporary human rights declarations cannot be derived from or grounded in accounts of well-being of the sort that interest theories rely upon. Buchanan claims that one can live what he describes as a "good life," in which one's needs are met, while being discriminated against or being of low caste status.[32]

Buchanan's arguments rest on two assumptions that we reject. The first assumption is that agency interests lie beyond the reach of a conception of well-being. This seems to us implausible. We argued the point against Buchanan already, in chapter 2. The heart of our position follows in the footsteps of Mill's observation that a life lacking in self-direction and the exercise of capacities to shape the broad contours of one's life is a life lacking in one of the principal sources of value and satisfaction.

---

[30] Waldron, "Is Dignity the Foundation of Human Rights?," 120.

[31] Allen Buchanan, "The Egalitarianism of Human Rights," *Ethics* 120, no. 4 (2010): 706–710.

[32] Ibid.; see also Allen Buchanan, *The Heart of Human Rights* (Oxford: Oxford University Press, 2013), 31–36.

The second assumption is that the status concerns raised by Buchanan and the shame and humiliation concerns raised by Waldron also lie beyond the reach of conceptions of well-being. This, too, we deny. Our richly detailed conception of well-being assigns a central place to the value of having the equal respect of others. Again, as we argued in chapter 2, this commitment to equal respect rules out certain forms of interaction where a person is treated as less than a moral equal. These forms of interaction are ruled out because such treatment is *bad for* the person whose experience is pervasively affected. These forms of treatment include marginalization, stigmatization, degradation, humiliation, and other manifestations of disrespect that are the inevitable products of invidious social hierarchies and unequal social and political standing.[33]

Thus, unlike Buchanan, we think that a conception of well-being can, and indeed should, include core elements that are responsive to the concerns raised by Waldron and Griffin, and that it is precisely this kind of well-being conception that is best suited to an interest theory of human rights. Indeed, the kinds of interest theories that in our view are implausible are the ones that suppose that the interests that individuals have in agency or equal respect fall outside of the core elements of a decent human life.

5.3. The Social Functions of Human Rights

A third challenge is leveled at both interest theories and control theories of human rights. The thrust of the critique is that neither the importance of securing the right-holder's control nor the importance of protecting the right-holder's well-being interests provides the rationale for the existence of some rights, including human rights.

Francis Kamm, for example, argues that the right to free speech does not fit well with the assumption that it is grounded in anything of specific concern to the right-holder. She presses her objection by picking up on a question raised by Joseph Raz. The issue is whether a journalist's right to free speech is best understood as grounded in its societal value or

---

[33] In chapter 2, we acknowledged that critics might think we have made a category mistake and that the primary reason that treatment as a moral equal matters morally is because failure to do so is wrong in itself, not how such treatment by others is experienced. We argued that interests affected by conduct that is inimical to equal moral status matter morally for a plurality of reasons, including reasons that capture the specific wrongness of treatment that is inconsistent with the characteristic features of a decent human life.

importance to the general public rather than in any well-being or control interest of the individual journalist right-holder.[34]

The issue has a long history. At least since Mill, arguments emphasizing the centrality of a public interest in open debate and democratic deliberation have been highly influential as accounts of the basis for a right of free expression. The proposed rationale is a societal one because the underlying value that grounds such a right accrues to society at large. This rationale rejects the assumption that what is focally important to protect in a right of free expression is the well-being of individual right-holders or their control over speech choices.

That there are contexts where a societal interest figures in the justification of rights is, we believe, undeniable. However, it is much too quick to conclude that the speaker has no important well-being interest at stake. It is not merely that individuals have some interest in speaking their minds. What matters from the perspective of the right-holder's well-being is the acquisition of knowledge and understanding that comes from participation in an interactive process of dialogue and discussion. Knowledge and understanding, a core element of well-being on our conception, constitutes the kind of interest that is among the grounds for the right to free speech.

Of course, an interactive process of dialogue and discussion also can advance political ends in a democracy, as many democratic theorists contend. However, the connection between a person's right to free speech and a core element of human well-being is more basic than the connection between that right and a societal interest in advancing democracy. It is more basic in the sense that the interest at stake in a core element of well-being is not contingent on membership in a democratic society. Core well-being interests are ones that all persons have reason to want for themselves, whatever else they might want, whatever their social circumstances. The enduring, universal value that knowledge and understanding has for the right-holder does not recede when democracy itself ebbs. Arguably, the protection of the interest can acquire even greater importance and urgency in conditions hostile to democracy.

The right-holder's universal interest in knowledge and understanding, of course, is shared by others engaged in the process. Presumably both speakers and listeners benefit from the cognitive gains accruing from active engagement and the contestation of ideas that free speech rights are designed to protect. However, this fact poses no problem for our defense

---

[34] Raz, *The Morality of Freedom*, 179–180, 247–249.

of an interest theory of human rights. What Kamm's free speech example shows is that a broader social purpose of human rights can be a part of their grounding.

If we are correct in concluding that individual rights can be understood as resting on more than one rationale, and thereby serving more than one function, then our version of the interest theory is unaffected by Kamm's point. At most, her arguments show that in some cases a right-holders' interests are not sufficient to explain the full weight and importance of such rights, and accordingly, it might be necessary to invoke some sort of larger social interest for a full justification.[35] Here and in our response to objections posed by dignity theories as well, we claim only that a right-holder's well-being interest is a necessary part of the rationale for human rights. For an interest theory to be plausible, it needs only to show the special importance of human rights *to right-holders*.

Moreover, on our view, the right to free speech is not an exceptional or unusual instance of what a full justification for a right requires. We suspect that in a general range of cases some broader social function is served by human rights. Even some influential interest theories of human rights appear to acknowledge a social function of human rights in addition to the function of rights in securing the well-being interests of right-holders.

For example, Henry Shue's theory begins with a claim that rights secure the right-holder's well-being interests, although in different ways. The function of human rights is to secure a basic level of well-being for right-holders. He says that basic human rights represent a "morality of the depths"; they specify "the line beneath which no one is to be allowed to sink."[36] Shue also describes the function of these basic human rights as preventing deprivation. Human rights serve the well-being interests of right-holders by providing "a shield . . . against at least some of the more devastating and more common of life's threats."[37]

However, Shue also observes that "a fundamental purpose of acknowledging any basic rights at all is to prevent, or eliminate, in so far as possible the degree of vulnerability that leaves people at the mercy of others."[38] Joseph Raz articulates much the same point about what we call the social function of human rights. He says that one of the most important

---

[35] Kamm, *Intricate Ethics*, 245. Cf. F. M. Kamm, "Rights," in *The Oxford Handbook of Jurisprudence and Philosophy of Law*, ed. Jules Coleman and Scott Shapiro (Oxford: Oxford University Press, 2002).

[36] Shue, *Basic Rights*, 18.

[37] Ibid.

[38] Ibid., 30.

functions of human rights is to distribute power away from the powerful to everyone else, including in particular those people who are especially vulnerable to the abuse of states, corporations, and other powerful international organizations.[39]

These remarks by Shue and Raz are not developed in detail, but we think that they contain the seeds of an account of the social function or larger societal purpose of human rights that pushes beyond the conception of an individual right-holder's well-being as providing their sole justification. Specifically, we think that they are best understood as directing our attention to the role human rights have in structuring power relations between social groups.

We can expand on these insights in several ways. Sometimes human rights alter social relations between groups by redistributing decisional power. Husbands may be divested of power over wives, racial minorities may be freed from the grip of legally sanctioned discriminatory housing or employment opportunities, and marginalized and subordinated groups subject to political disenfranchisement may gain a new measure of control over their own destinies. Human rights not only function to empower individuals; they undermine the structural basis of social hierarchies.

Moreover, reallocation of decisional authority is not the only mechanism through which this broader social function of human rights is achieved. When human rights protect against deprivation, they alter existing power dynamics by eliminating or reducing sources of vulnerability that powerful social groups and entities can exploit for their own advantage. For example, human rights that combat deprivation also eliminate or mitigate circumstances of desperation that effectively compel the most vulnerable social groups to accept deeply disadvantaging, exploitative employment and other unfair economic arrangements. In this way, human rights counteract the conditions which foster disadvantage and entrench subordinate social groups in positions of powerlessness where pathways of escape can narrow to the point of hopelessness. Human rights not only prevent deprivation and confer well-being gains on those who suffer deprivation. They also serve a larger social purpose in combating the conditions in which hopelessness abounds by disrupting unfair patterns of social interaction.

In short, it is not just the secure realization of well-being for individual right-holders that grounds many human rights. When human rights break up clusters of differential advantage and realign power relations between

---

[39] Raz, "Human Rights in the Emerging World Order," 226.

social groups, they eliminate group-level unfairness, thereby serving additional social justice aims. Human rights thus provide a bulwark not only against deprivation experienced by individuals but also provide a buffer against other forms of structural injustice that affect individuals as members of differentially positioned social groups. While the well-being interests of individual right-holders are a necessary and even central part of the grounds for all human rights, a fuller justification of human rights involves a recognition of the valuable social functions that human rights serve.[40] Within our overall theory of structural injustice, that social function is the role that human rights often play in preventing and undoing unfair patterns of disadvantage and unfair relations of power among differentially positioned social groups.

5.4. Institutional Counterpart Duties and General Responsibilities: A Pragmatic Approach

In this section, we consider how issues of specification of duties should be addressed in parallel with responsibilities to secure conditions of structural fairness. We begin by addressing the problem of how to specify institutional counterpart duties, elaborating on several steps in the development of a pragmatic approach that we introduced in chapter 3. We conclude by showing how human rights norms and fairness norms are intertwined in ways that offer practical guidance not available from thinking about human rights in isolation. Our approach is intended to be fit for the world as we find it and to serve as an alternative to the pre-institutional position defended by Onora O'Neill. We proceed under the quite general assumption that within the current geopolitical order, states have some special responsibility for human rights fulfillment. We defer until the next chapter questions about the normative uniqueness of states and the broader implications of the system of states for the assignment of counterpart duties.

5.4.1. The Recipient Orientation Objection: First Steps

There are a number of steps in the pragmatic process through which the content of duties can be made more determinate. The first three steps are

---

[40] Our view is in line with general doubts James Nickel raises about any approach that attempts to identify the sole function of human rights. James Nickel, "Assigning Functions to Human Rights," in *Human Rights: Moral or Political?*, ed. Adam Etinson (Oxford: Oxford University Press, 2018).

designed to respond to a problem about the specification of duties known as the *recipient orientation objection*. As Loren Lomasky puts the point of the objection, human need alone, no matter how profound, is insufficient grounds for any human right. That something can be shown to be important for a good life, or even vital to life itself, does not entail that someone has a claim against others for provision or assistance.[41] Lomasky's argument is directed against positive human rights that trigger duties of direct provision of goods necessary to meet some need. However, the force of the recipient orientation objection extends more broadly. It encompasses concerns about positive duties to protect the objects of negative rights. Joseph Raz, for example, claims that the fact that "something is of value to someone does not even begin to establish that I or anyone else has a duty to secure or protect his possession or enjoyment of that thing."[42]

The initial steps in a pragmatic process of duty specification respond to three parts of the recipient orientation objection. First, an implicit threshold question asks why the responsibility for securing the interest does not fall on the shoulders of the recipient herself. A critical part of the answer to this question is provided by the Structural Dependence Argument we developed in chapter 2. Some of what is necessary for the secure realization of individuals' well-being interests often lies beyond the capacities of individuals, acting on their own, to secure for themselves. In any reasonably complex form of social organization, some of the conditions for the successful realization of well-being can be provided only by social institutions and arrangements that can accomplish what individuals on their own cannot. These include everything from law enforcement protection of personal security to vaccine requirements for preserving health to school systems that make possible both childhood learning and longer-term development of critical understanding. They also include the institutional contribution to the creation and maintenance of background conditions that enable individuals to live self-determining lives, form and develop meaningful personal relationships, and interact with others in ways that affirm their standing as moral equals. What is at issue in the specification of counterpart duties, then, is not merely establishing that something is of great value to the recipient. In addition, the duties that correspond to the recipient's valued interest must have a clear institutional nexus.

Second, the recipient orientation objection challenges proponents of human rights to show that the burdens of the corresponding duties, whatever

---

[41] Lomasky, *Persons, Rights, and the Moral Community*, 85–94.
[42] Raz, "Human Rights in the Emerging World Order," 222; cf. 227.

they might involve, are tolerable and not inappropriately demanding of those upon whom they fall. We respond to this demandingness concern by incorporating Henry Shue's argument for limiting these duties to what he calls "standard threats." According to Shue's Standard Threats Proviso, "The social guarantees required by the structure of a right are guarantees, not against all possible threats, but only against what I will call standard threats . . . People are [not] entitled to social guarantees against every conceivable threat."[43] Standard threats are predictable and severe, but re-mediable.[44] The Standard Threats Proviso thus ratchets down the potential burdens imposed on duty-bearers to a reasonable and manageable level.

Third, a further argumentative step is required in light of the fact that even tolerable burdens associated with addressing standard threats will limit the availability of resources that might be dedicated to other purposes. As a consequence, a human rights scheme must meet a high standard of justification. We should not suppose human rights duties are triggered simply because they provide an added degree of protection or promotion that would not exist without them. It is not enough, for example, to argue for specific human rights or a portfolio of human rights on the grounds that individuals "will have a better chance for a good life in a society that respects and protects human rights."[45] That standard sets the threshold for justification too low, given the architectural role of human rights in our overall normative framework.

Human rights require a high threshold for justification because they make high-priority claims on the resources of others. They are entitlements that are deeply resistant to trade-offs for the sake of other social objectives. Given their presumptive weight for each right-holder, they preempt the ordinary balancing of benefits and burdens across persons. Human rights therefore restrict the options of all duty-bearers, including especially governments in the setting of public policies.[46] Because human rights have these constraining effects, there are good reasons to set a higher, more restrictive standard for deciding what matters require human rights protec-tion and how counterpart duties are specified.

---

[43] Shue, *Basic Rights*, 29, 32. The moniker for Shue's argument is ours.

[44] Ibid., 32.

[45] The quote is from James Nickel, but he merely mentions this way of thinking about the justification of human rights, seemingly without endorsement, given his more specific claim discussed below. Nickel, *Making Sense of Human Rights*, 54.

[46] Albert Weale, "The Right to Health versus Good Medical Care," *Critical Review of International Social and Political Philosophy* 15, no. 4 (2012): 473–493.

James Nickel proposes one such restrictive standard with which we largely concur. He argues that for anything to be the object of protection by a human right, an institutional system of rights protection must be an indispensable means, the only means, or a necessary means to protect the interest at stake.[47] For example, Nickel's standard requires us to consider whether some system of self-help within existing social practices, supplemented by charity, will be adequate to ensure regular and comprehensive satisfaction of any candidate interest.[48] If such a system offers sufficient protection against standard threats, then there is no justification for treating some interest-protecting (or interest-promoting) means as the object of a human right and the basis for imposing a duty on others. But if self-help is not an effective guarantee or if social reliance on charity is so spotty in its impact that it fails to provide comprehensive protection of interests, then some scheme of human rights protection or promotion of those interests is justified.[49] As Raz puts it, we need to distinguish the important values that human rights protect from the added value of having rights. In other words, justification of a scheme of human rights protection requires not only that such a scheme track normatively salient and important well-being interests. It also requires that the kind of protection and promotion of those values afforded by a scheme of rights be practically indispensable for the secure realization of those well-being interests.

We add a further clarification to this Practical Indispensability Argument. We need to be sure that we set the bar high enough that a scheme of human rights is indispensable in a very specific respect. That is, the scheme should ensure that no other institutional arrangement will secure the realization of core well-being interests for *all right-holders.* In other words, it is not enough that in the ordinary course of things core well-being interests are securely realized for most individuals and social groups. Human rights become especially normatively important when the core well-being interests of some social groups are at risk in such ways that comparably weighty interests of members of other social groups are not threatened.

5.4.2. Taking Stock

Thus far, the arguments surveyed in these first three steps lead us to conclude that the institutional duties associated with human rights are

---

[47] Nickel, *Making Sense of Human Rights*, 55–56.
[48] Ibid., 76–77.
[49] Ibid., 147.

circumscribed in the following ways. The normatively important well-being interests that generate the rights claims must be ones that cannot be secured adequately without the active involvement of social institutions (Structural Dependence Argument). The demand for active involvement of social institutions is limited further by the fact that they are required to address only those threats that are predictable and severe but remediable (Standard Threats Proviso). And finally, a scheme of human rights must be the only institutional option sufficient to deal with these threats because the peremptory force of human rights overrides all other policy options (Practical Indispensability Argument).

5.4.3. Specification of Institutional Counterpart Duties: The Holistic Assessment Argument

We still need more practical guidance about what is required of institutional agents such as states and for understanding what performance constitutes fulfillment of human rights claims. A threshold question, then, is how much can we, or should we, expect in the way of further specification? Opinions differ widely on this question.

O'Neill's pre-institutional approach sets a very high bar for specification, but we have already rejected her position for a range of other reasons in chapter 3. Requiring duties to be fully specifiable in the mythical state of nature imposes an implausible constraint for the world as we find it. It ignores altogether the social institutions that do not exist in this mythical state but that play such a huge role in both threatening and protecting well-being interests, leaving no room for taking account of social contingencies in the specification of duties.

John Tasioulas observes that human rights require a "tolerably determinate content independent of any subsequent institutional specification,"[50] but it is by no means clear what counts as tolerably determinate.

Allen Buchanan once took the problem of specification to be a serious challenge to the very idea of human rights with respect to health interests. He argued that prominent defenses of health care as a right suffer from "an embarrassing theoretical lacuna," namely "the lack of a principled specification of a decent minimum."[51] However, Buchanan and Kristen Hessler have since reached a quite different conclusion. They characterize any attempt to "delineate a universal, determinate standard defining the

---

[50] Tasioulas, "The Moral Reality of Rights," 76.
[51] Allen Buchanan, *Justice and Health Care* (Oxford: Oxford University Press 2009), 36.

precise scope and content of the human right to health care" as misguided. According to Buchanan and Hessler, the content of such a right is "necessarily vague and . . . the appropriate forum for specifying its content is through appropriate democratic procedures, and not by moral and political theory alone."[52]

Amartya Sen, by contrast, thinks that it is sufficient, given what he sees as the practical function of human rights and human rights standards, to be able to determine in real-world cases when human rights are being clearly violated or when the conditions for the realization of the underlying interest (capability, on his account) are patently not met. According to Sen, it is possible to make determinate judgments about clear violations or deficiencies even though we lack any identifiable bright line that marks the relevant threshold of satisfaction.[53]

These divergent positions proceed from a crucial premise. The assumption is that the only, or perhaps the most useful, way to think about what is required to fulfill counterpart duties is to view each duty as uniquely correlated with a specific human rights claim. According to this view, we can judge whether duty-bearers have fulfilled their human rights responsibilities only by reference to a specific standard of performance for each precisely individuated rights claim.

We do not suggest wholesale abandonment of this traditional approach, nor do we believe that nothing is gained by endorsing its underlying aspiration for precision. However, we do propose a complementary perspective that takes its cue from a different, more holistic way of seeing the justificatory relation between human rights and well-being interests.

For example, assume, as we do, that health is one of the core elements of well-being that figure centrally in the justification of human rights. The traditional approach is to start with the need to specify the content of each of the individuated rights justified by the importance of health for an individual's well-being, including most prominently the right to health care. On the holistic approach, however, we can start by asking a different question. We ask whether states, for example, have met their responsibility within a scheme of health-related human rights, each of which has a different object. (Here we follow conventional terminology, where the "object" of a right is the means by which a well-being interest that grounds the right is realized or secured.)[54] In many discussions of health, our attention

---

[52] Ibid., 203.

[53] Amartya Sen, *The Idea of Justice* (Oxford: Oxford University Press, 2009).

[54] Raz makes a distinction of this sort focusing on the object of a right. See Raz, "Human Rights in the Emerging World Order." Also see Matthew Liao and Adam Etinson, "Political and

is drawn to a cluster of more specific, supporting rights that secure the underlying interest.[55] The right to health care joins the right to food, water, a healthful environment and other rights in forming a cluster of rights that function to promote or protect health interests.

An implication of our holistic recalibration of how we assess what counts as human rights fulfillment is that it makes a certain kind of critical or skeptical stance less plausible. It makes less sense to insist on the precise specification of individuated rights in isolation from the contribution to health, for example, made by policies and activities that advance the objects of other health-related rights that are part of a cluster. While it is implausible to suppose that more emphasis on nutrition and food security could substitute for attention to access to clean water and sanitation services, there is quite a wide scope for combining options for reducing premature mortality and reducing excess morbidity. Whether it is ethically acceptable to exclude a specific cancer drug from universal health coverage is, for example, a critically important question. But trying to answer that question by focusing on whether its exclusion falls below a human rights standard set by rights to health care misses the moral mark. To suppose that we must necessarily focus on one object at a time is to ignore the fact that health goals are multiply realizable and that some degree of latitude in fulfillment is unavoidable. More generally, assessing the fulfillment of institutional counterpart duties, focusing on one object of human rights at a time, can lead to normatively distorted assessments of institutional agents. In many cases, a better way of judging their performance is to focus on how well a cluster of interest-related rights is served by a family of policies that influence health outcomes.

A related point is that there is no reason to limit our holistic assessment to a cluster of rights that is grounded primarily in a single well-being interest. There may be good reasons to incorporate into our holistic assessment how a state is fulfilling its duties with respect to health, for example, by taking into account the health benefits derived from the fulfillment of other human rights, grounded primarily in a different well-being interest. For example, human rights grounded in knowledge and understanding,

---

Naturalistic Conceptions of Human Rights: A False Polemic?," *Journal of Moral Philosophy* 9, no. 3 (2012): 327–352. Liao and Etinson distinguish between the aim or end or goal of a right, which we simply refer to as the well-being interest, and the various objects that are the means to its realization.

[55] Judith Jarvis Thomson treats property rights as a cluster of distinct claim rights. Judith Jarvis Thomson, *The Realm of Rights* (Cambridge, MA: Harvard University Press, 1990), 56–59. We speak of a cluster of distinct rights that serve common well-being interests.

another core element of well-being, such as rights to education and literacy, are highly instrumental in bringing about good health.[56]

Our holistic approach, then, incorporates two insights about the way well-being interests that ground human rights should inform the pragmatic task of specification of counterpart duties. First, in thinking about the fulfillment of a scheme of human rights as a whole, it is important to recognize that any single well-being interest is served by a cluster of differing rights with differing primary objects. Second, it is also important to recognize that any single well-being interest may also be served by success in realizing the objects of rights that are primarily grounded not in that specific interest, but in other well-being interests that have a strong, positive secondary impact.

The general point of this holistic assessment is this. The inability to draw bright lines demarcating the point at which each individuated right is fulfilled need not be fatal to the overall task of evaluating how well states or other agents fulfill their human rights duties with respect to the core elements of well-being that ground them. Our holistic approach to specification is a complimentary alternative to the traditional model by which how well institutional counterpart duties are fulfilled is assessed by focusing on only one object of a specific human right, in isolation.

A final point about our holistic approach to specification is that it should not be confused with other human rights theories with respect to the use of empirical evidence. Specifically, we want to be clear that our empirically driven arguments for how we undertake the specification of rights are different from various kinds of "bootstrap" arguments for identifying the panoply of human rights contained within a human rights portfolio.

The simplest bootstrap argument claims that we have sufficient reason to recognize the existence of another—usually more controversial—right by pointing to the instrumental support that the additional right provides for an interest that grounds the first, more widely accepted right. For example, more controversial rights of democratic participation are often defended on the grounds that they support other rights that protect universally recognized interests in personal security, promote peace, or prevent famine.[57] By contrast, using our example of the interdependence of health

---

[56] Ben-Shlomo and Kuth, "A Life Course Approach." The protective effect of education and literacy on good health and the protective effect of good health on cognitive development are well established. See Sabina Alkire and Andy Sumner, "Multidimensional Poverty and the Post-2015 MDGs," *Development* 56, no. 1 (2013): 46–51.

[57] See, e.g., Thomas Christiano, "An Instrumental Argument for a Human Right to Democracy," *Philosophy & Public Affairs* 39, no. 2 (2011): 142–176; Michael Doyle, "Kant, Liberal Legacies

and knowledge and understanding, we do not try to make the case for women's rights to education indirectly by reference to the health benefits that right would foster.

Our holistic argument should also not be confused with two other variations of a bootstrap argument that endorse an indivisibility of human rights thesis to enumerate the rights that are included in a human rights portfolio. There are strong and weak versions of the indivisibility thesis in the human rights literature. A strong version of this thesis supposes that because multiple rights within a portfolio of enumerated human rights provide some overlapping causal support for multiple well-being interests, they all stand or fall together.[58] A weak version of the indivisibility thesis argues for the existence of some candidate right as part of a portfolio of human rights on the grounds that, together with a second right, the interests that ground each right are more likely to be served better or more fully than they would be by a single right on its own.[59]

Our holistic argument does not aim to do what these interdependence arguments are designed to accomplish. In slightly different ways, each is intended to answer questions about what rights a justified portfolio of human rights must include. They first point to some important well-being interests served by some specific right and then parlay whatever causal support they can claim that another candidate right provides for that interest in order to bootstrap the inclusion of a new right in the portfolio. The causal support claimed in each of these three forms of interdependence argument differs. The first one claims that a second right instrumentally contributes to securing an interest served by the first right. The second one claims that the interest is impossible to secure without including the second right in the portfolio, and the third one claims that the interest that grounds the first right is normally not fully secured without including the second right in the portfolio.

---

and Foreign Affairs," *Philosophy and Public Affairs* 12 (1983): 205–235, 323–353; and Amartya Sen, *Development as Freedom* (New York: Anchor Books, 1999), 152.

[58] The 1993 Vienna Declaration is an example of the strongest version of the indivisibility thesis: "All human rights are universal, indivisible and interdependent and interrelated. The international community must treat human rights globally in a fair and equal manner, on the same footing, and with the same emphasis." See James Nickel, "Rethinking Indivisibility: Towards a Theory of Supporting Relations Between Human Rights," *Human Rights Quarterly* 30 (2008): 984–1001.

[59] Nickel points to the example of the 1968 Proclamation of Teheran: "Since human rights and fundamental freedoms are indivisible, the *full realization* of civil and political rights without the enjoyment of economic, social and cultural rights is impossible" (emphasis added). Ibid.

By contrast, our holistic argument does not rely on any of these three causal claims with the aim of answering questions about what rights there are. We aim only to address questions of how to approach the task of specifying the counterpart duties of whatever rights are included in the portfolio. Our holistic approach, then, is an interpretative strategy for specifying previously identified rights, not a strategy for identifying or enumerating a substantive list of rights.[60]

5.4.4. Responsibilities Beyond Counterpart Duties: The Linked Chain Argument

The counterpart duties that states have with respect to human rights claims do not exhaust their responsibilities for structural justice. We also need to ask how we should view human rights responsibilities that are not directly a part of the duties that fulfill human rights claims. We have in mind here more general responsibilities to prevent or undo the underlying unfair social conditions that make human rights violations so prevalent and pervasive. The close connection we see between human rights norms and fairness norms is spelled out in what we call the Linked Chain Argument.

The Linked Chain Argument unfolds against the backdrop of two premises set forth earlier in the book. First, there are responsibilities under our theory to address deficits or gaps in the core elements of well-being whenever their existence contributes to unfair power relations or helps to entrench unfair patterns of disadvantage. These responsibilities, as we argued in chapter 3, are justified on grounds that are independent of what is required to fulfill human rights claims, but failure to fulfill human rights is one significant way that deprivation can shade into unjust forms of advantage and power. Second, both forms of structural unfairness identified by our theory, unfair power relations and unfair patterns of disadvantage, are understood as important background conditions that make human rights violations more prevalent and more severe.

States thus have two interlocked, justice-related reasons for their responsibilities to address certain patterns of disadvantage and power relations: first, because these patterns are unfair and, second, because they are predictable incubators of human rights violations. At the same time, part and parcel of the responsibility of states to address structural unfairness is

---

[60] This process of enumeration as compared with specification is what James Griffin calls the task of a substantive theory of rights. James Griffin, "Towards a Substantive Theory of Rights." In *Utility and Rights*, ed. Raymond G. Frey (Oxford: Blackwell, 1984).

a responsibility to ensure that human rights deficits or differentials of well-being do not morph into unfair power or advantage.

The upshot is our Linked Chain Argument. The connection between the links of the chain with regard to states can be stated more fully as follows. The fulfillment of human rights claims is partly the duty of states, and the only reliable and durable way that these duties can be fulfilled is through combating structural injustice. At the same time, the only way that structural injustice can be combated is by making sure that deficits or gaps in well-being do not become vectors of unfair disadvantage or unfair power relations involving subordination, exploitation, or social exclusion.[61]

Our Linked Chain Argument has important implications for our original question about the specification of the duties that fulfill human rights claims. The choice among alternative policies for fulfilling human rights grounded in any of the core elements of well-being should be sensitive to the ways in which patterns of structural unfairness are affected by that choice. To the extent that one set of options for advancing some well-being interests also mitigates or prevents patterns of structural unfairness, we have reason to concentrate our efforts and resources there.[62]

Our Linked Chain Argument highlights the importance of attending to interdependent deprivations in well-being, not simply because it is better to

---

[61] Our Linked Chain Argument differs from other theories regarding the relation between human rights and structural justice. For example, Elizabeth Ashford defends the claim that systematic factors that result in human rights deficits are themselves instances of human rights violations rather than vectors of unfairness. Elizabeth Ashford, "Severe Poverty as a Systemic Human Rights Violation," in *Cosmopolitanism versus Non-cosmopolitanism*, ed. Gillian Brock (Oxford: Oxford University Press, 2013), 170. Samuel Moyn focuses on reasons to think that an absolute level of well-being secured by human rights is "not enough" as an account of the minimum universal demands of justice and that an exclusive focus on human rights sidelines equally important concerns about inequality. There are a few isolated references to others who take note of the kinds of linkage that we emphasize, but the main thrust of his argument is captured in his book's title. Moyn, *Not Enough*, 208, 210. Andrea Sangiovanni draws a connection between human rights and structural or systemic factors, but his aim differs from ours. He argues against two alternative conceptions of the subset of moral rights that should be counted as human rights. His position is that the rights that are the proper object of universal concern as distinctive matters of human rights are moral rights that are systematically violated, not all moral rights that are grounded in our common humanity (the orthodox conception) or the specific rights that have been identified in international law and practices (the political conception). Sangiovanni, *Humanity Without Dignity*, 191–192. John Christman's view seems closer to ours than these insofar as he sees human rights violations as deeply embedded in systematic patterns of injustice, but the centerpiece of his argument is the concern that a human rights focus obscures the appropriate remedy by singling out human rights violators for some sort of judicial remedy. John Christman, "Human Rights and Global Wrongs," in *Poverty, Agency, and Human Rights*, ed. Diana T. Meyers (Oxford: Oxford University Press, 2014), 322–323.

[62] For an earlier version of this argument, see Madison Powers, "Health Care as a Human Right: The Problem of Indeterminate Content," *Jurisprudence* 6, no. 1 (2015): 138–143.

reduce multiple deprivations, but for the sake of preventing and mitigating structural unfairness while simultaneously fulfilling human rights duties. The relevant point here is that deprivations in well-being that human rights are meant to guard against also matter because they carry the risk, whatever the cause, of shading into disadvantage and subordination. The risk is compounded under conditions of multiple deprivation. Our choice of options for fulfilling human rights duties should take this risk into account.

To stick with our health care example, this linked chain way of thinking provides yet another set of reasons for the inclusion of reproductive services in the specification of a right to health care as part of a cluster of health-related rights. Other things being equal, implementation of a health care right that is specified in a way that includes a range of reproductive services contributes to the fulfillment of rights grounded in two core well-being interests, self-determination as well as health. This way of killing two or more birds with one stone is a worthy objective, as we argued in chapter 2. Similarly, the holistic argument points to the importance of relying on multiple rights to secure each well-being interest. But specifying the right to health care to be inclusive of reproductive rights also does something else. It has the added benefit of mitigating against structural injustice by helping to alter power relations that seriously disadvantage women and perpetuate their subordination and exploitation. Instead of thinking about the content of counterpart duties that fulfill human rights claims only through the lens of the multiple, underlying well-being interests that are served by each right, or multiple rights that serve each well-being interest, we should opt for something more. In addition to ways of achieving what is specific to human rights fulfilment we should also opt to simultaneously serve a repertoire of more general responsibilities for combating structural unfairness.

Other examples make the same point. When thinking about social policies that advance rights pertaining to an economic standard of living, we should prefer policy options that avoid employment, social welfare, and other policies that leave some segments of the population too much at the mercy of the wealthy and the politically connected. Some state policies might do the bare minimum necessary to fulfill counterpart duties for economic rights, but still fall short of what is sufficient to combat economic exploitation and social exclusion or prevent unjust concentrations of power. Economic policies that have a better chance of mitigating unfair patterns of disadvantage and unfair power differentials are far preferable. For example, increasing the work options that women are able to pursue helps fulfill women's rights to a decent standard of living, but in addition it helps upend long-standing economic arrangements that serve preferentially the interests of men and maintain the subordinate status of women.[63] It is not enough simply to think about which among a number of feasible economic policy options best meets human needs or satisfies the immediate and focal demands of specific human rights. It is also critical to consider the impact of alternative policy options on structural unfairness.

Consider the implications of another example involving the mitigation or prevention of structural unfairness in the crafting of educational policies responsive to human rights claims. It is not enough on our view to make access to education available. Education must be made available in ways that do not saddle young adults with massive debt, and it must not be so different in quality that it gives some an enormous head start in life while undermining the options of others. The way educational access is organized must not set in motion the lifelong subordination of some social groups to others who, often from early childhood, have attended schools that lock in networks of power and privilege that exclude others. Nor should education be designed only with an eye to technical or managerial skills needed for success in the marketplace. Instead, education should be designed to prepare students for critical reflection and the making of informed choices in and about the political and social processes that shape their lives and determine their places within relations of power.

Human rights duties and other general responsibilities for structural fairness thus go hand in hand in our Linked Chain Argument. We should focus on addressing the factors that affect core elements of well-being in ways that recognize how deprivation (especially deprivation of multiple elements of well-being) contributes to structural unfairness and ultimately adversely affects the prospects for human rights fulfillment. Beyond the satisfaction of many human rights claims through what is minimally required for the fulfillment of the counterpart duties of protection against specific threats, we should think more expansively about the responsibility to address social structural conditions in order to combat the very conditions of power and disadvantage that make rights violations more prevalent.

---

[63] World Bank, "World Development Report: Gender Equality and Development, 2012" (2011). https://siteresources.worldbank.org/INTWDR2012/Resources/7778105-1299699968583/7786210-1315936222006/Complete-Report.pdf; and United Nations Commission on the Status of Women, "The Elimination and Prevention of All Forms of Violence Against Women and Girls," Report on the Fifty-Seventh Session (4–15 March 2013), Economic and Social Council Official Records, 2013, suppl. 7, http://undocs.org/E/2013/27.

Our conception of well-being, then, enters into our theory at multiple points, as a crucial part of the foundation of human rights, as an indicator of the high moral stakes that allow us to pick out the kinds of differentials in advantage and power of focal concern, and as paradigmatic examples of vectors of disadvantage and disempowerment. When thinking about the issues related to the specification of human rights, we not only have reasons to adopt a holistic rather than individuated approach to assessing what counts as the fulfillment and appropriate specification of institutional counterpart duties. We also have reasons to recognize that the responsibilities of states and other institutional agents to mitigate structural injustice go beyond the fulfillment of their counterpart duties to human rights. These responsibilities extend to fairness concerns as well, and these concerns can and should play a role in the pragmatic, empirically driven task of selecting pathways for the specification of those duties.

Our pragmatic approach to the specification of institutional counterpart duties and practical guidance for meeting broader responsibilities for combating structural injustice requires a deeper look at the role of nation-states. In the next chapter, we explore the rationales for assigning specific duties and general responsibilities to states and what makes them uniquely normatively positioned to undertake these complex, empirically informed tasks.

CHAPTER 6 | The Responsibility of States

OUR TASK IN THIS chapter is to consider the moral responsibility of nation-states to secure human rights and structural justice domestically, as well as responsibility to address the impediments to human rights fulfillment that flow from differentials of interstate and global institutional power. Our proposals do not proceed from an ideal of a fully just, or even reasonably just, global order. Nor do they rest on the assumption that the current nation-state system, suitably reformed, is the appropriate template from which such an ideal should be fashioned or that a system of nation-states is historically inevitable. Nor do they take sides on the question of whether a system of separate states is a natural response to human longings for communal solidarity among persons bound together by shared histories, cultural traditions, or other commonalities.

We do assume that a robust level of interaction between states, characterized by vastly different degrees of power and advantage, and subject to influence by a host of powerful non-state entities, will define the geopolitical context in which we are called upon to apply our theory. However, we make no assumption that current globalization trends will intensify or even continue indefinitely into the future or that the most powerful states today will retain their dominance.[1]

In section 6.1, we examine an argument intended to explain why states have no robust human rights responsibilities beyond their borders. The portion of the argument that we endorse is that only states have the institutional capacity and political legitimacy to do what is required to address

---

[1] The late nineteenth century experienced a high degree of global economic integration—obviously, much of it involuntary in an age of empire—that was fractured by World War I. That level of integration was not replicated until after World War II, when the identities of dominant parties and dependent states and enterprises again shifted. See Jeffry. A. Frieden, *Global Capitalism: Its Fall and Rise in the Twentieth Century* (New York: W. W. Norton, 2006).

the structural roots of human rights deficits comprehensively, and only then within their political jurisdiction. This argument provides a powerful explanation of why states have unique human rights responsibilities toward their own residents. Is also confirms our thesis about the ways in which human rights duties and responsibility for combating structural injustice are intertwined.

Because only states have the institutional capacities to adjust patterns of advantage and the politically legitimate authority to regulate relations of power that undermine the fulfilment of human rights, there are large gaps in human rights protections for many millions of people. We conclude this section by defending the Principle of Moral Equal Protection, which must be satisfied for the system of states to meet the minimum requirements of political legitimacy. We examine some options for meeting this challenge, given the division of moral labor within the states system, and we set the stage for arguments in the remainder of the chapter.

In section 6.2, we take up the position of "strong statists" who argue that the available rationales for addressing domestic inequalities cannot provide grounds for any egalitarian duties of justice beyond state borders. Strong statists make an exception to the more restrictive Hobbesian approach that rejects all duties of justice beyond national boundaries, inasmuch as they endorse some duties of transnational justice. However, such duties are limited to matters of human rights. We argue that strong statists fail to grasp the implications of their own position on human rights, in part because their position rests on empirically implausible assumptions about the effects of cross-border inequalities on human rights and in part because they make normatively indefensible assumptions about the burdens of justification strong statists must meet.

In section 6.3, we consider a different line of argument, which holds that pursuit of the reduction of transnational inequalities necessarily involves unjust interference with rights of national self-determination. We reject the empirical assumptions that undergird this argument, as well as the view of national self-determination and the principles of just interstate interaction derived from it.

In section 6.4, we consider a fourth argument against the extension of any state responsibility for inequality beyond its borders. This argument holds that even if there is significant cross-border impact and that impact is sufficient to trigger a high burden of justification, there is no action-guiding principle by which states can balance the interests of their own citizens and residents and the interests of non-nationals. We argue against this position by defending the Principle of Interstate Reciprocity. The principle establishes conditions under which the pursuit of national benefit, global advantage, and the exercise of power over others is morally constrained.

In section 6.5, we examine some ways in which the ability of states to discharge their domestic human rights duties and responsibilities for structural fairness are compromised by an overlay of global power relations. Low- and middle-income countries (LMICs), especially, are subject to unfair forms of control exercised by various supranational institutions, often in combination with powerful states and other non-state institutional agents. We discuss four distinct forms of unfairness inherent in these power relations.

6.1. The Normative Uniqueness of State Agency and Its Implications

The combination of two agential features of states helps to explain the current way of understanding the implicit division of moral labor within the existing system of states. These features explain, in particular, why it would be unjustified to extend robust state responsibility for the human rights of persons beyond their borders.[2]

First, states possess unique institutional capacities that, if exercised appropriately, allow them to implement and adjust social policies across a wide range of domestic activities affecting the distribution of advantages, power, risks, and opportunities. These wide-ranging capacities position states to take comprehensive steps to combat the multiple sources of structural unfairness and, in the process, mitigate the likelihood of human rights violations that routinely follow from unfair differentials of power and advantage. Second, only states satisfy the minimum moral criteria for political legitimacy and are thus uniquely, but conditionally justified in the exercise of the kind of power involved when they take such steps on behalf of their citizens.

Of course, not all states possess equally robust institutional capacities or exercise them well, but no other individual or institutional agent within the existing global order approximates the comprehensive set of capacities

---

[2] Our organization in this section is indebted to Saladin Meckled-Garcia, although we diverge on many specific points and the inferences we draw. See Saladin Meckled-Garcia, "On the Very idea of Cosmopolitan Justice: Constructivism and International Agency," *Journal of Political Philosophy* 16, no. 3 (2008): 245–247; and Saladin Meckled-Garcia, "Is There Really a Global Human Rights Deficit?," in *Cosmopolitanism versus Non-Cosmopolitanism*, ed. Gillian Brock (Oxford: Oxford University Press, 2013), 111–128.

possessed even by moderately well-functioning states. Although standards of political legitimacy are often unmet or only partially satisfied, here again no other existing kind of institutional agent is similarly positioned, at least as long as the system of separate states exists, to act in ways that could satisfy the minimum moral criteria for the exercise of coercive power.

6.1.1. Institutional Capacity

The first feature of state agency is the access of states to a multifaceted set of causal levers that enable them to make continuous adjustments in social policy and coordinate the decisions and actions of others.[3] States do so within an institutionalized "system of common public law" that only they possess.[4] Because of the comprehensive reach of this legal system, its institutionalized rules allow for the continuous and simultaneous adjustment of multiple social factors and coordination of numerous agents. Concretely, these adjustments achieve a wide range of policy goals, but the overarching normative point is that their actions determine on an ongoing basis how advantages are distributed and regulate the balance of power within social relations.[5]

Saladin Meckled-Garcia, for example, argues that states make adjustments in legal rules not only for the sake of routine policy goals, such as the facilitation of mutually beneficial economic transactions and economic efficiency, but also for the sake of various distributive goals.[6] Whether the state aims at securing some minimum level of well-being or standard of living, or seeks to moderate the gradient of inequality for some outcome of interest, the state is necessarily involved in the continuous adjustment of social advantages and the coordination of the activities of other moral agents.[7]

Meckled-Garcia's aim is to highlight the fact that states are squarely in the business of undertaking inherently redistributive tasks when they carry out their tasks of protecting and promoting human rights. We agree, but we place the normative emphasis on the fact that more is going on behind

---

[3] Rawls, *PL*, 267–268; Rawls, *JAF*, §§ 13.2 and 15.

[4] Rawls, *PL*, 265–267; cf. Miriam Ronzoni, "The Global Order: A Case of Background Injustice? A Practice-Dependent Account," *Philosophy and Public Affairs* 37, no. 3 (2009): 235; Meckled-Garcia, "On the Very Idea of Cosmopolitan Justice," 253–255.

[5] Rawls, *TOJ*, 6.

[6] Meckled-Garcia, "Is There Really a Global Human Rights Deficit?," 111, 116; Meckled-Garcia, "On the Very Idea of Cosmopolitan Justice," 246, 255–256, 265.

[7] Meckled-Garcia, "Is There Really a Global Human Rights Deficit?," 112, 123; Meckled-Garcia, "On the Very idea of Cosmopolitan Justice," 247, 249, 258, 263.

the scenes than a focus on economic redistribution reveals. States establish and periodically alter emerging patterns of advantage and power, and they can do so in a comprehensive manner through the multiple policy levers at their disposal. For example, states can facilitate the fulfillment of human rights claims to a minimum social welfare floor or decent standard of living through wage policy and the creation of social safety nets, including universal availability of affordable housing, food security, community-wide water and sanitation services, and access to health care and primary preventive health services. More broadly, states can employ a wide variety of policies to combat structural unfairness in the distribution of advantages and the concentration of political and economic power, which if unchecked, pose grave threats to these and indeed all human rights.

The impact on advantage and power is central to how states deploy their institutional capacities in service of human rights, including many social and economic rights. A state, for example, can employ a range of mechanisms that curb the power of employers over employees. These include regulation of terms of employment, minimum wages, pensions, worker safety, unemployment compensation, and disability insurance benefits, as well as the coordination of standards, mechanisms, and access to education necessary for employment.

States also adjust the power relationships among social groups more generally by setting the terms of franchise and political office, regulating equity and credit markets, enforcing anti-trust and consumer fraud rules, and developing standards for the formation and enforcement of contracts. State control over the rules of property ownership, inheritance, and transfer by gift have similar effects.[8] States also regulate sex, reproduction, family formation, protections for children, and the ways in which sexuality and gender figure in the workplace, commerce, and other public arenas. All of these regulatory activities, squarely in the purview of the state, can shape both the concentration and use of political, economic, and other forms of group-based power in ways that no other agent can.

When states implement public provision schemes they effectively remove power from some private actors, while regulatory schemes define the contours of its permissible use. States shape the conditions for human rights fulfillment, for example, when they create systems of public provision, as well as set market parameters for health care access and the protection and promotion of public health and safety. The establishment of

---

[8] Michael Blake, "Distributive Justice, State Coercion, and Autonomy," *Philosophy and Public Affairs* 30, no. 3 (2001): 257–296.

non-market mechanisms for achieving social welfare aims not only alters patterns of advantages that would otherwise accrue to those with substantial private resources; it also lessens the dependence of the poor and the weak on the preferences and goodwill of the rich and the powerful. Similar consequences for the concentration of power and advantage emerge when states impose schemes of taxation and undertake direct public expenditures for things such as roads and bridges, disaster relief, schools, and fire and rescue services. Only states through a system of public law can approximate the comprehensive task of establishing and maintaining the material and social conditions required for human rights fulfilment.

6.1.2. Political Legitimacy

The mere fact that states have the institutional capacity to alter and shape the dynamics of social structural processes is not sufficient to justify their exercise of such power. This brings us to the second agential feature of states. States possess a unique kind of normative standing that conditionally justifies the kind of power they possess over others.

Their exercise of coercive state power must satisfy requirements of political legitimacy. Rival theories of political legitimacy offer divergent accounts of the conditions under which states justifiably exercise their coercive authority over citizens and other residents under their territorial control.[9] While it is beyond the scope of our book to offer a defense of our approach or to explain our reasons for doubt about alternative theories, we adopt a deliberately modest standard of the minimum moral requirements for state legitimacy. Legitimate states, on our view, are ones that respect, promote, and protect the human rights of everyone within their borders and act with proper regard for the human rights of non-nationals over whom they have no direct political jurisdiction.[10]

---

[9] For example, some theories follow Locke in basing the right to rule on the consent of the governed, while others defend hypothetical consent models or focus on the link between the benefits received by citizens or services the states provide to its citizens. Still others, including ours, focus on the minimum moral requirements that a state must satisfy as a condition for legitimate exercise of its normative authority. For a survey see Fabienne Peter, "Political Legitimacy," *Stanford Encyclopedia of Philosophy*, ed. Edward N. Zalta (2010, rev., 2017), https://plato.stanford.edu/entries/legitimacy/.

[10] Our view follows the main contours of the position defended by Altman and Wellman. Andrew Altman and Christopher Heath Wellman, *A Liberal Theory of International Justice* (Oxford: Oxford University Press, 2009). However, there are other prominent arguments that proceed along similar lines but with more demanding standards. Allen Buchanan, for example, contends that "an entity has political legitimacy if and only if it is morally justified in wielding political power." Allen Buchanan, "Political Legitimacy and Democracy," *Ethics* 112, no. 4 (2002): 689. His account requires that basic human rights, including a demand for minimal

An important virtue of this deliberately modest account of political legitimacy is that it resonates with one of the centrally important instrumental reasons for the existence of states. While there are various elements of a plausible and more comprehensive rationale for the creation of political entities possessing the coercive power of the modern nation-state, the state's role as guarantor of the human rights of everyone subject to its jurisdiction is an uncontroversial element.[11]

The combination of comprehensive institutional capacity to make continuous adjustments of multiple structural conditions, including patterns of advantage and power, and the political legitimacy to use coercion to implement and coordinate the activities of other agents has important implications for the assignment of responsibility for human rights. This combination means that, within the existing global order, states are moral agents uniquely positioned to undertake the tasks necessary for the secure realization of human rights and, simultaneously, the successful prevention or amelioration of structural unfairness. No other institutional entities possess this combination of agential features that position them to carry out these interlocking tasks.

As this brief survey shows, states are unique in their ability to control the policy levers needed to manage a wide range of political and economic factors that, if left unchecked, readily morph into systematic disadvantage and unfair power relations. Also, states cannot effectively perform their task of securing human rights—which is essential to the justification of their existence and exercise of power—without also being in the business of preventing or mitigating both forms of structural unfairness. States can do and may do what no other individual, social group, or institution can or may do on its own within the existing global order.[12]

On our view, therefore, as we argued at the end of chapter 5, structural injustice and threats to human rights have to be theorized together as injustices, requiring states to address both responsibilities in tandem.

---

democracy, be protected, that a political entity not have come about through usurpation, and that states satisfy minimum external justice requirements, specifying conditions under which political entities should interact with one another. Allen Buchanan, *Justice, Legitimacy and Self-Determination* (Oxford: Oxford University Press, 2003), 266ff.

[11] Of course, this essential state function is rarely taken to be the sole rationale for the existence of states. Standard justifications for their existence also include their role in securing national defense, maintaining domestic order, and providing public goods and essential services.

[12] Meckled-Garcia, "On the Very Idea of Cosmopolitan Justice," 250.

6.1.3. Gaps in Responsibility for Human Rights and the Principle of Moral Equal Protection

The normative uniqueness of states in the existing global order and the implicit division of moral labor that results have deeply problematic implications. Many millions of people experience significant gaps in protection against threats that compromise the secure realization of human rights. There are at least four reasons why this is so.

First, as we have already noted, some states are not well-functioning entities. They lack either the capacities or the will to address the domestic roots of human rights violations and thus fail in their responsibilities to secure the human rights for all those residing in their borders. Second, refugees and migrants fleeing persecution and war are often viewed as stateless people, for whom no state takes comprehensive human rights responsibility. Third, some problems—climate change, for example—involve preservation of the global commons and are therefore beyond the institutional capacity or politically legitimate jurisdiction of individual states to address.[13] Fourth, transnational commercial, manufacturing, and investment activities can give rise to structural unfairness across states, resulting in human rights violations—for example, sweat shop labor abuses—within particular states as a result of the operation of global markets that no single state is in the position to address in a comprehensive way.

The upshot is that the global order is a fragile and porous system for protecting human rights and for addressing the structural conditions that put such rights at risk. How, then, should the system of states and its rigid division of moral labor be evaluated, and perhaps refined, in light of these gaps in human rights protection?

One way to proceed on the evaluative front is to extrapolate from the moral criteria for the political legitimacy of states. All states are subject to evaluation based on a premise central to the very idea of universal human rights: the vitally important interests that provide the rationale for human rights are of universal moral importance. Moreover, a widely shared assumption is that the notion of rightful enforceability is built into the concept of human rights. One aspect of rightful enforceability follows Mill's lead. To have a right is to have a valid claim against society at large for guaranteeing the object of that right.

---

[13] Madison Powers, "Moral Responsibility for Climate Change," in *Routledge Companion to Bioethics*, ed. John Arras, Elizabeth Fenton, and Rebecca Kukla (New York: Routledge, 2015).

When we combine the universality of human rights claims with the idea that such claims entail rightful enforceability, we end up with the Principle of Moral Equal Protection. Every bearer of universal human rights is therefore also the bearer of universal claims of rightful enforceability. If everyone is a member of a state that can and in fact does afford protection of human rights of those under its jurisdiction, then the Principle of Moral Equal Protection is satisfied. When states cannot or do not provide such protection or when, for the other reasons we described, individuals fall outside the envelope of effective state coverage, then the principle is violated and the legitimacy of the overall system of states is called into question. Within the existing global order, where states occupy an indispensable role as guarantors of human rights, those individuals not covered by state protection have been deprived of a key, front-line component of their claim of rightful enforceability. This constitutes a violation of the Principle of Moral Equal Protection that must be satisfied for the legitimacy of the system of states as a whole.

How then might we overcome, at least partially, the gaps in equal moral protection that arise from the moral division of labor within the existing global order, such that the system of states itself meets minimum demands of legitimacy? There are a number of possible remedies for some of the gaps, but each has its drawbacks and limitations.

One widely noted option involves the assignment of backup duties to well-functioning states.[14] This approach would address gaps due to the inability or unwillingness of some states to bear responsibilities to their own citizens or gaps due to statelessness. However, beyond the ability to respond to humanitarian crises, states generally lack the institutional capacity to tackle structural injustices that are often at the root of the human rights violations experienced by people living in dysfunctional or illegitimate states or who are stateless. Moreover, there is a lack of a clear principle for the assignment of backup responsibility. The plight of stateless people vividly illuminates the difficulty in assigning responsibility, beyond the usual platitudes about its being a collective duty of all states, where each state is charged with doing its share.

The backup duty approach also cannot solve problems that originate in cross-border market transactions or address issues pertaining to the global commons, such as preserving the Earth's atmosphere or protecting other planetary systems upon which we depend for our basic

---

[14] Miller, *National Responsibility and Global Justice*, 54, 251–259; Thomas Nagel, "The Problem of Global Justice," *Philosophy and Public Affairs* 33, no. 2 (2005): 132.

needs.[15] In such cases, supranational institutions might be established to address environmental problems requiring collective action or gaps that arise as a consequence of structural conditions of interstate commerce.[16] Problems that no single state caused and no one state acting on its own can address give rise to calls for states to assume duties to create and support such institutions, but they are notoriously open-ended, indeterminate duties, and any judgment as to whether a state has done its share—cutting its greenhouse gas emissions, for example—in fulfilling these duties is elusive.[17]

Moreover, such proposals must come to grips with the hard realities of just how many, different causal levers have to be brought under a single effective command in order to tackle problems such as climate change or, for that matter, problems that arise from a globalized economy. One likely consequence of creating genuinely effective supranational institutions, even for limited purposes, is the further erosion of the scope of state sovereignty, which, for all its limitations, remains important for addressing more localized issues of structural justice.

Even if we assume that some combination of backup responsibility and supranational institutions can go some distance toward satisfying the Moral Equal Protection Principle, it would do so by fundamentally altering the current global division of moral labor that its supporters think reasonable to sustain. We take up three arguments for the moral status quo in sections 6.2 through 6.4.

6.2. The Strong Statist Challenge

An approach to global justice widely known as "strong statism" invokes the tradition of Thomas Hobbes. Hobbes is known for the proposition that norms of justice arise within political society only once individuals become citizens subject to a common sovereign having the authority to promulgate and enforce requirements of justice. Hobbes's position is quite stark. In the proverbial state of nature, individuals are bound only by the

---

[15] Madison Powers, "Sustainability and Resilience," in *Encyclopedia of the Anthropocene*, vol. 4, ed. Dominick DellaSala and Michael Goldstein (Oxford: Elsevier, 2018), http://dx.doi.org/10.1016/B978-0-12-409548-9.10491-9.

[16] Ronzoni, "The Global Order: A Case of Background Injustice?"; Aaron James, *Fairness in Practice: A Social Contract for a Global Economy* (Oxford: Oxford University Press, 2012).

[17] For a thoughtful discussion of the issue, see Lief Wenar, "Responsibility for Severe Poverty," in *Freedom from Severe Poverty as a Human Right*, ed. Thomas Pogge (Oxford: Oxford University Press, 2007).

law of survival. This position is memorialized within the republican tradition and is also invoked by strong statists in the adage "extra rempublicam nulla justitia."

However, strong statists rarely make claims having the full strength of the pure Hobbesian approach, even when they characterize the global order of separate states in largely Hobbesian terms.[18] Strong statists typically endorse what we call the Human Rights Exception to a pure Hobbesian theory. Unlike Hobbes, they proceed from the assumption that there are some universal norms of justice upon which additional, purely domestic norms are layered.

For example, Rawls views human rights as universal requirements grounded in common humanity, while his egalitarian norms of fairness are grounded in one's status as a citizen of a particular nation.[19] Human rights norms take priority, and in his later work he goes so far as to describe them as lexically prior to his other principles.[20] Thomas Nagel similarly argues for the universal existence and moral priority of human rights which secure a minimum standard of well-being.[21] David Miller characterizes the division of norms in Nagel's theory as the difference between the non-comparative part of justice that sets minimum standards of human welfare and comparative principles that set limits on permissible inequalities between individuals or social groups.[22] The same point is sometimes described as a sufficientarian approach to global justice—where everyone "has enough" well-being, enough resources to meet basic needs, or enough to satisfy a threshold economic standard of living—combined with domestic egalitarianism, where additional principles constrain certain

---

[18] Nagel describes his approach as "Hobbesian in spirit." Nagel, "The Problem of Global Justice," 147.

[19] Rawls, *LOP*, 105–110, 118.

[20] Rawls, for example, supposes that universal human rights to a basic level of well-being are lexically prior to any distributive principles. Rawls, *LOP*, 65 n. 1. See also, Nagel, "The Problem of Global Justice," 130.

[21] Nagel, "The Problem of Global Justice," 132.

[22] David Miller uses this distinction to characterize Nagel's division between universal human rights and domestic egalitarian norms of justice. Miller, *National Responsibility and Global Justice*, 256. However, Miller is not a strong statist. He rejects the strong statist's way of distinguishing between global and purely domestic norms of justice. Unlike Nagel, Miller endorses the inclusion of some egalitarian norms of fairness in international cooperation as part of the global minimum of justice, along with human rights (251–252). Moreover, Miller's different way of categorizing norms of justice as either global or domestic reflects an underlying disagreement with Nagel's empirical premises. He sees no reason for the sharp divide, because chronic poverty and human rights violations often have their roots in "long-term structural causes" (235).

economic, political, or social inequalities.[23] All of these views, then, point to ways in which even strong statists carve out a human rights exception to the pure Hobbesian view.

6.2.1. Normative Uniqueness Arguments

The egalitarian norms strong statists view as applicable only within a politically unified association of citizens are not defined precisely, but the formulation proposed by Joshua Cohen and Charles Sabel captures the central point. "Strong statists" contend that "the existence of the state is necessary and sufficient to trigger *any* norms [of egalitarian justice] beyond humanitarianism's moral minimum."[24]

Nagel situates his discussion of the relevant inequalities of egalitarian concern under the heading of "socioeconomic justice." He provides no precise definition, but he cites Rawls's principles of distributive justice as norms that exemplify what he means by socioeconomic justice.[25] In addition, he offers some examples that go beyond a narrow focus on economic inequalities. They include "rights to democracy, equal citizenship, non-discrimination, equality of opportunity, and the amelioration, through public policy, of unfairness in the distribution of social and economic goods."[26]

Cohen and Sabel's characterization of strong statism is captured vividly in Nagel's wide-ranging list of purely domestic norms of justice. These norms all focus on some aspect of equality, including equal political standing and participatory rights, guarantees against certain forms of unequal treatment and social exclusion, as well as economic inequalities. Strong statism, then, endorses a wholesale exclusion of a large class of inequality-sensitive norms of justice from application to interactions that are outside national boundaries.

Moreover, strong statism also claims that no other norms of egalitarian justice are triggered by any other type of association. Thomas Nagel, for example, argues that egalitarian norms are generated only by associative relationships among citizens of a sovereign state.[27] Unlike human rights,

---

[23] Moyn, *Not Enough*; Lea Ypi, *Global Justice and Avant-Garde Political Agency* (Oxford: Oxford University Press, 2012), 44, 112, 119. Neither author's characterization of such theories comes with an endorsement.

[24] The label "strong statists" is from Joshua Cohen and Charles Sabel, "Extra Rempublicam Nulla Justitia?" *Philosophy and Public Affairs* 34, no. 2 (2009): 150.

[25] Nagel, "The Problem of Global Justice," 114–115, 122.

[26] Ibid., 127.

[27] Ibid.

which are universal moral requirements applicable to all human beings based on their status as human beings, inequality norms are applicable only to relations between co-nationals, and not the rest of the humanity, no matter how deeply intertwined the lives of people across national boundaries may be.[28] In other words, egalitarian norms apply only to associative relations among citizens, and no other kinds of relationships are sufficient to trigger such claims of justice.[29]

Brian Barry's strong statist position reflects both the presumptive normative uniqueness of associations among citizens and the view that all fairness norms are purely domestic in origin. In his response to critics who argue for the application of some norms of equality based on iterated patterns of economic interaction and mutual reliance across national boundaries, Barry claims that "trade, however multilateral, does not constitute a cooperative scheme of the relevant kind." It may be a mutually beneficial form of interaction, but it does not give rise to strongly egalitarian "duties of fair play."[30]

The strong statist position, then, is quite strong, both with regard to the necessity of associative relations among citizens of a state and the wholesale exclusion of all norms of fairness or equality from universal application. For an argument of this sort to work, its proponents have to give some account of what is normatively unique about relations among citizens of states. Lots of answers have been suggested, and we illustrate the basics of a few, but only with enough detail to facilitate understanding of the structure of their arguments.

Rawls, for example, emphasizes how the state is a special kind of cooperative venture established for the mutual benefit of all participating citizens and regulated by a common set of institutional rules.[31] Apart from the very specific social arrangements that make effective cooperation possible under these rules, and the joint efforts and contributions of different

---

[28] Ibid., 120, 132–133.

[29] Strong statism is a highly restrictive species of relational theories of justice. Such theories view some form of association as a necessary condition for the existence of any justice-based concerns about inequality, but strong statists go further. The only associative relationship triggering such duties is found within the context of states. For a discussion, see Andrea Sangiovanni, "Global Justice, Reciprocity, and the State," *Philosophy and Public Affairs* 35, no.1 (2007): 2–39; and Armstrong, *Global Distributive Justice*, 30–32. Non-relational theories, by contrast, make the case for the existence of certain globally applicable inequality-reducing requirements on the basis of common humanity, or the equal standing of all human beings, and not on the basis of specific, special relationships. Caney, *Justice Beyond Borders*, 111.

[30] Barry, "Humanity and Justice in Global Perspective," 233.

[31] Rawls, *TOJ*, 4, 109; Rawls, *JAF*, 5 and 25, respectively.

people that make cooperation more productive, there simply is no way to determine what an individual's just distributive share is.[32]

Another rationale for strong statism is grounded in assumptions about the prerequisites for democratic equality. In *Justice as Fairness*, Rawls restricts the application of his fairness principles to liberal democratic states. Rawls often focuses on distributional requirements appropriate for persons in their role as free and equal citizens of a democratic country, and not simply as human beings with various needs that must be met for the sake of a decent or dignified human life.[33] The argument turns on the instrumental importance of restraining economic inequalities in order to ensure political equality among citizens and preserve the integrity of democratic institutions. Extreme economic inequalities are assumed to pose a grave risk of entrenching political domination by the wealthy, allowing them to capture control of the democratic process and thereby fix the terms by which advantages are distributed in the future.[34] Outside of the context of democratic states, the rationale has no application.

Another argument supposes that there is something normatively unique about state coercion that triggers egalitarian distributive requirements. These requirements are said to emerge because citizens are owed a special justification for the coercive imposition of an economic and political order that infringes their autonomy.[35] Alternatively, state coercion is uniquely significant because of the special burden of justification that citizens in a democratic society owe to one another. Nagel, for example, argues that citizens of democratic states are joint authors of an institutional scheme of rules that involve comprehensive control over the framework of interaction between citizens, affecting many aspects of their lives, ordinarily over the course of their entire lives.[36] Citizens, therefore, are morally implicated in creating state policies having such a wide sweep and backed up by coercive measures.[37]

---

[32] Rawls, *TOJ*, 88, 109; 4, 53; Rawls, *JAF*, § § 14.1, 14.2; Rawls, *JAF*, 21.3.

[33] Rawls, *JAF*, §§ 13.6, 17.1.

[34] Ibid., §§ 15, 39.1; Rawls, *TOJ*, 470, 478.

[35] Blake, "Distributive Justice, State Coercion, and Autonomy"; Nicole Hassoun, *Globalization and Global Justice: Shrinking Distance, Expanding Obligations* (Cambridge: Cambridge University Press, 2012). For trenchant criticisms of coercion theories, see Andrea Sangiovanni, "The Irrelevance of Coercion, Imposition, and Framing to Distributive Justice," *Philosophy & Public Affairs* 40, no. 2 (2012): 102–103.

[36] Nagel, "The Problem of Global Justice," 123.

[37] Ibid., 128–130.

6.2.2. The Common Structure of Strong Statist Arguments

The comparative merits of different ways of justifying the claim that states are uniquely situated such that they are the sole locus of egalitarian norms are not of concern to our inquiry. However, two themes that run through much of the strong statist literature are important.

First, strong statists' arguments typically defend an associative rationale that depends on features of relations between persons that are generally absent outside the context of a single state. For example, concerns about the corrosive effect of great wealth differentials on democratic relations and the integrity of democratic institutions obviously matter in the domestic context, but given the lack of global democratic institutions, the rationale does not support the global extension of egalitarian norms.

All that this kind of argument can show is that relations that are unique to co-nationals do not justify the global extension of the specific egalitarian norms that these relations support. The argument delivers nothing like the knockout punch needed to rule out inequality-sensitive norms that our theory of structural injustice identifies as fundamental and equally at home both within a society and beyond it. Claims about what is normatively special about the relations between co-nationals do not run counter to our proposal for judging patterns of structural disadvantage as deeply and fundamentally unfair, wherever these patterns are located, so long as they have systematic impact on the core well-being prospects for a decent life of those affected by them. Nor do these claims register the basic wrongness, independent of citizenship status, of being in someone's grip, as a mere instrument of another's will, or being treated as an object of exploitation, or being made the subject of social exclusion.

The implications of these omissions are deeply counterintuitive. Strong statists offer no theoretical basis for concern about, or grounds for condemnation of, the existence of cross-border disadvantage affecting the most important aspects of life or the risk of exploitation of weak, fragile, or failed states by powerful states or non-state corporate entities.

Second, a background assumption shared by many strong statists is that inequalities in general are not unjust in the absence of some specific rationale for their being so. While human rights are justified on universally applicable grounds, the mere existence of global inequality is seen as morally unproblematic, as long as an individual floor of human well-being and other basic rights is secured. However, the norms of fairness and of human rights can be satisfied separately, as the statist supposes, only if they are both conceptually distinct and not practically intertwined.

Our argument throughout the book, especially in section 6.1, is that norms of fairness and of human rights are conceptually distinct but practically intertwined. One of the most important ways to discharge duties with respect to human rights involves combating the sources of structural unfairness in power and advantage, operating both within and across national borders, that are instrumental in compromising human rights. At the end of chapter 5, we suggested how thinking about both types of norms in tandem can aid the specification of the content of duties associated with human rights.

The theories of strong statists who endorse the Human Rights Exception have resources for reaching similar conclusions. Nagel not only accepts the existence of some secondary responsibility to secure the human rights of non-citizens when their own states fail in their responsibilities.[38] He also recognizes that proper regard for the human rights of non-nationals rules out complicit forms of interaction with and support for human rights violators. Moreover, he acknowledges that proper regard for human rights also places limits on the pursuit of national advantage and the reduction of domestic inequality when doing either is achieved by depriving non-nationals of their basic human rights.[39] Clearly, there is room, in principle, within the strong statist approach for the responsibility of states to address international, structural causes of human rights deficits experienced by non-nationals.

However, two objections to extending this strategy globally have to be overcome. The first objection builds on the claim that Nagel and other strong statists make about cross-border influences being too weak to constitute a substantial threat to human rights.[40] They might even supplement this objection by assuming that whatever impact there may be is well within the capacity of affected states to deal with on behalf of their own citizens. These are empirical claims, and we doubt that any such sweeping generalizations are plausible. We think the evidence in quite a few instances shows that some of the most significant causal pathways to human rights deficits are at work in the domestic context and globally, often for the same reasons. We consider a few concrete examples in section 6.5 and again throughout much of chapter 7.

The second objection can concede our empirical claims regarding impact and still reject any state responsibility to deal with cross-border

---

[38] Ibid., 132.
[39] Ibid.
[40] Rawls, *LOP*, 107–118; Nagel, "The Problem of Global Justice," 138.

structural causes of human rights deficits occurring elsewhere. This objection might appeal to the kinds of reasons we articulated in section 6.1. There, we maintained that only states are well positioned to comprehensively address social structural sources of human rights violations and only within the confines of their jurisdiction. However, the argument in 6.1 does not rule out that states have obligations to secure justice outside their jurisdictions. Just because there are some responsibilities that only states can take on *comprehensively* because of their institutional capacity and political legitimacy, it does not follow that states have no responsibilities to address structural causes linked to the human rights of non-citizens. Indeed, it may be the case that for some structural injustices, states are uniquely positioned to take on certain responsibilities for the human rights of non-nationals.

In section 6.4, we propose one such principle of interstate responsibility. But first we have to assess a different kind of argument. It may be claimed that even if there are instances in which states are uniquely positioned to take some specific steps to address the structural context of human rights deficits of non-nationals, it would be unjust for them to do so.

6.3. National Self-Determination Arguments

Rawls, in *The Law of Peoples*, rules out principles of justice pertaining to global inequality on the grounds that such principles would be incompatible with rights of national self-determination for "free and equal peoples."[41] For Rawls, inequalities of well-being, resources, and opportunity between nations, no matter how great, are treated as morally unproblematic.

In a similar vein, Nagel argues that the global economic order should be viewed as a "bargaining" relationship that involves forging agreements that are "like the contracts favored by libertarians."[42] Apart from ruling out fraud, coercion, and similar bargaining defects that make transactions unfair under the libertarian conception, states have primarily negative duties

---

[41] There is considerable debate about the concept of "peoples" who merit some presumption of a right of national self-determination. Presumably, Rawls's aim is to avoid constructing a theory of interstate justice that takes for granted the legitimacy of all and only the nation-states that happen to exist, no matter how morally problematic their origins. Critics, however, argue that Rawls falsely assumes a high degree of cultural and political homogeneity among peoples. Representatives of peoples may not speak for various groups who are marginalized, excluded from influence, or subordinated to the will of dominant groups. See Benhabib, *The Rights of Others*, 80–87; and Allen Buchanan, "Rawls's *Law of Peoples:* Rules for a Vanished Westphalian World," *Ethics* 110, no. 4 (2000): 698–700, 716–20.

[42] Nagel, "The Problem of Global Justice," 141.

not to be complicit in the activities of other states that undermine their realization of domestic justice.[43]

Rawls and Nagel reach similar conclusions, but Rawls's argument proceeds through a variant of the social contract device that he uses to generate principles of social justice for members of a single society. The parties to the hypothetical agreement choose principles on the assumption that they are "free and equal." The point is that each party values its status as an independent and self-directing agent, willing to acknowledge and reciprocally affirm claims for independence made by other parties to the contract. The outcome of the hypothetical agreement between peoples is meant to be a "reasonably just" system of international relations that any society has sufficient reason to endorse, given the aspiration of each to ensure for itself a high degree of independence in the conduct of its internal affairs.

Many details of Rawls's contract are subject to well-known criticisms, in particular objections to thinking about global justice entirely through the lens of societies rather than individuals, but his arguments, as well as Nagel's, offer useful starting points for thinking about an important subset of issues of global justice. An account of how sovereign states should relate to other sovereign states ought to be a part of any theory of global justice.[44]

Rawls illustrates his argument by imagining very different societies, each having their own priorities for such things as economic development, preservation of traditional ways of life, and population policy. Some societies choose rapid economic development and population policies that limit reproduction, both of which have the potential to expand the distributive shares of wealth and income and improve the standard of living for their people, but other societies do not. Affluent nations, for example, would object to any global distributive scheme that requires specific patterns of resource distribution across states. Their objection would rest on the assumption that they are entitled to whatever advantages accrue from their decisions to industrialize or limit population growth. Traditional agrarian countries and poor nations that value large families and a less individualistic, more cooperative mode of social organization also would object. They would object on grounds that other nations should not take it upon themselves to interfere in internal affairs in order to improve the

---

[43] Ibid., 143. There are secondary duties, discussed below, as well as other, less easily categorized duties that Nagel recognizes.

[44] See Benhabib, *The Rights of Others*, and Buchanan, "Rawls's *Law of Peoples*."

standard of living of other peoples according to the values that affluent, industrialized countries embrace.

Because representatives of nation-states are assumed to have reason to give high priority to national self-determination, both affluent states and poor states would object to any global distributive scheme that requires patterns of resource distribution across states, even for the sake of equalizing the opportunities of persons around the world. Instead, they would endorse a commitment to a global economic order in which contracts and bargains are upheld, along with rules that secure fair trade.

Notice that there are two quite distinct conclusions being run together in these discussions. One conclusion focuses on objections to the implementation of a global principle of resource distribution across states. Whether or not Rawls is correct to suppose that both rich and poor states would find such a principle objectionable, it is very different from a conclusion about what constitutes fair terms of interstate interaction. It is not reasonable for representatives of sovereign peoples, rich or poor, to agree to a global order whose terms are "seriously disadvantaging," even if, for the sake of argument, the implementation of a principle of distribution or redistribution would be rejected.[45]

Rawls, however, does not even entertain these fairness concerns because of empirical assumptions that the representatives of peoples are presumed to share. He assumes that the parties would agree that the causes and consequences of inequality between nations are almost wholly a function of what happens to and among citizens within nations. However, we think that under any empirically plausible model for selecting principles of interstate interaction, representatives of sovereign nations must be presumed to know that no state is immune to the effects of exogenous economic forces and that some states are especially vulnerable to both economic and geopolitical influences beyond their control.

In all countries, including the world's most developed and wealthiest nations, the well-being of their citizens is very much influenced by what happens in global markets for energy, food, capital and currency, as well as political decisions by powerful states with regard to their trade and investment priorities. Many organic, homegrown social justice movements in poor countries seek development, indeed the right to development on their own terms, not to be left behind or left alone. Moreover, low- and

---

[45] Buchanan, "Rawls's *Law of Peoples*," 705.

middle-income countries know that isolation is not a viable option and that what is needed instead is fair terms of interaction.

Countries truly committed to independence and national sovereignty would have ample reason to reject seriously disadvantageous conditions of interstate bargaining or one-sided imposition of terms of interaction, for example, terms that render them powerless to say no to external domination, exclusion, and exploitation. When crafting principles for the regulation of the global order, their representatives would therefore have strong reasons to take into account the importance of the mutual impact all nations have on the internal affairs of one another. They would endorse principles that set limits on the use of asymmetric bargaining power in order to protect the status of poorer, less powerful nations as equal, independent, and self-determining societies, and to implement their own specific conceptions of justice and the good.

The upshot is that Rawls's global principles regulating economic interaction and cooperation between states do not offer suitable protection for most nations of the world, as we know it. He falsely assumes that all that is required for genuine independence and national self-determination is a scheme of mutual forbearance, a broadly libertarian approach to market regulation, supplemented by a weak duty of humanitarian assistance.

The same objections apply to Nagel's broadly libertarian framework about what qualifies as fair in the interstate context. On his view, most forms of transnational agreement—between states or between entities based in separate states—should be viewed as ordinary contracts, subject only to market norms that rule out familiar transactional deficiencies such as fraud and coercion. Moreover, because of the presumption that what happens within a country is largely a function of internal policy decisions, and not a function also of global market dynamics, any duties of interstate assistance cannot be viewed as remedial duties of justice. Such duties are not ones designed to correct for unfairness in the process through which outcomes of transnational market transactions emerge. They are duties of humanitarian assistance.

By contrast, we believe that because there are sufficient effects of global interaction that radiate far beyond national boundaries, and because international rules that can mitigate those effects are required to maintain the independent, self-determining standing that Rawls's own theory demands, the libertarian tenor of principles of interstate justice proposed by Rawls and Nagel should be rejected. Globally, as well as domestically, there is a need for substantial moral restraints on wealthy nations pursuing greater wealth, seeking geopolitical and market power, and consolidating other forms of advantage that unfairly impinge on the national self-determination of low- and middle-income countries.

Even staunch defenders of the anti-egalitarian vision of interstate justice sometimes acknowledge the counterintuitive implications of their position. Nagel, for example, observes that it "seems highly arbitrary that the average individual born into a poor society should have radically lower life prospects than the average individual born into a rich one," but nevertheless he concludes that the position he defends is "accepted by most people in the privileged nations of the world," and moreover, it is "probably correct."[46]

There is a backstory of how the consensus Nagel supposes came into existence. In the 1970s, postcolonial states developed their own global development agenda known as the New International Economic Order (NIEO).[47] It called for collective self-determination of peoples, the right to development, and global reduction of economic inequality and inequality of power and influence in international institutions affecting the global economy. The resolution in support of the NIEO agenda was approved by the United Nations in 1978. It reiterated many ideas already contained in the International Covenant for Economic, Social, and Cultural Rights (ICESCR), which was proposed by the newly de-colonialized countries in 1966 and took effect in 1976. A centerpiece of ICESCR is the concept of collective self-determination of peoples, with a focus on "permanent sovereignty over resources" and their right not to be deprived by outsiders of "their own means of subsistence."[48]

Officials of the World Bank and the International Monetary Fund (IMF) were galvanized by these two UN actions, and many were candid about their intentions to deflect attention from the demands of postcolonial nations.[49] The World Bank in particular elevated the discussion of basic rights and added the aim of eliminating poverty to its public mission statement in an effort to "ethically outflank" calls for closing the gap between rich and poor nations.[50]

---

[46] Nagel, "The Problem of Global Justice," 126.

[47] UNESCO, Expert Meeting on Human Rights, Basic Needs, and the Establishment of a New Economic Order, Paris, June 19–23, 1978, UN Doc. SS78/Conf. 630/12. See also Victor McFarland, "The New International Economic Order, Interdependence, and Globalization," *Humanity* 6, no. 1 (2015): 217–233.

[48] International Covenant for Economic, Social, and Cultural Rights, UN General Assembly, *International Covenant on Economic, Social and Cultural Rights*, December 16, 1966, United Nations, Treaty Series, vol. 993.

[49] See Moyn, *Not Enough*, 119–145.

[50] Ibid., 121.

Many human rights advocates, however, resisted the efforts to delink human rights from broader issues of global and social justice. In 1980, Theo van Boven, the UN Human Rights division chief, told an assembled group of development specialists that it was imperative to abandon "the shallow approach to human rights, which neglects the deeper, structural causes of injustice."[51] Many knowledgeable human rights advocates today convey the same message. Philip Alston, in a widely cited "Report of the Special Rapporteur on Extreme Poverty and Human Rights," reiterates the importance of remedial action based on a proper understanding of the causal links between inequality, extreme poverty, and a host of human rights violations.[52]

By contrast, as Nagel suggests, the orthodox development community and influential philosophical theories are in broad agreement about the current division of moral labor within the existing global order. Our theory argues that their principles are predicated on assumptions that do not help us understand the world as it is or confront the moral problems that are so pervasive in it. We turn next to a consideration of an alternative principle that would do a better job of regulating unfair interstate differentials of power and advantage.

6.4. The Principle of Interstate Reciprocity

Meckled-Garcia argues that in the current geopolitical context, states would seem to be the only moral agents to whom claims of "justice proper" are addressed. By this, he means that states are under clear, reasonably determinate action-guiding duties to their citizens, requiring them to respond to the totality of accumulated inequalities that undermine their ability to protect and promote the human rights of their citizens. Failure to do so constitutes a violation of the human rights claims of its citizens.[53] Although states presumably have reasonably determinate, action-guiding duties to respect the human rights claims of citizens and non-citizens alike, non-nationals have no rights claims against states other their own for the promotion and protection of their human rights. A state's failure to attend to social conditions that affect the fulfillment of the human rights

---

[51] Quoted in ibid., 208.

[52] Philip Alston, "Report of the Special Rapporteur on Extreme Poverty and Human Rights," UN Doc. A/HRC/29/31, May 27, 2015.

[53] Meckled-Garcia, "Is There Really a Global Human Rights Deficit?," 112, 123; Meckled-Garcia, "On the Very Idea of Cosmopolitan Justice," 247, 249, 258, 263.

of non-nationals does not constitute a breach of duty owed to them, and therefore is not a human rights violation in the way that a failure to protect the rights of its own citizens is.

The challenge, then, is to determine whether we can identify some transnational activities that constitute a breach of a determinate duty in violation of the human rights of persons who have claims on states of which they are not citizens or legal residents. Meckled-Garcia's "justice proper" objection, then, comes down to this: there is no reasonably determinate principle by which the state's human rights responsibilities to its own citizens can be balanced against putative duties to address transnational inequalities that make human rights fulfillment within other countries more difficult. We argue directly against this position, and we begin by examining briefly a well-known, but in our view unsuccessful response to his challenge.

One line of argument that we reject asserts that the global order itself contributes to the intensification of global poverty in way that constitutes a violation of human rights. The argument is problematic for reasons we outlined in chapter 3. It equates foreseeable bad outcomes that could have been averted under feasible alternative institutional rules in the global order with human rights violations.[54] What seems to be missing in this formulation is the identification of any specific agent whose action or omission involves a breach of duty in violation of a right of an aggrieved party. The point is that there is a morally important gap between the existence of institutionally avoidable bad outcomes and a conclusion that a human rights violation or some other injustice has occurred. No matter how awful the global order might be, and no matter how much avoidable suffering it permits, what results is merely a social condition or state of affairs. There is no specific agent whose discrete act or omission, or even series of actions, can be identified as violating a clear, determinate action-guiding duty. States, by contrast, do have such duties to protect and promote the

---

[54] One author that Meckled-Garcia has in mind is Thomas Pogge, who argues that "any institutional order that foreseeably produces a reasonably avoidable excess of severe poverty and of mortality from poverty-related causes manifests a human rights violation on the part of those who participate in imposing this order." Thomas Pogge, "Severe Poverty as a Human Rights Violation," in *Freedom from Poverty as a Human Right*, ed. Thomas Pogge (Oxford: Oxford University Press, 2007), 30. He frames the rights violation claim in various ways. He argues that features of the present global order contribute to "vast excesses of severe poverty and premature poverty deaths" globally (30); violate the right to an adequate standard of living in UDHR Article 25 (11); involve a violation of a right to basic necessities (53); and violate rights by depriving people of their livelihoods (15). Sometimes Pogge says that the global order constitutes a human rights violation, suggesting that Meckled-Garcia's characterization is accurate, but in other places the accent is on the fact that it is being imposed (30), a signal that he is not making an agentless claim.

human rights of their citizens, and a failure to do so is an omission that is properly characterized as a human rights violation.

However, we argue that failures by states to protect their own citizens is not the only way that states can fail in their human rights duties. Violation by states of what we call the Principle of Interstate Reciprocity constitutes a similar morally culpable failure to show due regard for human rights, in this case of non-citizens.

6.4.1. Reciprocity and Fairness

Consider first how Rawls characterizes the overall framework within which we might think about interstate relations. He contends, quite plausibly, that any theory of fair terms of political and social cooperation across sovereign boundaries should conform to the "criterion of reciprocity" in the same way the criterion applies to a theory of fair cooperation within a single society.[55] By this generic notion of "reciprocity" he means the following: "These fair terms are those that a people sincerely believes other equal peoples might accept also; and should they do so, a people will honor the terms it has proposed even in those cases where that people might profit by violating them."[56] In the preceding section, we rejected Rawls's own account of transnational responsibilities that he believes constitute fair terms for the global order. Behind Rawls's criterion of reciprocity are, however, deeper assumptions that are worthy of exploration.

For Rawls, a commitment to an ideal of reciprocity is said to be a normative perspective located between impartiality and mutual advantage. Concretely, this means two things. First, the appropriate form of regard for others is not reducible to purely self-interested bargaining among parties seeking mutual advantage. Instead, a commitment to the ideal of reciprocity combines a reasonable concern for one's own interests and a willingness to honor terms that can require some degree of sacrifice of those interests for the sake of comparable interests of others. Second, the constraints on interaction that this commitment generates do not entail strict equality of treatment in all things, commonly taken as implied by impartiality. Instead, an ideal of reciprocity, following Ranier Forst,

---

[55] This generic account is different from Rawls's more demanding ideal of reciprocity, which he calls "reciprocity in the deepest sense." Rawls, *JAF*, § 21.4. It is offered as an interpretation of the Difference Principle, which requires that "[t]hose who gain are to do so on terms acceptable to those who gained less" (§ 36.2).

[56] Rawls, *LOP*, 35.

requires only "that none of the parties concerned may claim certain rights and privileges it denies to others."[57]

This generic explication of reciprocity does not provide a substantive account of the rights and privileges that none may claim if they deny them to others, but it does make clear the central point that there are some minimum reciprocal demands of justice due to moral equals. The substantive question then concerns specifying what rights and privileges may be asserted, either by individuals or their representatives, only on condition that others may assert them as well.

Consider the well-being interests that underwrite human rights. They are acknowledged as both especially weighty and of universal significance, simply in virtue of one's status as a human being. Persons cannot simultaneously claim a minimum level of rights protection of these interests for themselves, in virtue of being human beings, and deny to others who also share their status as human beings that same level of rights protection. Thus, if one thinks, as we do, that the minimum universal claims of justice include protection of well-being interests secured by human rights *and* the social protections afforded by a basic standard of structural fairness, then no individual can demand of others terms of sustained interaction that require a level of sacrifice of the very things that she thinks would be non-negotiable were others to make such demands upon her.

The more specific question, of course, pertains to the way we define the minimum demands appropriate to the terms of sustained, highly structured interaction among states. These minimum demands mark the limits of the kinds of sacrifices that the representatives of one country can demand of the representatives of another country in the process of reaching interstate agreements. Put another way, citizens would consider these minimum demands to be non-negotiable and, hence, not within the authority of their state representatives to surrender, as if they were little more than bargaining chips.

Richard Miller, for example, sheds light on the general shape of the problem of reciprocity in an interstate context. He refers to what he calls "reciprocity of reasons" in the way individuals should think about the conditions under which their governments should represent them and secure their interests in various global arenas of negotiation. Reciprocity requires "backing their own [government's] proposals with morally relevant reasons and giving weight, in proportion to seriousness, to relevantly

---

[57] Forst, "Towards a Critical Theory of Transnational Justice," 177.

similar reasons offered by [the governments of] others."[58] No one can consistently endorse an ideal of moral equality and at the same time instruct her government to prioritize the promotion and protection of her core well-being interests and simultaneously discount the very same claims when made by the representatives of nationals of other countries.

The arguments made throughout this book imply two practical conclusions. Citizens may not demand that their government press for national advantage and their well-being in ways that require sacrifice of the human rights of non-citizens that they would view as morally non-negotiable were such sacrifices demanded of them. Similarly, citizens may not demand that their government press for national advantage and their well-being in ways that create or sustain patterns of structural unfairness for non-citizens, that on our theory not only implicate the core elements of well-being and constitute unfair power relationships, but are unacceptable also because they routinely undermine and erode the secure realization of human rights.

We can now put these two ideas together in order to spell out our substantive Principle of Interstate Reciprocity.[59] This principle prohibits a nation from pressing for advantage for its own citizens when (i) the pursuit of national advantage undermines the human rights of citizens of other nations or constitutes unfair relations of power and (ii) forgoing the pursuit of advantage does not thereby put its own citizens' basic human rights at substantial risk or subject its citizens to unfair power relationships.

A few key points will elucidate the major implications of this principle. It does not involve a cosmopolitan or impartial concern for the overall welfare of all human beings. It does not rule out a nation's special concern for the overall welfare of its own citizens in pressing for favorable bargains or protecting them from unfair power relations. In fact, our interstate reciprocity criterion presupposes the acceptability of some self-interested international bargaining, but only within reciprocally recognized limits. Indeed, the principle takes for granted the widespread assumption that all nations, whether rich or poor, have sufficient reasons to promote the interests of their own citizens and, moreover, that they have a special, primary duty to ensure the satisfaction of the human rights of their own

---

[58] Richard Miller, *Globalizing Justice: The Ethics of Poverty and Power* (Oxford: Oxford University Press, 2010), 72.

[59] Just to be clear, this principle is in addition to whatever backup duties states have for securing the human rights of citizens of failed, fragile, or economically burdened states or any duties that ought to be assigned to supranational institutions.

citizens, as well as to protect them from subordination, exploitation, and exclusion by others.

The Principle of Interstate Reciprocity is especially important in a world of nations that differ greatly in wealth and other forms of power. It rules out forms of bargaining in which the morally non-negotiable human rights of the citizens of less powerful countries are not protected from serious threats or shielded from deeply unfair exercises of power that jeopardize those non-negotiable rights. No nation should acquiesce in the sacrifice required by such a bargain, and no nation should demand that kind of sacrifice from other, less powerful nations simply to preserve a vastly higher standard of living for its own citizens.

This principle rules out only forms of interstate bargaining and unilateral transnational activities that impose on others terms of interaction that implicate the core elements of human well-being. It does not remove all interstate negotiation from the realm of ordinary, less protective norms of market transactions. It does not rule out all differential advantages for citizens of prosperous countries or activities that might result in differential burdens on other countries. It does not rule out all power differentials across countries. It does rule out unilateral undertakings and modes of negotiation that pose serious threats to human rights. It does rule out forms of subordination, exploitation, and exclusion that are not only unfair by their very nature, but deeply unfair when the core elements of human well-being are at stake, and unjust also because of their causal link to human rights violations.

6.4.2. Double Standards in Agricultural Trade Policy and Climate Change

The current system of regulation of international agricultural trade illustrates the applicability of the Principle of Interstate Reciprocity to the kinds of cross-border transactions and unilateral activities that have garnered the attention of social movements, NGOs, and investigative journalists.[60] At the center of ongoing negotiations are debates over the way agricultural products are treated under international trade rules, codified in multilateral trade agreements, and enforced by the World Trade Organization (WTO).[61]

---

[60] The key points of this example are taken from Powers, "Food, Fairness, and Global Markets."
[61] Food and Agriculture Organization, "The Implications of the Uruguay Round Agreement on Agriculture for Developing Countries" (1995), http://www.fao.org/docrep/w7814e/w7814e05.htm#1.1.3.

On one side of the debate is a bloc of low- and middle-income nations led by the Group of 33, which includes India and China. This bloc argues that global market forces in agricultural trade often conflict with a variety of national social welfare policies and social justice aims, especially those intended to reduce hunger, malnutrition, and food insecurity. On the other side of the debate, a bloc of wealthier nations, including the US, the member states of the European Union, Australia, and Canada, oppose demands for latitude in deciding what government interventions are needed to protect farmers and consumers from the vicissitudes of global markets.

The Group of 33 insists that certain protections for food security programs in low- and middle-income nations be made permanent. The rules currently exempt many such nations from requirements to reduce their agricultural subsidies when they are needed to incentivize agricultural production and maintain enough food for stockholding programs designed to ensure food security.

The primary demand of the US and other affluent nations is the elimination of what is known as the "peace clause." The peace clause ensures that member nations cannot use WTO adjudication procedures to challenge policies that low- and middle-income nations defend as essential to their food security objectives. Bringing agricultural products within the full scope of WTO authority would expose food security programs to the threat of being overridden by the WTO if they were determined to be unduly restrictive of global trade.[62] Affluent nations are pushing such changes as a way of improving the competitive advantage of their own farmers in global commodities markets.

A key point of contention is the long-standing demand by the Group of 33 that wealthy nations eliminate both their own state subsidies for domestic agricultural products and the tariffs they impose on foreign food imports. Under current rules, wealthy nations are allowed to retain the very protectionist agricultural policies that low- and middle-income nations are often forced to abandon as a condition for gaining admission to the WTO and for obtaining loans from the International Monetary Fund (IMF).[63]

---

[62] Kirtika Suneja, "India Opposes US Proposal to Dismantle Price Support and Subsidies in World Trade Organization," *Economic Times* (September 25, 2015), http://articles.economictimes.indiatimes.com/2015-09-25/news/66884503_1_peace-clause-wto-members-subsidies.

[63] Stiglitz, *Globalization and Its Discontents*, 61–101; Darrel Moellendorf, "The World Trade Organization and Egalitarian Justice," in *Global Institutions and Responsibilities*, ed. Christian Barry and Thomas Pogge (Malden, MA: Blackwell, 2005), 148–149.

Critics point to the inherent unfairness of "double standards" in the rules that permit powerful, affluent nations to retain these trade advantages for themselves while perpetuating serious disadvantage for poorer nations.[64]

The unfairness of differential trade advantages built into these demands is highlighted by the fact that the kind of protectionist policies that wealthy countries retain for themselves and oppose for less wealthy countries are among the most damaging to the very goals that defenders of free trade emphasize. In particular, wealthy states have been able to insist on preserving direct price support payments to farmers "coupled" to their level of production.[65] The problem with coupled supports is that they create incentives for farmers in wealthy countries to produce more than the market demands, thereby artificially driving down global commodity prices. Artificially lowered commodity prices have knock-on effects that further harm the global poor. They deprive less affluent countries of agricultural revenue they would have had were markets not distorted by trade policies designed for the benefit of farmers in affluent nations.[66]

Moreover, wealthy nations often dump their excess production in poor nations at prices below the cost of local production, further disadvantaging farmers in developing countries, sometimes putting entire segments of domestic agricultural production out of business. By destroying the ability of farmers in less developed nations to compete effectively, artificially created global surpluses, either sold or given away as part of food aid programs, undermine rather than advance the goal of hunger relief and food security.[67]

---

[64] Oxfam, "Trade Report: Rigged Rules and Double Standards" (2002), http://policy-practice.oxfam.org.uk/publications/rigged-rules-and-double-standards-trade-globalisation-and-the-fight-against-pov-112391; ICTSD (International Centre for Trade and Sustainable Development), "Towards New Rules for Agricultural Markets?" (December 10, 2015), http://www.ictsd.org/bridges-news/bridges/news/towards-new-rules-for-agricultural-markets.

[65] Stefan Tangermann, "Farming Support: The Truth Behind the Numbers," *OECD Observer* (2013), http://www.oecdobserver.org/news/archivestory.php/aid/1223/Farming_support:_the_truth_behind_the_numbers.html#sthash.giLeoWad.dpuf.

[66] Oxfam, "A Recipe for Disaster" (2006), http://policy-practice.oxfam.org.uk/publications/a-recipe-for-disaster-will-the-doha-round-fail-to-deliver-for-development-114122.

[67] The UN estimate for one extended period in the 1990s is that the loss is as much as four times greater than capital inflow from trade liberalization. Oxfam offers estimates of the impact of surplus production on the depression of global prices that the poor receive for their agricultural exports, as a result of dumping. United Nations Committee on Trade and Development (UNCTAD), "Trade and Development Report, 1999," http://unctad.org/en/docs/tdr1999_en.pdf; See also Grant Potter, "Agricultural Subsidies Remain a Staple in the Industrial World," *Vital Signs*, (Worldwatch Institute, February 28, 2014), http://www.worldwatch.org/agricultural-subsidies-remain-staple-industrial-world-0.

Critics therefore argue that rules pertaining to global trade in agriculture products seem to get their priorities exactly backward.[68] Poorer nations have a stronger argument for protectionist policies than affluent countries because they confront a far graver threat of hunger and food insecurity. Moreover, they are subject to double standards imposed through the superior bargaining power of nations that control admission to the WTO and loan conditions for debtor nations. But it is wealthy nations that do not need market protections to meet the basic food and nutrition needs of their citizens that actually receive them. Global trade rules also enable wealthy nations to dump their subsidized goods into other countries, even though the substantial adverse effects on well-being would not be tolerated by affluent nations were the shoe on the other foot.[69]

Other examples of international negotiations that get their priorities backward include attempts to fashion treaties designed to reduce global greenhouse gas emissions that cause global warming. The hottest, poorest, most agriculturally dependent countries that have contributed the least to the problem are being hurt "first and worst" by global warming.[70] Nonetheless, a coalition of large-scale emitters has effectively blocked enforceable requirements to reduce greenhouse gas emissions. What hangs in the balance is the prospect of massive harm to the citizens of island and low-lying countries whose fate is almost entirely in the hands of nations that seek to preserve their higher standards of living at the expense of the global poor.[71] The stakes are enormous. Depleted aquifers, desertification, irregular rainfall, and increases in tropical disease will undermine health through loss of food security and adequate freshwater sources. Loss of coastline and submersion of low-lying areas will produce climate refugees, disrupting established patterns of personal relations and exposing large

---

[68] Paul B. Thompson, *The Ethics of Aid and Trade: US Food Policy, Foreign Competition and the Social Contract* (New York: Cambridge University Press, 1992).

[69] Kym Anderson and Will Martin, "Agricultural Trade Reform and the Doha Development Agenda," *World Economy* 28, no. 9 (2005): 1301–1327.

[70] Madison Powers, "Ethical Challenges Posed by Climate Change: An Overview," in *Moral Theory and Climate Change: Ethical Perspectives on a Warming Planet*, ed. Dale E. Miller and Ben Eggleston (London: Taylor & Francis/Routledge, 2020).

[71] Alex Kirby, "Climate Treaty Races Towards Hazy Future," Climate News Network (October 6, 2016), http://climatenewsnetwork.net/climate-treaty-hazy-future/?utm_source=Climate+News+Network&utm_campaign=83736d6ca0-Treaty_ratification10_6_2016&utm_medium=email&utm_term=0_1198ea8936-83736d6ca0-38767557; Oxfam, "Extreme Carbon Inequality" (2015), https://www.oxfam.org/sites/www.oxfam.org/files/file_attachments/mb-extreme-carbon-inequality-021215-en.pdf.

numbers of displaced people to loss of personal security, leaving them with radically reduced control over their own destinies.[72]

Needless to say, there are empirical disagreements about the likelihood, extent, and preventability of these impacts and normative disagreements over whether the impacts qualify as the kinds of structural injustice our theory identifies as centrally important. We simply note that the principle of interstate reciprocity provides a practical, action-guiding framework within which empirical data can be used to inform the balance between what powerful nations are entitled to do for the sake of their own citizens in light of the constraints imposed by comparable interests at stake for citizens of less powerful nations.

6.4.3. Conclusion

The Principle of Interstate Reciprocity cannot fill all of the gaps in human rights protection in a way that would fully satisfy the Principle of Equal Moral Protection. The principle does not address all of the failures of states that are currently unwilling or unable to fulfill the human rights duties they owe to all those living in their borders. However, adherence to the principle would go a long way toward eliminating the transnational sources of structural unfairness that contribute to human rights deficits in vulnerable nations. And it would deny leaders of failed or corrupt states some critical opportunities to enter into bargains that benefit themselves and other elites but harm their people. The human rights protection afforded by the global order would still be porous and fragile, but it would be less so if the Principle of Interstate Reciprocity were followed.

Because not all human rights deficits are fueled in whole or part by external factors, there would still be a need for more functional states to shoulder secondary responsibilities for the human rights of nationals of other countries. These states may have to step in where other states fail. However, the Principle of Interstate Reciprocity heads off some well-known obstacles to states meeting their human rights obligations at the front end, thereby reducing the likely need for after-the-fact interventions.

---

[72] IPCC 2014, "Summary for Policymakers," in *Climate Change, 2014: Mitigation of Climate Change*, ed. Ottmar Edenhofer et al., Contribution of Working Group III to the Fifth Assessment Report of the Intergovernmental Panel on Climate Change (Cambridge: Cambridge University Press, 2014), https://www.ipcc.ch/pdf/assessment-report/ar5/wg3/ipcc_wg3_ar5_summary-for-policymakers.pdf.

Moreover, we think that the principle offers practical, action-guiding direction for the here and now, constraining interstate bargaining and unilateral imposition of terms of interaction by the powerful over the weak.

That said, the principle's impact will fall short of what proponents of a comprehensive, democratically constituted global state would hope for. They will insist that nothing short of the creation of a politically unified, global institutional moral agent, vested with normative authority and institutional capacities of the sort now possessed only by separate states, can fully satisfy the requirements of our Principle of Equal Moral Protection. For those who reach this judgment, the Principle of Interstate Reciprocity might be endorsed as a principle of transitional justice. However, hopes for democratic supranational institutions have to be measured by the fact that existing institutions do not satisfy the most basic requirements of justice that warrant taking on such tasks, even to a limited degree.

6.5. The Power of Non-State Institutions in the Current Global Order

In both the global and domestic contexts discussed in this and the next two chapters, we emphasize the moral significance of power that can be and often is used to take control over the mechanisms that structure the primary terms of ongoing social interaction. This control by the powerful allows them to extract undeserved benefits from the vulnerable and the desperate. It also allows them to exclude subordinated groups from full participation in the activities and institutions that make possible a decent life. The power to exercise control over the social structure is the power to disregard the interests of subordinate groups, to marginalize their voices, to denigrate their demands as uninformed or unrealistic, and to impugn the motivations behind their demands as products of mere envy or unwarranted fear and suspicion of those in power.

The focus in section 6.4 was on non-reciprocal power relations between countries and their implications for human rights and the specification of human rights duties. In this section, we examine how other forms of global power relations affect the ability of states, particularly low- and middle-income countries, to discharge their domestic human rights duties and responsibilities for structural fairness. Our focus here is on how power is exercised by various supranational institutions, often in combination with powerful states and other non-state institutional agents, in ways that compromise what LMICs can do to protect and advance the interests of their own citizens.

We discuss four examples of unfair power, drawn from activists' complaints lodged against supranational institutions, their donor states, and corporate partners. We start with the mildest form of objection to their exercise of power and shift to more fundamental ones, and we explain why some objections are more important than others.

The least challenging objection to the global status quo expresses concern about the arbitrary use of power and the lack of institutional mechanisms for accountability. The antidote to this lack of accountability is the creation of procedural restraints, in particular the rule of law. Frank Lovett, for example, suggests that one concrete way of understanding what makes institutional power arbitrary is that the "potential exercise of power is not externally constrained by effective rules, procedures, or goals that are common knowledge to all the persons or groups concerned."[73]

This first complaint, when applied to the global arena, focuses on the absence of adequate and effective safeguards for checking the way supranational institutions exercise their power over LMICs. For example, reform-minded critics of the IMF and World Bank argue for greater transparency in decision-making, public disclosure of poverty reduction agreements (formerly known as structural adjustment agreements) entered into with individual countries, and the creation of independent oversight agencies.[74] They call for the institution of robust safeguards for guaranteeing clear practice guidelines in order to mitigate the risk of abuse of what is otherwise assumed to be legitimate power. There is no demand for democratic accountability, such that the composition of the body of power holders is subject to change, or for more or different countries to have seats at the governing table. Also, there is no demand that supranational institutions operate within stricter, independently defined moral limits circumscribing their range of permissible decisions, and there is no fundamental challenge to the right of these institutions to exercise power.

---

[73] Lovett, *A General Theory of Domination and Justice*, 96, 101, 213. Lovett and others in the republican political tradition characterize this as domination. "Domination should be understood as a condition experienced by persons or groups to the extent that they are dependent on those social relationships in which some other person or group wields arbitrary power over them" (2, 20, 119; the same language is used on each page cited). For a more general discussion, see Amy Allen, "Rethinking Power," *Hypatia*, 13, no. 1 (1998): 21–40; Amy Allen, *The Power of Feminist Theory: Domination, Resistance, Solidarity* (Boulder, CO: Westview Press, 1999); and Robert Dahl, "The Concept of Power," *Behavioral Science* 2, no. 3 (1957): 201–215.

[74] Alan Gelb, "World Bank Reorganization: To What End?" Center for Global Development (August 5, 2013), http://www.cgdev.org/blog/world-bank-reorganization-what-end.

A second, more challenging criticism goes further. It is aimed at conditions in which institutions and agents that hold power over matters of collective importance operate undemocratically. The heart of the objection is that those most affected by institutional decisions are excluded from participation in democratic decision-making. The institutions exercise power in ways that are undemocratic because their power is not "offset" or "checked" by the power of those affected by decisions to remove or revoke the authority of power holders through democratic processes.[75] The remedy is to expand the range of decisions that are subject to democratic control, in some cases changing the composition of institutional decision-making bodies in order to allow participation by affected parties who have been excluded from having a say.[76]

This second criticism appears prominently in the work of those who focus on the undemocratic nature of many global institutional power structures. A representative example of this objection is the complaint lodged against trade agreements that build in unfair advantages for developed nations. These advantages so weaken the bargaining power of poorer countries that key decisions affecting them are taken solely on the basis of power politics rather than consensual agreement.[77] This complaint assumes that, in order to have any chance for economic growth that comes from greater integration in the global economy, poorer countries are forced to accept whatever terms are on offer. They have no feasible option for changing the composition of the leadership body or any realistic pathway for exit from the trade regimes these institutions impose.[78] It is in effect a call for remedy through democratization. What is demanded is accountability through the creation of decision mechanisms that give people greater say in how their lives go, by altering the composition of institutional entities that govern important aspects of their lives.

This kind of argument is common among those who press for changes in the governing bodies of institutions such as the WTO, IMF, World

---

[75] Iris Young in some places treats domination as the opposite of democracy. Young, *Justice and the Politics of Difference*, 3. She defines domination as "institutional conditions that inhibit or prevent people from participating in determining their actions or the conditions of their actions" (28).

[76] Bohman, "Republican Cosmopolitanism."

[77] Moellendorf, "The World Trade Organization and Egalitarian Justice."

[78] Stiglitz, *Globalization and Its Discontents*, 61–101; Jürgen Habermas, "Warum Merkels Griechenland-Politik ein Fehler ist"; reprinted in English in *Social Europe* (June 25, 2015), https://www.socialeurope.eu/2015/06/why-angela-merkels-is-wrong-on-greece/.

Bank, or European Union.[79] A similar demand for greater participatory role in decisions affecting matters of global collective life sometimes extends beyond the democratization of subject-matter-specific supranational institutions. This sort of demand is frequently found in arguments for "cosmopolitan democracy."[80] Such proposals scale up traditional arguments for participation in decisions affecting collective life within a single republic to include participatory rights in matters affecting distinctively global forms of interaction or the global commons.

The demand for extending the reach of democratic control is not necessarily an argument for implementing a unitary world government empowered to address every matter of transnational significance. However, the implications of such a demand can often go well beyond what one might assume is required for regulating focal concerns such as global trade, sovereign debt, or economic development.

For example, effective regulation of the causes and consequences of climate change would likely require the creation of new supranational institutions having extensive powers over many aspects of domestic policy and cross-border interaction. Such institutions would necessarily require peremptory authority over sovereign states on a host of matters pertaining to the emission of greenhouse gases. To be effective, they would also have to have sufficient resources, coercive authority, institutional knowledge, and implementation capacities. These additional resources and new capacities would fundamentally alter the range of decisions currently left to separate states. To meet the second objection to the unjust exercise of power, new supranational institutions designed to regulate climate change would need to implement mechanisms for global democratic control over matters not now under any unified institutional control, democratic or otherwise. Put simply, these institutions would have to be governed in ways that ensured all nations were fairly represented, and not under the thumb of the global powerful or left to the judgment and discretion of politically unaccountable technocratic experts.[81]

The third kind of objection moves beyond a demand for democratic accountability. The core idea, elucidated by Philip Pettit, is that power is

---

[79] Buchanan, "Rawls's *Law of Peoples*"; Rakesh Mohan and Muneesh Kapur, "Emerging Powers and Global Governance: Wither the IMF?" (2015) IMF Working Paper 15/219, https://www.imf.org/external/pubs/ft/wp/2015/wp15219.pdf.

[80] Bohman, "Republican Cosmopolitanism."

[81] For an account of the multiple types and broad scope of decisions removed from national democratic control by the European Union, see Peter Mair, *Ruling the Void: The Hollowing of Western Democracy* (London: Verso, 2013), 99–137.

unjust when it can be exercised without justification.[82] Beyond the lack of institutional mechanisms for accountability, the deeper significance of this objection points to the lack of inherent substantive moral limits to the exercise of power. In other words, those who raise objections of this kind are posing a challenge to the subject matter jurisdiction of the power holder. Such objections have to do with a kind of overreach of authority, even in cases in which power is exercised by a democratically functioning deliberative body and the members of that body are subject to removal through democratic processes.

This third complaint is sometimes lodged against the IMF, often operating in conjunction with other regional development banks and private financiers of sovereign debt. It is an objection to the morally unjustified overreach of holders of institutional power. One familiar criticism of foreign lending institutions, for example, is that countries suffer devastating consequences when their domestic economies are forced to adopt budgetary austerity regimes as a condition of continued debt finance and other economic privileges (such as membership in the European Union).[83] Critics of these arrangements often base their objection to these externally imposed budgetary demands on the adverse impact austerity regimes have on the ability of states to protect human rights and secure social justice. For example, the argument often made is that foreign control over domestic social policies, including, for example, pension benefits, wage protections, and economic safety nets, imposes upon vulnerable and dependent nations a moral vision that those who are subject to such control do not share and, at any rate, have a right to determine for themselves.

In effect, the third objection is that institutional power is exercised without the substantive moral constraints needed to permit countries to pursue their own democratically chosen ideals of domestic social justice.[84] The criticism thus concedes that the IMF has some legitimate claim to institutional authority to deal with macroeconomic problems, but only within a narrowly defined portfolio, such as loan payment defaults that have the

---

[82] Philip Pettit, *A Theory of Freedom: From the Psychology to the Politics of Agency* (Oxford: Oxford University Press, 2001), 22.

[83] See Mark Blyth, *Austerity: The History of a Dangerous Idea* (Oxford: Oxford University Press, 2013).

[84] Ronzoni, "The Global Order: A Case of Background Injustice?," 247–249; Ngaire Woods and Amrita Narlikar, "Global Governance and the Limits of Accountability: The WTO, the IMF, and the World Bank," *International Social Science Journal* 53 (2001): 569–583;International Financial Institution Advisory Commission [aka the Meltzer Commission], "The Report of the International Financial Institution Advisory Commission" (2001), Library of Congress, Congressional Research Service, http://www.policyarchive.org/browse-publishers/480.

potential to cause worldwide economic instability. However, critics reject the authority of these supranational institutions to impose on debtor nations their own conception of social justice.[85]

The fourth and most fundamental complaint is that some power is simply illegitimate. It cannot be reclaimed or redeemed by procedural safeguards, transparency-ensuring mechanisms, democratic accountability, or the establishment of moral limits on its exercise. The demand is for nothing less than emancipation. In the case of rule over women by men in patriarchal societies, for example, the moral demand is not for clear rules, a greater voice by women in how they are ruled, or jurisdictional safeguards that ensure that men do not go beyond some established limits on the exercise of their authority over them. The demand is for an end to rule by men.

The demand for emancipation was at the core of the call for an end of colonial rule, and it is present as well in modern-day protests against the effective subordination of client states to the influence of regional or global superpowers. Demands for emancipation are also routinely part of the agenda of peasant farmer movements that seek food sovereignty and an end to what they see as illegitimate external control over critical aspects of their lives.[86]

It is often difficult to determine whether objections lodged against the IMF and various national and private banks amount to demands for moral limits on the exercise of their authority or demands for independence. Both focus on forms of control that are viewed as deeply unjust.

Nonetheless, the global demand for emancipation from illegitimate control extends further, and it includes demands against the supranational institutions that are, in turn, controlled by powerful foreign states. The objection also is lodged in contexts where there is an effective transfer of traditional state authority over the activities of civil society to non-state agents that exercise de facto control over important aspects of state governance and policy. Familiar examples include international financial

---

[85] For a history of how IMF policies eroded national sovereignty over economic policy and subordinated debtor states in the global South to a neoliberal vision of the relation between states and markets, see Jason Hickel, *The Divide: Global Inequality from Conquest to Free Markets* (New York: W. W. Norton, 2018). For a detailed explanation of how institutional components of the European Union, in particular the European Monetary Union, the European Central Bank, and the European Commission, in close cooperation with the IMF, had the same effect on national economic sovereignty of member states, for the same ideological ends, see Wolfgang Streeck, *How Will Capitalism End?* (London: Verso, 2017), 113–141; and Robert Kuttner, *Can Democracy Survive Global Capitalism?* (New York: W. W. Norton, 2018), 121–148.

[86] Institute for Agriculture and Trade Policy, "Towards Food Sovereignty: Constructive Alternatives to the World Trade Organization's Agreement on Agriculture" (2003), http://www.iatp.org/files/Towards_Food_Sovereignty_Constructive_Alternat.pdf.

rating agencies and multinational corporations. Some of these entities have annual revenues that exceed the gross domestic product (GDP) of many countries. As a consequence, they are often in the position to demand tax concessions and other policy prescriptions as a condition for investment. Economically weakened states—even middle-income states—are at the mercy of managers of hypermobile capital and purchasers of unskilled labor and commodities in monopsonistic global markets.

Moreover, the line between routine transnational corporate practices and criminal activity is often blurred. A coalition of UK and African equality and development campaigners, including Global Justice Now, estimates that illicit financial flows, which they define as the illegal movement of cash between countries, account for $68 billion a year, three times as much as the $19 billion Africa receives annually in aid.[87] Moreover, they estimate that African countries received $162 billion in 2015 in loans, aid, and personal remittances, while $203 billion was taken from the continent, either directly through multinationals repatriating profits or illegally by moving money into tax havens.[88]

In response, some civil society groups in vulnerable nations are proposing the elimination of global financial monopolies and the privileged position of the Bretton Woods institutions as lenders of last resort. They demand an end to power relations that make their countries and its peoples dependent upon the combination of demands for tax concessions from mega-lenders in capital markets and austerity and tax reduction policies imposed by the IMF and regional development banks.[89] In particular, they

---

[87] Global Justice Now, "Honest Accounts: 2017: How the World Profits from Africa's Wealth," http://www.globaljustice.org.uk/sites/default/files/files/resources/honest_accounts_2017_web_final_updated.pdf.

[88] Ibid. For an important and unprecedented collaboration among numerous investigative journalists exposing the corruption and complicity of banks and governments in moving money offshore, frequently illegally, see International Committee of Investigative Journalists, "The Panama Papers" (April 3, 2016), https://panamapapers.icij.org/; and International Committee of Investigative Journalists, "The Paradise Papers" (November 5, 2017), https://www.icij.org/investigations/paradise-papers/.

[89] The literature on how much the phenomenon of tax competition reduces the revenue to countries in each bracket of GDP reflects a great deal of ongoing controversy. It may or may not reduce revenue to some countries in ways that undermine their domestic agenda, and some countries may well be net beneficiaries of the tax competition phenomenon, at least for a time. But much of the literature reflects agreement that some countries are adversely affected and that most countries experience a loss in capacity to regulate their own economies free from the enormous constraints imposed as a consequence of the hypermobility of global capital. See http://www.gfintegrity.org/report/illicit-financial-flows-from-developing-countries-2001-2010/. Good discussions of both normative and empirical issues are found in Philipp Genschell, "Globalization, Tax Competition and the Welfare State," *Politics and Society* 30, no. 3 (2002): 245–272; Peter Dietsch, "Tax Competition and Its Effects on Domestic and Global Justice," in *Social Justice, Global Dynamics*, ed. Ayelet Banai, Miriam Ronzoni, and Christian

seek to eliminate the power of the IMF and World Bank to alter domestic social programs to suit their ideological preferences, power which they believe exacerbates the exposure of their compatriots to economic exploitation and political subordination.[90]

On our view, each of these four types of objection to global power relations, and its corresponding remedies, are applicable to certain kinds of global institutional entities, but in some cases the objections are too modest. We certainly want any *legitimate* power holder to exercise power according to transparent rules. However, the concentration of unaccountable power in undemocratic institutions is not only objectionable in itself but likely to promote and worsen the effects of other unfair exercises of globalized power.

Undemocratic institutions in the global arena create opportunities for exploitation and social exclusion in the same way that they do within the domestic context. The relational dynamics behind the tragedy of the natural resource curse and the global dumping of hazardous wastes are obvious examples discussed in the next chapter. Implementing clearer, more transparent rules for the exercise of power that should never have been vested in undemocratic institutions or multinational corporate entities in the first place provides no remedy at all.

The arguments in this section fundamentally challenge many assumptions upon which the current global order is predicated. Powerful states assert the right of national self-determination for themselves, but in effect they often fail to acknowledge the reciprocal claims of other states. Moreover, some if not most feel entitled to use their superior economic and political power to meet their own needs, perpetuate their advantages, and retain their dominance without effective challenge. Power elites tend to be confident in the reasonableness of their prerogatives to shape the terms of national and global economies and fight threats to geopolitical stability, as they deem best. Fundamental questions of fairness in the exercise of power over the world's poor and the vulnerable rarely come from these quarters. Such criticisms are more likely to percolate up from the ranks of the subordinate than emanate from the major sites where power

---

Schemmel (Oxford: Routledge, 2011); and Gabriel Zucman, *The Hidden Wealth of Nations* (Chicago: University of Chicago Press, 2015).

[90] The position of Greece is an obvious recent example of the combined power of private banks, assisted by Germany and other foreign governments, that not only demanded the implementation of a domestic austerity regime but were able to compel debtor nation to accept loan repayment terms that involved no economic penalty for banks that made improvident loans.

and privilege are exercised or from within the institutions that prepare the powerful to take their places in the world.[91]

6.6. Conclusion

In this chapter, we have argued that under the current global order, states are the only agents equipped with both the institutional capacity and the political legitimacy to address both structural unfairness and human rights in a fairly comprehensive manner. That provides reason to assign special responsibility to states that no other agents have. In addition, we have argued that as long as states are the primary vehicle for the pursuit of social justice within their borders and charged with the task of securing the human rights of their citizens, states are justified in their demand for constraints on the exercise of power by other states in establishing the terms of interstate interaction. Because states cannot address the multiple sources of structural unfairness and threats to human rights that originate beyond their borders, we have argued for the Principle of Interstate Reciprocity as a moral constraint on bargaining between powerful and vulnerable states.

We also have argued for the emancipation of sovereign states from illegitimate external power. That demand goes against the exercise of illegitimate power by individual states, a combination of states, undemocratic supranational institutions, corporate entities pursuing their own private good without any legitimate fiduciary relationship to the people whose lives they influence, or as often is the case, some combination of these external powers.

Finally, we have seen numerous ways in which patterns of differential power and advantage within the global order make it more difficult for states to meet their internal responsibilities for human rights and structural fairness. This erosion of state sovereignty and its adverse effects on the ability of states to pursue social justice is highlighted dramatically by findings in a raft of recent publications on the rise of economic inequality within states.[92] The rise of intrastate economic inequality is a global

---

[91] Paul Farmer, *Pathologies of Power* (Berkeley: University of California Press, 2004); Paulo Freire, *Pedagogy of the Oppressed, 30th Anniversary Edition*, trans. Myra Bergman Ramos (London: Bloomsbury Press, 2000).

[92] See, e.g., Branko Milanovic, *Global Inequality: A New Approach for the Age of Globalization* (Cambridge, MA: Harvard University Press, 2016); Thomas Piketty, *Capital in the Twenty-First Century* (Cambridge, MA: Harvard University Press, 2014); Joseph Stiglitz, *The Great Divide: Unequal Societies and What We Can Do About Them* (New York: W. W. Norton, 2015); Francois Bourguinon, *The Globalization of Inequality* (Princeton, NJ: Princeton University Press, 2015); and "World Inequality Report, 2018," https://wir2018.wid.world/.

phenomenon. While its most basic causes are matters of ongoing debate, there is widespread agreement that the combination of global market dynamics and geopolitical alignments creates the context within which repeatable patterns of social stratification arise within countries and sets parameters on the options for state solution.

The upshot is that the phenomenon of intrastate inequality, like inequality between states, is produced and sustained, in part, by the structure of the global order. As a consequence, the implications for the ability of states to secure human rights and structural fairness within their borders must be added to traditional concerns about the impact of global relations and institutions on interstate inequality. Moreover, as we have said many times throughout the book, it is not just about the money. The economists who track the global rise of intrastate economic inequality also point to trends of central interest under our theory. Greater intrastate economic inequality around the world is accompanied by the rise of social and political inequality, the exacerbation of power differentials, and the growing social distance between social groups, whose daily experiences and life prospects diverge so greatly.

CHAPTER 7 | Real-World Examples

THE AIM IN THIS chapter is to provide four compelling examples of routine, malignant forms of structural injustice. We have selected these examples in order to demonstrate how our theory draws support from and is responsive to circumstances of structural injustice around the world. Two examples are chosen from the US, which represents an economically advanced country publicly committed to democratic ideals and the rule of law, and two examples are drawn from low- and middle-income countries (LMICs) in the midst of economic and political transition.

These examples draw upon the perspectives of activists, journalists, and NGOs for reasons we described in chapter 2. In contrast to theories that defend norms of justice on the ground that they can command universal agreement within existing dominant ethical outlooks, we noted that our theory seeks to capture insights from and illustrate what drives the core complaints of social justice movements across a range of cultural and institutional settings.

In addition, we have chosen examples that reveal how every part of our theory comes into play. The examples illustrate how structural unfairness of power and advantage implicate many, if not all, of the core elements of well-being, often in ways that involve human rights violations. Sometimes what results are direct violations of human rights and sometimes violations of duties to protect.

We selected examples from both urban and rural settings, and from within the US and LMICs, for two reasons. First, a theory of structural injustice should have diagnostic relevance in both kinds of geographic settings and in countries that differ in the details of political and economic organization. Second, the fates of rural and urban areas are deeply intertwined, both within and across nations. In many respects, the dynamics of rural–urban interaction within countries resemble the global dynamics between many high-income countries and many middle- and low-income countries, where the separation of consumption and production follows a similar trajectory.

In sections 7.1 and 7.2, we examine environmental sacrifice zones in the US and in LMICs. In sections 7.3 and 7.4, we discuss urban settings, where most of the world's population now lives. We begin in 7.3 with the origins and current conditions of racially segregated cites of the US, and in 7.4 we turn to the realities of informal settlements (or slums) that define the trajectory of rapid urbanization in LMICs.

7.1. National Sacrifice Zones: From Appalachia to Warren County

Environmental activists in the 1970s first brought to widespread public attention the long-term effects of strip-mining coal, describing areas that were forever beyond reclamation as "sacrifice zones," and the term came to refer to other sites of environmental degradation.[1] The term was given a more technocratic, somewhat matter of fact gloss when the National Academies of Science adopted the phrase "national sacrifice zone," also in the 1970s. The National Academies used the term to describe ecological zones in which there is no probability of successful rehabilitation for human purposes, given existing technologies.[2]

The idea of sacrifice zones has since acquired greater currency among environmental justice movements in the US and beyond.[3] They are areas marked by the disproportionate concentration of especially hazardous activities such as mining and smelting, and of oil and gas wellheads and refineries, electronics manufacturing facilities, and insecure storage

---

[1] Department of Energy officials later picked up the term to describe other environmental hazards. Keith Schneider, "Dying Nuclear Plants Give Birth to New Problems," *New York Times* (October 31, 1988), http://www.nytimes.com/1988/10/31/us/dying-nuclear-plants-give-birth-to-new-problems.html?pagewanted=all.

[2] National Research Council (U.S.) Study Committee on the Potential for Rehabilitating Lands Surface Mined for Coal in the Western United States, *Rehabilitation Potential of Western Coal Lands* (Cambridge, MA: Ford Foundation Energy Policy Project; Ballinger, 1974), 85–86.

[3] For example, see three documentary films on sacrifice zones: an environmental activist film from Brazil by Emilie Romero, "The Sacrifice Zone: A Short Documentary" (2013), https://sacrificezone.wordpress.com/2013/02/12/about-2/; a film about an activist campaign against sacrifice zones in Germany and the Netherlands, Stichting Fossielvrij NL, "Sacrifice Zones in Germany and the Netherlands" (2016), https://gofossilfree.org/nl/sacrifice-zones-in-germany-and-the-netherlands/; and an Australian film about geographically concentrated gas production facilities, Great Artesian Basin Protection Group Inc., "Sacrifice Zone: A Movie About the Real Gas Crisis in Australia" (2017), https://chuffed.org/project/sacrificezone.

deposits or dumping sites of highly toxic chemical substances.[4] In addition to the byproducts from mining and energy extraction, the list of toxic substances includes e-wastes, mercury and lithium batteries, jet fuel, concentrated animal farm operations (CAFO) effluent and emissions, nuclear wastes, chemically saturated water discharged from factories, and airborne particulates absorbed by lungs, soil, and plants.[5]

Sacrifice zones are often known as "fence-line communities."[6] They are the "hot spots" of chemical pollution affecting those who live immediately adjacent to heavily polluting industries. These areas are described as sacrifice zones because they are among the most polluted and poisoned places on the planet. The most affected communities often see not only the land but also themselves as written off, the inevitable price of industrial progress.[7] The overwhelming empirical evidence shows that although sites of extraction are determined by where the resources are, the location of most toxic hazards is no accident. Moreover, the lack of monitoring and regulation, which is commonplace in extraction zones and other toxic sites, is frequently not a mere oversight or failure to plan for unintended, unexpected consequences.

The efforts of environmental justice movements, backed by decades of research and litigation, show that sacrifice zones in the US are concentrated in relatively powerless communities lacking both the economic and organizational resources to mount effective political resistance.[8] Such

---

[4] For example, see this discussion of the Apalachicola River, one of the most polluted bodies of water in the US, perhaps beyond the tipping point because of lax federal and tristate regulation. Earthjustice, "Conservationists Sue to Stop Toxic Coal Ash Pollution Leaking into Apalachicola River," http://earthjustice.org/news/press/2014/conservationists-sue-to-stop-toxic-coal-ash-pollution-leaking-into-apalachicola-river.

[5] CAFO, originally defined by the US Environmental Protection Agency, refers to a concentrated animal feeding operation. For discussion of CAFOs and ecological sacrifice zones, see http://www.cafothebook.org/theissue_9.htm.

[6] Lesley Fleischman and Marcus Franklin, "Fumes across the Fence-Line: The Health Impacts of Air Pollution from Oil & Gas Facilities on African American Communities" (NAACP Clean Air Task Force, 2017), http://www.naacp.org/wp-content/uploads/2017/11/Fumes-Across-the-Fence-Line_NAACP_CATF.pdf.

[7] See, e.g., J. W. Randolph, quoting from the coal production expert Jeff Goodall: "If we simply increase consumption, we will be condemning large areas of the country, including eastern Kentucky and southern West Virginia, to national sacrifice zones . . . The biggest problem with our bounty of coal is not what it does to our mountains or the atmosphere, but what it does to our minds. It preserves the illusion that we don't have to change our lives." J. W. Randolph, "Appalachia: National Sacrifice Zone," *Appalachian Voices* (June 27, 2006), http://appvoices.org/2006/06/27/1174/. Jeff Goodell, *Big Coal: The Dirty Secret Behind America's Energy Future* (Boston: Houghton Mifflin, 2007).

[8] References to extensive empirical documentation along with vivid firsthand stories from activists and residents of twelve US communities can be found in Steve Lerner, *Sacrifice Zones: The Front Lines of Toxic Chemical Exposure in the United States* (Cambridge, MA: MIT Press, 2010).

communities are the easiest, cheapest places to locate new production facilities. And for naturally occurring extraction sites, the inhabitants of surrounding areas are relatively easy to control socially and politically. Environmental activists have long complained that sacrifice zones are largely clustered in communities of color or of poor white people who live on the "wrong side of the tracks" and in "throw-away communities."[9] Indeed, many environmental historians trace the origins of the environmental justice movement in the US to citizens' resistance to the dumping of polychlorinated biphenyls (PCBs) in Warren County, North Carolina, followed by state plans to build a hazardous waste landfill for depositing the contaminated soil in Shocco, a rural town in Warren County. Of note, at the time of the PCBs dumping, Warren County was near the bottom of the state's counties in income and was 75 percent African American.[10]

7.1.1. The Legacy of Appalachia

Central to the idea of a sacrifice zone is the prospect of long-term, irreversible adverse effects on the people as well as the land. Most prominent in discussions about the impact on human beings is what happens to the education, health, and overall life prospects of the children living there, not only immediately but for many generations after the coal is stripped or the timber clear-cut. It is not only the land that is destroyed; it is also the future of the land's children.

Harry Caudill famously captures the essential complaint that deprivation in the development of knowledge and understanding affects the children of the Appalachian and Cumberland Plateau communities of Kentucky and Tennessee:

---

[9] Harry M. Caudill, *Night Comes to the Cumberlands: A Biography of a Depressed Area* (Boston: Little, Brown, 1963); John Gaventa, *Power* and *Powerlessness: Quiescence & Rebellion in an Appalachian Valley* (Urbana, University of Illinois Press, 1982). The underlying sentiment of abandonment is echoed but in more expansive terms by Chris Hedges and Joe Sacco in *Days of Destruction, Days of Revolt* (New York: Nation Books, 2014). They describe economically isolated, environmentally decimated communities across the country as "internal colonies" that have been reduced to "sacrifice zones," where their populations are treated as superfluous by corporate power and their fates are largely ignored by political elites.

[10] See Drew G. Murphy, "Environmental Justice and the Law" (January 17, 2017), https://drewgmurphy.com/2017/01/10/the-origins-of-environmental-justice/. This essay that appears on the Duke Environmental Justice webpage describes its mission to collect oral histories from activists. The banner on the homepage of their website, quoting Cary Grant, captures what we mean when we say that "what happens here happens elsewhere": "See it would be one thing if this was in one place . . . that you couldn't find any similarity anywhere else. Just take a look."

They [the mining companies] have produced what is probably the most seriously depressed region in the nation . . . They have brought economic depression, to be sure, and it lies like a gray pall over the whole land. But the deeper tragedy lies in the depression of the spirit which has fallen upon so many of the people, making them, for the moment at least, listless, hopeless and without ambition. The essential element of the plateau's malaise lies in the fact that for a hundred and thirty years [as of 1963] it has exported its resources, all of which—timber, coal, and even crops—have to be wrested violently from the earth. The nation has siphoned off hundreds of millions of dollars' worth of its resources while returning little of lasting value. For all practical purposes the plateau has long constituted a colonial appendage of the industrial East and Middle West, rather than an integral part of the nation generally. The decades of exploitation have in large measure exhausted the region . . . Even more ruinous than the loss of its physical resources is the disappearance of the plateau's best human material. Most of the thousands who left were the people who recognized the towering importance of education in the lives of their children . . . From the beginning, the coal and timber companies insisted on keeping all, or nearly all, the wealth they produced. They were unwilling to plow more than a tiny part of the money they earned back into the schools, libraries, health facilities, and other institutions essential to a balanced, pleasant, productive and civilized society."[11]

A variant of the concern about the impact of sacrifice zones on the well-being and future of children focuses on exposure to the high concentrations of toxins which these zones so frequently entail. The incidence of ill health from exposure to toxic chemicals is dose-response-dependent, meaning that those who live and work near the sites of effluent discharge and release of airborne pollutants are at greatest risk for the greatest magnitude of disease burden. The scope of the problem is in part a function of the nearly 120,000 chemicals used in homes and industrial workplaces, most of which have not undergone extensive testing for neurotoxicity, teratogenicity, and other health effects. The problem is also a function of chemical "intensification," meaning that "synthetic chemicals are fast becoming the largest constituents of waste streams and pollution around the world," thereby increasing the exposure of humans and habitats to chemical hazards.[12] Illnesses from exposure to industrial and agricultural chemicals

---

[11] Caudill, *Night Comes*, 325–326.
[12] United Nations Environment Programme (UNEP), "Global Chemicals Outlook" (2012), http://www.unep.org/chemicalsandwaste/what-we-do/policy-and-governance/global-chemicals-outlook.

are among the top five leading causes of death worldwide.[13] Health effects include cancer, cognitive impairment, organ damage, respiratory issues that can lead to pneumonia, and diarrhea and vomiting that can lead to dehydration.[14]

All people who live or work in close proximity to dangerous chemicals are at risk of suffering their ill effects, but children are especially vulnerable to them. Children are smaller and thus can be harmed by exposure levels that may not be toxic or as toxic to adults. Small children also are much more likely to put their hands into their mouths and thus are at increased risk of ingesting toxins that may be present in the ground, for example. Perhaps most important, many toxins, especially neurotoxins, have an outsized negative effect on the developing organism. This outsized effect is not limited to in utero exposure. The brain continues to develop well past birth, and exposures of the wrong sort at any time in the developmental trajectory can have disastrous effects on a range of functions, including cognitive capacities.

Another set of concerns about the impact of sacrifice zones on human well-being and especially, again, on prospects for future generations focuses on the overall social impact of an economy built on one-sided extraction of wealth in which those who benefit are largely social groups far from the site of extraction and its lasting environmental side effects. The broader, longer-term social consequences for the community include the downward pressure exerted on the tax base needed for infrastructure, the crowding out of alternative employment opportunities for young people coming up, the progressive deterioration of prevailing wages, and of course environmental degradation that imposes vast negative externalities on surrounding farmers and livestock producers.

Sacrifice zones are often single-industry communities, or "company towns." There is an extensive literature on the redistributive implications of this kind of non-diversified economic arrangement, especially for the local tax base.[15] When a local economy is heavily dependent upon a single employer or business sector, it loses political leverage against demands for

---

[13] One ranking of the ten most significant toxic chemical problems, based on estimated contribution to disease burden measured in Disability-Adjusted Life Years (DALYs), is available from Green Cross Switzerland and Pure Earth, "The World's Worst Pollution Problems, 2016: The Toxics Beneath Our Feet,"

[14] Children's Environmental Health Network, "Some Children Are at Greater Risk than Others," http://www.cehn.org/wp-content/uploads/2015/11/Some_Children_are_at_greater_risk14.pdf.

[15] See, e.g., Fiona McGillivray, *Privileging Industry: The Comparative Politics of Trade and Industrial Policy* (Princeton, NJ: Princeton University Press, 2004), especially chapter 7 on the redistributive effects of company towns.

tax concessions and other forms of publicly funded subsidy. These include demands for tax rate reductions, tax exemptions and a temporary moratorium on taxation or tax increases, the issuance of tax-free, publicly funded bonds for building private facilities, and demands for access roads and port facilities paid for by taxpayers.

When governments comply with these demands, the knock-on effects can be considerable. The revenue stream for future-oriented investment in infrastructure, public health, and education is diminished. Funds that might be used for promoting diversified economic development are diverted toward less economically beneficial uses. Company towns also skew local prevailing wages, resulting in long-term downward pressure on the incomes of workers in the region.[16] And if a local industry or the whole sector begins to fail, the tax base also craters. All of these effects are especially heavily borne by subsequent generations whose life prospects are dampened well after the heyday of a once-thriving industry passes.[17]

Coal and timber industries are not the only contributors to the sacrifice zones heavily concentrated in low-income rural communities in the US. The business model works wherever wealth can be extracted while leaving the health and environmental burdens behind for others to experience and address. There is a well-established pattern of a disproportionate concentration of environmentally destructive industries in the poorest areas in the rural southern US. The gravitational pull to the region is not entirely due to the fact that it is where many natural resources exist; other common denominators include lax regulatory laws, onerous legal requirements for successful lawsuits, and the overwhelming aim of political leaders to attract or retain jobs, even when these jobs are both hazardous to health and low-paying. Moreover, resource extraction is disproportionately concentrated in regions where the potentially offsetting power of organized community groups is weak and the economies are struggling. Industrial processing facilities and toxic waste dumps are sited in these communities as well, again especially in the rural southern US.[18]

---

[16] From 1984 to 2004, the average coal miner's per-shift productivity more than doubled, while wages declined by 20 percent (adjusted for inflation). Goodell, *Big Coal*.

[17] The long-term, cross-generational effects of company towns are described in John Gaventa's account of the evolving role of coal companies in Appalachian communities. He traces the shift from primary reliance upon state force to shape every aspect of daily lives of the miners during the era known as the Coal Wars to a new era of power, where the mining companies acquired control over all aspects of the machinery of the state and, hence, wholesale control of the immediate options and overall life prospects of the region's residents. See Gaventa, *Power and Powerlessness*, 47–83.

[18] This constellation of factors cited by activists is well documented in Robert Bullard, *Dumping in Dixie: Race, Class and Environmental Quality* (Boulder, Co: Westview Press, 1990).

7.1.2. Repeatable Patterns

The same incentivizing market dynamics and predictable systematic effects of geographically concentrated, highly polluting industries are found across the spectrum of industries. For example, large-scale poultry and livestock facilities tend to be located not simply where available land is cheap and plentiful, but where there are weak unions, a surplus of flexible labor, low prevailing wages, and weak labor and environmental laws. Local and regional labor markets are transformed in the same way they are in coal country. Regional hubs or clusters of poultry and livestock production facilities usually replace a diversified employment base. When there are only a few large employers in a regional market, prospective employees have limited economic alternatives and little bargaining power. The result is an expansion in the surplus of flexible labor, a cascading reduction of prevailing wages, and a corresponding shift in power that undermines the prospects of those living in these communities to exercise a significant degree of control over their own destinies.[19]

Significant environmental degradation is yet a further result, as runoff of fertilizer and animal waste pollutes the surrounding air, water, and soil.[20] This pattern holds as well in the geographic concentration of oil and gas production and refinery facilities. While some of the particulars are different, many of the enabling factors are similar, whether the industry is mining, concentrated animal production, logging, or oil and gas.

These industries are concentrated in economically distressed areas where the potentially offsetting power of organized citizens is weak. However, poverty and the powerlessness that it engenders are often not all that is in play.[21] Dozens of empirical studies show that in some instances, poverty is not even the centrally important variable. One representative

---

[19] Douglas H. Constance, "The Southern Model of Broiler Production and Its Global Implications," *Culture and Agriculture* 30, no 1. (2008): 17–31.

[20] Ibid. See also Larry L. Burmeister, "Lagoons, Litter and the Law: CAFO Regulation as Social Risk Politics," *Southern Rural Sociology* 18, no. 2 (2002): 56–87; and Pew Environment Group, *Big Chicken: Pollution and Industrial Poultry Production in America* (2011), http://www.pewtrusts.org/~/media/legacy/uploadedfiles/peg/publications/report/PEGBigChickenJuly2011pdf.pdf.

[21] One of the most frequently cited concentrations of oil refinery and other heavily polluting industrial facilities is the eighty-five-mile stretch of the Mississippi River between Baton Rouge and New Orleans. There are more than 140 industrial plants in this deep pocket of poverty and communities of color. It has earned the nickname "Cancer Alley," but as the environmental epidemiologist Ellen Silbergeld notes, the science is just not sufficiently fine-grained to sort through the confounding variables within such a small population. John McQuaid, "'Cancer Alley': Myth or Fact?," *Times-Picayune* (May 24, 2000, updated August 12, 2016), http://www.nola.com/politics/index.ssf/2000/05/cancer_alley_myth_or_fact.html.

study, for example, found that African American households with incomes between $50,000 and $60,000 live in neighborhoods that are, on average, more polluted than white neighborhoods of households with annual incomes of less than $10,000.[22] Another nationwide study found that people of color make up 56 percent of those living within two miles of the country's major commercial hazardous waste facilities, and they account for a whopping 69 percent of the population in neighborhoods in which multiple such facilities are clustered.[23]

Evaluating the health risks attributable to exposure to toxic chemicals produced in facilities sited in poor communities of color is complicated. The housing of many of the people affected is substandard, their jobs expose them to high levels of toxins, their family members bring toxic materials home on their work clothing, or crumbling infrastructure exposes them to other chemical hazards. However, for toxic sites other than ones associated with extraction, the evidence points to two further aspects of the correlation between race and poverty and sites of toxic pollution.

First, a class of "hyper-polluters—the worst-of-the-worst—account for a disproportionate amount of the toxic pollution and in doing so, they disproportionately expose communities of color and low-income populations to chemical releases."[24]

Second, there is the issue of which occurs first, polluters, who locate their facilities among the poor generally and poor communities of racial minorities, or people with few affordable options for housing who settle in heavily polluted locations. One study demonstrated that in the preponderance of commercial hazardous waste facilities sited from 1966 to

---

[22] Liam Downey and Brian Hawkins, "Race, Income, and Environmental Inequality in the United States," *Sociological Perspectives* 5, no. 4 (2008): 759–781.

[23] United Church of Christ, Commission on Racial Justice, Toxic Waste and Race in the United States, *A National Report on the Racial and Socioeconomic Characteristics of Communities Surrounding Hazardous Waste Sites* (New York: United Church of Christ, 1987); Robert Bullard et al., *Toxic Wastes and Race at Twenty* (New York: United Church of Christ, 2007).

[24] Mary B. Collins, Ian Munoz, and Joseph JaJa, "Linking 'Toxic Outliers' to Environmental Justice Communities," *Environmental Research Letters* 11 (2016), http://iopscience.iop.org/1748-9326/11/1/015004. The authors ask: "Are particular communities (low income and/or those of color) disproportionately impacted by producers who generate a disproportionate amount of pollution?" They point out that in discussions of the racism–poverty linkage to proximity to toxic hazard sites, the notion of disproportionality has two dimensions—disproportionality in the production of environmental harm (polluter disproportionality) and disproportionality in exposure. In the worst of the worst, both forms of disproportionality are in play. A small minority of producers, polluting at levels far exceeding group averages, generate the majority of overall exposure to industrial toxics. Of 15,758 industrial sites, only 809 "toxic outlier" sites—about 5 percent of the total—were responsible for 90 percent of the pollution. Moreover, these toxic outliers disproportionately expose communities of color and low-income populations to chemical releases. The authors refer to the linked phenomenon as "double disproportionality."

1995, the polluters sited their facilities in existing poor communities, especially communities of color. They located either where there were heavy concentrations of low-income and non-white residents or where "white flight" was already well under way.[25]

Community awareness of multi-source toxic exposure, together with the community perception that low-income communities of color have a bulls-eye on their backs, has led to a larger social movement that has applied the umbrella label "environmental racism" to the wider constellation of concerns.[26]

The environmental justice movement in the US has expanded its understanding of the racial dimensions of industrial toxic exposure beyond the highly publicized problems in the refinery districts of the Mississippi Delta and the landfills of Warren County, North Carolina. In 1991, the First National People of Color Environmental Leadership Summit was held in Washington, DC. The outcome was a list of seventeen environmental justice principles that recognized the parallels between the racially disproportionate effects of the ways in which toxic substances are produced, stored, and concentrated in communities of color in the US and in communities of color in the global South.[27]

7.2. The Globalization of Sacrifice Zones

What happens with sacrifice zones in the US happens everywhere. At the front end, many of the same market incentives and political dynamics are at work, with very similar long-term consequences for land and future generations at the back end. In LMICs, however, there are some twists to the story that often exacerbate the adverse effects on well-being and entrench even deeper differentials of power and advantage.

---

[25] Paul Mohai and Robin Saha, "Which Came First, People or Pollution? Assessing the Disparate Siting and Post-Siting Demographic Change Hypotheses of Environmental Injustice," *Environmental Research Letters* 10, no. 11 (2015), (http://iopscience.iop.org/1748-9326/10/11/115008.

[26] For an informative history of this movement and its focus on the effects on children, see Corliss Wilson Outley, "The Challenge of Environmental Justice for Children: The Impact of Cumulative Disadvantageous Risks," *Environmental Justice* 23, no. 4 (2006): 49–56. See also Robert Bullard, "Environmental Justice: It's More than Waste Facility Siting," *Social Science Quarterly* 77, no. 3 (1996): 493–499.

[27] The principles are available in David Naguib Pellow, *Resisting Global Toxics: Transnational Movements for Environmental Justice* (Cambridge, MA: MIT Press, 2007), app., 245–247.

7.2.1. The Natural Resource Curse

We start with a puzzle in developmental economics, the answer to which Appalachian and Mississippi Delta communities will grasp readily from firsthand experience. Economists and observers of international politics and trade have long noticed that some poor nations blessed with natural resources—especially when blessed with large amounts of one scarce resource—often fare worse economically than other poor nations. This is known as the resource curse.[28] Why should the presence of rich reserves of resources be so commonly associated with poor economic performance and the perpetuation of poverty? One would think that an abundance of natural resources needed by the developed world would offer a low- or middle-income country an exceptional opportunity to get out of poverty.

However, the truth is more complicated. Foreign investors in extractive industries—in particular those that extract non-renewable resources—have few incentives to remain present for the long term, invest in a country's economic future, or work toward a more democratic political culture. The pattern is familiar. Foreign investors extract profits from a country's resources while simultaneously depleting them. They produce goods for the global affluent, invest little to improve the local economy or relieve poverty, leave behind environmental degradation, convert smallholders to low-wage transient workers, and dispossess many traditional landholders.[29] The presence of vast stores of natural resources invites exploitation from the outside while simultaneously enabling autocratic leaders and their cronies to finance their own lifestyles and build up arms and infrastructure that allow them to remain in power through repression and elaborate systems of bribery and patronage.[30]

It is this enabling role of the foreign investor that gives the global South version of the sacrifice zone its special and devastating twist. In addition to the dire consequences for local communities of extractive industries in the rural US, the collaboration between foreign investors and governments often leads to a tightening of the grip of regimes already notorious for human rights violations, now economically incentivized to double down

---

[28] Paul Collier, *The Plundered Planet: Why We Must—and How We Can—Manage Nature for Global Prosperity* (Oxford: Oxford University Press, 2010).

[29] Ibid.; Macartan Humphreys, Jeffery Sachs, and Joseph Stieglitz, *Escaping the Resource Curse* (New York: Columbia University Press, 2007); Worldwatch Institute, "The Hidden Shame of the Global Industrial Economy" (2004), http://www.worldwatch.org/node/543.

[30] Collier, *The Plundered Planet*, 132–159; Leif Wenar, "Property Rights and the Resource Curse," *Philosophy and Public Affairs* 36, no. 1 (2008): 2–32; Lief Wenar, *Blood Oil: Tyrants, Violence, and the Rules That Run the World* (Oxford: Oxford University Press, 2015).

on those violations.[31] Governments' efforts to secure the well-being of their citizens are not necessarily in the economic self-interest of foreign investors. For example, governmental policies might require foreign investors to attend to the working conditions of those they employ and mitigate the negative externalities that their activities impose on others. Foreign investors, of course, do have an interest in the state's guarantee of a stable business climate. However, the nature of that interest is not what many outsiders might expect. The overwhelming economic incentive is to support governmental policies that get out of the way of doing business, clearing the path of regulatory hurdles, labor protests, and opposition from landowners and riparian right-holders.

The World Bank has been notably sympathetic to the interests of foreign investors over the interests of local constituencies. Since 2003 the World Bank has maintained a registry known as the "Doing Business Report." It ranks 189 countries based on the ease of doing business. In 2014, the Bank claimed to have inspired over a quarter of the 2,100 reforms registered since its creation. However, the "reforms" intended to improve the ease of doing business typically involve lower labor and environmental standards, reduced taxation of corporations, diminished business contributions to social security funds, and easier and cheaper transfers of public lands.[32] The registry has drawn heavy criticism from local social movements and NGOs from around the world. A coalition of 260 human rights groups, trade unions, and civil society groups recently urged the Bank to eliminate the "Doing Business" registry. However, at the insistence of the wealthy G8 countries, the Bank instead instituted a similar registry for global agricultural land investment, known as "Enabling the Business of Agriculture."[33]

---

[31] It is important to note the parallels between the historical US experience and the contemporary systemic violence and threats to personal security so common now in extractive industries within some LMICs. The history of US coal mining at the earliest phases of exploration and production is marked by the legacy of violent suppression of protest and resistance by armed private security forces and state police. The 1914 Colorado Coalfield War, culminating in the Ludlow Massacre and the 1921 Blair Mountain Uprising in Logan, West Virginia, and the 1912–1913 Paint Creek–Cabin Creek Strike in Kanawha County, West Virginia, are three important examples of the bloody incidents of the Coal Mine Wars between 1890 and 1930. Students of the Paint Creek incident will recall the leadership role of Mary Harris Jones (aka Mother Jones). Western states incidents are well documented in Thomas G. Andrews, *Killing for Coal: America's Deadliest Labor War* (Cambridge, MA: Harvard University Press, 2010), and West Virginia incidents (although a bit thin on the Blair Mountain incident) are discussed in David Corbin, *Gun Thugs, Rednecks, and Radicals: A Documentary History of the West Virginia Mine Wars* (Oakland, CA: PM Press, 2011).

[32] Peiley Lau, "The World Bank's Doing Business Rankings: Relinquishing Sovereignty for a Good Grade," http://www.oaklandinstitute.org/ world-bank%E2%80%99s-doing-business-rankings-relinquishing-sovereignty-good-grade.

[33] GRAIN, "The G8 and Land Grabs in Africa" (March 11, 2013), https://www.grain.org/article/ entries/4663-the-g8-and-land-grabs-in-africa.

7.2.2. Do the Benefits Offset the Burdens?

Why then might some developmental economists and institutions such as the World Bank and the IMF be so enthusiastic about promoting direct foreign investment in LMICs, even in sectors prone to the known hazards associated with the natural resource curse? The answer, in short compass, is impact on gross domestic product (GDP).

GDP is a measure of aggregate economic production in a country. Other things being equal, a rise in GDP translates into a rise in the standard of living and therefore the overall well-being of a country. Moreover, a predictive feature of much economic theory, increasingly backed up by a considerable amount of empirical evidence, points to the importance of increased GDP as a vehicle for poverty relief. So far, so good. Often GDP does go up with the development of new extractive industries, just as proponents of greater foreign direct investment in developing economies hope for and predict. But GDP is often a poor proxy for how well a country or segments of its population are faring. GDP can go up even if most of the wealth departs the country, leaving gross national product (GNP)— the amount of money that stays within the nation—unimproved. In fact, that scenario is one of the main problems that the natural resource curse identifies. Much of the wealth that is created by extractive industries does not come from the sale of raw materials such as diamonds, minerals, oil, and gas. Firms based in developed countries often pay little for those resources, and most of the market value is added through the processes of manufacture and fabrication. The real profits to be had are in the commercially tradable finished goods sold to the global affluent, profits generated through processes and transactions that occur outside the countries where the natural resources were extracted.[34]

Moreover, much of the wealth that does stay in the country does not get distributed to the poor or invested for the sake of improving the well-being of future generations. The standard scenario is one in which political cronies, corrupt government officials, and the rising urban middle classes capture most of whatever is left of the economic gains from direct foreign investment in extractive industries.

Economists refer to such costs as "negative externalities," costs imposed on parties "external" to the exchange. Economic theory objects to negative externalities because overall efficiency is undermined when the true social cost of an activity fails to be reflected in the market price. For us,

---

[34] Rodrik, *The Globalization Paradox.*

what matters are issues of fairness when the costs of a market transaction are borne by people other than those who are the parties to it and who share its benefits. Standard examples of costs include environmental degradation and adverse health effects from industrial or agricultural pollution. In such cases, parties to the transaction can prosper by offloading the costs of doing business, including the resultant health and environmental risks, onto others. This offloading of costs can be and often is a key component of an overall seriously unfair pattern of advantage in economies heavily structured by the way a single industry—particularly an extractive industry—is organized.

Another common negative externality or side effect of state-sponsored foreign direct investment in extractive industries is the rural poor's dispossession of traditional ancestral lands. Often, those whose lands are taken for the private purposes of others have no legal title to back up the claim to their homes. The United Nations estimates that 4 billion people live outside the protection of basic rules of law establishing rights to property and remedies for dispute resolution.[35] In theory, these lands are held in common by the citizens of a country. However, they are easily expropriated by the state, which then makes the lands available for use by local elites or foreign business interests that pay the state for mining rights or for establishing large agricultural enterprises.

Grossly unequal systems of property ownership are unfair and unacceptable for obvious reasons. They are particularly problematic for the rural poor because a lack of any publicly known, regularly enforced system of transferable property rights works to ensure that the rural poor remain poor. Not having legal title to ancestral lands not only means high risk of dispossession. It also means that the consequences of dispossession are all the greater. It limits access to credit, undermines opportunities for economic improvement, and leaves the poorest segment of society at the absolute mercy of ruling elites and foreign businesses. Ultimately, the lack of legal title undermines the prospects of the rural poor and the prospects of subsequent generations for leading self-determining lives, now and even more so when the resources are depleted.

There is a second respect in which GDP is often a seriously misleading indicator of a country's well-being. GDP measures only current aggregate

---

[35] United Nations Commission on the Legal Empowerment of the Poor, *Making the Law Work for Everyone*, vol. 1: *Report of the Commission on the Legal Empowerment of the Poor* (2008), https://www.un.org/ruleoflaw/blog/document/making-the-law-work-for-everyone-vol-1-report-of-the-commission-on-legal-empowerment-of-the-poor/.

economic output. Building prisons and selling cigarettes increase current aggregate economic output—GDP—but not all increases in GDP are on a par in terms of the more basic aim of improving human well-being, now and over the long haul. Increases in GDP fail to register the possibility that, over the long term, economic activities that initially enhance GDP will be self-defeating. Extractive industries, as we have seen, leave behind environmental degradation and environmentally mediated health risks of the sort we described in the US context. Much of the burden falls on the next generation, whose health is affected adversely at critical developmental stages and where the resources needed to address their problems have been "plundered" (in Paul Collier's famous phrase).

Moreover, the same kinds of problems that plague company towns seriously damage the economies of entire nations. The focus on a single export commodity often results in what is commonly known as the "commodity trap," a condition in which a country lacking a diversified economy has few economic alternatives. Over time, this approach can lock in a variety of long-term disadvantages.[36] Economies that are too narrowly based on non-renewable resources or another single commodity lose out in a multitude of ways. They are more significantly subject to precipitous losses from currency fluctuations and often devastating, sudden reductions of income from commodity price drops.

Even members of the middle classes of LMICs are often made more vulnerable over the longer term by a phenomenon known as the "Dutch Disease." In the Dutch Disease, intense activity in one sector of the economy, typically a natural resource or monocrop agricultural industry, results in reduced activity in other sectors of the economy. This is because the global sale of the natural resource or single commodity generally strengthens a developing nation's currency. The strengthened currency makes other exports from the country more expensive for international buyers, and thus less competitive on the world market.[37] From the standpoint of economic elites, the lack of competitiveness of other exports may be of little consequence, as they are prospering from the enhanced revenues generated by the concentrated export. But for many low- and middle-income segments of society whose purchasing power is thereby eroded, a strengthened currency is often a huge problem. Moreover, because these redistributive effects tend to be long-term, current gains in

---

[36] Rodrik, *The Globalization Paradox*, 156.

[37] "What the Dutch Disease Is, and Why It's Bad," *The Economist* (November 5, 2014), http://www.economist.com/blogs/economist-explains/2014/11/economist-explains-2.

GDP for the fortunate few have to be analyzed to determine not only the current impact on inequalities in wealth and well-being but also the impact on future generations.[38]

7.2.3. The New Natural Resource Curse

Wealthy nations and multinational corporations are not only looking for energy sources, strategic minerals, and rare earth material. They are searching the world over for dwindling land and water resources. Especially attractive are lands that can be leased or purchased in low-income countries where land is extremely cheap and governance is weak.[39] The primary purpose is to establish large-scale agricultural production facilities designed to feed the citizens of wealthier countries. Critics argue that we are witnessing a "global land grab"—a pattern of resource acquisition that threatens the long-term food security of the global poor and makes more fragile the land tenure of many of the world's most vulnerable people.[40]

Purchasing or leasing land in poorer countries offers foreign investors the prospect of substantial economic gains without having to make significant long-term financial commitments to the economic well-being and environmental quality of the communities in which they operate. Moreover, it is not clear how beneficial such arrangements are for the host countries, even in the short term. Studies of the prevailing modes of purchase and leasing arrangements show that often these agreements are entered into by governments for little or no direct economic remuneration, offering little beyond the vague and unenforceable promise of overall increase in GDP.[41]

---

[38] Dani Rodrik has identified empirically a more general problem, namely that staking the lion's share of an economic development strategy on international trade can have profound redistributive effects within developing countries. For every dollar of increase in a developing country's GDP achieved through increased international trade, roughly $50 of income is transferred from the lowest economic strata to the middle- and upper-income strata. In addition, the same groups of people with the lowest skills tend to get hit hardest with each successive upward tick in GDP. Rodrik, *The Globalization Paradox*, 55–61.

[39] Center for Human Rights and Global Justice, *Foreign Land Deals and Human Rights: Case Studies on Agricultural and Biofuel Investment* (New York: NYU School of Law, 2010).

[40] Karl Klare, *The Race for What's Left: The Global Scramble for the World's Last Resources* (New York: Picador Books, 2012), 183–208; Michael Kugelman and Susan L. Levenstein, *The Global Farms Race: Land Grabs, Agricultural Investment, and the Scramble for Food Security* (Washington, DC: Island Press, 2013); Fred Pearce, *The Land Grabbers: The New Fight Over Who Owns the Earth* (Boston: Beacon Press, 2012).

[41] "An Online Repository of Open Land Contracts," https://www.openlandcontracts.org/. This website hosts a massive databank of contract documents and details regarding acquisition.

There is much yet to learn about the ultimate extent and impact of the global land grab.[42] Still, some analysts and activists are already chronicling harms that some developing countries are experiencing.[43] They include smallholders' dispossession of existing farmlands, deforestation for the sake of opening new land to cultivation, the displacement of local agricultural production with large-scale export crops, greater dependency on agricultural imports as local production withers, and increased susceptibility to global price shocks due to a narrowing of the agricultural and overall economic base.[44] Some of these harms have a direct negative effect on the local cost of food, an especially harsh outcome for many of the world's poor for whom food is 50 to 70 percent of their household budget. Moreover, analysis of the prevailing new modes of ownership and leasing arrangements suggest that they are following the pattern of other extractive industries in taking the lion's share of the economic benefit out of the country.[45] In the worst cases, these new modes of ownership and leasing also leave behind soil degradation and groundwater depletion that undermine long-term agricultural productivity necessary to meet the future food needs of the country.[46]

As we have already noted, the lack of any publicly known, regularly enforced system of transferable property rights virtually guarantees that the rural poor remain poor and powerless, leaving them at the mercy of ruling political elites and foreign businesses.[47] Efforts to make foreign

---

[42] A 2010 World Bank study found that the annual acquisitions in 2008 were around 10 million acres, but the estimate for the first eleven months of 2009 jumped to 110 million. World Bank, "Protecting Land Rights Is Key to Large-Scale Land Acquisitions" (2010), https://reliefweb.int/report/world/protecting-land-rights-key-successful-large-scale-land-acquisitions.
See also Till Buckner, "The Myth of the African Land Grab," *Foreign Policy* (October 20, 2015), http://foreignpolicy.com/2015/10/20/the-myth-of-the-african-land-grab/. Estimates of the global scale of foreign investment in large-scale agricultural projects in developing nations vary for a number of reasons. Market conditions change quickly; some deals turn sour; some estimates involve double-counting from assimilated news reports; and most transactions lack public transparency.

[43] Human Rights Watch, *Waiting Here for Death: Forced Displacement and "Villagization" in Ethiopia's Gambella Region* (New York: Human Rights Watch, 2012).

[44] See, e.g., Olivier De Shutter, "How Not to Think of Land-Grabbing: Three Critiques of Large-Scale Investments in Farmland," *Journal of Peasant Studies* 38, no. 2 (2011): 249–279; Richard Schiffman, "Hunger, Food Security, and the African Land Grab," *Ethics & International Affairs* 27, no. 3 (2013): 239–249; Beth Robertson and Per Pinstrup-Anderson, "Global Land Acquisition: Neo-Colonialism or Development Opportunity," *Food Security* 2 (2010): 271–283; Human Rights Watch, *Waiting Here for Death*; and Center for Human Rights and Global Justice, *Foreign Land Deals and Human Rights*.

[45] "An Online Repository of Open Land Contracts."

[46] Joseph Stiglitz, Jean-Paul Fitouss, and Amartya Sen, *Mismeasuring Our Lives: Why GDP Doesn't Add Up* (New York: New Press, 2010).

[47] Robertson and Pinstrup-Anderson, "Global Land Acquisition," 275–276; Worldwatch Institute, "The Hidden Shame of the Global Industrial Economy." Even the most ardent supporters of foreign

acquisition easier have had the effect of further undermining legal ownership rights, even though the importance of such rights is well known.[48] When the poor have secure legal rights, they are much better positioned to prevent government complicity with foreign investors.[49] In many contexts, these legal ownership rights cannot easily be overridden by authoritarian governments. They create legal protections of land and water from devastation by those who have little long-term stake in environmentally sustainable and socially beneficial enterprises.[50]

Whether in its newer global land grab manifestation or its traditional extractive industry mode, the natural resource curse is an especially pernicious instance of negative externalities imposed on third parties by the market agreements entered into by others. It may benefit some individual parties to market transactions, but the potential for disastrous impact on the global poor, who are but bystanders at best and objects of direct displacement at worst, is a form of systematic disadvantage imposed by a powerful combination of domestic political leaders and foreign investors.

7.2.4. Global Dumping and Outsourcing: Toxics and Trash

The global poor are at systemic risk for the deprivation of core elements of well-being not only from the removal of resources from a region or country. They are also at increased risk from the hazardous materials arriving from abroad as a consequence of globalized markets. Global dumping of hazardous wastes is an example. The bulk of electronic waste produced in both the US and Europe is unaccounted for in official registries created to track it. According to some estimates, as much as 80 percent of e-waste generated in the US and 75 percent generated in Europe bypass international registries.[51] According to other estimates, 50 to 80 percent of the

---

direct investment in large-scale agricultural production facilities as a way of enhancing economic growth put this risk at the forefront of their downside concerns. World Bank, "Protecting Land Rights Is Key to Large-Scale Land Acquisitions.".

[48] GRAIN, "The G8 and Land Grabs in Africa."

[49] Rachael Knight et al., "Protecting Community Lands and Resources: Evidence from Liberia, Mozambique and Uganda" (Namati and International Development Law Organization, 2012), http://namati.org/wp-content/uploads/2012/06/protecting_community_lands_resources_inter_ FW.pdf.

[50] Michael Lipton, *Land Reform in Developing Countries: Property Rights and Property Wrongs* (London: Routledge, 2009).

[51] Karin Lundgren, "The Global Impact of e-Waste: Addressing the Challenge," International Labour Office, Programme on Safety and Health at Work and the Environment (SafeWork), Sectoral Activities Department (SECTOR), (2012), http://www.saicm.org/Portals/12/Documents/ EPI/ewastesafework.pdf.

e-waste collected for recycling in the US is exported to LMICs, especially Asian and West African countries.[52] Electronic wastes contain dangerous neurotoxins to which even small exposures are devastating. The same problem arises with batteries that are used in automobiles and consumer electronics.

Whole industries have grown up in the port cities of poor nations around waste management. The process of disassembly and recycling not only harms the health of the desperate people who agree to do the dirty work that the global affluent wish to avoid, a problem of market exploitation. It also affects the health of everyone in the urban communities that abut the waste management facilities, as well as the health of family members and others who have close contact with the workers. The imported e-waste also poisons the land and pollutes the air of outlying rural areas where the unusable remains of the recycling process are deposited.

Other forms of waste from industrial processes and residential communities are similarly loaded on large container ships bound for poor nations where the land is cheap and environmental laws are less onerous. These are not simply rare or irregular events but part and parcel of well-developed global market practices.[53] Nor are these the activities of criminal associations (which do their bit in all this), but rather mainstream activities that even some economists have commended as a reasonable pathway for economic development. Lawrence Summers, for example, while director of the World Bank, notoriously argued that the developing world was under-polluted, by which he meant that from a strictly market perspective, it made sense for the developed world to offload its garbage to places where land and labor are cheap and transaction costs, including the costs associated with environmental and health safety, are low.[54] This stark economic assessment, of course, overlooks the more basic ways in which global structural arrangements of this sort undermine the core dimensions of well-being, including health, personal security, and knowledge and

---

[52] M. Khurrum Bhutta, Adnan Omar, and Xiaozhe Yang, "Electronic Waste: A Growing Concern in Today's Environment," *Economics Research International* (2011), http://dx.doi.org/10.1155/2011/474230.

[53] For accounts of global dumping and siting of hazardous industrial facilities in LMICs, see Pellow, *Resisting Global Toxics*; and Jo Ann Carmin and Julian Agyeman, *Environmental Inequalities Beyond Borders: Local Perspectives on Global Injustices* (Cambridge, MA: MIT Press, 2011). For a specific example, see Elizabeth Rosenthal, "Lead from Old U.S. Batteries Sent to Mexico Raises Risks," *New York Times* (December 8, 2011), http://www.nytimes.com/2011/12/09/science/earth/recycled-battery-lead-puts-mexicans-in-danger.htm.

[54] Some have argued that he was being satirical, but here is the memo. Judge for yourself. http://www.whirledbank.org/ourwords/summers.html.

understanding, of the global poor. It also overlooks how these negative externalities undermine the self-determination of the poor who must live under hazardous conditions that they can scarcely improve or avoid.

Not only are the wastes generated by prosperous consumer societies sent abroad while the benefits remain at home, but even the manufacture of some of the more dangerous products is outsourced to developing nations. Globalization thus provides the affluent with new opportunities to make their own problems the problems of others. What is at issue in extractive industries, dumping, and outsourcing are global practices in which the benefits of technological progress are concentrated among the global affluent while the risks are borne increasingly by the poor, both at home and abroad.

7.3. Segregated Cities: "Two Societies, . . . Separate and Unequal"

We now turn from examples of sacrifice zones located largely in rural areas to examples of structural injustice in cities and settlements. In the present section, we focus on the origins and current realities of segregated cities in the United States and, in section 7.4, on the structural features of urban settlements or slums in low- and middle-income countries.

Racial injustice in the US has a long history. Its permutations run through slavery, the Jim Crow era, and the period of the Great Migration, when 4 million blacks left the South for northern industrial cities between 1910 and 1970. The current story cannot be fully told without reference to this historical context, but we begin our narrative with a discussion of what came next. Our starting point is the 1968 release of the Kerner Commission Report.[55] President Johnson appointed the commission in the aftermath of nearly three years of intermittent outbreaks of violence in major urban areas.[56] The report became an immediate national bestseller, and its central message and stark language are familiar to those who have studied the development of urban America.[57] Its executive summary concluded:

---

[55] The Report of the National Advisory Commission on Civil Disorders is widely known as the Kerner Commission Report, named for its chair, Illinois governor Otto Kerner, Jr.

[56] The commission was charged with answering three questions about the riots: "What happened? Why did it happen? What can be done to prevent it from happening again and again?" (Lyndon B. Johnson, July 29, 1967). See John T. Woolley and Gerhard Peters, eds., "Remarks upon Signing Order Establishing the National Advisory Commission on Civil Disorders," The American Presidency Project, University of California, Santa Barbara.

[57] See, e.g., Richard Rothstein, *The Color of Law: A Forgotten History of How Our Government Segregated America* (New York: W. W. Norton, 2017); Julian E. Zelizer, "Fifty Years Ago, the

Our nation is moving toward two societies, one black, one white—separate and unequal . . . Segregation and poverty have created in the racial ghetto a destructive environment totally unknown to most white Americans. What white Americans have never fully understood—but what the Negro can never forget—is that white society is deeply implicated in the ghetto. White institutions created it, white institutions maintain it, and white society condones it.

Though the language is from an earlier era, the core findings of the Kerner Report retain their relevance today.[58] Combined with the details of subsequent research, they reveal how so many were locked into place, both geographically and in their relative social position. The continuing normative importance of place—how African Americans got there and why they stayed—is underscored by Patrick Sharkey. The heart of his argument is that "[i]nequality stems from place itself and is located in the urban neighborhoods that generations of African-Americans have called home . . . [O]ver 70 percent of the African-American residents of America's poorest and most segregated neighborhoods are the children and grandchildren of those who lived in similar neighborhoods forty years ago."[59]

We focus on the evolution of US racial divisions that are the product of social control, social exclusion, and economic exploitation, leading to the production and perpetuation of deleterious effects on human well-being. More specifically, we look at residential housing patterns, economic conditions, and policing.[60]

Government Said Black Lives Matter: The Radical Conclusions of the 1968 Kerner Report," https://bostonreview.net/us/julian-e-zelizer-kerner-report; and Nikole Hannah-Jones, "Living Apart: How the Government Betrayed a Landmark Civil Rights Law," *Pro Publica* (June 25, 2015), https://www.propublica.org/article/living-apart-how-the-government-betrayed-a-landmark-civil-rights-law.

[58] Members of the commission were African American. "Negro" is anachronistic, and the term "ghetto" is normatively loaded in ways it was not then. However, the definition of "ghetto" was intended to demonstrate the origins of the affected communities: "an area within a city characterized by poverty and acute social disorganization, and inhabited by members of a racial or ethnic group under conditions of involuntary segregation."

[59] Quoted by Richard Florida, "The Persistent Geography of Disadvantage," *City Lab*, https:// www.citylab.com/equity/2013/07/persistent-geography-disadvantage/6231/.

[60] Chapter 2 of the Kerner Report presents the results of a survey of residents of twenty-three cities where riots occurred, in which the residents were asked to rank their grievances. Twelve of the most recurrent grievances were categorized according to level of intensity. Grievances within the first level of intensity were (1) police practices; (2) unemployment and underemployment; and (3) inadequate housing. Our focus on police practices also includes the administration of justice, which appears as a separate item in the survey. Our focus on economic conditions includes

7.3.1. The Modern Origins of Segregated Residential Housing Patterns

We begin with housing. Four factors were crucial in shaping not only the segregated character of cities but the economic conditions of its black residents: redlining, restrictive covenants, installment sales contracts, and the siting of public housing.

"Redlining" refers to racially discriminatory banking and insurance practices, including the denial of mortgage loans, homeowner insurance, and access to credit more generally in neighborhoods having a significant presence of African Americans. However, redlining from its inception was not simply a practice created and implemented by private financial institutions seeking to limit their exposure to the risks of transactions in lower-income communities. The practice acquired its name from the red ink on the "residential security maps" used by the Federal Home Loan Bank Board to designate neighborhoods as poor credit risks because of the presence of African Americans. The Federal Housing Authority (FHA) adopted these maps when it was created in 1934, not simply as the basis for offering financial advice to private lenders but to designate areas where it would not make loans or ensure private bank mortgages.

The exclusionary policies were not adopted solely on the assumption that race was a suitable proxy for lending risk. A 1938 manual for the FHA encouraged officials to avoid mixing "inharmonious racial or nationality groups" and "the occupancy of properties except by the race for which they are intended."[61] Similar discriminatory intention was reflected in other policies. The FHA would not lend to or insure private mortgages for a black person seeking to buy property in a white neighborhood. It even went so far as to bar African Americans from obtaining bank mortgages in suburban subdivisions that were privately financed without FHA construction loan guarantees.

The exclusionary effects of official government policies were compounded by the pervasive use of restrictive racial covenants that forbade property sales to blacks and other minorities, most typically Jews. Here too, these were not merely cumulative effects of private market decisions. The FHA refused federally subsidized construction loans to suburban subdivision developers unless they excluded African Americans.[62] The

---

employment matters but also lack of educational opportunity, inadequate social safety nets, and neighborhood business practices, all of which fall within the other nine major grievances.

[61] Hannah-Jones, "Living Apart."

[62] For example, the FHA insisted that Levittown, a famous subdivision built in 1947, not sell homes to blacks. Each deed also included the prohibition in future resales. Kenneth T. Jackson, *Crabgrass Frontier* (New York: Oxford University Press, 1985).

FHA's official policy, as well as the policy of the Veterans Administration, supported racial covenants until 1950 by "refusing to underwrite loans that would bring 'incompatible' racial groups into newly created white areas."[63] Change came only when the US Supreme Court struck down laws permitting restrictive covenants, but the Court did so on the grounds that they interfered with white sellers' rights, not the rights of black buyers.[64]

The combination of federal policy and the exercise of anti-competitive market power in the private sector left African Americans with few options. They could rent, but generally at above-market prices because of the lack of housing stock in neighborhoods where landlords would rent to them. Or they could purchase homes through installment contracts. The buyers built up no equity as they would have with mortgages, and they acquired legal title only when the lease-purchase amount was paid in full. With high rates and fees, buyers ended up paying exorbitant prices.[65] The further consequence was that moving elsewhere meant losing everything they had invested.

The other residential option was public housing projects. Here too, African Americans were bound to place. Public housing projects were located in the same segregated, depressed neighborhoods as the few other housing alternatives open to them.

In a review of this history and its durable impact on the intersection of race and poverty, Paul Jargowsky summarizes the result: "Given that the housing stock lasts for decades, these policies build *a durable architecture of segregation* that ensures that racial segregation and the concentration of poverty is entrenched for years to come."[66] In city after city, the pattern was repeated—from Ferguson to Baltimore to Cleveland and elsewhere.[67]

---

[63] See, e.g., Hannah-Jones, "Living Apart." By one estimate, 98 percent of the loans the FHA insured between 1934 and 1962 went to white borrowers.

[64] However, some real estate agent organizations adopted "codes of ethics" that banned sales to African Americans outside of black areas. Hannah-Jones, "Living Apart."

[65] Ta-Nehisi Coates, "The Case for Reparations," *Atlantic* (June 2014), https://www.theatlantic.com/magazine/archive/2014/06/the-case-for-reparations/361631. See also Arnold Hirsch, *Making the Second Ghetto: Race and Housing in Chicago, 1940–1960* (Chicago: University of Chicago Press, 1998).

[66] Paul Jargowsky, "Race & Inequality: Architecture of Segregation, Civil Unrest, the Concentration of Poverty, and Public Policy" (August 7, 2015), https://tcf.org/content/report/architecture-of-segregation/ (emphasis mine).

[67] Rothstein, *The Color of Law*; Jamelle Bouie, "How We Built the Ghettos: A Brief Introduction to America's Long History of Racist Housing Policy," *Daily Beast* (March 13, 2014), http://www.thedailybeast.com/how-we-built-the-ghettos.

7.3.2. Geographic Dispersion and Reconcentration of Poverty: 2000 to the Present

The intersection of race and socioeconomic position in the United States today is complex and often misunderstood. One mistake is the equation of the conditions of all black Americans with the extreme poverty of the inner cities. The majority of African Americans do not reside in the inner cities, and they are not below the official poverty level.[68] The opposite mistake is the assumption that the socioeconomic position of African Americans has improved greatly and that the problems associated with high concentrations of poverty in the inner cities are receding. The major economic indicators, including wealth and income, show otherwise. Poverty among blacks is more geographically dispersed, for example, moving rapidly into the inner suburban rings of metropolitan areas and reconcentrating with the same predictable adverse effects that are manifested in the inner cities.

Consider first the economic indicators of racial disparities in poverty rates, income, and wealth. The proportion of African Americans who are living in poverty is 27 percent, compared with an overall 11 percent, and 38 percent of black children live in poverty, compared with 22 percent of all children in the US.[69] In 1984, the white-to-black wealth ratio was 12 to 1. By 2009, the wealth gap grew to more than 19 to 1.[70]

The wealth gap is a particularly important indicator of differential well-being. Individual wealth—as well as family wealth—is a source of resilience and opportunity. For example, it reduces financial impediments for individuals seeking preventive and acute medical care for themselves and their families. It lessens the risk of eviction or mortgage foreclosure, and it enables parents and grandparents to contribute financially to the education or home purchase of young adults.

---

[68] Alana Semuels, "No, Most Black People Don't Live in Poverty—or Inner Cities," *Atlantic* (October 12, 2016), https://www.theatlantic.com/business/archive/2016/10/trump-african-american-inner-city/503744/.

[69] US Census Bureau, American Community Survey, 2016.

[70] These disproportionate losses are due primarily to decreased real estate value, the principal asset of most black households. Patrick Sharkey, "Neighborhoods and the Black–White Mobility Gap" (2009), http://www.pewtrusts.org/~/media/legacy/uploadedfiles/wwwpewtrustsorg/reports/economic_mobility/pewsharkeyv12pdf.pdf. A separate study by researchers at the Institute on Assets and Social Policy at Brandeis University found that from 1984 to 2009, the median net worth of white households grew to $265,000 over the twenty-five-year period compared with just $28,500 for black households. In addition, the study found that whites were five times more likely to inherit money than blacks, and their typical inheritances were ten times as big. Thomas Shapiro, Tatjana Meschede, and Sam Osoro, "The Roots of the Widening Racial Wealth Gap: Explaining the Black–White Economic Divide," Research and Policy Brief (February 2013), http://iasp.brandeis.edu/pdfs/Author/shapiro-thomas-m/racialwealthgapbrief.pdf.

Another important, but often neglected indicator of well-being and overall life prospects is the concentrated poverty rate—the share of poor residents living in poor neighborhoods. Extreme-poverty neighborhoods are ones where 40 percent or more of the population lives below the federal poverty line. The number of people living in these areas has nearly doubled since 2000, rising from 7.2 million to 13.8 million.[71] In addition, the number of high-poverty neighborhoods, defined as ones with poverty rates in the range of 20 to 40 percent, have also increased since 2000, and the overall result is that 55 percent of poor people in the United States now live in a high-poverty or extreme-poverty area.[72]

The reconcentration of poverty has had a disproportionate effect on non-whites. For example, among the residents of extreme-poverty neighborhoods, 70 percent are predominantly minority members. More than one-fourth of the black poor and nearly one-sixth of the Hispanic poor live in a neighborhood of extreme poverty, compared with one in thirteen of the white poor.[73] Moreover, concentrated poverty, along with new predominantly minority communities, spreads beyond the urban core. Today, more African Americans live in the suburbs than in the cities, but suburban areas, especially the inner rings, are now among the fastest-growing extreme-poverty neighborhoods.[74] By 2014, there were almost three times as many extreme-poverty suburban neighborhoods as there were in 2000, and poor black residents were more than three and a half times more likely than whites to live there.[75]

The increase in extreme- and high-poverty neighborhoods is significant in ways that may not be apparent to those who do not study the effects of concentrated poverty. It has durable adverse effects on well-being that go beyond the effects produced simply by being poor or growing up in a poor household. Multiple adverse impacts on every aspect of well-being—due simply to living in neighborhoods with concentrated poverty rates—kick

---

[71] Elizabeth Kneebone and Natalie Holmes, "U.S. Concentrated Poverty in the Wake of the Great Recession" (March 31, 2016), https://www.brookings.edu/research/u-s-concentrated-poverty-in-the-wake-of-the-great-recession/; Paul A. Jargowsky, "Concentration of Poverty: An Update," The Century Foundation, *Blog of the Century* (April 9, 2014), http://tcf.org/blog/detail/concentration-of-poverty-an-update.

[72] Kneebone and Holmes, "U.S. Concentrated Poverty."

[73] Paul Jargowsky, "Race & Inequality."

[74] Elizabeth Kneebone and Alan Berube, *Confronting Suburban Poverty in America* (Washington, DC: Brookings Institution, 2013).

[75] Kneebone and Holmes, "U.S. Concentrated Poverty."

in when the neighborhood poverty rate exceeds about 20 percent and tapers off when the rate reaches approximately 40 percent poverty.[76]

The multiple adverse effects—neighborhood effects, as they are known—are well documented.[77] For example, as many studies demonstrate in great detail, concentrated poverty and poor neighborhood schools go hand in hand, resulting in educational disadvantages and substantial achievement gaps for children. Areas of concentrated poverty affect learning and cognitive development in other ways as well. Such communities separate their residents from the civic life of the broader community, increasing social isolation and reducing opportunities for learning about the world and for social networking opportunities. Exposure to art, music, and a wider range of people, professions, and cultures does far more to advance preparedness for classroom learning than being able to sound out the alphabet.[78]

In addition, there is a high prevalence of physical and mental illness and high death rates in areas of concentrated poverty.[79] The reasons are various. These areas are associated with concentrated environmental hazards in old and poorly constructed housing stock, as well as harmful emissions produced by surrounding industries. Racially isolated neighborhoods, in particular, typically lack local primary care providers and ready access to routine and preventive health care even when residents have health care coverage through programs like Medicaid.[80] Residents are exposed to a higher level of violence, not only undermining short-term personal security but having lifelong effects on their capacity for trust and the development of other social skills necessary for establishing durable, rewarding personal relationships.[81]

---

[76] George C. Galster, "The Mechanism(s) of Neighborhood Effects: Theory, Evidence, and Policy Implications," presentation at the ESRC Seminar, St. Andrews University, Scotland, February 4–5, 2010.

[77] For an in-depth review of the literature on the effects of concentrated poverty, see the Federal Reserve System and the Federal Reserve System and Brookings Institution, *The Enduring Challenge of Concentrated Poverty in America: Case Studies from Communities Across the U.S.* (Richmond, VA: Federal Reserve System and Brookings Institution, 2008).

[78] David Grissmer et al., "Fine Motor Skills and Early Comprehension of the World: Two New School Readiness Indicators," *Developmental Psychology* 46 (5) (2010): 1008–1017; Tamara Wilder, Whitney C. Allgood, and Richard Rothstein, "Narrowing the Achievement Gap for Low-Income Children: A 19-Year Life Cycle Approach," table 11 (2008), http://www.epi.org/files/page/-/pdf/wilder_allgood_rothstein-narrowing_the_achievement_gap.pdf.

[79] For a review of converging research from developmental psychology, neuroscience, public health, economics, and sociology on the effects of concentrated poverty on children across generations, see Patrick Sharkey, *Stuck in Place: Urban Neighborhoods and the End of Progress Toward Racial Equality* (Chicago: University of Chicago Press, 2013).

[80] Wilder, Allgood, and Rothstein, "Narrowing the Achievement Gap," table 10.

[81] Sharkey, *Stuck in Place*.

There are, then, three distinct implications to bear in mind when thinking about the reconcentration of poverty. First, it is worse for the 55 percent of poor Americans who live in these neighborhoods than it is for the poor in less disadvantaging social circumstances. This means that a significant percentage of poor Americans are being left behind in ways beyond what income and household wealth differentials alone reveal. The adverse effects of individual or household poverty are thus compounded by social structural arrangements that thwart access to social programs and public resources that can counteract the long-term deprivation and disadvantage that accompany poverty.

Second, blacks of all ages and income levels are far more likely to live in areas of concentrated poverty than whites.[82] This means that many more affluent African Americans experience much of the adverse structural impact of an impoverished environment than whites of comparable socioeconomic status.

Third, poor children are much more likely than poor adults to live in poor neighborhoods, and black children are far more likely than white children to live in neighborhoods with poverty rates of 20 percent or more.[83] This means that the durable adverse effects of living in areas marked by severe deprivation and deep disadvantage take hold early and often last a lifetime.

Poverty is bad for human well-being, but concentrated poverty is far worse. Concentrated poverty is worse still for the African American community, even for those who do not bear the added burdens of personal poverty. This is the case because a higher proportion of non-poor blacks suffer from the lingering effects of urban and suburban communities created along racially exclusionary lines. And concentrated poverty tends to be especially bad for children in comparison with adults. Patterns of racial segregation leave more black children caught in the grip of circumstances beyond their making.[84]

---

[82] John Eligon and Robert Gebeloff, "Segregation, the Neighbor That Won't Leave," *New York Times* (August 21, 2016). They used the 20 percent figure as the defining threshold; https://www.nytimes.com/2016/08/21/us/milwaukee-segregation-wealthy-black-families.html?smid=nytcore-ipad-share&smprod=nytcore-ipad.

[83] For example, "Over the course of childhood, two out of three black children (66 percent) born from 1985 through 2000 were raised in neighborhoods with at least a 20 percent poverty rate, compared to just 6 percent of white children." Sharkey, "The Black–White Mobility Gap."

[84] Research by Raj Chetty and colleagues provides strong evidence that children who experience the disadvantages of growing up in and surrounded by poverty will continue to bear the burden of those disadvantages into adulthood. Raj Chetty et al., "Where Is the Land of Opportunity? The Geography of Intergenerational Mobility in the United States," NBER Working Paper 19843, June 2014; Raj Chetty and Nathaniel Hendren, "The Impacts of Neighborhoods on Intergenerational Mobility: Childhood Exposure Effects and County-Level Estimates," NBER, May 2015.

7.3.3. The Poor (Neighborhoods) Pay More (and Get Less)

The adverse effects of concentrated poverty extend beyond obvious factors like failing, underfunded schools, crumbling infrastructure, dangerously polluted water systems, and geographic isolation from primary transportation hubs.[85] Community residents, neighborhood activists, and legal aid lawyers also have firsthand experience with a web of laws that benefit others at the expense of disadvantaged communities. David Caplovitz's classic book, *The Poor Pay More*, provides a comprehensive account of the predatory institutions dedicated to the extraction of wealth from the poor and vulnerable with little legal accountability for their commercial practices.[86] The predatory lending practices prior to the Great Recession are among the most well-known schemes deliberately designed to exploit the residents of low-income communities, especially ones predominantly made up of African Americans.

While most know that the housing stock in poor neighborhoods of color is dilapidated and unsafe, it is also true that this is not a matter of mere neglect or the simple inability of the poor to pay higher rents for better housing. In fact, rents in poor neighborhoods typically approximate those in other neighborhoods where the housing stock is in far better shape. As a result, along with reduced maintenance costs, housing in poor neighborhoods yields higher returns to landlords.[87]

Other routinely exploitative businesses concentrated in lower-income areas include a phalanx of financial institutions targeting low-income communities.[88] They include rent-to-own companies, usurious pawnshops, consumer finance companies, and payday lenders. These financial institutions all benefit from laws that make default judgments (uncontested court orders) more likely, inflate recovered damages far in excess of actual loss, and permit wage garnishments that can often take up to 65 percent of a debtor's wages with no recourse.[89] They also take advantage of a system

---

[85] Furman Center, "Research Brief: Race and Neighborhoods in the 21st Century," *Research & Policy* (January 30, 2015), http://furmancenter.org/thestoop/entry/research-brief-race-and-neighborhoods-in-the-21st-century.

[86] David Caplovitz, *The Poor Pay More: Consumer Practices of Low-Income Families* (New York: Free Press, 1967).

[87] Matthew Desmond, *Evicted* (New York: Broadway Books, 2016).

[88] See, e.g., community activist organizations such as the umbrella organization Action Center on Race and the Economy (ACRE) that target the "financial elite responsible for pillaging communities of color, devastating working class communities and harming our environment," https://www.acrecampaigns.org/about.

[89] For a summary, see Monica Steinisch, "You Can Avoid Wage Garnishment" (Financial Resource Center, 2015), http://resourcecenter.cuna.org/331/article/2615/html.

of legal notification of pending lawsuits that lawyers refer to as "sewer service,"[90] so named because the formal notice process of pending legal action routinely fails to reach the defendants.

Some financial institutions also extract high profits by a practice of loan "flipping." Loans are refinanced multiple times and the accrued interest is folded into the principal, resulting in annual percentage rates of up to 250 percent in some jurisdictions. Added into the mix are insurers that sell "monthly-debit ordinary" life insurance only in low-income neighborhoods, often door to door, at higher rates and with lesser benefits than risk-based underwriting warrants. The list goes on, but the combined effect is a massive wealth transfer from the poor to the middle class and the affluent.

These processes of wealth extraction layer on top of the structural constraints on household revenue. Employment discrimination based on race is very much a part of the fabric of US economic life, along with high levels of underemployment.[91] Moreover, the increasing reliance on informal labor has replaced many regular employment arrangements for unskilled workers, especially African Americans and non-white Hispanics.[92] Added to this pattern of depressed household revenue from discrimination and the transformation of labor markets are the effects of the 1990s promise to "end welfare as we know it." This policy shift has deprived many people of the kinds of safety nets that are necessary to meet the most basic needs for food, shelter, medical care, and the transportation and material goods necessary to send children to school.[93] Here, the adverse effects are often especially felt by women and children. It is sometimes

---

[90] State of California Department of Justice, "Attorney General Kamala D. Harris Announces Suit Against JP Morgan Chase for Fraudulent and Unlawful Debt-Collection Practices," https://oag.ca.gov/news/press-releases/attorney-general-kamala-d-harris-announces-suit-against-jpmorgan-chase.

[91] The unemployment rate for African Americans has been roughly double that of whites since the 1950s. Drew Desilver, "Black Unemployment Rate Is Consistently Twice That of Whites," PEW Research Center, http://www.pewresearch.org/fact-tank/2013/08/21/through-good-times-and-bad-black-unemployment-is-consistently-double-that-of-whites/. In addition, numerous studies show discriminatory attitudes toward job applicants when applications include indictors of race, such as an "African-American-sounding" name. National Bureau of Economic Research, "Employers' Replies to Racial Names," http://www.nber.org/digest/sep03/w9873.html. A broader range of factors is discussed by Devah Pager and Hana Shepherd, "The Sociology of Discrimination: Racial Discrimination in Employment, Housing, Credit, and Consumer Markets," *Annual Review of Sociology* 34, no. 1 (2008): 181–209. https://doi.org/10.1146/annurev.soc.33.040406.131740.

[92] Demetra Smith Nightingale and Stephen A. Wandner, "Informal and Nonstandard Employment in the United States: Implications for Low-Income Working Families," Urban Institute, Brief 20, August 2011.

[93] Semuels, "No, Most Black People."

said that "black men get locked up while black women get locked out [evicted]."[94]

7.3.4. Policing

The *Washington Post* maintains a database cataloging every fatal shooting nationwide by a police officer in the line of duty, based "on news reports, public records, social media and other sources." The database includes whatever information is available about the circumstances of the shooting, as well as demographic data.[95] It illustrates what is already widely known: fatal interactions between police and the public disproportionately impact poor men and women in communities of color. The protest banner reading "Hands Up, Don't Shoot" vividly captures activists' understanding of the context of these shootings. The message of the movement Black Lives Matter is that all too often black lives don't matter within US society, at least not nearly as much as white lives do.

It is now commonly said that the problem is structural. One feature of this claim is that even though the disproportionate racial impact is stark, the individual motive behind these fatalities is not necessarily explicit racial animus. Even non-white officers may harbor beliefs that lead them to view black men with suspicion in ways that provoke more aggressive, preemptive police actions. This phenomenon affects black men in neighborhoods marked by high crime rates. But it also affects black men in expensive cars driving through affluent, predominantly white suburbs, when nothing other than skin color signals a threat to public safety or the security of police officers.

An array of other institutionalized race-based policing policies disproportionately affect poor neighborhoods of color. They are often described by law enforcement officials and politicians as war zones.[96] The assumption is that the situation in urban America, in both inner cities and inner suburban neighborhoods like Ferguson, is so dire that ordinary approaches to policing have to give way to more aggressive tactics. The "broken-windows approach," for example, was widely adopted and defended on

---

[94] Desmond, *Evicted.*

[95] "Fatal Force," *Washington Post,* https://www.washingtonpost.com/graphics/2018/national/police-shootings-2018/?utm_term=.4a05471e6c1a.

[96] This explicitly military approach was the brainchild of Los Angeles police chief Daryl Gates, who modeled the now ubiquitous SWAT team approach on tactics used by American soldiers in Vietnam. See Barry Friedman, *Unwarranted: Policing Without Permission* (NY: Farrar, Straus & Giroux, 2017), 54–58.

grounds that aggressive enforcement of minor offenses deters more serious crimes.[97]

The wartime mentality escalates beyond the intrusiveness of large-scale monitoring and surveillance in these neighborhoods. Today, in many midsized to large cities, serving criminal warrants and other routine police activities are often performed in highly militarized fashion, complete with techniques adapted from recent overseas wars, the deployment of military-grade equipment, and the use of profiling strategies designed to identify the "bad guys" in advance of any overt hostility.[98] Echoing the central message of James Baldwin's "Report from Occupied Territory," the police presence in communities of color is often referred to as "The Occupation."[99]

Fatal shootings and other aggressive, preemptive policing policies are components of a larger structural phenomenon that the Black Lives Matter movement identifies. The movement's founders characterize its purposes in their manifesto, proclaiming that the movement should be seen as "an intervention specifically created to address anti-blackness in all its historic and contemporary manifestations."[100] It points to their belief that the larger society endorses, at least passively, attaching diminished importance to black lives in numerous ways. Christopher Lebron describes the general phenomenon animating Black Lives Matter as "one of America's greatest failures—the dis-valuation of black lives, the prevalent sense that black lives were inconsequential and disposable."[101]

The argument for enhanced efforts to contain urban violence through aggressive policing has its historic roots in the Jim Crow era portrait of blackness as animalistic, lacking impulse control, and subhuman.[102] The contemporary version of this fear-driven white sentiment is captured by sociologist John DiLulio's characterization of the superpredator archetype, reiterated and popularized by a generation of politicians eager to establish their credentials as tough on crime. The implication of the containment strategy is that all that white America has to do to protect itself is

---

[97] James Q. Wilson, "Broken Windows," *Atlantic*, March 1982.

[98] Friedman, *Unwarranted*.

[99] Nikole Hannah-Jones, "Yes, Black America Fears the Police. Here's Why," *Pro Publica* (March 4, 2015), https://www.propublica.org/article/yes-black-america-fears-the-police-heres-why.

[100] Christopher J. Lebron, *The Making of Black Lives Matter* (New York: Oxford University Press, 2017), 174.

[101] Ibid., 44.

[102] Ibid., 22; Michele Alexander, *The New Jim Crow*, 2nd ed. (New York: New Press, 2012).

to stay clear of the bad neighborhoods and let the police do whatever needs to be done to control the problems and the responsible populations.[103]

The shift toward mass incarceration is the most obvious end result of the containment model, but there is more to it than that. Underneath the phenomenon of affluent black motorists being stopped by police for "driving while black," particularly in whiter, more affluent neighborhoods, is an extension of the broad-brush suspicion of blackness. It is rooted in white fear that bad things will happen if containment policies fail, leading to hypervigilance against the threat that black people will go where they do not belong.[104]

Municipalities also extract disproportionate revenue from the poor through a system of fines and court cost levies, often for petty offenses that are not enforced in other communities.[105] Stop-and-frisk techniques and arrests for obstructing doorways and sidewalks—practices almost exclusively confined to poor communities of color—not only serve their intended purpose of intimidation but pay the salaries of numerous clerks, court officers, and ancillary police department personnel. These widespread practices often generate a high proportion of the municipal revenues in small jurisdictions. One of the most widely publicized examples is contained in the US Justice Department report in the wake of the Michael Brown shooting in Ferguson, Missouri.[106] However, it is simply a high-profile example of a widespread technique for generating municipal revenues without having to raise taxes on politically more influential citizens who will hold them accountable at the ballot box.[107]

In sum, the origin and perpetuation of the conditions of black Americans living predominantly in segregated metropolitan areas have multiple causes, with a diversity of agents exhibiting a range of moral postures toward the disadvantaged. Taken together, the conditions of black America, in particular those of poor communities of color, is a function of multiple, overlapping factors that reinforce disadvantage, exploitation, social control, and social exclusion in a systematic manner. No black person can

---

[103] Paul Butler, *Chokehold: Policing Black Men* (New York: New Press, 2017), 117–148.

[104] James Forman, *Locking Up Our Own* (New York: Farrar, Straus & Giroux, 2017), 197–215.

[105] John F. Pfaff, *Locked In* (New York: Basic Books, 2017).

[106] United States Justice Department, Civil Rights Division, "Investigation of the Ferguson Police Department" (March 4, 2015), https://www.justice.gov/sites/default/files/opa/press-releases/attachments/2015/03/04/ferguson_police_department_report.pdf.

[107] Pfaff, *Locked In*; Matt Taibbi, *The Divide: American Injustice in the Age of the Wealth Gap* (New York: Spiegel and Grau, 2014), 85–139.

fully escape the insidious effects. Some of these factors are fear-driven and rooted in racial animus, however far from the surface of consciousness these motives might be in some instances. This is straightforward subordination of a racially defined community, with some individuals exhibiting a clear desire to exclude a subject population from the mainstream of social life.

For others, there is a level of moral indifference that valorizes a social ideal in which people are expected to attend to their families and immediate circle of friends and expect the same from others.[108] An especially callous variant of this libertarian ideal of "live and let live" involves a self-serving falsification of the true relationship of the privileged to the disadvantaged. Particularly problematic are individuals who benefit from this pattern of social insularity and exclusion, for example, by avoiding the taxes that would be required to bring public infrastructure and schools up to a standard commensurate with what is available in advantaged communities.

For others still, there is money to be made. Exploitation is the central form of unfairness manifested. Real estate practices—from redlining to installment sales to subprime predatory lending—is but one illustration. Many business owners benefit from having at the ready a large pool of day laborers who work outside of the formal economy that underwrites the expectation of middle-class whites for legally enforceable minimum wages, worker safety protections, a measure of job security, and at least some employee benefits.

No one can deny that there have been important changes for the better with regard to racial justice in the US since the 1960s. However, too many things of consequence remain the same. A 2016 report from New York University's Furman Center surveys the conditions in urban America, where race, place, and concentrated poverty intersect, and its conclusion echoes the stark language of the Kerner Report: "Segregation in the 21st century, in other words, continues to result not only in separate but also in decidedly unequal communities."[109]

---

[108] Young, *Responsibility for Justice*, 81–84.
[109] Furman Center, "Research Brief."

7.4. Urban "Slums": The Proliferation of Informal Human Settlements

Precarious human settlements—"slums" in the vernacular of activists and global policy analysts—typically situated on the peripheries of large urban centers in the global South, are sites of extreme, multidimensional deprivation. The differentials of power and life prospects between residents of these settlements and their more prosperous neighbors who reside and work in the sleek modern buildings in the background are stark. Activists and others with long-term, firsthand experience emphasize the similarity of patterns of human devastation and environmental destruction in slums around the world.[110]

7.4.1. Urbanization and the Urbanization of Poverty

For the first time in history more than half the world's population lives in urban areas. More than 90 percent of future urban population growth is expected to occur in LMICs, with the overwhelming majority of newly urbanized residents located in slums.[111] This is because the urbanization of LMICs has been accompanied by the urbanization of poverty. In 2003, the widely cited UN-Habitat report estimated that 1 billion people were living in informal settlements that lacked basic services and projected that the urban slum population would increase to 2 billion people before midcentury.[112] Indeed, most of the world's poor are no longer found in rural areas, because they migrate to the mega-cities and large cities of Asia, Africa, and Latin America.[113]

This pattern of the urbanization of the poor is more complicated than either the raw numbers or the projections suggest. For example,

---

[110] UN-Habitat, *The Challenge of Slums, Global Report on Human Settlements* (London: Earthscan, 2003); Mike Davis, *Planet of Slums* (London: Verso, 2006).

[111] United Nations, "World Urbanization Prospects: The 2014 Revision," Population Division of UN Department of Economic and Social Affairs(2014), https://esa.un.org/unpd/wup/publications/files/wup2014-highlights.pdf.

[112] UN-Habitat, *The Challenge of Slums*.

[113] Martin Ravallion, "On the Urbanization of Poverty," Policy Research Working Paper no. 2586, World Bank (2001), http://documents.worldbank.org/curated/en/577771468739538398/On-the-urbanization-of-poverty. There are many estimates of the sizes of many of the world's largest slums in the world. See, e.g., World Economic Forum, https://www.weforum.org/agenda/2016/10/these-are-the-worlds-five-biggest-slums/. Also, the fastest-growing urban centers are not mega-cities, but medium and small cities with less than 1 million inhabitants, which account for 59 percent of the world's urban population https://doi.org/10.1016/j.jue.2015.09.002.

the majority of the world's poor no longer reside in low-income countries; they live in middle-income countries, mirroring the overall global trend toward increased intrastate inequality.[114] Moreover, although the percentage of the global urban population has been declining, the absolute numbers of slum dwellers continue to grow, and the trend toward regional concentration of urban poverty in the world's two poorest regions—South Asia and sub-Saharan Africa—is expected to continue.[115]

In addition, the global rise of slums has confounded the expectations of long-term observers of urbanization and globalization trends. Historically, income growth and urbanization tended to go hand in hand.[116] This time, things are different. We are witnessing a new pattern of "urbanization without growth."[117] While the correlation between urbanization and income remains weakly positive overall, the relationship is negative in poorer countries, such as those in Latin America and sub-Saharan Africa.[118]

There is no shortage of (not necessarily incompatible) explanatory hypotheses for the global phenomenon of urban slum growth. There is, however, widespread agreement about the conditions in slums and how they contribute to extreme deprivation, foster human rights violations, enable and exacerbate economic exploitation, institutionalize existing informal patterns of subordination and social exclusion, and involve state violence.[119]

---

[114] "World Urbanization Prospects: The 2014 Revision."

[115] Slum Almanac, 2015–2016, https://unhabitat.org/slum-almanac-2015-2016/; *State of the World's Cities, 2012/2013: Prosperity of Cities* (London: Earthscan, 2013).

[116] J. Vernon Henderson, "Cities and Development," *Journal of Regional Science* 50, no. 1 (2010): 515–540.

[117] Marianne Fay and Charlotte Opal, "Urbanization without Growth: A Not-So-Uncommon Phenomenon," Policy Research Working Paper 2412, World Bank (2000), https://openknowledge.worldbank.org/handle/10986/21373.

[118] David Castells-Quintana, "Malthus Living in a Slum: Urban Concentration, Infrastructure and Economic Growth," *Journal of Urban Economics* 98, issue C (2017): 158–173. Recent surveys estimate that a quarter of the urban population around the world lives in slums, but in sub-Saharan Africa, the percentage is 59. Moreover, 7 of the 10 million more people added to the urban population of sub-Saharan Africa each year end up in slums, compared with only 2 million who leave. Slum Almanac, 2015–2016.

[119] See, e.g., Michael Lipton, *Why Poor People Stay Poor: A Study of Urban Bias in World Development* (Cambridge: Cambridge University Press, 1977); Daron Acemoglu and Simon Johnson, "Disease and Development: The Effect of Life Expectancy on Economic Growth," *Journal of Political Economy* 115, no. 6 (2007): 925–985; and Remi Jedwab, Luc Christiaensen, and Marina Gindelsky, "Demography, Urbanization and Development: Rural Push, Urban Pull and . . . Urban Push?" *Journal of Urban Economics* 98 (2017): 6–16.

7.4.2. Definitions and Characteristics of Slums

The term "slum" has a long history. In the nineteenth century, as today, it designated a particular kind of low-income urban community, where living conditions were "squalid" and "degrading."[120] Although there are concerns that the term tends to further stigmatize the inhabitants of these communities, even activists themselves often adopt it.[121] Every part of the world has its own nomenclature: the *favelas* of Brazil, the *villas miserias* of Buenos Aires, the *colonias populares* of Mexico City, the *conventillos* of Quito, the *barriad`as* of Lima, the *umjondolos* of Durban, the *intra-murios* of Rabat, the *bidonvilles* of Abidjan, the *baladis* of Cairo, the *gecekondus* of Ankara, and so on. Whatever the terminology, descriptions and definitions emphasize the degraded and degrading conditions, and they nearly always begin with depictions of housing, how the dwellings are fabricated, and where they are located.

One of the most widely cited descriptions of slums is that of Mike Davis in his influential book, *Planet of Slums*: "The urban poor . . . are every-where forced to settle on hazardous and otherwise unbuildable terrains—over-steep hillslopes, river banks and floodplains. Likewise, they squat in the deadly shadows of refineries, chemical factories, toxic dumps, or in the margins of railroads and highways."[122]

The Slum Almanac produced by the UN describes slums in a similar manner. "Slums are marginalised, large agglomerations of dilapidated housing often located in the most hazardous urban land—e.g. riverbanks; sandy and degraded soils, near industries and dump sites, in swamps, flood-prone zones and steep slopes—disengaged from broader urban systems and from the formal supply of basic infrastructure."[123]

The UN-Habitat's operational definition of slum dwellers picks up on five common features in the report of an Expert Group Meeting convened in 2002. It describes a slum household as "a group of individuals living under the same roof lacking one or more of the following conditions: (1) access to improved water; (2) access to improved sanitation facilities;

---

[120] *The New Shorter Oxford English Dictionary*, vol. 2 (Oxford: Clarendon Press, 1993).

[121] Some community groups and NGOs include Slum/Shack Dwellers International and the International Federation of Slum Dwellers. Alternative labels, such as "informal settlements" and "subaltern cities," are also used. See Alan Gilbert, "The Return of the Slum: Does Language Matter?," *International Journal of Urban and Regional Research* 31, no. 4 (2007): 697–713; and Ananya Roy, "Slumdog Cities: Rethinking Subaltern Urbanism," *International Journal of Urban and Regional Research* 35, no. 2 (2011): 223–238.

[122] Davis, *Planet of Slums*, 323.

[123] Slum Almanac, 2015–2016.

(3) sufficient living area—not overcrowded; (4) structural quality/durability of dwellings; and (5) security of tenure." We consider briefly what the first four of these conditions entail; we address the fifth condition in more detail. We also discuss the precarious nature of the informal subsistence economy of slums, as well as the power differentials that not only produce and reproduce slum conditions but manifest in the pervasive threat of arbitrary state action and routine exposure to both private and state-sanctioned violence, especially for women.

The first and second conditions involve deficiencies in water and sanitation. The most common standards by which water and sanitation requirements are judged are quite modest. For example, under the WHO/United Nations Children's Fund (UNICEF) standard, pit latrines with slabs qualify as improved sanitation. However, pit latrines have been shown to provide inadequate protection against communicable disease in densely populated areas. They are especially unsanitary for women and girls and are a source of gender-based violence.[124] A lack of piped water is ubiquitous, and many surveys show that residents view access to clean water sufficient for bathing, cooking, and drinking as their most pressing need.[125]

The third condition is overcrowding. It is difficult to convey with words alone—pictures and films are far better—just how intense the overcrowding is. The conditions in Kenya, where 60 to 80 percent of its urban population lives in slums, are representative of the problem. In Nairobi, informal slum settlements cover just 6 percent of the total residential land area, yet they house 60 to 80 percent of the city's population.[126]

The fourth condition is the lack of durably constructed dwellings. Slums everywhere are put together out of a hodgepodge of locally available, found objects. Among the most common are the leftover or discarded materials out of which modern urban life for the more affluent is constructed. Included are metal scraps, used oil drums, chemical containers, wood timbers or pieces of plywood, molded or water-damaged insulation, cardboard boxes and packing strips, tarp, concrete fragments, straw, polythene bags, corrugated zinc, and broken car doors. Residents

[124] Anne Nakagiri et al., "Are Pit Latrines in Urban Areas of Sub-Saharan Africa Performing? A Review of Usage, Filling, Insects and Odour Nuisances," *BMC Public Health* 16: 120 (2016), https://doi.org/10.1186/s12889-016-2772-z.

[125] E.g., Priti Parikh, Himanshu Parikh, and Allan McRobie, "The Role of Infrastructure in Improving Human Settlements," *Proceedings of the Institution of Civil Engineers: Urban Design and Planning* 166, no. 2 (2013): 101–118.

[126] UN-Habitat, World Habitat Day (WHD) Background Paper (2014), https://unhabitat.org/wp-content/uploads/2014/07/WHD-2014-Background-Paper.pdf.

pick through rubbish heaps and industrial dumping sites for anything that can be used to cobble together a small structure that can be nestled for support against tunnel walls, earthen berms, vertical bridge beams, or crumbling, partially standing ruins of abandoned buildings. These contemporary slum dwellings are not like the tenements of an earlier era of industrialized urbanization, but makeshift shelters that are easily and regularly destroyed by floods, wind, and fire.

This brings us to the fifth and perhaps most striking fact about slum dwellings. The only locations available to slum residents to construct their dwellings are abandoned, uninhabitable, or simply unclaimed scraps of otherwise economically unmarketable land near factories, waste dumps, and other sources of highly toxic pollution or on low-lying areas.[127] They are built in settlements that are "informal" in the sense that the land on which the dwellings are constructed are either public lands or unclaimed lands for which neither the occupants nor other parties hold legal title.

The consequences of informal occupancy are numerous. The occupants have no legally enforceable rights and can be evicted without any recourse or due process. They cannot accumulate wealth by investing in their homes, and they cannot use these legally undocumented assets to borrow money for business enterprises or the education of their children. The lack of a system for acquiring and documenting ownership rights is thus a massive impediment to upward and outward economic mobility. Most slum residents have no realistic choice but to remain in the slums. Many repeatedly suffer the loss of their makeshift home, the one asset they have struggled to acquire, and are forced to start over to obtain shelter in whatever way they can find.

In many instances, the slums are constructed outside of the municipal jurisdiction of the cities. That means that there is usually no entity or agency having clear responsibility for providing essential services such as piped water, sanitation, garbage collection, and police protection. Of course, this lack of formal authority does not entail that the municipal governments make no efforts. Some do, but often they are under-resourced or poorly managed. However, the fact that entire communities, often containing hundreds of thousands of people scattered around urban areas, are not part of any formal system of registry means that government accountability is weak or non-existent.

---

[127] Geoffrey Payne, Tony Piaskowy, and Lauren Kuritz, "Land Tenure in Urban Environments," United States Agency for International Development (2014), www.land-links.org/issue-brief/land-tenure-in-urban-environments/.

Not only does the informal system of land tenure impose durable economic consequences on the residents of slums, it also exposes them to state and private party violence. Residents are subject to the arbitrary actions of both governments, who view them as lawbreakers, and powerful commercial developers. Commercial developers, themselves often criminal enterprises, can simply force out the current residents and build commercial enterprises on sites that previously had no economic value.[128] The very fact of rapid urbanization creates upward price pressure on even the most marginal of urban peripheral land, resulting in the wholesale displacement of communities for development and infrastructure projects, from the construction of dams, to housing renovations, to the building of Olympic Games facilities.[129]

In the largest slums in Nairobi, for example, the majority of housing is controlled by landlords who, although they have no legal claim to the land, are major political figures who either bribe officials to look the other way or even establish formal ownership rights for them. Not only do these landlords earn high economic rents, they also block alternative patterns of redevelopment that would benefit the slum dwellers or provide formalization of their land rights.[130]

There are good reasons to think that the Kenyan experience, though more systematically studied than many other urban slums, is hardly unique. The informal land system is a global phenomenon. According to the United Nations' Global Land Tool Network, 70 percent of land in most developing countries is held under a category other than registered freehold.[131] One widely regarded estimate calculates that 85 percent of the urban residents of the developing world occupy property illegally.[132]

---

[128] Leilani Farha, "Statement of the UN Special Rapporteur on Adequate Housing as a Component of the Right to an Adequate Standard of LIVING and on the Right to Non-Discrimination in This Context," 2nd Latin America and Caribbean Regional Forum on Adequate Housing, "Vivienda para la Vida," Monterrey, Mexico, May 6, 2015.

[129] See http://globalinitiative-escr.org/wp-content/uploads/2013/05/Issue-Brief-1-Forced-Eviction.pdf. For an exemplary case study, see Greg Bankoff, "Constructing Vulnerability: The Historical, Natural and Social Generation of Flooding in Metropolitan Manila," *Disasters* 27, no. 3 (2003): 224–238.

[130] J. Vernon Henderson, Anthony J. Venables, Tanner Regan, and Ilia Samsonov, "Building Functional Cities," *Science* 352, no. 6288 (May 20, 2016): 946–947, doi: 10.1126/science.aaf7150.

[131] Christiaan Lemmen, "The Social Tenure Domain Model: A Pro-Poor Land Tool," International Federation of Surveyors, UN-Habitat, Global Land Tool Network (2010), http://www.fig.net/resources/publications/figpub/pub52/figpub52.pdf. See also https://landportal.info/book/thematic/urban-tenure.

[132] Winter King, "Illegal Settlements and the Impact of Titling Programmes," *Harvard International Law Review* 44, no. 2 (2003): 433–471, at 471.

Women often bear a disproportionate share of the burden of inadequate, impermanent shelter. Close to one-third of the world's women are homeless or live in inadequate dwellings, and in many countries a majority of homeless women have escaped from domestic violence.[133] Even where some degree of land right formalization has occurred, women are often left out. Limited property rights affect more than 80 percent—about 1 billion—of urban women. About 35 percent of these women live in countries where the formal property rights of women are not equal to those of men, most prevalently in South Asia, the Middle East, and North Africa. Another 300 million live in countries where there are legally recognized property rights for women but social pressure, threats, or legal systems that allow customary law to trump statutory law, prevent women from exercising their legal rights and using their assets to obtain credit.[134] The relationship between domestic violence, homelessness among women, and unequal property rights is complex. Domestic violence is both a cause of homelessness and a consequence of it. For example, one study in India found that 7 percent of women who owned land and housing experienced domestic abuse, compared with nearly 50 percent of women who did not.[135]

There is also evidence that women are disproportionately the victims of forced evictions in informal settlements and suffer greater adverse consequences than men when they are. This is because women are less likely than men to abandon the dependent young and older family members when families are evicted.[136]

7.4.3. The Informal Economy

Informality of land tenure is an important part of a larger system of informal legal and economic arrangements characteristic of life in slums. Employment as traditionally defined has given way to a constellation of informal work practices that lie outside the formal wage-based economy. These practices include everything from piecework production (e.g., peeling garlic cloves or disassembling electronic devices) to scavenging

---

[133] UN-Habitat, Shelter and Sustainable Human Settlement Division, "Why Focus on Women?," mirror.unhabitat.org/content.asp?typeid=19&catid=423&cid=1507.

[134] Bethany Martin-Breen, "In the Developing World, Property Rights for Women Are About More than Just Housing," Rockefeller Foundation blog (November 5, 2014), https://www.rockefellerfoundation.org/blog/developing-world-property-rights-women/.

[135] Ibid. Obviously, it is difficult to say which way the causal arrow points.

[136] UN-Habitat, *Forced Evictions—Towards Solutions?* Second Report of the Advisory Group on Forced Evictions to the Executive Director of UN-Habitat (Nairobi: AGFE, 2007), 38.

for recyclables in piles of garbage or polluted waterways. Most survive by working short-term jobs with no formal labor contract, benefits, job security, or legal protections against exposure to toxic substances or regulation of hazardous machinery or industrial processes. The basis of livelihood in slums is often characterized as informal survivalism. As Mike Davis vividly portrays it, "Those living in poverty often work and live with thoughts of survival in mind . . . Their struggle is a daily reality, and they don't bother with financial success, because it seems so far out of reach at the moment . . . They are consumed with thoughts of worry, even panic, over income and if their job will hold out one more day."[137]

The informal economy of slums is simply the most extreme example of a larger global transition from a wage economy to a highly precarious informal labor system. That transition is summarized by a joint report of the World Trade Organization and the International Labour Organization in the following way: "In many developing economies job creation has mainly taken place in the informal economy, where around 60% of workers find income opportunities. However, the informal economy is characterized by less job security, lower incomes, an absence of access to a range of social benefits and fewer possibilities to participate in formal education and training programmes—in short, the absence of key ingredients of decent work opportunities."[138]

Women face different, often more difficult challenges to survival in the informal economy, which, in urban areas, is where much of women's paid work resides. For example, in sub-Saharan Africa, an estimated 84 percent of women's non-agricultural employment is in the informal sector.[139] Poor women in slums often seek ways to make money within the home or at very close proximity for the sake of their children, and they earn far less than men in informal employment. Although even in urban slums women outlive men, they end up having to support a household alone. Women thus bear what is often called "triple responsibilities"—caring for children, earning a livelihood, and managing the household, which involves

[137] Mike Davis, "Dealing with Poverty" (2009), https://hubpages.com/politics/Dealing-with-Poverty.

[138] Marc Bacchetta, Ekkehard Ernst, and Juana P. Bustamante, "Globalization and Informal Jobs in Developing Countries," International Labour Office and the World Trade Organization (2009), https://www.wto.org/english/res_e/booksp_e/jobs_devel_countries_e.pdf. For a review of labor informalization around the world, see Kuttner, *Can Democracy Survive?*, 97–148.

[139] UN-Habitat, *State of the World's Cities, 2008/2009: Harmonious Cities* (London: Earthscan, 2008), 88.

spending considerable time obtaining food, water, and fuel, as well as finding the money to pay for them.[140]

Home-based microenterprises are widely celebrated in some policy circles as important vehicles for escaping poverty and facilitating women's independence. However, the evidence is mixed at best. Often it is not poor women who take up these new work options, but rather displaced salaried employees. The trend has been described not as new "opportunities" but as "forced entrepreneurialism foisted on former salaried employees by the decline of formal sector employment."[141] Moreover, while some microenterprises result in an improvement of household income, "generally speaking, the incomes generated from these enterprises, the majority of which tend to be run by women, usually fall short of even a minimum living standard and involve little capital investment, virtually no skills training, and only constrained opportunities for expansion into a viable business."[142] Also, the default rate among many microentrepreneurs is high and business failures are common. Many women report dissatisfaction with the precariousness of these survivalist enterprises. They express the hope that their children will find employment in the formal sector, where they can expect a set wage and a measure of job security.[143]

It is possible that the modernization hypothesis—that slums are a transitional phenomenon that over time will be eradicated by markets—will prove correct. If so, in the aggregate and over time, more people will benefit from urbanization than will be harmed. But those who are being hurt, the losers in this transition, are the millions upon millions of current slum dwellers who are trapped in terrible circumstances that allow others to extract benefit from their misfortune. The one-two punch of informal housing and an informal economy constitutes a serious structural

---

[140] United Nations Population Fund, "State of the World Population (2007): Unleashing the Potential of Urban Growth," 38, https://www.unfpa.org/sites/default/files/pub-pdf/695_filename_sowp2007_eng.pdf. For a discussion of the time burden on women and girls imposed by the daily need to secure water, see United Nations Development Programme, *Human Development Report, 2006: Beyond Scarcity: Power, Poverty, and the Global Water Crisis* (Geneva: UNDP, 2006), 47. For a discussion of earlier childbirth among poor urban women, see *State of the World's Cities, 2006/2007: The Millennium Development Goals and Urban Sustainability*, (London: Earthscan, 2006), 127.

[141] Alejandro Portes and Kelly Hoffman, "Latin American Class Structures: Their Composition and Change during the Neoliberal Era," *Latin American Research Review* 38, no. 1 (2003): 55.

[142] Christian Rogerson, "Globalization or Informalization? African Urban Economies in the 1990s," in *The Urban Challenge in Africa: Growth and Management of Its Large Cities*, ed. Carole Rakodi (Tokyo: United Nations University Press, 1997), 348.

[143] Abhijit V. Banerjee and Esther Duflo, *Poor Economics: A Radical Rethinking of the Way to Fight Global Poverty* (New York: Public Affairs, 2011).

impediment to the prospects of upward and outward mobility for slum dwellers, especially women, whose burdens differ in both magnitude and kind from those generally born by men.

7.4.4. Multidimensional Deprivation

Among the most widely discussed consequences of life in slums is the adverse impact on health. There are many well-known linkages between health deprivation and deeply disadvantaging social conditions, and these linkages are demonstrated amply by studies of health outcomes of residents of slums across the world.[144]

As we discussed in section 7.3, poor health outcomes are strongly associated with living in areas of high concentration of poverty and other markers of disadvantage and deprivation, even among residents of non-poor households. There are many obvious reasons for these neighborhood effects on health. People who live in slums share a multitude of environmental and other risks that people who live in other LMIC urban areas do not, or not to the same degree. Trauma from accidents precipitated by the collapse of unstable dwellings built upon unstable hillsides or floodplains is commonplace, as are injury and death from violence.

Because of poor sanitation, lack of clean water, and exposure to untreated human waste and toxic industrial dumping, the occurrence of infectious diseases that cause diarrhea and other symptoms that directly affect malnutrition is magnified.[145] Infectious diseases also spread wider and faster because of residential density and low rates of immunization.

Hunger and malnutrition are major problems.[146] A large percentage of people's caloric intake derives from nutritionally inadequate food sold by street vendors. Food insecurity and hunger are constantly hovering.

---

[144] Unless otherwise indicated, the health effects described in this subsection are based on a recent, comprehensive literature review. Alex Ezeh et al., "The History, Geography, and Sociology of Slums and the Health Problems of People Who Live in Slums," *Lancet* 389, no. 1006 (October 16, 2016), http://www.thelancet.com/series/slum-health.

[145] WHO/UNICEF Joint Monitoring Programme, "Progress on Sanitation and Drinking Water: 2015 Update and MDG Assessment" (2015), http://www.wssinfo.org/; Robert Bain et al., "Global Assessment of Exposure to Faecal Contamination Through Drinking Water Based on a Systematic Review," *Tropical Medicine and International Health* 19, no. 8 (August 2014): 917–927; World Health Organization, "Water for Health: Taking Charge" (2001), http://www.who.int/water_sanitation_health/wwdreport.pdf?ua=1; Centers for Disease Control and Prevention, "Global Water Sanitation, and Hygiene"(updated 2015), http://www.cdc.gov/healthywater/global/wash_statistics.html.

[146] Hema Swaminathan and Arnab Mukherji, "Slums and Malnourishment: Evidence from Women in India," *American Journal of Public Health* 102, no. 7 (2012): 1329–1335, doi: 10.2105/AJPH.2011.300424.

Slum dwellers are also more likely than other urban residents to lack access to even the most basic public health services and medical care. Neuropsychiatric disorders associated with the extraordinary stress of daily life in slums and respiratory illness caused by indoor cooking with solid fuels in densely populated, poorly ventilated clusters of households are also both regular features of slum life. It is no wonder that life expectancy is much lower and the mortality of children under five years of age is much higher for the urban poor than for other urban residents.[147]

This brief inventory of adverse effects on health joins the many other dimensions of deprivation that matter, including themes already discussed. They include lack of physical security, education, the economic basis for subsistence living, social isolation, and loss of self-determination.

7.4.5. Power and Deprivation

In his widely cited address in the Kangemi slum of Nairobi, Kenya, Pope Francis referenced many of the same conditions identified by the UN-Habitat definition and in this section.[148] The Pope characterizes the conditions of slum dwellers by what he calls "the dreadful injustice of urban exclusion":

> These are wounds inflicted by minorities who cling to power and wealth, who selfishly squander while a growing majority is forced to flee to abandoned, filthy and run-down peripheries . . . These realities . . . are not a random combination of unrelated problems. They are a consequence of new forms of colonialism . . . where a minority believes that it has the right to consume in a way which can never be universalized . . . I would propose a renewed attention to the idea of a respectful urban integration, as opposed to elimination, paternalism, indifference or mere containment.[149]

The Pope's characterization of social exclusion and disadvantage, and how it serves the interests of the powerful at the expense of the poor and the vulnerable, mirrors a recurrent theme in the case studies that accompanied

---

[147] World Health Organization, Urban HEART (Urban Health Equity Assessment and Response Tool, Kobe, Japan, WHO Commission on Social Determinants of Health, 2010), http://www.who.int/kobe_centre/publications/urban_heart/en/.

[148] For example, he listed the lack of toilets, sewers, drains, refuse collection, electricity, roads, schools, hospitals, and access to drinking water.

[149] For the full text, see Edward Pentin, "Full Text of Pope Francis' Address at Kangemi Slum," *National Catholic Register*, 2015, http://www.ncregister.com/blog/edward-pentin/full-text-of-pope-francis-address-at-kangemi-slum.

the 2003 UN-Habitat Report. The report noted as an example the reproach that slum dwellers sense in the language used by the non-slum dwellers of Bogotá, who "would appear to view the impoverished urban groups as undesirables, expressed in the specific terms applied to describe them—desechable (disposable) . . . that are highly associated with delinquency, unproductiveness and uselessness."[150]

This reference to the indifference shown to the lives of slum dwellers is echoed in Katherine Boo's book, *Behind the Beautiful Forever.* She reports that the boys of the Annawadi slum in Mumbai "have accepted the basic truths: that in a modernizing, prosperous city, their lives were embarrassments best confined to small spaces, and their deaths would not matter at all."[151]

Human deprivation, rooted in and sustained by conditions of powerlessness and public indifference, is a theme voiced also by the poorest of the global poor around the world. In interviews with thousands of poor individuals in over fifty countries in both urban and rural settings, the authors of a three-volume study entitled *Voices of the Poor* found that "[a]gain and again, powerlessness seems to be at the core of a bad life . . . Powerlessness is described as the inability to control what happens, the inability to plan for the future, and the imperative of focusing on the present."[152] This concern about powerlessness fits our notion of the importance of a self-determining life to well-being. Moreover, many of those interviewed attributed their condition of powerlessness to factors beyond a mere confluence of unfortunate circumstances. Many cited the arbitrary power of local and state institutions and powerful private actors who thwart their efforts to gain access to social services, earn a living, or escape their harsh circumstances.[153]

We conclude our discussion with a point regarding the "nexus between gender and daily mobility, and the ways in which this nexus coalesces to further embellish the existing power-asymmetries . . . in the developing countries."[154] The heart of this problem is that control over women's lives—where they can go, what they can do, who they can associate with,

---

[150] UN-Habitat, *The Challenge of Slums*, 205.

[151] Katherine Boo, *Behind the Beautiful Forevers: Life, Death, and Hope in a Mumbai Undercity* (New York: Random House, 2012), 236.

[152] Deepa Narayan et al., *Voices of the Poor*, vol. 2: *Crying Out for Change* (Oxford: Oxford University Press, 2000), 36.

[153] Ibid., 25.

[154] Tanu Priya Uteng, *Gender and Mobility in the Developing World*, background paper, World Development Report, 2012 (Washington, DC: World Bank, 2011), 4.

and the risks to physical safety they must endure—is a function of the configuration of urban space and urban modes of travel that is not merely a product of the inattentiveness of men in power to the needs of women. This structural constraint on women is also often a product of a "web of cross-cutting power relations," forged and embedded in patriarchal cultural traditions, enforced within households, and reinforced by state deference to the preferences of men who wish to control women by controlling their movements. In some cases, this state reinforcement goes so far as to make control by men over the movements of women explicitly legal.[155]

Moreover, because women undertake most of the household tasks of securing food, fuel, and water, they face obstacles that do not affect men in quite the same way. Women need more time than men to safely accomplish these tasks because they face the dangers of sexual assault and harassment on public transport, the lack of police protection, and the large swaths of slums that are unsafe to walk in. Women in these environments find it necessary to take self-imposed precautionary measures that limit the times and locations of their movements, and ultimately limit their work opportunities, their associations with others, and their overall ability to lead more self-determining lives. These constraints on women's lives are created by some men, acquiesced in by others, and sustained by men who disvalue the lives of women and their claims to social equality, self-determination, and setting their own terms of personal engagement with others.

Slum life, in short, is not merely bad; it is often unjust in its inception and its effects. For women, slum life is even more confining than it is for the men also caught in its grip.

7.5 Conclusion

The four examples in this chapter confirm a central theme of this book. There are things that powerful, advantaged social groups are willing to do, or at least let happen, to members of other less powerful, less advantaged social groups that they would not be willing to do or let happen to members of their own social group. This starkly differential concern for human well-being lies at the heart of many of the most malignant forms of structural injustice, in which group-based unfairness and human rights violations are so often intertwined. It is reflected in the powerful message

---

[155] Ibid., 18–20.

of Black Lives Matter, the demands of environmental activists from around the world who see themselves as inhabitants of sacrifice zones, and the despair among residents of slums who endure the taunts of those who see them as "desechable" (disposable) and the message that "their deaths would not matter at all."

CHAPTER 8 | Resistance to Injustice

Activism and Social Movements

AS WE NOTED IN chapter 6, the system of reliance on nation-states to protect human rights and address ongoing injustice fails many millions of people. The institutional capacity or the legitimacy of authority in some states is so badly compromised that they are ill-equipped to undertake comprehensive steps to avoid structural unfairness and fulfill human rights within their borders. Secondary duties of other states to step in where these states are unable or unwilling to secure conditions of domestic justice are triggered only after the injustice is especially grave. Even then, it is not clear who has the normative responsibility and authority to act, especially when no available agent has sufficient willingness or institutional capacity to provide the necessary remedies.

Moreover, many transnational sources of injustice lie beyond the jurisdictional reach of any state. Adherence to the Principle of Interstate Reciprocity proposed in chapter 6 is intended to set limits on interstate bargaining that would otherwise result in human rights violations or structural conditions that breed those violations. However, no supranational agency has the normative authority or institutional capacity to enforce the principle, and global collective action problems such as climate change are likely to exacerbate global structural injustice without the creation of new types of global institutional agents.

These gaps in responsibility for addressing structural injustice are particularly acute in the multipolar world of the twenty-first century. Things have changed. We have new sources of concentrated power, new threats that may originate outside of established political boundaries, and a growing cross-border traffic of economic migrants, investors, tax avoiders, electronic data, pollution, diseases, weapons, ideologies, military and intelligence-gathering aircraft, climate and conflict refugees, and natural resource prospectors.

The multipolar world, of course, is centrally composed of states, but it also includes domestic patriarchies, global and domestic power structures within which states are embedded, supranational institutions established and directed by great powers, multinational business entities, and various secular and religious hierarchies. Many of these non-state entities are often the architects of policies implemented by state institutions, and in numerous ways they sometimes eclipse, orchestrate, or usurp crucial exercises of state power. The upshot is that many states are not in good enough working order to handle problems originating within their jurisdictions or problems that originate beyond state borders and extend across them.

Because there are currently problems of structural injustice that no agent has the willingness, capacity, or authority to solve, we seem to be caught in a dilemma. We can either wait until the right sort of global institutional agency is created or try to figure out what we can and indeed may do under these conditions. We need to figure out the remedies and enforcement options that non-state agents can and indeed may pursue in the here and now, instead of deferring hopes of resolution to some indeterminate future when the right sort of institutional agency is created. We have to consider the role of individuals and groups, acting on their own at times or working together within social movements to resist injustice. Often there is no other recourse, especially when states are part of the problem or are simply overwhelmed by other power centers.

Identifying what non-state agents can and may do is not easy. The normative authority that individuals have to step into the breach is morally clouded, especially when ordinary avenues of democratic change are partially, or even largely foreclosed and individual capacities for affecting change on a large scale are uncertain. In this chapter, we examine some strategies of resistance that aggrieved individuals and social groups have adopted. We consider the justification for their pursuit, especially when states are ineffective or unwilling guarantors of structural justice and human rights, along with the conditions under which the targeting of non-state entities is justified.

In section 8.1, we consider what Rawls had to say about civil disobedience and other forms of social protest, only to conclude that the restrictions that he imposed on their exercise do not apply to the world as we find it. In later sections, we use Rawls's framing to help bound the reach of our own inquiry into permissible resistance to injustice.

In section 8.2, we turn our attention to what means and what goals are appropriate for non-state agents who want to resist human rights violations and structural unfairness. Widely discussed and frequently utilized means of resistance include "name and shame" media strategies, boycotts, divestment campaigns, blockades and other legally non-compliant activities, and defensive actions. Goals for resistance efforts include the creation of incentives for non-state entities to initiate change in their conduct, disruption of business as usual, and self-defense or the defense of others. In all of these efforts the ultimate aim is to transform power relations and realign reward structures, sometimes with the effect of stripping beneficiaries of unjust gains.

In section 8.3, we shift from means and goals to targets of resistance. We consider factors relevant for making legitimate targeting decisions, as well as a range of objections. Objections include the charge of undemocratic vigilantism, unfair selective targeting, harm to third parties, and undermining the value of the rule of law.

In section 8.4, we end the chapter and the book with a brief reflection on participation in social justice movements as a vehicle for the realization of the core elements of well-being, which are at present inadequately secured by existing social arrangements, within and across nations.

8.1. Individual Responsibility in a Nearly Just Society

Rawls provides one of the most carefully worked out models of the moral division of labor between states and individuals, but only within a domestic context. Even here, it offers little help with many real-world problems of structural injustice. In chapter 4, we discussed the diagnostic limitations of Rawls's heavily idealized theory. In this chapter we consider why the way Rawls sets up the problem of structural injustice has enormous consequences for how the responsibility of individuals is understood.

As we have already noted, what it means for Rawls's theory to be an ideal theory can be understood in several senses. His theory is intended only for societies characterized by moderate scarcity, not for economies where severe scarcity is commonplace, as is the case in many low- and even some middle-income countries. His theory is also not designed for societies that lack basic economic safety nets or where basic human rights are not protected, and thus the range of issues for which the assignment of responsibility is relevant is truncated. Because each society is treated as a relatively closed, self-contained unit of analysis, there is no need to take account of its impact on other societies when issues of responsibility are under consideration. Nor is there any need to take account of any external impact originating from other political entities or caused by exogenous economic forces. Because the theory is intended only for well-ordered societies that conform to ideals of equality under the rule of law, issues of responsibility directly related to structural racism and structural gender inequalities, for example, are not in play. Equally significant for purposes of thinking about responsibility is Rawls's assumption that a well-ordered society, in which his account of the moral division of labor is applicable, is a well-functioning democracy in which all citizens have comparable opportunities to influence government policy.

Under these idealized conditions, realizing and maintaining social conditions that satisfy the requirements of social justice are the responsibility of states. They are uniquely positioned to alter the structural factors bearing on differential socioeconomic life prospects. Because the society envisioned by Rawls is a "nearly just" one,[1] the responsibility of citizens is largely a matter of supporting just institutions. As we observed in chapters 3 and 6, his background assumption is that human rights violations and discriminatory treatment based on race, gender, or other invidious characteristics are not in play. The society is not riddled with unfair power relationships resulting in group-based domination or involving conditions ripe for exploitation or social exclusion. The context in which the relevant forms of structural injustice arise is so morally cleansed of deep injustices that the duty of citizens to support just institutions involves little more than compliance with generally fair rules. When structural injustice occurs, it arises only at the margins and is quickly addressed by governmental adjustments.

The range of permissible responses by citizens to structural injustice in nearly just societies is, as a consequence, quite limited. What Rawls says about civil disobedience and other forms of legitimate protest reflects the kinds of responses to injustice that he views as warranted in contexts that match his idealized assumptions. Rawls's widely cited duty to support "just institutions" does not rule out acts of protest or civil disobedience by individuals seeking to vindicate their own claims of justice or the claims of others.[2] In this respect, Rawls follows pretty much the standard line of liberal theorizing about the conditional obligations of citizens to obey the law. However, Rawls views civil disobedience, like all legitimate forms

---

[1] Rawls, *TOJ*, 319, 322.
[2] Ibid., 96–100.

of protest in a nearly just society, as a form of democratic dialogue with others.[3] Its only morally legitimate purpose is to persuade other citizens of the moral necessity for reform achievable through democratic processes. Aimed as they are at educating other citizens, all protests and acts of civil disobedience must be public. Rawls's further constraint on justified forms of protest is that those engaged in acts of civil disobedience should accept any corresponding legal penalty.[4]

In the scenario Rawls constructs, the moral gravity of the situation is generally modest and democratic processes function well. The only acceptable form of opposition to policies and practices is democratic dialogue aimed at incremental changes in the rules through processes that are open and fair. Because aggrieved individuals and groups can fully rely on the state to implement remedies for the injustices they suffer, there is no case for direct action or resistance designed to disrupt the status quo. And because the state can exercise comprehensive control over the levers of well-being and social relations, there is no reason to assume that, in some circumstances, other agents of injustice need to be held accountable directly.

Rawls's strictures on the purpose, manner, and target of protests have no place, however, in a world in which many people live in states that do not even approximate these idealized conditions. Nor do they have a place in a world in which injustices are not only domestic but also global, with weaker states and their poorest residents often not positioned to hold their own fates in their own hands. Rawls's theory is not applicable to the world as we know it. And in this world, we need a different way of thinking about how individuals and groups should respond to structural injustices that are far more expansive than the restricted options that Rawls's theory admits.

8.2. Means and Goals of Resistance in Less Ideal Circumstances

Our interest in the appropriate responses to structural injustice lies in the vast territory between Rawls's nearly just society and extreme forms of oppression, such as brutal authoritarian regimes, the institution of slavery, and foreign occupation. In those circumstances, justifiable resistance may well include the use of armed force as a central strategy for combating

---

[3] Ibid., 321.
[4] Ibid., 323.

injustice, but this is not a territory we address. We also set aside any discussion of issues related to the destruction of physical property as a form of resistance. These issues are deeply interwoven with the ethics of armed conflict and the use of force, and the kinds of just cause necessary to warrant activities that pose great risk of loss of human life and physical injury, topics which we do not address.

We are interested in ways of resisting injustice that neither aim for the overthrow of an oppressor nor intend merely to influence or contribute to democratic deliberation. As the phrase "resisting injustice" implies, we are focused on strategies designed to combat active, ongoing, or emerging injustice. We do not weigh in on a related, quite complex set of issues regarding what should be done to vindicate claims of historical injustice. For example, we do not address morally appropriate strategies for pressing demands for reparations for slavery.[5] Nor do we discuss theories of rectification that focus on compensation for injuries, except insofar as theories of compensatory justice can be used analogously to illuminate questions about the kinds of burdens or losses that might justifiably be imposed on contributors to and beneficiaries of injustice as a result of efforts to resist ongoing injustice.

Our understanding of resistance is quite broad. Some definitions restrict the concept of resistance to those activities that are counter to law, but ours does not.[6] Resistance certainly includes, but it is not limited to, activities involving non-compliance with the law. It often emerges out of grassroots social movements that combine the efforts of many into a politically unified force.[7] However, resistance is not necessarily an organized endeavor, at least at the outset. Resistance as we use the term also applies to the actions of individuals who are in a position to utilize their knowledge and capacities as leverage for social change but not necessarily with an

---

[5] For representative discussions, seeJeremy Waldron, "Superseding Historic Injustice," *Ethics* 103, no. 1 (1992): 4–28; Bernard R. Boxill, "A Lockean Argument for Black Reparations," *Journal of Ethics* 7, no. 1 (2003): 63–91; David Lyons, *Confronting Injustice: Moral History and Political Theory* (Oxford: Oxford University Press, 2013); and Coates, "The Case for Reparations."

[6] Simon Caney, "Responding to Global Injustice: On the Right of Resistance," *Social Philosophy & Policy* 32, no. 1 (2015): 53.

[7] We do not offer a definition of a social movement. Most sociological conceptions emphasize the collective, organized nature of a movement, its responses to established power other than ones limited to electoral politics or lobbying, and a collective agenda of demands, though the timing of their emergence and unanimity regarding the movement's goals differ on various conceptions. For some well-known theories, see Mario Diani, "The Concept of Social Movement," *Sociological Review* 40, no. 1 (1992): 1–25; Charles Tilly, *Social Movements, 1768–2004* (Boulder, CO: Paradigm, 2004); and Sidney Tarrow, *Power in Movement: Collective Action, Social Movements and Politics* (Cambridge: Cambridge University Press, 1994).

expectation that they will have an impact on the normal course of electoral politics and legislative advocacy. We have in mind investigative journalists and the advocacy and activism of many NGOs. Whether acts of resistance are part of spontaneous or organized social movements or the acts of a single moral agent, resistance is a bottom-up response to injustice.

Resistance can take many forms, but a common denominator is the resolve of those affected by injustice, or those who witness it firsthand, to refuse to stand idly by and let it happen or wait until someone else, including the state, comes along to fix the problem. The ultimate aim of all direct resistance efforts is to get contributors to structural injustice to either change the way they do things or to stop doing what they are doing.[8]

8.2.1. Organizational Insights from the Ethics of Armed Conflict

Although discussions of the moral limits on the use of armed force is outside the scope of our inquiry, they do reveal some of the key types of considerations that are relevant to the contexts of interest to us. Among the most important are international norms for "armed conflicts in which peoples are fighting against colonial domination, alien occupation or racist regimes." These are contained in the 102 articles of Protocol I, which in 1977 reaffirmed and supplemented the Geneva Convention on Protection of Victims of International Armed Conflicts.[9]

Some articles deal with eligible means. Articles 43 and 44 regulate the activities of guerrilla forces, requiring clothing or emblems that make them recognizable as combatants while preparing for or during an attack. Article 35 bans weapons that "cause superfluous injury or unnecessary suffering," as well as means of warfare that "cause widespread, long-term, and severe damage to the natural environment."

---

[8] Various legal theorists draw the line between civil disobedience and activities directed toward private entities in different ways. Joseph Raz, for example, does not count breaches of law that protest the decisions of private agents such as trade unions, banks, and private universities as acts of civil disobedience. Joseph Raz, *The Authority of Law: Essays on Law and Morality* (Oxford: Clarendon Press, 1979), 264. Brownlee argues that civil disobedience can include challenges to such decisions. Kimberley Brownlee, *Conscience and Conviction: The Case for Civil Disobedience* (Oxford: Oxford University Press, 2012). Our interest is orthogonal to these definitional debates because we are interested in activities directed at both states and private entities, as well as activities that do and do not break the law.

[9] Protocol Additional to the Geneva Conventions of 12 August 1949, and Relating to the Protection of Victims of International Armed Conflicts (Protocol I), 8 June 1977, ICRC, International Committee of the Red Cross.

Other articles deal with eligible goals. Article 64 prohibits military activities from having the objective of acquiring resources for their own benefit or diverting them from essential purposes of the population. Articles 73 and 76 prohibit efforts to impose collective punishments on segments of the population, especially vulnerable members of the community, or engage in criminal acts under the ruse of pursuing legitimate military objectives.

A third class of articles deals with eligible targets. For example, Articles 56 and 53 outlaw attacks on dams, dikes, nuclear generating stations, and places of worship. Articles 51 and 54 outlaw indiscriminate attacks on civilian populations and the destruction of food, water, and other materials needed for survival.

In what follows, we adopt the tripartite organizational structure of Protocol I. In contexts that fall somewhere between a nearly just Rawlsian democracy and extreme conditions of structural injustice exemplified by brutal authoritarian regimes, we explore justified means, goals, and targets of resistance.

We focus on various means that social movements and other non-state agents of social change have employed or considered employing. Our main question is this. What can and may be done by individuals or coalitions of individuals when democratic processes are clogged or laws and prevailing cultural norms not only permit unjust conduct but often also insulate its perpetrators from adverse consequences?

In the remainder of this section, we examine four broad categories of means: naming and shaming; boycotts and disinvestment campaigns; blockades and other direct actions in violation of the law; and organizing for self-defense and the defense of others. These means of responding to injustice can be categorized by the extent to which they involve escalation of moral significance in five dimensions: (i) increasing use of techniques designed to pressure others to do what they otherwise would not do willingly; (ii) disruption of the status quo in ways that risk undermining the value of a web of established social expectations and reliance upon existing norms; (iii) potential for harm to third parties and unintended adverse societal consequences, including failure to mitigate the injustice; (iv) likelihood of damaging effects on democratic processes and public deliberation; and (v) risk of breakdown of civil order and deference to the rule of law upon which civil order and accountable power depend. We begin at the lowest rung on the ladder and move upward to more morally complex responses to structural injustice.

8.2.2. Naming and Shaming

Some responses to injustice are meant primarily to shine a light on the problem. They prick the conscience of persons who may not have thought deeply about an issue or who have failed to fully grasp the relevant facts or their implications. These responses aim at moral persuasion as a primary vehicle for capturing public attention and improving the quality of public dialogue. If all works well, legislative and other kinds of governmental decision-making are affected in ways that may in some respect or other mitigate the injustice. Many different strategies are employed to address injustice through public dialogue, including peaceful protest marches, op-ed essays, hunger strikes, and university teach-ins.

By contrast, although tactics designed to name and shame may be used to influence public debate, they are not always directed to public decision-making within deliberative bodies, nor do they necessarily aim to succeed through consciousness-raising or improvement in the quality of general moral reflection and deliberation. Naming and shaming can be intended to directly change the decision-making and actions of private sector actors. The idea behind this use of naming and shaming is to induce change by leveraging external incentives or disincentives in the choice architecture of private decision-makers. Often the aim is to get private decision-makers to move in a direction not pointed to by their own moral compasses. It would be great if hearts and minds were changed as well or if legislative reform ensued, but these are not the primary mechanisms through which naming and shaming is expected to work. Rather, the strategy is intended to capitalize on its ability to alter how decision-makers believe they appear in the eyes of others. For example, the racist employer might bow to public pressure and refrain from making overtly racist remarks and modify hiring practices, but still subscribe to white supremacist views.

There is, however, a critical relationship between naming and shaming and public dialogue. In order for shame to do its work, existing public opinion has to conform to the perspective of the social critic, or more likely, existing moral horizons have to be altered such that conduct widely accepted as reputable comes to be seen by enough people as dishonorable. In other words, naming and shaming does not replace moral persuasion of the general public and may well depend on it to be effective.

Naming and shaming can be an especially potent response in circumstances in which the source of the injustice straddles political jurisdictions. A naming and shaming campaign against sweatshop labor is a case in point. Its justification is closely linked to the fact that the pathways to a democratic solution are largely foreclosed, not necessarily because of state complicity in injustice but simply because sweatshop labor is an international phenomenon that escapes the normative authority and institutional capacity of any state to comprehensively solve on its own. The problem is inherent in the business model. Most retailers and fabricators of clothing operate on the basis of short-term contracts. Contracts are for "just in time production" of consumer products that have a short life in the fashion world. Global buyers offload the market risks onto the fabricators, who own the physical facilities and bear the burdens of employment and environmental regulation. The buyers are free to contract for services elsewhere. And they can do so usually in a matter of months because, at the site of production, they own nothing, hire no employees, and do not have a long-term stake that harnesses them to local laws, regulations, and taxation.

The effectiveness of naming and shaming is a matter of debate. Moral fatigue among consumers can be quick to set in, especially when the cumulative impact of such campaigns is awareness among members of the public that just about every item of their clothing, all of their electronic devices, and much of their food is sourced in ways that take advantage of and exacerbate structural injustices, and that their consumer goods would likely cost more were they to insist on products being free from unjust practices. Still, naming and shaming is often one of the few potentially effective forms of resistance available because of global gaps in institutional remedies.

8.2.3. Boycotts and Divestment Campaigns

The next step up the ladder of moral complexity involves boycotts and divestment campaigns. As with naming and shaming, the aim of boycotts and divestment campaigns is to alter the incentives of those in positions of power in order to pressure them to change their behavior. Typically, the focus is on purchasers and sellers that are involved in harmful, unjust business practices or that support or sustain the unjust activities of others. With boycotts, the incentives for producers and sellers are changed by changing the purchasing decisions of consumers, while in disinvestment campaigns these incentives are altered by changing the practices of investors and shareholders, and ultimately of the firms that engage in conduct the campaigners find objectionable. Often, the aim of boycotts and divestment campaigns is not to get others to do what they do in a more just manner but to get them to stop what they are doing. For example, the aim is to stop them from using coal as an energy source or from buying up farmland and water resources in poor regions of the world for the benefit of the global affluent.

Critics often object to boycotts and divestment campaigns, though more seems to be written about the former than the later. The core objection is that those who mount these campaigns use market power to achieve fundamental social change that the critics believe should be pursued through democratic means. By taking direct action to put an end to the unjust conduct of others, activists bypass the use of democratic processes aimed at enacting legally enforceable rules. Moreover, unlike naming and shaming, which is often initiated by the exposés of NGOs or investigative journalists, boycotts and divestment campaigns work by issuing and acting on threats. Instead of using embarrassment and shame as incentives to motivate others to alter their behavior, threats of economic reprisal are the centerpiece of the tactic.

Arguably, threatening behavior is morally different from naming and shaming, which typically relies on public consciousness-raising or moral persuasion as a means to pressure corporations to alter their practices. An uncharitable description would be that boycotts rely upon intimidation, bullying, and unaccountable power exercised at will by groups whose social agendas can vary greatly in terms of their moral character.

Objections of this sort sometimes suggest that boycotts in particular can often take the form of vigilantism, a morally tainted substitution of private power to achieve a broad social agenda that ought to be realized, if at all, through democratic means.[10] The vigilantism objection rests on the assumption that, at least within a democracy, the use of market power by organized groups to achieve changes in the social and economic order interferes in unacceptable ways with problems that should be dealt with through democratic deliberation. The critics assume that deliberation is morally superior in procedural terms because decisions affecting work and commerce are matters of collective concern, and therefore ought to be reserved for collective determination.

A further worry raised by critics is that efforts to realign incentive structures for the sake of a focal objective can have adverse ripple effects that, in principle, require democratic deliberation and government policy to weigh and address. What is needed, and what deliberation and policy can supply, are mechanisms that allow for appropriate adjustments to be made

---

[10] Waheed Hussain, "Is Ethical Consumerism an Impermissible Form of Vigilantism?," *Philosophy and Public Affairs* 40, no. 2 (2012): 113–143.

over time in order to mitigate or curtail unintended social consequences. For example, opponents of those who advocate boycotting non-renewable sources of energy point to the negative impacts such boycotts would have on both low- and middle-income US consumers who benefit from cheap energy and workers in these industries who stand to lose their only means of livelihood. Only democratic bodies can balance the fuller range of social considerations at stake. For both procedural and outcome-oriented reasons, the argument is that democratic processes are better vehicles for social change than organized efforts to mobilize consumers to use market power to achieve a narrow social agenda.

Moreover, boycotts and divestment campaigns not only pose the risk of getting complex policy choices wrong or disrupting the salutary deliberative aims of democracy. The use of private market power to effect change is especially risky for additional moral reasons. Critics note that boycotts in particular have been used for morally dubious or socially contentious aims, such as dissuading pharmacies from stocking contraceptives or pressuring employers to adopt benefits policies that discriminate on the basis of sexual orientation. The history of boycotts, for example, includes European boycotts against Jewish merchants in the 1930s. They were used, as Waheed Hussain puts it, to deprive people of their basic rights to free religious expression by making it economically impossible to exercise such expression.[11] Our theory, however, condemns boycotts and divestment campaigns whenever they are used as instruments for creating and sustaining the kinds of structural unfairness, like social exclusion, that our theory counts among its central concerns.

These strands of the vigilantism objection, in our view, do not involve risks that are unique to market-based strategies for redressing structural injustices. The risks that it identifies inhere in all exercises of power, whether public or private. Both noble and ignoble objectives are often blocked or achieved on the basis of the balance of power in legislative venues. Democratic processes offer no guarantee that the very same unjust results will not emerge from legislative decisions. After all, there is a considerable overlap between the consumer constituency that is able to carry the day in its use of market power and the voter constituency that has the power to determine legislative outcomes. For example, the same constellations of power at work in the 1930s consumer boycotts against

---

[11] Ibid., 117–118.

Jewish merchants also achieved their objectives by voting into office the National Socialist, or Nazi, Party.

On our view, the vigilantism worry that boycotts are inherently problematic rests on assumptions that miss key moral differences and rely on a politically unrealistic understanding of power. Consider what is at stake, for example, when democratic processes are held captive to powerful economic interests that block economic justice or when patriarchal constituencies use the law to consolidate the subordination of women. These social agendas are similar in intent and outcome to the boycotts of Jewish businesses. All these agendas aim to subordinate, marginalize, and exploit the powerless, whether through laws or boycotts. The moral character of these uses of boycotts and political processes is fundamentally different from social agendas that aim to use boycotts or laws to do the opposite. While the former clearly runs counter to ideals of democratic equality, the latter are in alignment.

It also matters morally if market power is used by the democratically disempowered for purposes of combating otherwise unfair and largely inescapable power relations or used by the powerful to retain their power and use it for socially exclusionary purposes. The same point applies to the use and misuse of democratic processes. Exclusionary purposes are unjust uses of power in both arenas.

More troubling is the worry that boycotts and disinvestment campaigns are poor vehicles for dealing with the full panoply of social issues that democratic deliberation is in principle designed to address. Market power aims to stop some objectionable conduct without simultaneously addressing the broader social considerations and consequences with which the conduct may be intertwined. For example, social movements might get an oil extracting company to increase the technical investment it makes in environmental safety, but their success neither mitigates the fallout for workers who might be displaced as a result nor prevents related increases in energy costs. Companies responding to economic threats can only stop what they are doing. They cannot solve the attendant social problems. In most cases, only a legislative or other government solution can address the full range of issues of social justice as a package deal.

The problem with this objection is that it suffers from a lack of political realism. Even when state action—for example, entering into international free trade agreements—results in worker displacement or an increase in the price of some consumer goods, democratic institutions in many countries do not step in to deal with the collateral damage. They do not always ramp up social safety nets to address employment issues or implement subsidies to augment lost consumer purchasing power of low- and middle-income families. There is simply no reasonable expectation, based on the way things are, that democratic processes that have the normative authority and institutional capacity to address broader issues of justice will necessarily or even often do so. At best, the argument counsels a form of social advocacy that puts the ancillary issues on its agenda and, if possible, works to create positive incentives for other private decision-makers to pick up the slack. It is therefore not very convincing to object that social movements cannot pursue a tactic that may have consequences they cannot remedy when in fact those having the power in democratic arenas to remedy the collateral damage do not do so.

Whether boycotts hold great promise as effective tools for combating structural injustice and human rights violations is another matter. This is not simply a strategic issue but an ethical concern. As Hussain correctly points out, the overwhelming concentration of market power resides in the affluent consumers of the world. They differentially benefit from many of the practices and power relations that organizers of boycotts seek to pressure manufacturers and retailers to curtail or relinquish.[12] We can see where the bulk of market power resides by observing that the most affluent 20 percent of the global population accounts for more than 80 percent of consumer spending.[13] Unless the affluent are willing to act contrary to their economic self-interests, they are likely to overwhelm the efforts of those who seek to leverage market power to alter the practices of manufacturers and retailers in ways that address structural injustices but increase the costs or decrease the diversity of consumer goods. An overlapping concentration of political power within the global affluent classes likewise overwhelms democratic efforts to get the most privileged to do what they are likely to view as contrary to their self-interests. To paraphrase Martin Luther King, Jr., power and advantage are never given up voluntarily; fairness must be demanded by the powerless and the disadvantaged.[14]

Market leverage deployed on behalf of a social justice agenda thus suffers from some of the same defects of democratic processes, and for

---

[12] Ibid., 120.

[13] McKinsey Global Institute, "Urban World: The Global Consumers to Watch" (2016), https://www.mckinsey.com/global-themes/urbanization/urban-world-the-global-consumers-to-watch/~/media/57c6ad7f7f1b44a6bd2e24f0777b4cd6.ashx.

[14] King said that "freedom is never voluntarily given by the oppressor; it must be demanded by the oppressed." Martin Luther King, "Letter from Birmingham City Jail," in *A Testament of Hope: The Essential Writings and Speeches of Martin Luther King*, Jr., ed. James Melvin Washington (New York: HarperCollins, 1991), 292.

many of the same reasons. The effectiveness of both strategies is limited by the imbalanced distribution of power, generally, and this points to a larger critique of overreliance upon market-based social justice strategies. The experience of fair-trade initiatives reveals numerous instances of unintended consequences. For example, in some cases, marketing to the tiny segment of consumers of conscience has resulted in increased profits (though not so much in terms of market share) for some well-intentioned companies and an improved standard of living for their workers. While it is an undeniably good thing to pull a few people out of poverty, these small-scale interventions, spurred by consumer campaigns, do little or nothing to address the structural root causes of global poverty.[15] The bottom line here is that we should be wary of all strategies that put too much faith in our ability to shop our way to social justice.

8.2.4. Blockades, Data Hacks, and Other Violations of Law

Resistance movements focused on climate change and environmental degradation are especially interested in strategies that involve activities that do not comply with the law. Such movements are growing rapidly around the world. Many proponents argue that democratic avenues are blocked as a result of a combination of shortsightedness on the part of the public, the self-interests of politically and economically dominant social groups, and even a failure to recognize that inaction will result in massive human rights deficits. As a consequence, these movements endorse direct-action techniques that involve blockades, obstructive encampments, and putting movement participants at risk of physical harm—for example, where ground is being broken for new carbon-intensive infrastructure projects.

The global umbrella of the movement is sometimes referred to as "Blockadia," a name taken from an encampment of activists who were mostly drawn from First Nation communities in Canada. These activists are seeking to stop the construction of the TransCanada pipeline in order to prevent what they see as the destruction of their local environment and the unjustified perpetuation of a business model that has drastic implications for the entire planet. As evidence of the political logjam and moral intransigence of the dominant political class, the activists point out the role of their prime minister in the global promotion of Canadian tar sands. More

---

[15] Ndongo Samba Sylla, "Fairtrade Is an Unjust Movement That Serves the Rich," *Guardian* (September 5, 2014), https://www.theguardian.com/global-development/2014/sep/05/fairtrade-unjust-movement-serves-rich

generally, the activists note the state's deep involvement with financing, permitting, and using its eminent domain authority to acquire land that private owners refuse to sell.[16]

In Canada, Australia, Greece, and elsewhere activists are standing in front of bulldozers, chaining themselves to construction fences, and blocking oil tankers from entry to deep-water ports. Organizations such as 350.org prominently endorse and help with the coordination of such efforts on the grounds that we face a planetary crisis, that democratic institutions are inadequate to the task of doing enough, soon enough, to avert an environmental and human rights catastrophe. All of these activities target both private and state entities simultaneously, often employing tactics that are known to violate the law.

There are many more examples. Much of what has been brought to light by investigative journalists and NGOs about global tax evasion, the movement of dark money, and shell corporations designed to shield from accountability foreign investments that pension funds and hedge funds claim not to be making has involved violations of confidentiality that are often legally protected. The hidden aspects of the international arms trade are brought to light by a variety of hackers, data pirates, and whistle blowers who also have violated confidentiality or other legal duties.[17] Community activists and even some state and local agencies shield and provide support to undocumented persons. These activities, too, are in violation of some laws.

Put aside the possibility that in some cases some of these activities are strategically ineffective or even counterproductive and instead assume that they sometimes offer promise where other forms of democratic activism or resistance are likely to fail. Assume also that activists' estimates of the moral stakes are correct and that what hangs in the balance are human rights violations or other significant structural injustices that facilitate human rights violations. Imagine, then, the formation of the Global Environmental Resistance Movement (GERM)—a kind of Greenpeace on steroids. What moral warrant would carbon-intensive nations have in using coercion to suppress the resisters?

This is, of course, a complicated question. We could use any number of alternative examples to raise the issue of moral justification for legal

---

[16] Ed Struzik, "Canada's Trudeau is Under Fire for His Record on Green Issues," *Yale Environment 360* (January 19, 2017), http://e360.yale.edu/features/canada_justin_trudeau_environmental_policy_pipelines.

[17] International Committee of Investigative Journalists, "The Panama Papers" (April 3, 2016), https://panamapapers.icij.org/.

non-compliance, and it may be instructive to think about the general question through the lens of a different set of facts. But one familiar approach to the question is found in the account of political legitimacy we discussed in chapter 6. Political legitimacy, as we said there, is a normative standard by which we judge whether a state's exercise of coercion is permissible.

One specific implication of political legitimacy bears on our GERM example. As we noted earlier, there are divergent philosophical accounts of the minimum normative standards that states must satisfy in order for them to legitimately use coercion and for individuals to be placed under a presumptive duty to comply. We endorse a deliberately weak one. A state's use of coercion and the presumptive requirements to obey its commands are justified only when a state meets certain minimum standards of justice: it must respect and protect the human rights of its citizens and show due respect for the human rights of all other human beings.

Neither this account nor any other more demanding theory of political legitimacy argues for the absurd claim that state use of coercion is never justified unless there is perfect compliance with every last human right or for the equally implausible claim that no one under a state's jurisdiction has any presumptive reason to comply with its commands unless the state is fully just. The reason is that we should not assume that political legitimacy is an all-or-nothing matter. A state would be justified, say, in using coercion to prevent and punish rape, but not justified in using coercion to secure for some privileged groups the economic benefits derived from human rights violations.

Whether any particular set of grievances constitute the kinds of injustices that trigger presumptive reasons for engaging in illegally prohibited forms of resistance, and whether all of the prerequisite conditions for doing so are satisfied, has to be answered on a case-by-case basis. Proponents of such activities bear a heavy burden of justification. For example, without filling in much more of the story, local objections to constructing a dam that destroys a trout stream or complaints against building a bridge across an environmentally sensitive wetland would not meet that burden.

Socially disruptive activities that violate the law require more stringent justification because they take another step up the ladder of moral significance. They involve more forceful techniques designed to pressure others to do what they otherwise would not do willingly. Moreover, these activities may disrupt not only what is unjust in the status quo but also what is socially valuable about established social expectations and existing norms. They may also expose innocent third parties to potential harm and create new opportunities for unintended adverse societal consequences that laws are intended to prevent. Legally prohibited forms of resistance pose the additional risk of damaging respect for democratic processes and for the rule of law, upon which civil order and accountable power depend. Despite these risks, however, a blanket rejection of such strategies as always unjustifiable is, in our view, not defensible.

8.2.5. Self-Defense and Defense of Others

The final rung up the ladder is an even more contentious form of resistance to injustice. Self-defense, unlike blockades, is not necessarily a violation of the law in all jurisdictions. However, because bodily force is involved, it is commonplace for legal systems to recognize only a limited right of defense of oneself or others. When social activists engage in what they understand to be self-defense or the defense of others, their actions may or may not be considered lawful. Yet even in circumstances where full-scale armed conflict aimed at overthrowing those in power is not justifiable, methods for self-defense or defense of others are sometimes defended by social movements. These defenders argue that they are necessary to put an end to activity that is seriously harmful to innocent people, including state-sanctioned violence.

Defensive measures may be particularly fitting responses to structural injustices when some social groups are threatened by and experience physical violence and psychological intimidation in ways not faced by other groups, and the state fails in its duty to protect the physical security of the threatened groups. Indeed, the moral case for self-defense or defense of others is strongest when states are powerless or unwilling to take adequate steps to prevent harm to group members. The case is particularly strong when agents of the state exceed their authorization to use force and are the front-line perpetrators of the threatened harm. To be sure, the line of demarcation between circumstances in which such injustices warrant full-scale armed conflict to repel those currently in government or otherwise wielding the apparatus of the state and circumstances under which only self-defense is appropriate is not always easy to draw. But because it is difficult to do so does not mean that there are no cases where the right of self-defense is justified but wholesale, armed conflict is not.

To some readers this line of argument might seem at odds with the positions taken by well-known practitioners of non-violent resistance, but that impression would be mistaken. Gandhi coined the term "civil resistance" as an alternative to standard references to non-violent resistance in part to emphasize that self-defense and defense of others should not be an option surrendered lightly.[18] His argument is that this option is important where it is imminently necessary to disempower those who misuse an otherwise rightful grant of power or do not merit the kind of power they exercise, including power that involves the persistent threat of arbitrary exercises of force for purposes of subordination. This sort of conduct fundamentally differs from the use of force, restrained by the rule of law, for legitimate purposes of law enforcement or public safety.

Gandhi's point is not inconsistent with his strong commitment to non-violence, which he defends on both strategic and moral reasons. For Gandhi, even the immediate goal of self-defense against an imminent threat is preferably achieved peacefully. However, he recognized that peaceful means are not always an option. What is possible for successful defense in particular circumstances is not entirely up to the resisters to choose.

The emphasis on "civil" then is meant to indicate that whenever forceful resistance is necessary, its use should be restrained by the aim of preserving the civil character of society, even when the tactics employed are designed to undermine some uses of the adversary's sources of power. The function of forceful civil resistance is purely defensive, time-limited, and directed against an imminent threat. Unlike armed conflict, it is not aimed at the coercive transformation of society or seizing control of the machinery of government. The triggering threats are not viewed as warranting the creation of a standing militia, composed of lawful, clearly identifiable armed combatants, as they are defined under the Geneva protocol. And certainly, it is not to be deployed for punitive purposes, to extract revenge, or to terrorize or demoralize the communities of those who unjustly employ violence or the threat of violence against them.

There are historical and contemporary examples that illustrate the basic idea, though our task is not to weigh in on which ones are or have been justified. Civil rights workers in the Mississippi Freedom Rides of 1961 faced imminent threats of death, and while they eschewed violence as a means of achieving their goals, they traveled with armed protection during the most dangerous parts of the trip. Leaders of peaceful protests in Tahir Square organized armed groups to repel pro-regime, out-of-uniform attackers on horseback.

---

[18] Many of the normative and factual claims in this section owe a great debt to Adam Roberts's introduction to and other essays in *Civil Resistance and Power Politics: The Experience of Non-violent Action from Gandhi to the Present*, ed. Adam Roberts and Timothy Garton Ash (Oxford: Oxford University Press, 2009).

The practitioners of civil resistance in these examples are fundamentally unlike the private, armed militias that have appeared in some western states of the US. These militias also claim to be engaging in self-defense, but they assert the illegitimacy of both federal authority and any police jurisdiction over the land where the militias reside. Their posture is not defensive, and their tactics are not short-term responses to focal, imminent threats. Rather, these militias embrace objectives that align more with the Geneva Convention definition of armed combatants. Their uprisings and armed standoffs with authorities are viewed as serving purposes going well beyond immediate goals of self-defense. These differences make such movements fundamentally different from what US civil rights activists and most of the leaders of the Arab Spring uprisings envisioned.

Even when a social movement seeks the removal of an oppressive regime, the types of justifiable activity that fall under the umbrella of self-defense are normatively distinct. Gandhi, for example, embraced the aim of ousting illegitimate authority, but he viewed participants who were involved in strictly self-defense efforts as engaged in a morally different kind of activity than freedom fighters. As we have already noted, Gandhi argued that self-defense is not an option to be surrendered lightly. However, he argued even more vociferously that it was not an option to be exercised without circumspection. Gandhi also cautioned that self-defense activities should not be pursued in ways that conflate its narrow objectives with more aggressive strategies meant to address the full range of grievances. For example, defense of others might justify forceful restraint of rogue police engaged in a malicious beating of an unarmed citizen, but it does not provide a reason to fire shots at police cruisers in order to deter such behavior, even in neighborhoods where such beatings are perceived as a systemic, daily fact of life.

8.3. Targets of Resistance: Contributors and Beneficiaries

Self-defense is a singular category of potentially justified resistance in at least one respect. Would-be resisters know the immediate perpetrators of the injustice. The specific unjust acts whose consequences they wish to prevent through self-defense are clear. This is not always true for the other three types of resistance strategies that social movements and other non-state agents of social change might employ in response to human rights violations and other structural injustices. In the case of naming and shaming, boycotts and divestment, and blockades, data hacks, and other violations of law, we need some desiderata for determining the appropriate targets of resistance, especially when the targets include non-state entities. An equally thorny issue concerns the basis for selecting targets where there are multiple contributors to injustice and some priorities have to be made. These and other moral complexities have given rise to a family of objections to targeting non-state entities based on claims of unfairness in the selection of targets.

8.3.1. The "All or None" Objection

A threshold objection asks why justice movements should pick out one target when there are arguably many causal contributors to the injustice and all bear some measure of fault. The more specific objection is that it is unfair to single out one contributor unless all contributors are made to bear a share of responsibility proportionate to their contribution. Fairness, these critics argue, requires holding responsible all or none. Moreover, even if resisters do have all contributors to the injustice in their sights, determining the proportionate contribution of each often eludes the epistemic abilities of social movement activists, and the epistemic challenge alone leaves acts of resistance open to the unfairness objection.[19]

In thinking about the burdens and losses that resisters justifiably may impose on their targets, an analogy to legal theories of compensation for injury is helpful. The arguments in the tort liability and resistance to injustice contexts are structurally similar. Both involve holding some contributors accountable in ways that have significant economic impact while other contributors escape these consequences. Judges deciding complex tort cases regularly dismiss the "all or none" objection. We argue that it should be rejected not only in law but also in determining whom it is acceptable for social movements to target and hold accountable for injustice.

Imagine a number of manufacturing companies that over the course of many years dump chemical effluent into a river. The cumulate effect is a toxic soup that damages farmland downstream. Suppose that some companies are no longer in business, some companies profited greatly, and other companies barely made ends meet. Suppose also that some companies are known to have dumped a lot of chemical effluent, while

---

[19] David Miller, "Global Justice and Climate Change: How Should Responsibilities Be Distributed? Parts I and II," in *Tanner Lectures on Human Values 28*, ed. G. B. Peterson (Salt Lake City: University of Utah Press, 2008), 119–156; Eric Posner and Cass Sunstein, "Global Warming and Social Justice: Do We Owe the World for Climate Change?," *Regulation* 31, no. 1 (2008): 14–20.

it is uncertain how much other companies dumped. Courts do not accept in-principle and as determinative the defendants' claims that it is unfair to assign liability without clear criteria for apportioning damages on the basis of contribution or that it is unfair to hold liable the companies still in business or those having "deep pockets" sufficient to pay damages. Instead, courts point to the plaintiffs' competing claims of unfairness and conclude that it would be a graver injustice to leave injured parties without recourse to remedy by letting everyone off the hook simply because all contributors cannot be held accountable in proportion to their contribution.

The analogous moral point is that we should reject the "all or none" complaint made by companies targeted by resistance campaigns that it is unfair that they should sustain a loss of share value or other economic opportunity when other similarly situated companies are off the hook. As in the tort liability context, potential targets of resistance are not all situated similarly with regard to likelihood of impact or satisfaction. Moreover, resistance movements cannot be expected to have the resources to address all perpetrators of the same injustice or of the same kind of injustice all at once. If a name and shame campaign targets one garment manufacturer for its labor exploitation practices, that manufacturer has no basis for complaint based on the fact that other exploiting companies were not targeted and therefore did not also face loss of share value or economic opportunity as a consequence. If grassroots organizations attempt to blockade the construction of a massive new carbon-intensive energy facility, resulting in costly delays or even cancellation of the project, the public or private owners have no grounds to object based on the fact that their competitor's existing facilities continue to operate without the economic burdens created by resisters.

8.3.2. Two Tiers of Targeting Considerations

Of course, resistance is justified only if the targeted entity either contributed to an injustice, or benefited from an injustice, or both. These are matters determined on the basis of the specifics of the case. But assume that a threshold determination that an entity is in fact appropriately connected to injustice is satisfied. We then need some criteria for determining targeting. We propose two tiers of considerations to aid decision-making.

The first tier focuses on strategic considerations that should be taken into consideration in selecting targets. Importantly, each of these considerations is supported by moral reasons. Moral backing matters because of the expectation that the campaign's means of resistance will impose economic or other losses on its target, and also possibly on other parties. Even if all the gains at issue are considered morally undeserved in the larger scheme of things, the imposition of corresponding losses is not always ethically straightforward. This is because the gains may have arisen under conditions in which there was an existing social expectation that what the agents are doing was not part of an unjust social practice. Existing social expectations, though not decisive, are entitled to some moral weight because people plan their lives around them.

The second tier of considerations focuses on morally compounding factors that provide additional reasons for selecting particular beneficiaries of injustice as targets of resistance activities. We examine four categories of ill-gotten gains realized through one or more forms of compounding injustice: complicity in other injustices; anti-democratic conduct; anti-competitive conduct; and accountability avoidance. The categories are not meant to be mutually exclusive, but they merit separate discussion because of the different moral salience of each.

8.3.3. First-Tier Considerations

Four first-tier strategic considerations are relevant to the threshold identification of potential targets for resistance campaigns. The first strategic consideration is the scale or magnitude of a potential target's contribution to injustice. Consider, for example, large retailers that operate extensive, exploitative global supply chains or polluters responsible for massive environmental degradation and harm to public health.

The second strategic consideration is the magnitude of the profits or other benefits a potential target derives from its contribution to injustice. There is no perfect correlation between magnitude of harm and magnitude of benefit, but both are relevant factors.

The third strategic consideration takes account of the prospect of victory, understood as the likelihood of achieving the aims of the campaign. This is not merely a matter of going after the low-hanging fruit. Because it is likely that losses will be imposed on the potential target, and possibly also on other parties, it is important to prioritize resistance activities that have a better chance of succeeding so that these harms are not incurred needlessly, without benefit to others.

The fourth strategic consideration is the likelihood of broader impact, beyond the immediate aims of the campaign, if the campaign is successful. For example, a successful boycott of a large, highly visible retail chain that sources its fresh tomatoes from farms that fail to pay a living wage and subject their workers to human rights abuses is successful if the retail chain changes its supply chain practices and restricts purchasing to farms with appropriate labor practices. If successful, this kind of campaign is also likely to have a broader, catalytic or domino effect on other retail purchasing decisions.[20] Targeted resistance on this ground also offers the prospect of avoiding needless harm to other potential targets and third parties, as well as the prospect of being effective in mitigating injustice on a larger scale.

Other things being equal, strategic targeting of entities for which most or all of these four boxes are checked is backed by powerful moral reasons. The main moral reasons behind the first, third, and fourth considerations are the importance of avoiding the imposition of harm on others when it is unlikely that the resistance efforts will be successful and the importance of selecting targets that are likely to result in the greatest reduction of the injustice that motivates the resistance efforts in the first place.

The moral reasons for including the magnitude of benefit received from the injustice as a consideration in selecting targets are somewhat different. At the very least, those who benefit greatly from injustice are poorly positioned to object that they are being unfairly targeted. It is arguably the case that, where possible, those who benefit more from injustice should be held to greater account than those who benefit less. Also, if what is at stake for the potential target is significant, the resistance activity may be able to secure some relief from the injustice in a timelier way and with fewer resources, leaving open the possibility of turning to other targets more quickly.

We do not think, however, that a strict algorithm of the sort often used to calculate the proportionate share of compensatory duties is a helpful approach to thinking about targeting resistance to structural injustice. Consider a familiar way of thinking about the appropriate response to injustice called the "wrongful benefits approach." It is modeled on legal theories of unjust enrichment, which require agents to surrender or "disgorge" the benefits received from an injustice.[21] The intuitive idea is that individuals are under a presumptive duty to compensate victims of injustice by returning the full value of the ill-gotten gains, and individuals who

---

[20] See, e.g., Coalition of Immokalee Workers, "Modern Farmer Article Traces History of Fair Food Movement . . ." (December 18, 2015), http://ciw-online.org/blog/2015/12/modern-farmer-article/.

[21] David Brooks, "On Living in an Unjust Society," *Journal of Applied Philosophy* 6, no. 1 (1989): 31–42.

fail to do so are blameworthy.[22] Thus, intrinsic to the wrongful benefits approach is the need to calculate the full value of what each beneficiary of the injustice has received, in order to determine what each owes to the victims.

However, we are not suggesting that a *precise* magnitude of benefit is relevant to targeting decisions, both because we have general reservations about the feasibility of the wrongful benefits approach, as others have argued,[23] and because our purpose and the purpose of that approach are quite different.

On the general feasibility point, the idea of an exact calculation of ill-gotten gains is confounded by the fact that the benefits any entity receives from structural injustice are a function of complex social processes. They are not analogous to the traceable benefits derived from single transactions, for example, where we can calculate the undeserved benefit derived from the receipt of a stolen painting. Moreover, the benefits from structural injustice are not merely monetary, but include a bundle of social privileges and elevated social standing that come with being a member of a dominant social group.

For these general reasons we have reservations about the wrongful benefits approach. We have an additional reservation, however, that is specific to our context. The problem we are addressing is fundamentally different from the one the wrongful benefits approach was designed, however ineffectively, to address. The wrongful benefits approach operates through a perspective on what beneficiaries owe the victims of injustice in order to make amends or compensate for the harm others have suffered. By contrast, our focus is on what the victims and their advocates may take back from the beneficiaries, or get them to make changes in the way they accrue benefits, without the beneficiaries having preemptive moral grounds for opposition. Accordingly, we have no rationale for or interest in precise magnitudes of benefit, because we are not seeking compensation for some specific quantum of undeserved gains. For us, what matters is that a target has made and continues to make a large contribution to injustice and, in the process, receives a large benefit. It is this fact that explains why targets lack grounds for complaint should the burdens created by resistance fall heavier upon them than other contributing

---

[22] Ibid., 36; Daniel Butt, "On Benefitting from Injustice," *Canadian Journal of Philosophy* 37, no. 1 (2007): 129–152.

[23] Avery Kolers, "The Priority of Solidarity to Justice," *Journal of Applied Philosophy* 31, no. 4 (2014): 420–425.

beneficiaries. Calculations are not relevant, because compensation is not the point. Rather, the point is to decide whether there is adequate justification for the imposition of loss on some but not all contributing beneficiaries of injustice.

8.3.4. Second-Tier Considerations

In many cases there will be multiple entities that contributed to and benefited from structural injustice in ways that meet the threshold desiderata of the first tier of considerations. How might the process of target selection be refined? We argue that there are certain additional features of the behavior of some beneficiaries of injustice that make targeting the gains they receive from the injustice particularly appropriate.

We turn now to the second tier of considerations for targeting companies that satisfy the first tier. These entities, especially private sector targets of strategies intended to affect their market share and disrupt business as usual, will object to being singled out. How might we go about a process of target selection that diffuses those objections? We argue that a more refined basis for targeting should take into consideration not only whether beneficiaries have benefited from structural injustice but also if they have in some way contributed to the injustice in morally objectionable ways. We discuss four factors that provide additional reasons for selecting particular beneficiaries to be targets of resistance activities.

8.3.5. Passive Complicity in Injustices by Others

The first factor to consider in targeting decisions is *passive* complicity in the injustices perpetrated by others. Different definitions of complicity have been used for different practical purposes, and so it is important for us to stipulate what we have in mind by complicity in this context. We begin by drawing a contrast to one such account. A familiar way of being implicated as a complicit party in an injustice is by being a participant in a joint project defined by a common end. Each participant is complicit by doing her or his part to support the shared end through whatever means available. This account is meant to elucidate, for example, what is involved in the assignment of responsibility for the extermination of Jews and other victims in the Nazi Holocaust, not only to those who masterminded and ran the Nazi death camps, but also to local police, managers of the railroads, train conductors, and others who shared the ends of Nazi executioners and did their part to facilitate the killing.

We want a weaker standard that still points to a significant way in which those who have some less direct connection to injustices are morally implicated. A passively complicit agent on our account knows the ends of the perpetrators and is aware of the unjust means used to achieve them. She does not necessarily share those ends, or as Howard McGary puts it, complicit agents "need not see themselves as interested in another's interest."[24] The complicit agent does, however, need the perpetrators to succeed in achieving at least some aspects of their ends in order to get what she wants. All things being equal, she would prefer that her ends were achieved by different means that were not unjust, but she takes no steps to make that happen.

On our account, then, the passively complicit agent need not share the ends of the perpetrators of the injustice, but she allows herself to benefit from their pursuit of them, without protest or complaint. In this sense, the complicit agent passively supports the ends of the other. Importantly, the complicit agent would not alter her own actions in pursuit of the benefits she seeks or forgo the benefits secured by the unjust actions of others in order to disrupt the unjust means employed by the other. The complicit agent is not directly involved in a collective injustice. She is not like the guards in the death camps, or even like those who helped round up or transport Jews to the camps. At the same time, however, she has a different moral posture in relation to both the means and the ends of the injustice than those who truly are merely innocent bystanders. Here are three examples of how this complex idea of complicity works.

In the first example, a mining company is engaged in the extraction of minerals in a brutal autocratic country where atrocities regularly occur. The autocrat responsible for the atrocities needs the proceeds from the mining industry in order to stay in power. The company does not commit the atrocities. It is not interested in the autocrat's preference for using brutal techniques to secure social control, nor is it interested in his authoritarian objective. The company is interested, however, in the autocrat's success in maintaining a stable and tightly controlled business environment. Though the company's executives know how that business environment is secured, the company nonetheless continues to reap the benefits of what the autocrat does. If disrupting the autocrat's preferred techniques of maintaining social control meant forgoing the lucrative mining contract, the company would not do so.

---

[24] Howard McGary, "Morality and Collective Liability," *Journal of Value Inquiry* 20, no. 2 (1986): 158.

The second example involves a clothing retailer that contracts with garment fabricators in a low-income country. The retailer knows that the fabricators rely on an intrusive private police force to keep down labor unrest. The retailer is not in any way directly involved with the activities or tactics of the private police force. It would be perfectly satisfied, and even prefer, if favorable workplace conditions were achieved in some other way. Nonetheless, because of the benefits the contractual arrangements bring to the company, it will continue contracting with the fabricators as long as favorable workplace conditions are maintained.

The third example is more nuanced. Consider some white Americans. They are aware that aggressive police tactics in poor urban neighborhoods of color are routine. They do not personally participate in the disproportionate killing of unarmed black men, nor do they necessarily share the attitudes of white supremacists who actively support these unjust means of social control. However, they are unwilling to sacrifice anything of personal value to alleviate these injustices. For example, they are unwilling to pay more taxes or redistribute public revenue to help reduce police brutality or improve infrastructure or opportunities in minority communities. Nor are they willing to demand more restraints on police misconduct, because they value the sense of personal security that they feel results when police are given a wide berth.

8.3.6. Anti-Democratic Conduct

The second factor in targeting decisions is anti-democratic conduct. The essence of this concern involves unfair uses of power of the sort discussed in the preceding chapter, where undue influence is exerted over the electoral process, legislative deliberation, or executive decision-making.

Making massive campaign contributions to candidates in order to secure self-serving legislative and other governmental outcomes is an obvious instance. The problematic feature is that private entities use their resources in ways that corrupt democratic processes. Massive contributions on the part of a relatively small number of donors steer the agenda of government away from its proper focus on the common good and toward policies that inure to the private benefit of the contributors. Those who make massive campaign contributions in effect participate in rigging the rules of economic and social life by commandeering public sources of power for their own purposes.

Of particular concern is the exercise of such influence to ensure that businesses do not have to pay the full social costs of their activities.

Market transactions produce spillover effects—market externalities, as economists refer to them—positive or negative, affecting the interests of those who are not parties to the agreements. Negative externalities include economic costs or risks imposed on others as a consequence of the agreements entered into by the parties to the transaction. For example, an industrial factory produces chemicals that are used in consumer products or a factory farm produces hogs that are raised for food. Unless the costs of illness from air pollution produced by the chemical plant or the environmental damage to drinking water from wastes from the hog farm are factored into the prices that consumers pay, the true cost to society is not reflected in those prices. The resulting harms or the increased risks of harm are not voluntarily accepted by those on whom they fall. In most instances, they are imposed and not readily avoidable by individuals acting on their own. Mitigating or preventing these risks typically requires government action either through taxation that is sufficient to deter the offending behavior or the enforcement of legal prohibitions on the creation of negative externalities.[25] The use of campaign funding to secure key votes necessary to defeat environmental and health regulations, or to block access to private legal remedies, is precisely the sort of anti-democratic conduct that makes a private entity an especially appropriate target of resistance.

8.3.7. Anti-Competitive Conduct

The third factor relevant to the identification of targets is anti-competitive conduct. Anti-competitive conduct is a paradigmatic way in which an unfair system of advantages gets put into place. Although each instance might not implicate core elements of well-being in a significant way, anti-competitive conduct is the sort of activity that over time runs counter to both the common good and the well-being of the less powerful. Defenders of markets routinely recognize that, for economic power to be legitimately exercised, it must not be concentrated in ways that undermine free market processes. This is because inappropriate concentrations of market power undermine the basis of claims made on behalf of the legitimacy of markets. Markets are often viewed as justified only to the extent that they have the potential to advance the social good.

---

[25] For classic discussions of the problem and divergent solutions (i.e., taxation vs. regulation), see, e.g., Arthur C. Pigou, *The Economics of Welfare* (London: Macmillan, 1920); and Ronald Coase, "The Problem of Social Cost," *Journal of Law and Economics* 3, no. 1 (1960): 1–44.

Often anti-competitive conduct and anti-democratic conduct overlap. An illustration involves what economists refer to as "rent-seeking behavior."[26] Powerful self-interested entities seek economic gains, not by performing well in competitive markets but by using leverage over governmental agencies to capture opportunities for themselves. This not only creates unfair advantages for some competitors at the expense of others; it does so through undue influence over public, governmental decision-making. The rent-seeker uses its resources—often its political capital—to obtain economic gain without returning any benefits to society through wealth creation or efficient overall use of society's resources.

Examples include lobbying for subsidies to realize profits that entities could not otherwise earn in strictly competitive markets or securing single-source, non-competitive governmental contracts. Often these arrangements are argued for on grounds of national security or claims of unique expertise. But whatever the merits of such arguments, these arrangements generally have the seriously anti-competitive effects of allowing the entities who benefit from them to dominate the current marketplace and repel new market entrants.

Other anti-competitive conduct involves the use of state power as an instrument of business enterprise. For example, banks can effectively use government as a debt collector and indemnifier of economic losses. States often pressure debtor nations to repay in full money they have been lent, even though the lending institutions had good reason to know at the outset of the high likelihood of default. Lending money in circumstances in which lenders know that they will never experience a loss, no matter how much economic risk is involved, is an example of what economists call "moral hazard." Individuals impose the costs of their improvident, but likely profitable conduct on third parties that did not consent to the risk in the circumstances.

The raft of subprime mortgage loans, marketed to low- and middle-income families in the run-up to the 2008 economic crisis in the US is another example. Banks had considerable assurance that the sheer size of the loan portfolio meant that they would be viewed by regulators as too big to fail and, if need be, that a taxpayer-funded bailout would likely be forthcoming. In addition, because of US Justice Department guidelines, well known to white-collar crime defense and finance industry lawyers, executives also understood that they were likely too big to jail.

---

[26] Anne O. Krueger, "The Political Economy of the Rent-Seeking Society," *American Economic Review* 64, no. 3 (1974): 291–303.

Businesses also use agencies of the state to assist in the global promotion of harmful activities or substances, especially ones dangerous enough to be outlawed or heavily regulated at home. Tobacco products, pesticides, and fracking technology are examples familiar to advocacy groups.

Not only are states sometimes treated as instruments of business interests, but international agencies also often serve private purposes, sometimes even with partial funding from industry. We discussed one often-cited example in chapter 7, the World Bank's controversial "ease of doing business index." NGOs around the world describe the index as a guide to and incentive for massive deregulation of environmental, health, and land acquisition laws in order to shelter foreign investors from having to internalize the costs of their operations and to circumvent laws designed to protect land and water rights of the poor.

We have illustrated but a few of the ways the private sector commandeers government power for its own economic benefit. Most of the means it employs not only create and sustain unfair advantages for the already privileged but are also profoundly undemocratic.

8.3.8. Accountability Avoidance

The fourth factor is whether a potential target of resistance is engaged in one or more informational techniques of accountability avoidance. The conduct we have in mind includes the propagation of false and misleading information to consumers, voters, and government regulators. Is also includes efforts to undermine legal and civic avenues for vindicating rights and gaining access to information necessary to hold corporate entities accountable in the marketplace, legislatures, or the judicial system. Here too, this conduct not only unfairly positions some entities in relation to others but more generally undermines the public good.

Examples include consumer product safety disinformation campaigns that are designed to hide the health or economic consequences of products, and political propaganda campaigns intended to advance a rent-seeking agenda by convincing the public that only private business can efficiently deliver certain services. Other examples of accountability avoidance include the ongoing repudiation of climate science by companies even when internal documents show that they do not believe their own claims; and companies' payment of academic researchers to put their imprimatur on junk science or promulgate statistically misleading information. Other efforts to evade both marketplace and regulatory accountability include the suppression of research findings, or cherry-picking data to hide risks, and funding public relations campaigns to deflect attention from the role of harmful consumer products, such as soda in obesity, by highlighting the importance of exercise and personal responsibility.

Media manipulation orchestrated by private sector actors for the sake of advancing their own business interests is another form of accountability avoidance. It takes many forms, including the growth of ideologically driven media outlets that use a stable of like-minded commentators to get out the message. Here too, the aim is to deflect attention from the real nature, causes, and consequences of existing social conditions and, in the process, attempt to absolve those who profit from the ideology.

Among the newer means of manipulating public opinion are social media tools—bots, for example—that are designed to skew the public's perception of prevailing opinion. Some analyses of Twitter feeds during the Brexit debate estimate that a significant proportion of retweets in the final days before the vote were generated by bots.[27] These machine-generated contributions to public debate give the false impression of the range of opinion actually held by members of the public and are intended to affect outcomes by the creation of a false sense of an emerging consensus.

Businesses also rely upon "Astroturfing," a process by which a small number of people pass themselves off as a membership-driven organization using techniques that mimic real grassroots advocacy. Astroturf organizations influence public opinion through websites and television ads that make economically self-interested industry talking points seem as if they represent an organic groundswell of informed, civically engaged opinion mobilized on behalf of the public interest.

One last set of examples involves the misuse of the legal system to intimidate, bankrupt, and silence critics and whistleblowers. Public interest groups are often peppered with frivolous, time-consuming, and expensive litigation known as "slap suits." Industry advocates, acting through tax-exempt legislative drafting organizations, are the architects of state laws designed to avoid accountability in both the marketplace and the courtroom by, for example, constraining the actions of potential whistle blowers or critics. A proliferation of agricultural gag laws across the US makes it a crime to film agricultural facilities, even from the air or from external premises. Some ag gag laws have even been expanded to provide

---

[27] Yuriy Gorodnichenko, Tho Pham, and Oleksandr Talavera, "Social Media, Sentiment and Public Opinions: Evidence from #Brexit and #USElection," NBER Working Paper 24631, May 2018.

the same informational shield to fracking sites and the disposal or release of hazardous materials and industrial or agricultural wastes.

All four of these second-tier considerations are important markers of corporate bad citizenship that help make them appropriate targets of resistance movements. These considerations point to efforts to rig the system in order to create unfair advantages and substitute the pursuit of private gain for the pursuit of the common good. And often they involve the exercise of private power over matters that are of public interest in decision-making arenas meant for collective, democratic decision-making.

8.3.9. A Cautionary Note

We close this section on appropriate targets for active resistance on a note of caution. It is important to distinguish between two types of beneficiaries of activities that contribute to structural injustices, based on differences in their economic options. We have been focusing on targets that are primary contributing beneficiaries, but there are secondary ones as well. Consider the differences between the circumstances of coal companies and the miners who work for them. Both miners and their employers know or should know of the harmful effects of continued reliance on high-carbon-footprint energy sources and how the associated burdens disproportionately impact disadvantaged groups and future generations. Both contribute to the problem and both benefit from it. But there is a critical difference between the two. Coal company executives and their political allies have options. Although they may incur some losses, they generally have the resources to choose to move their capital investments to other industries that do not contribute to structural injustice. The miners, by contrast, are captive, secondary beneficiaries. They cannot simple walk away.

The coal industry's critique of divestment campaigns and other efforts to alter the energy mix, which they refer to as a "war on coal," often emphasizes the devastating impact on the welfare of miners and their families when mines are closed. It is true that divestment strategies and other resistance efforts, if successful, set in motion a process that social movements cannot control. In many cases, the losses that are imposed cannot be confined to executives or shareholders. People, miners in this instance, stand to lose the only feasible employment options they have. It may be the case that, all things considered, the trade-off between protecting the planet and protecting jobs is justified, but the imposition of loss on captive beneficiaries remains morally consequential nonetheless. Captive contributing beneficiaries are in a morally different position but it is usually not possible for divestment campaigners to calibrate their actions in ways that impose losses only on the subset of beneficiaries that have the capital mobility and resources to withstand or survive them.

Assuming that there is an all things considered justification for fossil fuel divestment campaigns, or name and shame strategies against retailers that profit from exploitative global supply chains, morally responsible resistance requires high-profile attention to potential solutions that compensate for or prevent the imposition of losses on captive contributing beneficiaries. The problem is particularly acute when the participants in social movements are drawn largely from groups that are less likely to experience the harms expected to accompany the success of the movement. Our argument, then, is that morally responsible resistance requires serious efforts to limit the collateral damage to the interests of captive beneficiaries.

8.4. Conclusion: Well-Being and Social Movements

Our theory of structural injustice is built around a particular conception of human well-being. This concept has illuminated not only our account of human rights but also our account of structural unfairness. We close our book by returning to the core elements of well-being to illuminate yet one more point. Resistance to structural injustice can not only put the well-being of those who engage in it at risk. Resistance can also advance the core elements of well-being for activists, their communities, and society more broadly.

Although resistance is at its core intended to improve the well-being and well-being prospects of those who suffer from structural injustice, it is worth noting that the well-being of those who participate in resistance activities is sometimes put at risk in the process. Because of this possibility, it is also worth considering how participation in social movements that work to resist injustice can sometimes have positive effects on the core elements of human well-being of the resisters, their communities, and the wider society. These positive effects are different in important ways from the hoped-for, long-term improvements in well-being that result when social movements are successful in achieving their objectives.

First, participation contributes to the good of personal attachment. It builds personal ties of loyalty, trust, friendship, and solidarity.[28] Members of social groups who exist on the margins of society, without the protection

---

[28] Cynthia Townley, "Trust and the Curse of Cassandra (an Exploration of the Value of Trust)," *Philosophy in the Contemporary World* 10, no. 2 (2003): 105–111.

and consideration accorded to more privileged members, often find in resistance movements avenues of emotional connection so often foreclosed
to them. Solidarity realized through resistance is not necessarily rooted in
notions of the shared identity of members of a defined social group, for
example, based on race or gender, but rather in the shared experience of
oppression or disadvantage.[29]

Second, participation also engenders respect from others, at least within
social movements that explicitly reject the hierarchical patterns of relationship characteristic of structurally unjust societies.

Third, social movements guided by robust deliberative processes bring
to bear a diversity of experiences that increase the knowledge and understanding of those who participate in them. They can generate a kind of
knowledge that is ordinarily unavailable to members of dominant social
groups who have little firsthand connection to members of subordinated
groups whose experiences differ. The beneficial effect arises out of the fact
that "the social location of the knower affects what and how she knows."[30]
The standpoint of those who have borne the brunt of social exclusion or exploitation yields insights into power relations that readily escape those in
positions of power and privilege.[31] The reliability of one's own knowledge
depends heavily on interaction with others whose experiential knowledge
base differs from one's own.[32] Even among social groups that have firsthand experience of domination and marginalization, differences in standpoint emerge along racial, gender, and other axes of power relations.[33]

---

[29] Tommie Shelby, "Foundations of Black Solidarity: Collective Identity or Common
Oppression," *Ethics* 112, no. 2 (2002): 231–266.

[30] Elizabeth Anderson, "Feminist Epistemology and Philosophy of Science," in *The Stanford
Encyclopedia of Philosophy*, Fall 2012 ed., Edward N. Zalta, https://plato.stanford.edu/archives/
sum2012/entries/feminism-epistemology/.

[31] Sometimes it is not simply what is not known because of experiential differences but "invested
ignorance" in which the ignorance is "systematically produced and sustained to misrepresent
reality in ways that not coincidentally sustain patterns of . . . privilege" (Townley, "Trust and
the Curse," x). Cf. Charles Mills, who conceptualizes whites as engaged in a kind of cognitive
dysfunction that serves their purposes by preventing them from understanding the social
relations of domination in which they are engaged. Charles Mills, "White Ignorance," *Race and
Epistemologies of Ignorance*, ed. Shannon Sullivan and Nancy Tuana (Albany: State University of
New York Press, 2007), 11–38.

[32] Linda Martín Alcoff, "On Judging Epistemic Credibility: Is Social Identity Relevant?"
Engendering Rationalities, ed. Nancy Tuana and Sandra Morgen (Albany: State University of
New York Press, 2001), 53–80; Elizabeth Anderson, "Epistemic Justice as a Virtue of Social
Institutions," *Social Epistemology: A Journal of Knowledge, Culture and Policy*, 26, no. 2
(2012): 163–173.

[33] Linda Alcoff and Elizabeth Potter, "Introduction: When Feminisms Intersect Epistemology,"
Feminist Epistemologies, ed. Linda Alcoff and Elizabeth Potter (New York: Routledge,
1993), 1–14.

Deliberation and discussion among persons occupying differing social positions can increase their understanding of the dynamics of advantage and power.[34] It can help dispel the socially distorting patterns of false consciousness that contribute to the subordination of social groups and correct for adaptive preferences engendered by the necessity of coping with the harsh realities of one's condition.[35]

Fourth, participation in deliberative processes offers new opportunities to take charge of aspects of life often left to the discretion of others. From within the relationships and experiences forged in social movements, individuals can lead more self-determining lives, assume more control over their own destinies, and discover ways to navigate through the web of power relations in order live life more on their own terms. Participation in social movements can both illuminate and motivate efforts to break through deeply ingrained, internalized barriers that provide short-term rewards for silence and submission.[36]

Fifth, in circumstances in which lack of personal security is a fact of daily existence, organized efforts to counter the institutionally unchecked violence and intimidation of the vulnerable, especially when they speak out or participate in public protests, can add some measure of personal security.

Sixth, whether participation overall is beneficial for health is a complex question, and it is linked to the larger issue of whether participation in resistance efforts has net well-being benefits.[37] The pursuit of justice can be exhausting and overwhelming, and it can invite retaliation. The struggle for justice can be extremely hazardous to one's health. Many have died and many more have suffered injury. But many have found hope where hope has seemed beyond reach.

---

[34] Helen Longino, *The Fate of Knowledge* (Princeton, NJ: Princeton University Press, 2002). For an older but insightful take on false consciousness, see Oscar Wilde's remark, "Misery and poverty are so absolutely degrading, and exercise such a paralyzing effect over the nature of men, that no class is ever really conscious of its own suffering." Oscar Wilde, *The Soul of Man under Socialism and Selected Critical Prose*, ed. Linda Dowling (London: Penguin, [1891] 2001).

[35] For a general argument along similar lines, see Elizabeth Anderson, "Epistemic Justice as a Virtue of Social Institutions," *Social Epistemology: A Journal of Knowledge, Culture and Policy* 26, no. 2 (2012): 163–173.

[36] Ann Cudd describes the phenomenon in detail. One illustrative remark reveals how people are often embedded in incentive structures that affect choices in ways that keep them locked in positions of powerlessness. "The oppressed are co-opted through their own short-run rational choices to reinforce the long-run oppression of their social group." Ann Cudd, *Analyzing Oppression* (Oxford: Oxford University Press, 2006), 21–22.

[37] For a discussion of some of these downsides, see Daniel Silvermint, "Resistance and Well-being," *Journal of Political Philosophy* 21, no 4. (2013): 421–422.

BIBLIOGRAPHY

Acemoglu, Daron and Simon Johnson. "Disease and Development: The Effect of Life Expectancy on Economic Growth." *Journal of Political Economy* 115, no. 6 (2007): 925–985.

Ackrill, J. L. "Aristotle on Eudaimonia." In *Essays on Aristotle's Ethics*, edited by A. O. Rorty, 15–33. Berkeley: University of California Press, 1980.

Adorno, Theodor. *History and Freedom: Lectures, 1964–1965*. Edited by Rolf Tiedemann. Cambridge: Polity, 2006.

Alcoff, Linda. "The Problem of Speaking for Others." *Cultural Critique*, no. 20 (1991–1992): 5–32.

Alcoff, Linda and Elizabeth Potter. "Introduction: When Feminisms Intersect Epistemology." In *Feminist Epistemologies*, edited by Linda Alcoff and Elizabeth Potter, 1–14. New York: Routledge, 1993.

Alcoff, Linda Martín. "On Judging Epistemic Credibility: Is Social Identity Relevant?" In *Engendering Rationalities*, edited by Nancy Tuana and Sandra Morgen, 53–80. Albany: State University of New York Press, 2001.

Alexander, Michele. *The New Jim Crow*, 2nd ed. New York: New Press, 2012.

Alkire, Sabina and Andy Sumner. "Multidimensional Poverty and the Post-2015 MDGs." *Development* 56, no. 1 (2013): 46–51.

Allen, Amy. *The Power of Feminist Theory: Domination, Resistance, Solidarity*. Boulder, CO: Westview Press, 1999.

Allen, Amy. "Rethinking Power." *Hypatia* 13, no. 1 (1998): 21–40.

Alston, Philip. "Report of the Special Rapporteur on Extreme Poverty and Human Rights." UN Doc. A/HRC/29/31. May 27, 2015.

Altman, Andrew and Christopher Heath Wellman. *A Liberal Theory of International Justice*. Oxford: Oxford University Press, 2009.

Anderson, Elizabeth. "Epistemic Justice as a Virtue of Social Institutions." *Social Epistemology: A Journal of Knowledge, Culture and Policy* 26, no. 2 (2012): 163–173.

Anderson, Elizabeth. "Feminist Epistemology and Philosophy of Science." In *The Stanford Encyclopedia of Philosophy*, Fall 2012 ed., edited by Edward N. Zalta. https://plato.stanford.edu/archives/sum2012/entries/feminism-epistemology/.

Anderson, Elizabeth. "John Stuart Mill and Experiments in Living." *Ethics* 102, no. 1 (1991): 4–26.

Anderson, Elizabeth. "Justifying the Capabilities Approach to Justice." In *Measuring Justice*, edited by Harry Brighouse and Ingrid Robeyns, 81–100. Cambridge: Cambridge University Press, 2010.

Anderson, Elizabeth. *Private Government: How Employers Rule Our lives (and Why We Don't Talk About It)*. Princeton, NJ: Princeton University Press, 2017.

Anderson, Elizabeth. "What Is the Point of Equality?" *Ethics* 109, no. 2 (1999): 287–337.

Anderson, Kym and Will Martin. "Agricultural Trade Reform and the Doha Development Agenda." *World Economy* 28, no. 9 (September 13, 2005): 1301–1327.

Andrews, Thomas G. *Killing for Coal: America's Deadliest Labor War*. Cambridge, MA: Harvard University Press, 2010.

Aristotle. *The Complete Works of Aristotle: The Revised Oxford Translation*. Edited by Jonathan Barnes. Princeton, NJ: Princeton University Press, 1984.

Armstrong, Chris. *Global Distributive Justice: An Introduction*. Cambridge: Cambridge University Press, 2012.

Ashford, Elizabeth. "Duties Imposed by the Right to Basic Necessities." In *Freedom from Poverty as a Human Right*, edited by Thomas Pogge, 183–218. Oxford: Oxford University Press, 2007.

Ashford, Elizabeth. "Severe Poverty as a Systemic Human Rights Violation." In *Cosmopolitanism versus non-cosmopolitanism*, edited by Gillian Brock, 129–155. Oxford: Oxford University Press, 2013.

Bacchetta, Marc, Ekkehard Ernst, and Juana P. Bustamante. "Globalization and Informal Jobs in Developing Countries." International Labour Office and the Secretariat of the World Trade Organization, 2009. https://www.wto.org/english/res_e/booksp_e/jobs_devel_countries_e.pdf.

Baier, Kurt. "Justice and the Aims of Political Philosophy." *Ethics* 99, no. 3 (1989): 771–790.

Bain, Robert, Ryan Cronk, Rifat Hossain, Sophie Bonjour, Kyle Onda, Jim Wright, Hong Yang, et al. "Global Assessment of Exposure to Faecal Contamination Through Drinking Water Based on a Systematic Review." *Tropical Medicine and International Health* 19, no. 8 (August 2014): 917–927.

Banerjee, Abhijit V. and Esther Duflo. *Poor Economics: A Radical Rethinking of the Way to Fight Global Poverty*. New York: Public Affairs, 2011.

Bankoff, Greg. 'Constructing Vulnerability: The Historical, Natural and Social Generation of Flooding in Metropolitan Manila.' *Disasters* 27, no. 3 (2003): 224–238.

Barry, Brian. "Humanity and Justice in Global Perspective." In *NOMOS XXIV, Ethics, Economics and the Law*, edited by J. Roland Pennock and John W. Chapman, 219–252, New York: Harvester Wheatsheaf, 1982.

Barry, Christian and Laura Ferraciola. "Young on Responsibility and Structural Injustice." *Criminal Justice Ethics* 32, no. 3 (2013): 247–253.

Beitz, Charles. *The Idea of Human Rights*. Oxford: Oxford University Press, 2009.

Benhabib, Seyla. *The Rights of Others: Aliens, Residents and Citizens*. Cambridge: Cambridge University Press, 2004.

Ben-Shlomo, Y. and Kuth, D. A. "A Life Course Approach to Chronic Disease Epidemiology: Conceptual Models, Empirical Challenges, and Interdisciplinary Perspectives." *International Journal of Epidemiology* 31, no. 2 (2002): 285–293.

Berger, Fred. *Happiness, Justice and Freedom: The Moral and Political Philosophy of John Stuart Mill*. Berkeley: University of California Press, 1984.

Berlin, Isaiah. *Four Essays on Liberty*. Oxford: Oxford University Press, 1969.

Bhutta, M. Khurrum, Adnan Omar, and Xiaozhe Yang. "Electronic Waste: A Growing Concern in Today's Environment." *Economics Research International*, 2011. http://dx.doi.org/10.1155/2011/474230.

Blackstone, William. *Commentaries on the Laws of England*, 1753.

Blake, Michael. "Distributive Justice, State Coercion, and Autonomy." *Philosophy and Public Affairs* 30, no. 3 (2001): 257–296.

Blyth, Mark. *Austerity: The History of a Dangerous Idea*. Oxford: Oxford University Press, 2013.

Bohman, James. "Republican Cosmopolitanism." *Journal of Political Philosophy* 12, no. 3 (2004): 336–352.

Boo, Katherine. *Behind the Beautiful Forevers: Life, Death, and Hope in a Mumbai Undercity*. New York: Random House, 2012.

Bouie, Jamelle. "How We Built the Ghettos: A Brief Introduction to America's Long History of Racist Housing Policy." *Daily Beast*, March 13, 2014. http://www.thedailybeast.com/how-we-built-the-ghettos.

Bourguinon, Francois. *The Globalization of Inequality*. Princeton, NJ: Princeton University Press, 2015.

Boxill, Bernard R. "A Lockean Argument for Black Reparations." *Journal of Ethics* 7, no. 1 (2003): 63–91.

Brock, Gillian. *Global Justice: A Cosmopolitan Account*. Oxford: Oxford University Press, 2009.

Brock, Gillian. "Needs and Global Justice." *Royal Institute of Philosophy, Supplement* 57 (2005): 51–72.

Brooks, David. "On Living in an Unjust Society." *Journal of Applied Philosophy* 6, no. 1 (1989): 31–42.

Brownlee, Kimberley. *Conscience and Conviction: The Case for Civil Disobedience*. Oxford: Oxford University Press, 2012.

Buchanan, Allen. "The Egalitarianism of Human Rights." *Ethics* 120, no. 4 (2010): 679–710.

Buchanan, Allen. *The Heart of Human Rights*. Oxford: Oxford University Press, 2013.

Buchanan, Allen. "Justice and Charity." *Ethics* 97, no. 3 (1987): 558–575.

Buchanan, Allen. *Justice and Health Care: Selected Essays*. Oxford: Oxford University Press, 2009.

Buchanan, Allen. *Justice, Legitimacy, and Self-Determination: Moral Foundations for International Law*. Oxford: Oxford University Press, 2003.

Buchanan, Allen. "Political Legitimacy and Democracy." *Ethics* 112, no. 4 (2002): 689–719.

Buchanan, Allen. "Rawls's *Law of Peoples*: Rules for a Vanished Westphalian World." *Ethics* 110, no. 4 (2000): 697–721.

Buchanan, Allen, Dan W. Brock, Norman Daniels, and Dan Wikler. *From Chance to Choice*. Cambridge: Cambridge University Press, 2000.

Buckner, Till. "The Myth of the African Land Grab." *Foreign Policy*, October 20, 2015. http://foreignpolicy.com/2015/10/20/the-myth-of-the-african-land-grab/.

Bullard, Robert. *Dumping in Dixie: Race, Class and Environmental Quality*. Boulder, CO: Westview Press, 1990.

Bullard, Robert. "Environmental Justice: It's More than Waste Facility Siting." *Social Science Quarterly* 77, no. 3 (1996): 493–499.

Bullard, Robert et al. *Toxic Wastes and Race at Twenty*. New York: United Church of Christ, 2007.

Burmeister, Larry L. "Lagoons, Litter, and the Law: CAFO Regulation as Social Risk Politics." *Southern Rural Sociology* 18, no. 2 (2002): 56–87.

Butler, Paul. *Chokehold: Policing Black Men*. New York: New Press, 2017.

Butt, Daniel. "On Benefitting from Injustice." *Canadian Journal of Philosophy* 37, no. 1 (2007): 129–152.

Caney, Simon. *Justice Beyond Borders*. Oxford: Oxford University Press, 2005.

Caney, Simon. "Responding to Global Injustice: On the Right of Resistance." *Social Philosophy and Policy* 32, no. 1 (2015): 51–73.

Caplovitz, David. *The Poor Pay More: Consumer Practices of Low-Income Families*. New York: Free Press, 1967.

Carmin, Jo Ann and Julian Agyeman. *Environmental Inequalities Beyond Borders: Local Perspectives on Global Injustices*. Cambridge, MA: MIT Press, 2011.

Castells-Quintana, David. "Malthus Living in a Slum: Urban Concentration, Infrastructure and Economic Growth." *Journal of Urban Economics* 98, issue C (2017): 158–173.

Caudill, Harry. *Night Comes to the Cumberlands: A Biography of a Depressed Area*. Boston: Little, Brown, 1963.

Center for Human Rights and Global Justice. *Foreign Land Deals and Human Rights: Case Studies on Agricultural and Biofuel Investment*. New York: NYU School of Law, 2010.

Centers for Disease Control and Prevention. "Global Water Sanitation, and Hygiene." Updated December 17, 2015. http://www.cdc.gov/healthywater/global/wash_statistics.html.

Chetty, Raj et al. "Where Is the Land of Opportunity? The Geography of Intergenerational Mobility in the United States." NBER Working Paper 19843, June 2014.

Chetty, Raj and Nathaniel Hendren. "The Impacts of Neighborhoods on Intergenerational Mobility: Childhood Exposure Effects and County-Level Estimates." NBER, May 2015.

Children's Environmental Health Network. "Some Children Are at Greater Risk than Others." http://www.cehn.org/wp-content/uploads/2015/11/Some_Children_are_at_greater_risk14.pdf.

Christiano, Thomas. "An Instrumental Argument for a Human Right to Democracy." *Philosophy and Public Affairs* 39, no. 2 (2011): 142–176.

Christman, John. "Autonomy and Personal History." *Canadian Journal of Philosophy* 21, no. 1 (1991): 1–24.

Christman, John. "Human Rights and Global Wrongs." In *Poverty, Agency, and Human Rights*, edited by Diana T. Meyers, 321–345. Oxford University Press, 2014.

Coalition of Immokalee Workers. "Modern Farmer Article Traces History of Fair Food Movement . . " December 18, 2015. http://ciw-online.org/blog/2015/12/modern-farmer-article/.

Coase, Ronald. "The Problem of Social Cost." *Journal of Law and Economics* 3, no. 1 (1960): 1–44.

Coates, Ta-Nehisi. "The Case for Reparations." *Atlantic*, June, 2014. https://www.theatlantic.com/magazine/archive/2014/06/the-case-for-reparations/361631/.

Cohen, Jean. *Globalization and Sovereignty*. Cambridge: Cambridge University Press, 2012.

Cohen, Joshua. "Minimalism About Human Rights: The Most We Can Hope For?" *Journal of Political Philosophy* 12, no. 2 (2004): 190–213.

Cohen, Joshua and Charles Sabel. "Extra Rempublicam Nulla Justitia?" *Philosophy and Public Affairs* 34, no. 2 (2009): 147–175.

Collier, Paul. *The Plundered Planet: Why We Must—and How We Can—Manage Nature for Global Prosperity*. Oxford: Oxford University Press, 2010.

Collins, Mary B., Ian Munoz, and Joseph JaJa. "Linking 'Toxic Outliers' to Environmental Justice Communities." *Environmental Research Letters* 11 (2016). http://iopscience.iop.org/1748-9326/11/1/015004.

Constance, Douglas H. The Southern Model of Broiler Production and Its Global Implications." *Culture and Agriculture* 30, no. 1 (2008): 17–31.

Corbin, David. *Gun Thugs, Rednecks, and Radicals: A Documentary History of the West Virginia Mine Wars*. Oakland, CA: PM Press, 2011.

Crisp, Roger. "Aristotle's Inclusivism." *Oxford Studies in Ancient Philosophy* 12 (1994): 111–136.

Cruft, Rowen, Liao, Matthew, and Renzo, Massimo, eds. *Philosophical Foundations of Human Rights*. Oxford: Oxford University Press, 2015.

Cudd, Ann E. *Analyzing Oppression*. New York: Oxford University Press, 2006.

Dahl, Robert. "The Concept of Power." *Behavioral Science* 2, no. 3 (1957): 201–215.

Darwall, Stephen. *The Second-Person Standpoint: Morality, Respect, and Accountability*. Cambridge, MA: Harvard University Press, 2006.

Davis, Mike. "Dealing with Poverty." 2009. https://hubpages.com/politics/Dealing-with-Poverty.

Davis, Mike. *Planet of Slums*. London: Verso, 2006.

De Shutter, Olivier. "How Not to Think of Land-Grabbing: Three Critiques of Large-Scale Investments in Farmland." *Journal of Peasant Studies* 38, no. 2 (2011): 249–279.

Desilver, Drew. "Black Unemployment Rate Is Consistently Twice That of Whites." PEW Research Center. http://www.pewresearch.org/fact-tank/2013/08/21/through-good-times-and-bad-black-unemployment-is-consistently-double-that-of-whites/.

Desmond, Matthew. *Evicted*. New York: Broadway Books, 2016.

Diani, Mario. "The Concept of a Social Movement." *Sociological Review* 40, no. 1 (1992): 1–25.

Dietsch, Peter. "Tax Competition and Its Effects on Domestic and Global Justice." In *Social Justice, Global Dynamics*, edited by Ayelet Banai, Miriam Ronzoni, and Christian Schemmel, 94–113. Oxford: Routledge, 2011.

Donnelly, Jack. *Universal Human Rights in Theory and Practice*, 3rd ed. Ithaca, NY: Cornell University Press, 2013.

Downey, Liam and Brian Hawkins. "Race, Income, and Environmental Inequality in the United States." *Sociological Perspectives* 51, no. 4 (2008): 759–781.

Doyle, Michael. "Kant, Liberal Legacies and Foreign Affairs." *Philosophy and Public Affairs* 12, nos. 3, 4 (1983): 205–235, 323–353.

Easterly, William. *The Tyranny of Experts: Economists, Dictators, and the Forgotten Rights of the Poor*. New York: Basic Books, 2013.

Eligon, John and Robert Gebeloff. "Segregation, the Neighbor That Won't Leave." *New York Times*,August21,2016.https://www.nytimes.com/2016/08/21/us/milwaukee-segregation-wealthy-black-families.html?smid=nytcore-ipad-share&smprod=nytcore-ipad.

Etinson, Adam. *Human Rights: Moral or Political?* Oxford: Oxford University Press, 2018.

Elster, Jon. *Sour Grapes: Studies in the Subversion of Rationality*. New York: Cambridge University Press, 1983.

Ezeh, Alex, Oyinlola Oyebode, David Satterthwaite, Yen-Fu Chen, Robert Ndugwa, Jo Sartori, Blessing Mberu, et al. "The History, Geography, and Sociology of Slums and the Health Problems of People Who Live in Slums." *Lancet*, 389, no. 1006 (October 16, 2016). http://www.thelancet.com/series/slum-health.

Farha, Leilani. "Statement of the UN Special Rapporteur on Adequate Housing as a Component of the Right to an Adequate Standard of Living and on the Right to Non-Discrimination in This Context." 2nd Latin America and Caribbean Regional Forum on Adequate Housing, "Vivienda para la Vida," Monterrey, Mexico, May 6, 2015.

Farmer, Paul. *Pathologies of Power*. Berkeley, CA: University of California Press, 2004.

"Fatal Force." *Washington Post*. https://www.washingtonpost.com/graphics/2018/national/police-shootings-2018/?utm_term=.4a05471e6c1a.

Fay, Marianne and Charlotte Opal. "Urbanization Without Growth: A Not-So-Uncommon Phenomenon." Policy Research Working Paper 2412. World Bank, 2000. https://openknowledge.worldbank.org/handle/10986/21373.

Federal Reserve System and the Brookings Institution. *The Enduring Challenge of Concentrated Poverty in America: Case Studies from Communities Across the U.S.* Richmond, VA: Federal Reserve System and Brookings Institution, 2008.

Feinberg, Joel. "The Nature and Value of Rights." *Journal of Value Inquiry* 4, no. 4 (1970): 243–257.

Finnis, John. *Natural Law and Natural Rights*. Oxford: Oxford University Press, 1980.

Fleischman, Lesley and Marcus Franklin. "Fumes Across the Fence-Line: The Health Impacts of Air Pollution from Oil & Gas Facilities on African American Communities." NAACP Clean Air Task Force, 2017. http://www.naacp.org/wp-content/uploads/2017/11/Fumes-Across-the-Fence-Line_NAACP_CATF.pdf.

Florida, Richard. "The Persistent Geography of Disadvantage." *City Lab*, July 25, 2013. https://www.citylab.com/equity/2013/07/persistent-geography-disadvantage/6231/.

Food and Agriculture Organization. "The Implications of the Uruguay Round Agreement on Agriculture for Developing Countries." 1995. http://www.fao.org/docrep/w7814e/w7814e05.htm#1.1.3).

Forman, James. *Locking Up Our Own*. New York: Farrar, Straus & Giroux, 2017.

Forst, Ranier. "A Critical Theory of Human Rights: Some Groundwork." In *Critical Theory in Critical Times*, edited by Penelope Deutscher and Christina Lafont, 74–88. New York: Columbia University Press, 2017.

Forst, Ranier. "Towards a Critical Theory of Transnational Justice." In *Global Justice*, edited by Thomas Pogge, 169–187. Oxford: Blackwell, 2001.

Frankfurt, Harry. "Freedom of the Will and the Concept of a Person." In *The Importance of What We Care About: Philosophical Essays*. Cambridge: Cambridge University Press, 1998.

Fraser, Nancy. "Behind Marx's Hidden Abode: For an Expanded Conception of Capitalism." In *Critical Theory in Critical Times*, edited by Penelope Deutscher and Christina Lafont, 141–159. New York: Columbia University Press, 2017.

Freire, Paulo. *Pedagogy of the Oppressed*, 30th Anniversary Ed. Translated by Myra Bergman Ramos. London: Bloomsbury Press, 2000.

Fricker, Miranda. *Epistemic Injustice: Power and the Ethics of Knowing*. Oxford University Press, 2007.

Frieden, Jeffry A. *Global Capitalism: Its Fall and Rise in the Twentieth Century*. New York: W. W. Norton, 2006.

Friedman, Barry. *Unwarranted: Policing Without Permission*. New York: Farrar, Straus & Giroux, 2017.

Furman Center. "Research Brief: Race and Neighborhoods in the 21st Century." *Research & Policy*, January 30, 2015. http://furmancenter.org/thestoop/entry/research-brief-race-and-neighborhoods-in-the-21st-century.

Galster, George C. "The Mechanism(s) of Neighborhood Effects: Theory, Evidence, and Policy Implications." Presentation at the ESRC Seminar, St. Andrews University, Scotland, February 4–5, 2010.

Gaventa, John. *Power* and *Powerlessness: Quiescence & Rebellion in an Appalachian Valley*. Urbana: University of Illinois Press, 1982.

Gelb, Alan. "World Bank Reorganization: To What End?" Center for Global Development, August 5, 2013. http://www.cgdev.org/blog/world-bank-reorganization-what-end.

Genschell, Philipp. "Globalization, Tax Competition and the Welfare State." *Politics and Society* 30, no. 3 (2002): 245–272.

Geuss, Raymond. *History and Illusion in Politics*. Cambridge: Cambridge University Press, 2001.

Gilabert, Pablo. *From Global Poverty to Global Equality*. Oxford: Oxford University Press, 2012.

Gilbert, Alan. "The Return of the Slum: Does Language Matter?" *International Journal of Urban and Regional Research* 31, no. 4 (2007): 697–713.

Global Justice Now. "Honest Accounts, 2017: How the World Profits from Africa's Wealth." http://www.globaljustice.org.uk/sites/default/files/files/resources/honest_accounts_2017_web_final_updated.pdf.

Goodell, Jeff. *Big Coal: The Dirty Secret Behind America's Energy Future*. Boston: Houghton Mifflin, 2007.

Gorodnichenko, Yuriy, Tho Pham, and Oleksandr Talavera. "Social Media, Sentiment and Public Opinions: Evidence from #Brexit and #USElection." NBER Working Paper 24631, May 2018.

GRAIN. "An Online Repository of Open Land Contracts." https://www.openlandcontracts.org/.

GRAIN. "The G8 and Land Grabs in Africa," March 11, 2013. https://www.grain.org/article/entries/4663-the-g8-and-land-grabs-in-africa.

Grant, Ruth W. *John Locke's Liberalism*. Chicago: University of Chicago Press, 1991.

Great Artesian Basin Protection Group Inc. "Sacrifice Zone: A Movie About the Real Gas Crisis in Australia," 2017. https://chuffed.org/project/sacrificezone.

Green Cross Switzerland and Pure Earth. "The World's Worst Pollution Problems, 2016: The Toxics Beneath Our Feet." http://www.worstpolluted.org/.

Grissmer, David, Sophie M. Aiyer, William M. Murrah, Kevin J. Grimm, and Joel S. Steele. "Fine Motor Skills and Early Comprehension of the World: Two New School Readiness Indicators." *Developmental Psychology* 46, no. 5 (2010): 1008–1017.

Griffin, James. *On Human Rights*. Oxford: Oxford University Press, 2008.

Griffin, James. "Towards a Substantive Theory of Rights." In *Utility and Rights*, edited by Raymond G. Frey, 137–160. Oxford: Blackwell, 1984.

Griffin, James. *Well-Being: Its Meaning, Measurement, and Moral Importance*. Oxford: Oxford University Press, 1986.

Habermas, Jürgen. "Warum Merkels Griechenland-Politik ein Fehler ist." *Süddeutsche Zeitung*. June 22, 2015. http://www.sueddeutsche.de/wirtschaft/europa-sand-im-getriebe-1.2532119. Reprinted in English in *Social Europe*, June 25, 2015. https://www.socialeurope.eu/2015/06/why-angela-merkels-is-wrong-on-greece.

Hamlin, Alan and Zofia Stemplowska. "Theory, Ideal Theory, and the Theory of Ideals." *Political Studies Review* 10, no. 1 (2012): 48–62.

Hannah-Jones, Nikole. "Living Apart: How the Government Betrayed a Landmark Civil Rights Law." *Pro Publica*, June 25, 2015. https://www.propublica.org/article/living-apart-how-the-government-betrayed-a-landmark-civil-rights-law.

Hannah-Jones, Nikole. "Yes, Black America Fears the Police. Here's Why." *Pro Publica*, March 4, 2015. https://www.propublica.org/article/yes-black-america-fears-the-police-heres-why.

Hart, H. L. A. "Are There Any Natural Rights?" *Philosophical Review* 64, no. 2 (1955): 175–191.

Hart, H. L. A. *Essays on Bentham: Studies in Jurisprudence and Political Theory*. Oxford: Clarendon Press, 1982.

Haslanger, Sally. "What Is a (Social) Structural Explanation?" *Philosophical Studies* 173, no. 1 (2016): 113–130.

Hassoun, Nicole. *Globalization and Global Justice: Shrinking Distance, Expanding Obligations*. Cambridge: Cambridge University Press, 2012.

Hayward, Tim. "On Prepositional Duties." *Ethics* 123, no. 2 (2013): 264–291.

Hedges, Chris and Joe Sacco. *Days of Destruction, Days of Revolt*. New York: Nation Books, 2014.

Heinaman, Robert. "The Improvability of Eudaimonia in the *Nicomachean Ethics*." *Oxford Studies in Ancient Philosophy* 23, suppl. (2002): 99–145.

Henderson, J. Vernon. "Cities and Development." *Journal of Regional Science* 50, no. 1 (2010): 515–540.

Henderson, J. Vernon, Anthony J. Venables, Tanner Regan, and Ilia Samsonov. "Building Functional Cities." *Science* 352, no. 6288 (May 20, 2016): 946–947. doi: 10.1126/science.aaf7150.

Hickel, Jason. *The Divide: Global Inequality from Conquest to Free Markets*. New York: W. W. Norton, 2018.

Hirsch, Arnold. *Making the Second Ghetto: Race and Housing in Chicago, 1940–1960*. Chicago: University of Chicago Press, 1998.

Human Rights Watch. *Waiting Here for Death: Forced Displacement and "Villagization" in Ethiopia's Gambella Region*. New York: Human Rights Watch, 2012.

Humphreys, Macartan, Jeffery Sachs, and Joseph Stieglitz. *Escaping the Resource Curse*. New York: Columbia University Press, 2007.

Hurka, Thomas. *Perfectionism*. Oxford: Oxford University Press, 1993.

Hussain, Waheed. "Is Ethical Consumerism an Impermissible Form of Vigilantism?" *Philosophy and Public Affairs* 40, no. 2 (2012): 113–143.

ICTSD (International Centre for Trade and Sustainable Development). "Towards New Rules for Agricultural Markets?" December 10, 2015. http://www.ictsd.org/bridges-news/bridges/news/towards-new-rules-for-agricultural-markets.

Ignatieff, Michael. *Human Rights as Politics and Idolatry*. Princeton, NJ: Princeton University Press, 2001.

Institute for Agriculture and Trade Policy. "Towards Food Sovereignty: Constructive Alternatives to the World Trade Organization's Agreement on Agriculture." 2003. http://www.iatp.org/files/Towards_Food_Sovereignty_Constructive_Alternat.pdf.

International Committee of Investigative Journalists. "The Panama Papers." April 3, 2016. https://panamapapers.icij.org/.

International Committee of Investigative Journalists. "The Paradise Papers." November 5, 2017. https://www.icij.org/investigations/paradise-papers/paradise-papers-International.

International Covenant for Economic, Social, and Cultural Rights, UN General Assembly, *International Covenant on Economic, Social and Cultural Rights*, December 16, 1966, United Nations, Treaty Series, vol. 993.

International Financial Institution Advisory Commission. "The Report of the International Financial Institution Advisory Commission." Library of Congress, Congressional Research Service, 2001. http://www.policyarchive.org/browse-publishers/480.

IPCC. 2014. "Summary for Policymakers." In *Climate Change, 2014: Mitigation of Climate Change*, edited by Ottmar Edenhofer et al. Contribution of Working Group III to the Fifth Assessment Report of the Intergovernmental Panel on Climate Change. Cambridge: Cambridge University Press, 2014. https://www.ipcc.ch/pdf/assessment-report/ar5/wg3/ipcc_wg3_ar5_summary-for-policymakers.pdf.

Jackson, Kenneth T. *Crabgrass Frontier*. New York: Oxford University Press, 1985.

Jaggar, Alison. "Are My Hands Clean? Responsibility for Global Gender Disparities." In *Poverty, Agency, and Human Rights*, edited by Diana T. Meyers, 170–194. Oxford: Oxford University Press, 2014.

James, Aaron. *Fairness in Practice: A Social Contract for a Global Economy*. Oxford: Oxford University Press, 2012.

James, Susan. "Realizing Rights as Enforceable Claims." In *Global Responsibilities: Who Must Deliver on Human Rights?*, edited by Andrew Kuper, 79–93. London: Routledge, Taylor & Francis, 2005.

Jargowsky, Paul A. "Concentration of Poverty: An Update." The Century Foundation: *Blog of the Century*, April 9, 2014. http://tcf.org/blog/detail/concentration-of-poverty-an-update.

Jargowsky, Paul A. "Race & Inequality: Architecture of Segregation, Civil Unrest, the Concentration of Poverty, and Public Policy." August 7, 2015. https://tcf.org/content/report/architecture-of-segregation/.

Jedwab, Remi Luc Christiaensen and Marina Gindelsky. "Demography, Urbanization and Development: Rural Push, Urban Pull and . . . Urban Push?" *Journal of Urban Economics* 98 (2017): 6–16. https://doi.org/10.1016/j.jue.2015.09.002.

Kamm, F. M. *Intricate Ethics: Rights, Responsibilities, and Permissible Harm.* New York: Oxford University Press, 2007.

Kamm, F. M. "Rights." In *The Oxford Handbook of Jurisprudence and Philosophy of Law*, edited by Jules Coleman and Scott Shapiro, 486–513. Oxford: Oxford University Press, 2002.

Kant, Immanuel. *Metaphysical Elements of Justice.* 1797. Translated by John Ladd. Indianapolis: Hackett, 1999.

Kant, Immanuel. *The Metaphysics of Morals.* 1797. In *Practical Philosophy.* Edited and translated by M. J. Gregor. Cambridge: Cambridge University Press, 1999.

Kar, Dev and Sarah Freitas. "Illicit Financial Flows from Developing Countries: 2001–2010." http://www.gfintegrity.org/report/illicit-financial-flows-from-developing-countries-2001-2010/.

King, Martin Luther. "Letter from Birmingham City Jail." In *A Testament of Hope: The Essential Writings and Speeches of Martin Luther King, Jr.* Edited by James Melvin Washington. New York: HarperCollins, 1991.

King, Winter. "Illegal Settlements and the Impact of Titling Programmes." *Harvard International Law Review* 44, no. 2 (2003): 433–471.

Kirby, Alex. "Climate Treaty Races Towards Hazy Future." Climate News Network, October 6, 2016. http://climatenewsnetwork.net/climate-treaty-hazy-future/?utm_source=Climate+News+Network&utm_campaign=83736d6ca0-Treaty_ratification10_6_2016&utm_medium=email&utm_term=0_1198ea8936-83736d6ca0-38767557.

Klare, Karl. *The Race for What's Left: The Global Scramble for the World's Last Resources.* New York: Picador Books, 2012.

Kneebone, Elizabeth and Alan Berube. *Confronting Suburban Poverty in America.* Washington, DC: Brookings Institution, 2013.

Kneebone, Elizabeth and Natalie Holmes. "U.S. Concentrated Poverty in the Wake of the Great Recession." March 31, 2016. https://www.brookings.edu/research/u-s-concentrated-poverty-in-the-wake-of-the-great-recession/.

Knight, Rachael et al. "Protecting Community Lands and Resources: Evidence from Liberia, Mozambique and Uganda." Namati and International Development Law Organization, 2012. http://namati.org/wp-content/uploads/2012/06/protecting_community_lands_resources_inter_FW.pdf.

Kolers, Avery. "The Priority of Solidarity to Justice." *Journal of Applied Philosophy* 31, no. 4 (2014): 420–433.

Kramer, Matthew. "Some Doubts About Alternatives to the Interest Theory." *Ethics* 123, no. 2 (2013): 245–263.

Kraut, Richard. *What Is Good and Why: The Ethics of Well-being.* Cambridge, MA: Harvard University Press, 2007.

Krueger, Anne. "The Political Economy of the Rent-Seeking Society." *American Economic Review* 64, no. 3 (1974): 291–303.

Kugelman, Michael and Susan. L. Levenstein. *The Global Farms Race: Land Grabs, Agricultural Investment, and the Scramble for Food Security.* Washington, DC: Island Press, 2013.

Kuttner, Robert. *Can Democracy Survive Global Capitalism?* New York: W. W. Norton, 2018.

Kutz, Christopher. *Complicity: Ethics in a Global Age.* Cambridge: Cambridge University Press, 2000.

Laborde, Cecile. "Republican Global Distributive Justice: A Sketch." *European Journal of Political Theory* 9, no. 1 (2010): 48–69.

Lau, Peiley. "The World Bank's Doing Business Rankings: Relinquishing Sovereignty for a Good Grade." http://www.oaklandinstitute.org/world-bank%E2%80%99s-doing-business-rankings-relinquishing-sovereignty-good-grade.

Lazarus, Liora. "The Right to Security." In *Philosophical Foundations of Human Rights*, edited by Rowen Cruft, Matthew Liao, and Massimo Renzo, 423–444. Oxford: Oxford University Press, 2015.

Lear, Jonathan. *Aristotle: The Desire to Understand.* Cambridge: Cambridge University Press, 1988.

Lebron, Christopher J. *The Making of Black Lives Matter.* New York: Oxford University Press, 2017.

Lemmen, Christiaan. "The Social Tenure Domain Model: A Pro-Poor Land Tool." International Federation of Surveyors, UN-Habitat, Global Land Tool Network. 2010. http://www.fig.net/resources/publications/figpub/pub52/figpub52.pdf.

Lerner, Steve. *Sacrifice Zones: The Front Lines of Toxic Chemical Exposure in the United States.* Cambridge, MA: MIT Press, 2010.

Liao, S. Matthew. "Human Rights as Fundamental Conditions for a Good life." In *Philosophical Foundations of Human Rights*, edited by Rowan Cruft, S. Matthew Liao, and Massimo Renzo, 79–100. Oxford: Oxford University Press, 2015.

Liao, S. Matthew and Etinson, A. "Political and Naturalistic Conceptions of Human Rights: A False Polemic?" *Journal of Moral Philosophy* 9 (2012): 327–352.

Lipton, Michael. *Land Reform in Developing Countries: Property Rights and Property Wrongs.* London: Routledge, 2009.

Lipton, Michael. *Why Poor People Stay Poor: A Study of Urban Bias in World Development.* Cambridge: Cambridge University Press, 1977.

John Locke, *Two Treatises of Government.* 1699. Edited by Peter Laslett. Cambridge: Cambridge University Press, 1988.

Lomasky, Loren E. *Persons, Rights, and the Moral Community.* New York: Oxford University Press, 1987.

Longino, Helen. *The Fate of Knowledge.* Princeton, NJ: Princeton University Press, 2002.

Lovett, Frank. *A General Theory of Domination and Justice.* Oxford: Oxford University Press, 2010.

Lukes, Steven. *Power: A Radical View*, 2nd ed.. London: Macmillan, 2005.

Lundgren, Karin. "The Global Impact of e-Waste: Addressing the Challenge." Programme on Safety and Health at Work and the Environment (SafeWork), International Labour Office, Sectoral Activities Department (SECTOR), 2012. http://www.saicm.org/Portals/12/Documents/EPI/ewastesafework.pdf.

Lyons, David. *Confronting Injustice: Moral History and Political Theory.* Oxford: Oxford University Press, 2013.

Macklin, Ruth. "Dignity Is a Useless Concept." *British Medical Journal* 327 (2003): 1419.

Mair, Peter. *Ruling the Void: The Hollowing of Western Democracy.* London: Verso, 2013.

Manne, Kate. *Down Girl: The Logic of Misogyny*. New York: Oxford University Press, 2018.

Margalit, Avishai. *The Decent Society*. Cambridge, MA: Harvard University Press, 1996.

Martin-Breen, Bethany. "In the Developing World, Property Rights for Women Are About More than Just Housing." Rockefeller Foundation blog, November 5, 2014. https://www.rockefellerfoundation.org/blog/developing-world-property-rights-wome.

May, Thomas. "The Concept of Autonomy." *American Philosophical Quarterly* 31, no. 2 (1994): 133–144.

McFarland, Victor. "The New International Economic Order, Interdependence, and Globalization." *Humanity* 6, no. 1 (2015): 217–233.

McGary, Howard. "Morality and Collective Liability." *Journal of Value Inquiry* 20, no. 2 (1986): 157–165.

McGillivray, Fiona. *Privileging Industry: The Comparative Politics of Trade and Industrial* Policy. Princeton, NJ: Princeton University Press, 2004.

McKinsey Global Institute. "Urban World: The Global Consumers to Watch." 2016. https://www.mckinsey.com/global-themes/urbanization/urban-world-the-global-consumers-to-watch/~/media/57c6ad7f7f1b44a6bd2e24f0777b4cd6.ashx.

McQuaid, John. "Cancer Alley': Myth or Fact?" *Times-Picayune*, May 24, 2000, updated August 12, 2016. http://www.nola.com/politics/index.ssf/2000/05/cancer_alley_myth_or_fact.html.

Meckled-Garcia, Saladin. "Is There Really a Global Human Rights Deficit?" In *Cosmopolitanism versus Non-Cosmopolitanism*, edited by Gillian Brock, 111–128. Oxford: Oxford University Press, 2013.

Meckled-Garcia, Saladin. "On the Very idea of Cosmopolitan Justice: Constructivism and International Agency." *Journal of Political Philosophy* 16, no. 3 (2008): 245–271.

Milanovic, Branko. *Global Inequality: A New Approach for the Age of Globalization*. Cambridge: MA: Harvard University Press, 2016.

Mill, John Stuart. *The Collected Works of John Stuart Mill, Volume X: Essays on Ethics, Religion, and Society*. Edited by John M. Robson. Introduction by F. E. L. Priestley. Toronto: University of Toronto Press; London: Routledge & Kegan Paul, 1985.

Mill, John Stuart. *The Collected Works of John Stuart Mill, Volume XVIII: Essays on Politics and Society, Part I*. Edited by John M. Robson. Introduction by Alexander Brady. Toronto: University of Toronto Press; London: Routledge & Kegan Paul, 1977.

Mill, John Stuart. *The Collected Works of John Stuart Mill, Volume XXI: Essays on Equality, Law, and Education*. Edited by John M. Robson. Introduction by Stefan Collini. Toronto: University of Toronto Press; London: Routledge & Kegan Paul, 1984.

Miller, David. "Global Justice and Climate Change: How Should Responsibilities Be Distributed? Parts I and II." In *Tanner Lectures on Human Values 28*, edited by G. B. Peterson, 119–156. Salt Lake City: University of Utah Press, 2008.

Miller, David. *National Responsibility and Global Justice*. Oxford: Oxford University Press, 2007.

Miller, David. *Principles of Social Justice*. Cambridge, MA: Harvard University Press, 1999.

Miller, Richard. *Globalizing Justice: The Ethics of Poverty and Power*. Oxford: Oxford University Press, 2010.

Mills, Charles W. "Criticizing Critical Theory." In *Critical Theory in Critical Times*, edited by Penelope Deutscher and Christina Lafont, 233–250. New York: Columbia University Press, 2017.

Mills, Charles W. "'Ideal Theory' as Ideology." *Hypatia* 20, no. 3 (2005): 165–168.

Mills, Charles W. "White Ignorance." In *Race and Epistemologies of Ignorance*, edited by Shannon Sullivan and Nancy Tuana, 11–38. Albany: State University of New York Press, 2007.

Moellendorf, Darrel. "The World Trade Organization and Egalitarian Justice." In *Global Institutions and Responsibilities*, edited by Christian Barry and Thomas Pogge, 148–149. Malden, MA: Blackwell, 2005.

Mohai, Paul and Robin Saha. "Which Came First, People or Pollution? Assessing the Disparate Siting and Post-Siting Demographic Change Hypotheses of Environmental Injustice." *Environmental Research Letters* 10, no. 11 (2015): 115008. http://iopscience.iop.org/1748-9326/10/11/115008.

Mohan, Rakesh and Muneesh Kapur. "Emerging Powers and Global Governance: Wither the IMF?" IMF Working Paper 15/219, 2015. https://www.imf.org/external/pubs/ft/wp/2015/wp15219.pdf.

Moore, G. E. *Principia Ethica*. 1903. Edited by T. Baldwin. Cambridge: Cambridge University Press, 1993.

Moyn, Samuel. *Not Enough: Human Rights in an Unequal World*. Cambridge, MA: Belknap Press, 2018.

Murphy, Drew G. "Environmental Justice and the Law." January 17, 2017. https://drewgmurphy.com/2017/01/10/the-origins-of-environmental-justice/.

Nagel, Thomas. "Personal Rights and Public Space." *Philosophy and Public Affairs* 24, (1995): 83–107.

Nagel, Thomas. "The Problem of Global Justice." *Philosophy and Public Affairs* 33, no. 2 (2005): 113–147.

Nakagiri, Anne, Charles B. Niwagaba, Philip M. Nyenje, Robinah N. Kulabako, John B. Tumuhairwe, and Frank Kansiime. "Are Pit Latrines on Urban Areas of Sub-Saharan Africa Performing? A Review of Sage, Filling, Insects and Odour Nuisances." *BMC Public Health, 2016* 16, no. 120. https://doi.org/10.1186/s12889-016-2772-z.

Narayan, Deepa, Robert Chambers, Meera K. Shah, and Patti Petesch. *Voices of the Poor*, vol. 2: *Crying Out for Change*. Oxford: Oxford University, 2000.

National Bureau of Economic Research. "Employers' Replies to Racial Names." January 27, 2109. http://www.nber.org/digest/sep03/w9873.html.

National Research Council (U.S.) Study Committee on the Potential for Rehabilitating Lands Surface Mined for Coal in the Western United States. *Rehabilitation Potential of Western Coal Lands*. Cambridge, MA: Ford Foundation Energy Policy Project; Pensacola, FL: Ballinger, 1974.

Nickel, James. "Assigning Functions to Human Rights." In *Human Rights: Moral or Political?*, edited by Adam Etinson, 145–159. Oxford: Oxford University Press, 2018.

Nickel, James. *Making Sense of Human Rights*, 2nd ed. Malden, MA: Blackwell, 2007.

Nickel, James. "Rethinking Indivisibility: Towards a Theory of Supporting Relations Between Human Rights." *Human Rights Quarterly* 30, no. 4 (2008): 984–1001.

Nozick, Robert. *Anarchy, State and Utopia*. New York: Basic Books, 1974.

Nussbaum, Martha. *Creating Capabilities*. Cambridge, MA.: Belknap Press, 2011.

Nussbaum, Martha. *Frontiers of Justice: Disability, Nationality, Species Membership.* Cambridge, MA: Harvard University Press, 2006.

Nussbaum, Martha. *Women and Human Development: The Capabilities Approach.* Cambridge: Cambridge University Press, 2000.

Nussbaum, Martha. "Women and the *Law of Peoples.*" *Politics, Philosophy & Economics* 1, no. 3 (2002): 283–306.

O'Neill, Martin. "What Should Egalitarians Believe?" *Philosophy & Public Affairs* 36, no. 2 (2008): 119–156.

O'Neill, Onora. "The Dark Side of Human Rights." *International Affairs* 81, no. 2 (2005): 427–439.

O'Neill, Onora. *Towards Justice and Virtue.* Cambridge: Cambridge University Press, 1996.

Ostrom, Elinor. *Governing the Commons.* Cambridge: Cambridge University Press, 1990.

Outley, Corliss Wilson. "The Challenge of Environmental Justice for Children: The Impact of Cumulative Disadvantageous Risks." *Environmental Justice* 23, no. 4 (2006): 49–56.

Owen, G. E. L. "*Tithenai ta phainomena.*" 1961, In *Logic, Science and Dialectic*, 239–251. London: Duckworth, 1986.

Oxfam. "Extreme Carbon Inequality." 2015. https://www.oxfam.org/sites/www.oxfam.org/files/file_attachments/mb-extreme-carbon-inequality-021215-en.pdf.

Oxfam. "A Recipe for Disaster." 2006. http://policy-practice.oxfam.org.uk/publications/a-recipe-for-disaster-will-the-doha-round-fail-to-deliver-for-development-114122.

Oxfam. "Trade Report: Rigged rules and Double Standards." 2002. http://policy-practice.oxfam.org.uk/publications/rigged-rules-and-double-standards-trade-globalisation-and-the-fight-against-pov-112391.

Pager, Devah and Hana Shepherd. "The Sociology of Discrimination: Racial Discrimination in Employment, Housing, Credit, and Consumer Markets." *Annual Review of Sociology* 34, no. 1 (2008): 181–209. https://doi.org/10.1146/annurev.soc.33.040406.131740.

Parekh, Serena. "Getting to the Root of Gender Inequality: Structural Injustice and Political Responsibility." *Hypatia* 26, no. 4 (2011): 672–689.

Parfit, Derek. *Reasons and Persons.* Oxford: Oxford University Press, 1986.

Parikh, Priti, Himanshu Parikh, and Allan McRobie. "The Role of Infrastructure in Improving Human Settlements." *Proceedings of the Institution of Civil Engineers—Urban Design and Planning* 166, no. 2 (2013): 101–118.

Passmore, John. "Civic Justice and Its Rivals." In *Justice*, edited by Eugene Kamenka and Alice Erh-Soon Tay, 25–49. London: Edward Arnold, 1979.

Pasternak, Avia. "Voluntary Benefits from Wrongdoing." *Journal of Applied Philosophy* 31, no. 4 (2014): 377–391.

Payne, Geoffrey, Tony Piaskowy, and Lauren Kuritz. "Land Tenure in Urban Environments." United States Agency for International Development, 2014. www.land-links.org/issue-brief/land-tenure-in-urban-environments/.

Pearce, Fred. *The Land Grabbers: The New Fight over Who Owns the Earth.* Boston: Beacon Press, 2012.

Pellow, David Naguib. *Resisting Global Toxics: Transnational Movements for Environmental Justice.* Cambridge, MA: MIT Press, 2007.

Pentin, Edward. "Full Text of Pope Francis' Address at Kangemi Slum." *National Catholic Register*, November 27, 2015. http://www.ncregister.com/blog/edward-pentin/full-text-of-pope-francis-address-at-kangemi-slum.

Peter, Fabienne. "Political Legitimacy." In *Stanford Encyclopedia of Philosophy*, 2010, ed., revised 2017, edited by Edward N. Zalta. https://plato.stanford.edu/entries/legitimacy/.

Pettit, Philip. *A Theory of Freedom: From the Psychology to the Politics of Agency.* Oxford: Oxford University Press, 2001.

Pew Environment Group. "Big Chicken: Pollution and Industrial Poultry Production in America." 2011. http://www.pewtrusts.org/~/media/legacy/uploadedfiles/peg/publications/report/PEGBigChickenJuly2011pdf.pdf.

Pfaff, John F. *Locked In*. New York: Basic Books, 2017.

Pigou, Arthur C. *The Economics of Welfare*. London: Macmillan, 1920.

Piketty, Thomas. *Capital in the Twenty-First Century*. Cambridge, MA: Harvard University Press, 2014.

Pinkard, Terry. Review of *Kritik von Lebensformen* by Rahel Jaeggi. *European Journal of Philosophy* 25, no. 2 (2017): 540–546.

Pogge, Thomas, ed. *Freedom from Poverty as a Human Right*. Oxford: Oxford University Press, 2007.

Pogge, Thomas. "Severe Poverty as a Human Rights Violation." In *Freedom from Poverty as a Human Right*, edited by Thomas Pogge, 11–53. Oxford: Oxford University Press, 2007.

Posner, Eric and Cass Sunstein. "Global Warming and Social Justice: Do We Owe the World for Climate Change?" *Regulation* 31, no. 1 (2008): 14–20.

Portes, Alejandro and Kelly Hoffman. "Latin American Class Structures: Their Composition and Change During the Neoliberal Era." *Latin American Research Review* 38, no. 1 (2003): 41–82.

Potter, Grant. "Agricultural Subsidies Remain a Staple in the Industrial World." *Vital Signs.* Worldwatch Institute, February 28, 2014. http://www.worldwatch.org/agricultural-subsidies-remain-staple-industrial-world-0.

Powell, Rhonda. "The Relational Concept of Security." DPhil diss., University of Oxford, 2006.

Powers, Madison. "Ethical Challenges Posed by Climate Change: An Overview." In *Moral Theory and Climate Change: Ethical Perspectives on a Warming Planet*, edited by Dale E. Miller and Ben Eggleston. London: Taylor & Francis/Routledge, 2020.

Powers, Madison. "Food, Fairness, and Global Markets." In *Oxford Handbook of Food Ethics*, edited by Anne Barnhill, Mark Budolfson, and Tyler Dogget, 367–398. New York: Oxford University Press, 2018.

Powers, Madison. "Health Care as a Human Right: The Problem of Indeterminate Content." *Jurisprudence* 6, no. 1 (2015): 138–143.

Powers, Madison. "Moral Responsibility for Climate Change." In *Routledge Companion to Bioethics*, edited by John Arras, Elizabeth Fenton, and Rebecca Kukla, 133–146. New York: Routledge, 2015.

Powers, Madison. "Social Justice." In *Encyclopedia of Bioethics*, 4th ed., edited by Bruce Jennings, 2966–2973. Farmington Hills, MI: Macmillan, 2014.

Powers, Madison. "Sustainability and Resilience." In *Encyclopedia of the Anthropocene*, vol. 4, edited by Dominick DellaSala and Michael Goldstein, 29–37. Oxford: Elsevier, 2018. http://dx.doi.org/10.1016/B978-0-12-409548-9.10491-9.

Powers, Madison and Ruth Faden. "Health Capabilities, Outcomes, and the Political Ends of Justice." *Journal of Human Development and Capabilities* 12, no. 4 (2011): 565–570.

Powers, Madison and Ruth Faden. "Racial and Ethnic Disparities in Health Care: An Ethical Analysis of When and How They Matter." In *Unequal Treatment: Confronting Racial and Ethnic Disparities in Health Care*, edited by Brian D. Smedley, Adrienne Y. Stith, and Alan R. Nelson, 463–475. Committee on Understanding and Eliminating Racial and Ethnic Disparities in Health Care, Board on Health Sciences Policy. Washington, DC: National Academy of Sciences, Institute of Medicine, 2002.

Powers, Madison and Ruth Faden. *Social Justice: The Moral Foundations of Public Health and Health Policy*. New York: Oxford University Press, 2006.

Powers, Madison and Ruth Faden. "Social Practices, Public Health, and the Twin Aims of Justice: Responses to Comments." In "Symposium on Social Justice: The Moral Foundations of Public Health and Health Policy." *Public Health Ethics* 6, no. 1 (2013): 45–49.

Powers, Madison, Ruth Faden, and Yashar Saghai. "Liberty, Mill, and the Framework of Public Health Ethics." *Public Health Ethics* 5, no. 1 (2012): 6–15.

Proclamation of Teheran. International Conference on Human Rights, 22 Apr.–13 May 1968, ¶ 13, U.N. Doc. A/CONF.32/41 (1968). http://www.unhchr.ch/html/ menu3/b/ b_tehern.htm.

Protocol Additional to the Geneva Conventions of 12 August 1949, and Relating to the Protection of Victims of International Armed Conflicts (Protocol I), 8 June 1977. International Committee of the Red Cross. https://ihl-databases.icrc.org/ihl/INTRO/470.

Putnam, Daniel. "Equality of Intelligibility." In *The Equal Society: Essays on Equality in Theory and Practice*, edited by George Hull, 91–112. Lanham, MD: Lexington, 2015.

Randolph, J. W. "Appalachia: National Sacrifice Zone." *Appalachian Voices*, June 27, 2006. http://appvoices.org/2006/06/27/1174/.

Ravallion, Martin. "On the Urbanization of Poverty." Policy Research working paper WPS 2586, World Bank, 2001. http://documents.worldbank.org/curated/en/ 577771468739538398/On-the-urbanization-of-poverty.

Rawls, John. *Justice as Fairness: A Restatement*. Cambridge, MA: Harvard University Press, 2001.

Rawls, John. *The Law of Peoples*. Cambridge, MA: Harvard University Press, 1999.

Rawls, John. *Political Liberalism*. Columbia University Press, 1995.

Rawls, John. *A Theory of Justice*. 1971. Cambridge, MA: Harvard University Press, 1999.

Raz, Joseph. *The Authority of Law: Essays on Law and Morality*. Oxford: Clarendon Press, 1979.

Raz, Joseph. "Human Rights in the Emerging World Order." In *Philosophical Foundations of Human Rights*, edited by Rowen Cruft, Matthew Liao, and Massimo Renzo, 217–231. Oxford: Oxford University Press, 2015.

Raz, Joseph. *The Morality of Freedom*. Oxford: Clarendon Press, 1986.

Reiman, Jeffrey. "The Structure of Structural Injustice: Thoughts on Iris Marion Young's *Responsibility for Justice*." *Social Theory and Practice* 38, no. 4 (2012): 738–751.

Renzo, Massimo. "Human Needs, Human Rights." In *Philosophical Foundations of Human Rights*, edited by Rowen Cruft, Matthew Liao, and Massimo Renzo, 570–587. Oxford: Oxford University Press, 2015.

Roberts, Adam and Timothy Garton Ash, eds. *Civil Resistance and Power Politics: The Experience of Non-violent Action from Gandhi to the Present.* Oxford: Oxford University Press, 2009.

Robertson, Beth and Per Pinstrup-Anderson. "Global Land Acquisition: Neo-Colonialism or Development Opportunity." *Food Security* 2, no. 3 (2010): 271–283.

Rodrik, Dani. *The Globalization Paradox.* New York: W. W. Norton, 2010.

Rogerson, Christian. "Globalization or Informalization? African Urban Economies in the 1990s." In *The Urban Challenge in Africa: Growth and Management of Its Large Cities*, edited by Carole Rakodi, 337–370. Tokyo: United Nations University Press, 1997.

Romero, Emilie. "The Sacrifice Zone: A Short Documentary." 2013. https://sacrificezone.wordpress.com/2013/02/12/about-2/.

Ronzoni, Miriam. "The Global Order: A Case of Background Injustice? A Practice-Dependent Account." *Philosophy and Public Affairs* 37, no. 3 (2009): 229–256.

Rosenthal, Elizabeth. "Lead from Old U.S. Batteries Sent to Mexico Raises Risks." *New York Times*, December 8, 2011. http://www.nytimes.com/2011/12/09/science/earth/recycled-battery-lead-puts-mexicans-in-danger.htm.

Rothstein, Richard. *The Color of Law: A Forgotten History of How Our Government Segregated America.* New York: W. W. Norton, 2017.

Roy, Ananya. "Slumdog Cities: Rethinking Subaltern Urbanism." *International Journal of Urban and Regional Research* 35, no. 2 (2011): 223–238.

Sample, Ruth. *Exploitation, What It Is and Why It Is Wrong.* Lanham, MD: Rowman & Littlefield, 2003.

Sandel, Michael. *Justice: What's the Right Thing to Do?* New York: Farrar, Straus & Giroux, 2010.

Sangiovanni, Andrea. "Global Justice, Reciprocity, and the State." *Philosophy and Public Affairs* 35, no. 1 (2007): 3–39.

Sangiovanni, Andrea. *Humanity Without Dignity: Moral Equality, Respect, and Human Rights.* Cambridge, MA: Harvard University Press, 2017.

Sangiovanni, Andrea. "The Irrelevance of Coercion, Imposition, and Framing to Distributive Justice." *Philosophy & Public Affairs* 40, no. 2 (2012): 79–110.

Scanlon, T. M. *Why Does Inequality Matter?* Oxford: Oxford University Press, 2018.

Schiffman, Richard. "Hunger, Food Security, and the African Land Grab." *Ethics & International Affairs* 27, no. 3 (2013): 239–249.

David Schmidtz. "Nonideal Theory: What It Is and What It Needs to Be." *Ethics* 121, no. 4 (2011): 772–796.

Schneider, Keith. "Dying Nuclear Plants Give Birth to New Problems." *New York Times*, October 31, 1988. https://www.nytimes.com/1988/10/31/us/dying-nuclear-plants-give-birth-to-new-problems.html?pagewanted=all.

Semuels, Alana. "No, Most Black People Don't Live in Poverty—or Inner Cities." *Atlantic*, October 12, 2016. https://www.theatlantic.com/business/archive/2016/10/trump-african-american-inner-city/503744/.

Sen, Amartya. *Development as Freedom.* New York: Anchor Books, 1999.

Sen, Amartya. *The Idea of Justice.* Oxford: Oxford University Press, 2009.

Shapiro, Thomas, Tatjana Meschede, and Sam Osoro. "The Roots of the Widening Racial Wealth Gap: Explaining the Black–White Economic Divide." Research and Policy

Brief, February 2013. http://iasp.brandeis.edu/pdfs/Author/shapiro-thomas-m/racialwealthgapbrief.pdf.

Sharkey, Patrick. "Neighborhoods and the Black–White Mobility Gap." 2009. http://www.pewtrusts.org/~/media/legacy/uploadedfiles/wwwpewtrustsorg/reports/economicmobility/pewsharkeyv12pdf.pdf.

Sharkey, Patrick. *Stuck in Place: Urban Neighborhoods and the End of Progress toward Racial Equality.* Chicago: University of Chicago Press, 2013.

Shelby, Tommie. "Foundations of Black Solidarity: Collective Identity or Common Oppression." *Ethics* 112, no. 2 (2002): 231–266.

Shue, Henry. *Basic Rights: Subsistence, Affluence, and U.S. Foreign Policy*, 2nd ed. Princeton, NJ: Princeton University Press, 1996.

Shue, Henry. "Mediating Duties." *Ethics* 98, no. 4 (1988): 687–704.

Silvermint, Daniel. "Resistance and Well-being." *Journal of Political Philosophy* 21, no. 4 (2013): 405–425.

Simmons, A. John. "Ideal and Nonideal Theory." *Philosophy and Public Affairs* 38, no. 1 (2010): 5–36.

Singer, Peter. "Famine, Affluence, and Morality." *Philosophy and Public Affairs* 1, no. 3 (1975): 229–243.

Skorupski, John. *The Domain of Reasons.* Oxford: Oxford University Press, 2010.

Smith Nightingale, Demetra and Stephen A. Wandner. "Informal and Nonstandard Employment in the United States: Implications for Low-Income Working Families." Brief 20. The Urban Institute, Washington, DC, August 2011.

Sreenivasan, Gopal. "Duties and Their Direction." *Ethics* 120, no. 3 (2010): 465–494.

Sreenivasan, Gopal. "A Hybrid Theory of Claim-Rights." *Oxford Journal of Legal Studies* 25 (2005): 257–274.

State of California Department of Justice. "Attorney General Kamala D. Harris Announces Suit Against JPMorgan Chase for Fraudulent and Unlawful Debt-Collection Practices." https://oag.ca.gov/news/press-releases/attorney-general-kamala-d-harris-announces-suit-against-jpmorgan-chase.

Steinisch, Monica. "You Can Avoid Wage Garnishment." Financial Resource Center, 2015. http://resourcecenter.cuna.org/331/article/2615/html.

Stichting Fossielvrij NL. "Sacrifice Zones in Germany and the Netherlands." 2016. https://gofossilfree.org/nl/sacrifice-zones-in-germany-and-the-netherlands/.

Stiglitz, Joseph. *Globalization and Its Discontents.* New York: W. W. Norton, 2003.

Stiglitz, Joseph. *The Great Divide: Unequal Societies and What We Can Do About Them.* New York: W. W. Norton, 2015.

Stiglitz, Joseph, Jean-Paul Fitouss, and Amartya Sen. *Mismeasuring Our Lives: Why GDP Doesn't Add Up.* New York: New Press, 2010.

Streeck, Wolfgang. *How Will Capitalism End?* London: Verso, 2017.

Struzik, Ed. "Canada's Trudeau Is Under Fire for His Record on Green Issues." *Yale Environment 360*, January 19, 2017. http://e360.yale.edu/features/canada_justin_trudeau_environmental_policy_pipelines.

Suneja, Kirtika. "India Opposes US Proposal to Dismantle Price Support and Subsidies in World Trade Organization." *Economic Times*, September 25, 2015. http://articles.economictimes.indiatimes.com/2015-09-25/news/66884503_1_peace-clause-wto-members-subsidies.

Swaminathan, Hema and Arnab Mukherji. "Slums and Malnourishment: Evidence from Women in India." *American Journal of Public Health* 102, no. 7 (2012): 1329–1335. doi: 10.2105/AJPH.2011.300424.

Sylla, Ndongo Samba. "Fairtrade Is an Unjust Movement That Serves the Rich." *Guardian*, September 5, 2014. https://www.theguardian.com/global-development/2014/sep/05/fairtrade-unjust-movement-serves-rich.

Taibbi, Matt. *The Divide: American Injustice in the Age of the Wealth Gap.* New York: Spiegel & Grau, 2014.

Tangermann, Stefan. "Farming Support: The Truth Behind the Numbers." *OECD Observer*, 2013. http://www.oecdobserver.org/news/archivestory.php/aid/1223/Farming_support:_the_truth_behind_the_numbers.html#sthash.giLeoWad.dpuf.

Tarrow, Sidney. *Power in Movement: Collective Action, Social Movements and Politics.* Cambridge: Cambridge University Press, 1994.

Tasioulas, John. "The Moral Reality of Rights." In *Freedom from Poverty as a Human Right,* edited by Thomas Pogge, 75–101. Oxford: Oxford University Press, 2007.

Tasioulas, John. "On the Foundations of Human Rights." In *Philosophical Foundations of Human Rights,* edited by Rowen Cruft, Matthew Liao, and Massimo Renzo, 45–70. Oxford: Oxford University Press, 2015.

Tawney, R. H. *Equality,* 4th ed. Introduction by Richard Titmuss. London: Unwin Books, 1964.

Taylor, Paul C. *Race: A Philosophical Introduction,* 2nd ed. Cambridge: Polity Press, 2013.

Temkin, Larry S. "Inequality." *Philosophy and Public Affairs* 15, no. 2 (1986): 99–121.

Thompson, Paul B. *The Ethics of Aid and Trade: US Food Policy, Foreign Competition and the Social Contract.* New York: Cambridge University Press, 1992.

Thomson, Judith Jarvis. *The Realm of Rights.* Cambridge, MA: Harvard University Press, 1990.

Tilly, Charles. "Inequality, Democratization, and De-democratization." *Sociological Theory* 21, no. 1 (2003): 37–43.

Tilly, Charles. *Social Movements, 1768–2004.* Boulder, CO: Paradigm, 2004.

Townley, Cynthia. "Trust and the Curse of Cassandra (An Exploration of the Value of Trust)." *Philosophy in the Contemporary World* 10, no. 2 (2003): 105–111.

UNESCO. Expert Meeting on Human Rights, Basic Needs, and the Establishment of a New Economic Order, Paris, June 19–23, 1978, UN Doc. SS78/Conf. 630/12.

UN-Habitat. *The Challenge of Slums: Global Report on Human Settlements.* London: Earthscan, 2003.

UN-Habitat. *Forced Evictions—Towards Solutions?* Second Report of the Advisory Group on Forced Evictions to the Executive Director of UN-Habitat. Nairobi: Advisory Group on Forced Evictions, 2007.

UN-Habitat, Shelter and Sustainable Human Settlement Division. "Why Focus on Women?" mirror.unhabitat.org/content.asp?typeid=19&catid=423&cid=1507.

UN-Habitat. *State of the World's Cities, 2006/2007: The Millennium Development Goals and Urban Sustainability.* London: Earthscan, 2006.

UN-Habitat. *State of the World's Cities, 2008/2009: Harmonious Cities.* London: Earthscan, 2008.

UN-Habitat. *State of the World's Cities, 2012/2013: Prosperity of Cities.* London: Earthscan, 2013.

UN-Habitat. World Habitat Day (WHD) Background Paper. 2014. https://unhabitat.org/wp-content/uploads/2014/07/WHD-2014-Background-Paper.pdf.

United Church of Christ Commission for Racial Justice. *Toxic Wastes and Race in the United States: A National Report on the Racial and Socioeconomic Characteristics of Communities Surrounding Hazardous Waste Sites*. New York: United Church of Christ, 1987.

United Nations. "World Urbanization Prospects: The 2014 Revision." Population Division of UN Department of Economic and Social Affairs, 2014. https://esa.un.org/unpd/wup/publications/files/wup2014-highlights.pdf.

United Nations Commission on the Legal Empowerment of the Poor. *Making the Law Work for Everyone*, vol. 1: *Report of the Commission on the Legal Empowerment of the Poor*, 2008. https://www.un.org/ruleoflaw/blog/document/making-the-law-work-for-everyone-vol-1-report-of-the-commission-on-legal-empowerment-of-the-poor/.

United Nations Commission on the Status of Women. "The Elimination and Prevention of All Forms of Violence Against Women and Girls." Report on the Fifty-Seventh Session (4–15 March 2013). Economic and Social Council Official Records, 2013, suppl. 7. http://undocs.org/E/2013/27.

United Nations Committee on Trade and Development (UNCTAD). "Trade and Development Report, 1999." http://unctad.org/en/docs/tdr1999_en.pdf.

United Nations Development Programme (UNDP). *Human Development Report, 2006: Beyond Scarcity: Power, Poverty, and the Global Water Crisis*. Geneva: UNDP, 2006.

United Nations Environment Programme (UNEP). "Global Chemicals Outlook." 2012. http://www.unep.org/chemicalsandwaste/what-we-do/policy-and-governance/global-chemicals-outlook.

United Nations General Assembly. "Universal Declaration of Human Rights." 1948. http://www.un.org/en/universal-declaration-human-rights/index.html.

United Nations Population Fund. "State of the World Population (2007): Unleashing the Potential of Urban Growth." https://www.unfpa.org/sites/default/files/pub-pdf/695_filename_sowp2007_eng.pdf.

United States Census Bureau. *2016 American Community Survey*. https://www.census.gov/programs-surveys/acs.

United States Justice Department, Civil Rights Division. "Investigation of the Ferguson Police Department." March 4, 2015. https://www.justice.gov/sites/default/files/opa/press-releases/attachments/2015/03/04/ferguson_police_department_report.pdf.

Uteng, Tanu Priya. *Gender and Mobility in the Developing World*. Background paper, World Development Report, 2012. Washington, DC: World Bank, 2011.

Valentini, Laura. "Cosmopolitan Justice and Rightful Enforceability." In *Cosmopolitanism versus Non-Cosmopolitanism*, edited by Gillian Brock, 8–26. Oxford: Oxford University Press, 2013.

Valentini, Laura. "Ideal vs. Non-Ideal Theory: A Conceptual Map." *Philosophy Compass* 7, no. 9 (2012): 654–664.

Valentini, Laura. *Justice in a Globalized World*. Oxford: Oxford University Press, 2012.

Vallier, Kevin. "Social Injustice as Emergent Property." *Bleeding Heart Libertarians* (blog). May 22, 2013. http://bleedingheartlibertarians.com/2013/05/social-injustice-as-emergent-property/.

Vienna Declaration and Programme of Action, U.N. GAOR, World Conference on Human Rights, 48th Sess., 22d plen. mtg., part I, ¶ 5, U.N. Doc. A/CONF.157/24 (1993), reprinted in 32 I.L.M. 1661 (1993).

Waldron, Jeremy. *Dignity, Rank, and Rights*. Oxford: Oxford University Press, 2012.

Waldron, Jeremy. *God, Locke, and Equality*. Cambridge: Cambridge University Press, 2002.

Waldron, Jeremy. "Is Dignity the Foundation of Human Rights?" In *Philosophical Foundations of Human Rights*, edited by Rowen Cruft, Matthew Liao, and Massimo Renzo, 117–137. Oxford: Oxford University Press, 2015.

Waldron, Jeremy. "Superseding Historic Injustice." *Ethics* 103, no. 1 (1992): 4–28.

Weale, Albert. "The Right to Health versus Good Medical Care." *Critical Review of International Social and Political Philosophy*" 15, no. 4 (2012): 473–493.

Wenar, Lief. *Blood Oil: Tyrants, Violence, and the Rules That Run the World*. Oxford: Oxford University Press, 2015.

Wenar, Lief. "The Nature of Rights." *Philosophy and Public Affairs* 33, no. 3 (2005): 223–253.

Wenar, Leif. "Property Rights and the Resource Curse." *Philosophy and Public Affairs* 36, no. 1 (2008): 2–32.

Wenar, Lief. Responsibility for Severe Poverty." In *Freedom from Poverty as a Human Right*, edited by Thomas Pogge, 255–274. Oxford: Oxford University Press, 2007.

Wertheimer, Alan. *Exploitation*. Princeton, NJ: Princeton University Press, 1996.

"What the Dutch Disease Is, and Why It's Bad." *The Economist*, November 5, 2014. http://www.economist.com/blogs/economist-explains/2014/11/economist-explains-2.

Whitehouse, Peter, Eric Juengst, Maxwell Mehlman, and Thomas Murray. "Enhancing Cognition in the Intellectually Intact." *Hastings Center Report* 27, no. 3 (1997): 14–22.

WHO/UNICEF Joint Monitoring Programme. "Progress on Sanitation and Drinking Water: 2015 Update and MDG Assessment." 2015. http://www.wssinfo.org/.

Wilde, Oscar. *The Soul of Man under Socialism and Selected Critical Prose*. 1891. Edited by Linda Dowling. London: Penguin, 2001.

Wilder, Tamara, Whitney C. Allgood, and Richard Rothstein. "Narrowing the Achievement Gap for Low-Income Children: A 19-Year Life Cycle Approach." 2008. http://www.epi.org/files/page/-/pdf/wilder_allgood_rothstein-narrowing_the_achievement_gap.pdf.

Wilson, James Q. "Broken Windows." *Atlantic*, March 1982. https://www.theatlantic.com/magazine/archive/1982/03/broken-windows/304465/.

Wolff, Jonathan and Avner De-Shalit. *Disadvantage*. New York: Oxford University Press, 2007.

Woods, Ngaire and Amrita Narlikar. "Global Governance and the Limits of Accountability: The WTO, the IMF, and the World Bank." *International Social Science Journal* 53 (2001): 569–583.

Woolley, John T and Gerhard Peters. "Remarks upon Signing Order Establishing the National Advisory Commission on Civil Disorders." American Presidency Project. Santa Barbara: University of California.

World Bank. "Protecting Land Rights Is Key to Large-Scale Land Acquisitions." 2010. https://reliefweb.int/report/world/protecting-land-rights-key-successful-large-scale-land-acquisitions.

World Bank. "World Development Report: Gender Equality and Development. 2012." 2011. https://siteresources.worldbank.org/INTWDR2012/Resources/7778105-1299699968583/7786210-1315936222006/Complete-Report.pdf.

World Economic Forum. "These Are the World's Five Biggest Slums." October 19, 2016. https://www.weforum.org/agenda/2016/10/these-are-the-worlds-five-biggest-slums/.

World Health Organization. Preamble to the Constitution of the World Health Organization as Adopted by the International Health Conference, New York, June 19–22, 1946.

World Health Organization. Urban HEART (Urban Health Equity Assessment and Response Tool). Kobe, Japan. WHO Commission on Social Determinants of Health, 2010. http://www.who.int/kobe_centre/publications/urban_heart/en/.

World Health Organization. "Water for Health—Taking Charge." 2001. http://www.who.int/water_sanitation_health/wwdreport.pdf?ua=1.

"World Inequality Report, 2018." https://wir2018.wid.world/.

World Summit Outcome Document, Article 143, 2005; and United Nations General Assembly Resolution 66/290.

Worldwatch Institute. "The Hidden Shame of the Global Industrial Economy." 2004. http://www.worldwatch.org/node/543.

Young, Iris Marion. "Equality of Whom? Social Groups and Judgments of Justice." *Journal of Political Philosophy* 9, no, 1 (2001): 1–18.

Young, Iris Marion. *Inclusion and Democracy*. New York: Oxford University Press, 2000.

Young, Iris Marion. *Justice and the Politics of Difference*. Princeton, NJ: Princeton University Press, 1990.

Young, Iris Marion. *Responsibility for Justice*. Oxford: Oxford University Press, 2011.

Ypi, Lea. *Global Justice and Avant-Garde Political Agency*. Oxford: Oxford University Press, 2012.

Zelizer, Julian E. "Fifty Years Ago, the Government Said Black Lives Matter: The Radical Conclusions of the 1968 Kerner Report." *Boston Review*, May 4, 2016. https://bostonreview.net/us/julian-e-zelizer-kerner-report.

Zucman, Gabriel. *The Hidden Wealth of Nations*. Chicago: University of Chicago Press, 2015.

INDEX

advantage
    definition of, 16–17n
    disparities in, 52
    economic class and, 87–88
    intersection of group memberships
        and, 107
    Rawls on, 89
    relative social position and, 101–4
    social groups and, 87–88, 107
    See also systematic disadvantage
Africa, sub-Saharan, urban poverty in,
    220–21, 223, 225, 230
agricultural gag laws, 265–66
agricultural production facilities in
    LMICs, 202–4
agricultural trade, regulation of, 172–75
Alston, Philip, 167
anti-competitive conduct of targets of
    resistance, 262–64
Appalachia, as sacrifice zone, 190–93
Aristotle
    conception of well-being of, 20–21,
        22–23, 24
    on courage, 25
    on justice, 57–58n1
    Politics, 52
    on self-determination, 41
    theological principle example of,
        21–22n13
armed conflict, ethics of, 240–41
assessment of fulfillment of human rights
    duties, 136–41
associative rationale of strong statism, 160

Astroturfing, 265
asymmetric impact of unjust structural
    arrangements, 92
Augustinian Doctrine, 67n17
avoidance of accountability of targets of
    resistance, 264–66

backup responsibility, assignment of,
    154, 171n59
backward-looking accounts of
    deprivation, 55–56
Baldwin, James, "Report from Occupied
    Territory," 217
Barry, Brian, 61, 62, 158
bearers of rights. *See* right-holders
Beitz, Charles, 48–49
beneficence
    duties of, as imperfect, 63
    theories of, 53–54
benefit received from injustice,
        targets of resistance and, 256,
        257–59, 266–67
Berlin, Isaiah, 39–40
Black Lives Matter, 6, 216, 217
blackness, stereotypes and suspicion
    of, 217–18
blockades, 248–51
bonds of personal attachment, as core
    element of well-being, 37–38
Boo, Katherine, *Behind the Beautiful
    Forever,* 231
bootstrap arguments for identifying
    human rights, 139–40

deontological approach to disrespect, 35–37
deprivation of well-being
backward-looking accounts of, 55–56
beneficence and, 53–54
in childhood, 90–91
choiceworthy option availability and, 91
direct moral concern for, 15
disadvantage, unfair power relations, and, 15–16
disadvantage compared to, 16–17
as input and output of normative phenomena, 20
Linked Chain Argument and, 142–43
Structural Dependence Argument and, 26–27
in urban slums, 229–32
Difference Principle of Rawls, 87–88, 169n55
dignity-based theories of human rights
justificatory roles of dignity and, 125–26
moral status question and, 124–25
overview of, 116–17, 124
specific rights and, 125–28
Dilulio, John, 217–18
disadvantage. *See* systematic disadvantage
disrespect and well-being, 33–37. *See also* equal respect
divestment campaigns, 243–48, 266–67
domination. *See* subordination or domination
dumping of hazardous wastes in LMICs, 204–6
Dutch Disease, 201–2
duties
accountability and, 64–66
assignment and specification of, 68, 132
imperfect, 63, 66–67n16
perfect, 63
See also counterpart duties
duty-bearers
assessment on fulfillment of responsibilities of, 137–41
moral claims on, 119–20
status of, 120

economic classes
advantage and, 87–88
market power and, 247
Rawls on, 103–4
social distance between, 52
social position and, 85–86
Tawney on, 103–4
See also poverty; relative social position
economic policies
GDP focus of, 199–202
to mitigate unfairness, 143–44
economic production and relative social position, 102–4
economic systems
anti-competitive conduct in, 262–64
closed, 109–11
Dutch Disease, 201–2
market-based strategies to resist injustice, 243–48
negative externalities in, 199–200, 204, 205–6, 261–62
in sacrifice zones, 192–94, 201
in urban slums, 226–29
See also economic classes
education, for knowledge and understanding, 30–31
educational policies to mitigate unfairness, 144
egalitarian norms and strong statism, 157–60
egalitarian view of justice, 65n13
electronic waste, dumping of, 205
emancipation from illegitimate control, demand for, 182–84
empirical approach to universal endorsement, 44–48
enforcement of justice norms. *See* rightful enforceability of justice norms
environmental degradation. *See* sacrifice zones
environmental racism, 196
equality, assumption of, 83–84
equal respect
as core element of well-being, 33–37
decent life and, 43–44
participation in social movements and, 268
social relations and, 37
well-being and, 128

essential dimensions, terminology
    of, 25n22
ethical outlook
    definition of, 44–45n49
    divisions in, 51–52
    interpretive approach and, 48–50
ethics
    of armed conflict, 240–41
    practical, 5
ethnicity. *See* race
exclusion. *See* segregated cities; social
    exclusion
exploitation
    definition of, 18
    disrespect and, 36
    of poor neighborhoods, 214–16
    resource curse and, 197–98
    unfairness and, 78
extractive industries in sacrifice zones
    foreign direct investment in, 197–98
    GDP and, 199–202
    mining, 190–93, 197–98n31
extractive practices in poor
    neighborhoods, 214–16

Fair Equality of Opportunity Principle of
    Rawls, 76–77, 87–88
fairness norms
    assumptions in, 83–84
    human rights norms and, 75–77,
        83–84, 141–45
    Interstate Reciprocity Principle
        and, 169–72
    intuitive case for, 77–78
    moral salience and, 79–81, 84
    multiple realizability and, 70
    power relations and, 81–84
    Rawls on, 60–61
    strong statism and, 157–59
    well-being and, 56
fair-trade initiatives, 247–48
false consciousness, 269
Federal Housing Authority (FHA), 208–9
fence-line communities, 189
Ferguson, Missouri, 209, 216–17, 218
First National People of Color
    Environmental Leadership
    Summit, 196
food security programs, 172–75
foreign direct investment

in agricultural production
    facilities, 202–5
negative externalities of, 199–200
resource curse and, 197–98, 199, 202–5
Forst, Ranier, 75, 169–70
Francis (pope), 230–31
free expression, right of, 128–30

gains, ill-gotten, and targets of
    resistance, 257–59
Gandhi, Mahatma, 251–52, 253
GDP (gross domestic product) in sacrifice
    zones, 199–202
gender
    informal economy and, 227–29
    intersectionality and, 107–8
    judgments of moral worth and, 49–50
    in power relations, 79, 231–32
    power relations and, 81–83
    relative social position and, 93–94, 105–6
    social exclusion and, 79
    in urban slums, 226
    See also women
Geneva Conventions, 126, 240–41
genuine rights, 63–64
global institutional factors, 98
globalization
    assumptions about, 146
    dumping of hazardous wastes
        and, 204–6
    formation of structural injustices and, 4
    of sacrifice zones, 196
    See also global order
Global Justice Now, 183
global land grab, 202–4
global order
    as intensifying global poverty, 168–69
    intrastate economic inequality
        and, 185–86
    Moral Equal Protection Principle
        and, 154–55
    power of non-state institutions
        in, 177–85
    protection of human rights and, 153
    states in, 185
    See also globalization; Interstate
        Reciprocity Principle
global warming, 175–76, 180, 248–49
goals of resistance, 241
good, prudential conception of, 22

moral importance and stringency
criteria for, 59–63
overview of, 74–75
rightful enforceability of, 71–74
in theory of structural injustice, 62–63
See also claimability and specificity
criteria for justice norms;
fairness norms
justification
of core elements of well-being, 119
of human rights schemes, 134–35
of justice norms, 118
of legal non-compliance, 250–51
of selection of targets of
resistance, 255–59
of theory of structural justice, 50–53
See also universal endorsement
approaches to well-being

Kamm, Frances, 124, 128–30
Kant, Immanuel, 69, 70, 72–73, 120
Kenya, urban slums in, 223, 225, 230
Kerner Commission Report, 206–7
King, Martin Luther, Jr., 247
knowledge and understanding
as core element of well-being, 29–32
neighborhood effects on, 212
participation in social movements
and, 268–69
right of free expression and, 129–30
Kraut, Richard, 21–22

land in LMICs
informal occupancy of, 224–26
ownership of, 200, 203–4
purchasing or leasing of, 202–4
Law of Peoples, The (Rawls), 162
Lebron, Christopher, 217
legal systems
institutional capacity of states
and, 149
law violations as resistance to
injustice, 248–51
misuses of, 265–66
policing in segregated cities
and, 216–19
right of defense of self or others in, 251
systematic influence of, 97–98
two-tier system of, 105
legitimate states, definition of, 152

life insurance, "monthly-debt
ordinary," 215
life prospects
conceptions of, 19
disadvantage experienced in childhood
and, 90–91
as probabilistic notion, 16
systematic disadvantage and, 16–17
See also decent life
Linked Chain Argument, 141–45
LMICs. *See* low- and middle-income
nations
loans
"flipping," 215
installment contracts, 209
predatory, 214
subprime mortgage, 263
Locke, John
on resistance to injustice, 73, 74
on states and rights, 67–68
Lomasky, Loren, 132–33
Lovett, Frank, 178
low- and middle-income nations (LMICs)
agricultural trade policy and, 172–75
dumping of hazardous wastes in, 204–6
human rights duties of, 177–78
purchasing and leasing land in, 202–4
resource curse of, 197–98, 199, 202–5
urbanization of, 220–21

malnutrition in urban slums, 229–30
market-based strategies to resist
injustice, 243–48
market systems. *See* economic systems
Marx, Karl, 85–86, 102
McGary, Howard, 260
means of resistance
blockades, data hacks, and violations of
law as, 248–51
boycotts and divestment campaigns
as, 243–48
moral significance of, 241
naming and shaming as, 242–43
overview of, 241
self-defense and defense of others
as, 251–54
Meckled-Garcia, Saladin, 149–50, 167–68
media manipulation, 265
microenterprises, home-based, 228
militias, private armed, 253

Mill, John Stuart
  on justice and rights, 59–60, 72
  on self-determination, 38–39,
    121, 127
Miller, David, 49–50, 156–57
Miller, Richard, 170–71
Mills, Charles, 104–5
minimalist position on human
    rights, 46–48
minimally decent life, 43, 75–76n31
mining
  history of, in US, 197–98n31
  sacrifice zones and, 190–93
  as target of resistance, 266–67
Mississippi Freedom Rides, 252
Mississippi River Delta, 194–95n21, 196
modernization hypothesis, 228–29
Moral Equal Protection Principle, 154–55,
    176, 177
moral goodness, 22n16
moral hazard, 263
moral importance criteria for justice
    norms, 59–63
moral significance
  captive contributing beneficiaries
    and, 267
  of choice and choiceworthy
    options, 89–91
  complicit agents and, 259–61
  defense of self or others and, 251
  deprivation of well-being and, 15
  fairness norms and, 79–81, 84
  interpretive approach and, 49–50
  justice and, 57
  of legal non-compliance, 249–51
  limits to exercise of power and, 180–82
  "livce and let live" ideal and, 219
  means of resistance and escalation
    of, 241
  natural law conception of norms of, 66
  normative innovation and, 66–69
  other-regarding, 29–30
  respect and, 36–37
  in selection of targets of resistance,
    255–56, 257, 259
  of state responsibility, 10–11,
    146–48, 152
  of structural influence on groups, 87–91
moral status question, 124–25
mortgage loans, subprime, 263

multiple realizability, specificity and
    problem of, 69–70
Mumbai, urban slums in, 231

Nagel, Thomas
  individual inviolability and, 48–49
  national self-determination and,
    162–63, 165–66, 167
  strong statism and, 156–58, 159, 161
naming and shaming, as resistance to
    injustice, 242–43
National Academies of Science, 188
national self-determination
    arguments, 162–67
nation-states. *See* states
natural law conception of moral norms, 66
natural resource curse, 197–98,
    199, 202–5
near-inescapable impact of unjust
    structural arrangements, 92–95
nearly just society of Rawls, 19–20,
    112–13, 236–38
negative duties or rights, 63–64
negative externalities, 199–200, 204,
    205–6, 261–62
neighborhood effects, 211–12, 229
New International Economic Order
    (NIEO), 166–67
Nickel, James, 135
non-citizens/non-nationals, state
    responsibility for human rights of,
    161–62, 167–68
non-comparative justice, 75–76
non-relational theories of justice, 65n13,
    157–58n29
normative agency, 40–41n40
normative innovation, sphere of, 66–69
norms. *See* fairness norms; human rights
    norms; justice norms
Nussbaum, Martha, 89

objects of rights, 137–38
oil and gas production facilities in
    sacrifice zones, 194–96
O'Neill, Onora, 63–65, 66, 132, 136
oppression, extreme forms of, 238–39
overcrowding of urban slums, 223

parental rights, 123n19
Passmore, John, 57–58

patriarchal power relations, 231–32
PCBs (polychlorinated biphenyls),
    dumping of, 189–90
peace clause, 173
perfect duties, 63
personal attachments
    as core element of well-being, 37–38
    decent life and, 43–44
    participation in social movements
        and, 267–68
personal security
    as core element of well-being, 31–33
    participation in social movements
        and, 269
pervasive impact of unjust structural
    arrangements, 95–97
Pettit, Philip, 180–81
policing
    in segregated cities, 216–19
    in urban slums, 224
political legitimacy of states,
    151–52, 249–50
political standing and participation, and
    equal respect, 34–35
pollution
    "hyper-polluters," 195
    in sacrifice zones, 188–89, 191–92,
        195–96, 204–6
    siting of facilities and, 195–96
polychlorinated biphenyls (PCBs),
    dumping of, 189–90
positive rights, 64–65
poultry and livestock facilities in sacrifice
    zones, 194–96
poverty
    food security programs and, 172–75
    gender and, 223
    hunger and, 229–30
    intersection of race and, 209–11
    reconcentration of, 211–13
    urbanization of, 220–21
    women in, 215–16, 222–23,
        226, 227–29
poverty rate, concentrated, 211
Powell, Rhonda, 32
power
    arbitrary use of, 178
    coercive state, 151–52, 159, 250
    illegitimate use of, 182–84
    moral limits to exercise of, 180–82

power relations
    anti-democratic conduct of targets of
        resistance and, 261–62, 263
    global, 177–85
    intersection of group memberships
        and, 107
    market-based strategies to resist
        injustice and, 243–48
    relative social position and, 101–4
    social functions of human rights
        and, 130–32
    systematic disadvantage and,
        17–18, 82–83
    unfairness and, 18, 20, 78, 81–84
    urban slums and, 230–32
    See also exploitation; power; social
        exclusion; subordination or
        domination
practical ethics, 5
Practical Indispensability Argument, 135
practical reason, 29–30, 68
pragmatic approach to structural justice
    and human rights
    elasticity and, 69–70
    Holistic Assessment Argument, 136–41
    Linked Chain Argument, 141–45
    overview of, 66–69, 145
    recipient orientation objection, 132–35
pre-institutional benchmark of existence
    of human rights, 66–69, 136
principles
    Difference, 87–88, 169n55
    Fair Equality of Opportunity,
        76–77, 87–88
    Moral Equal Protection, 154–55,
        176, 177
    theological, of Aristotle, 21–22n13
    See also Interstate Reciprocity
        Principle
production, economic, and relative social
    position, 101–4
profound impact of unjust structural
    arrangements, 95
property ownership
    in sacrifice zones, 200, 203–4
    in slums, 224–26
    by women, 226
protectionist trade policies, 172–75
Protocol Additional to the Geneva
    Conventions, 240–41